A RIGHT TO INCLUSION AND EXCLUSION?

This volume of essays, situated at the interface between legal doctrine and legal and political philosophy, discusses the conceptual and normative issues posed by the right to inclusion and exclusion which the EU claims for itself when enacting and enforcing immigration and asylum policy under the Area of Freedom, Security and Justice. In particular, the essays probe how this alleged right acquires institutional form; how the enactment and enforcement of the EU's external borders render possible and undermine the claim to such a right; and how the fundamental distinctions that underpin this alleged right, such as inside/outside and citizen/alien, are being disrupted and reconfigured in ways that might render the EU's civic and territorial boundaries more porous. The volume is divided into three parts. A first set of essays delves into the empirical aspects that define the institutional context of the EU's alleged *jus includendi et excludendi*. A second set of essays is theoretical in character, and critically scrutinises the basic distinctions that govern this alleged right. The third set of essays discusses politico-legal alternatives, exploring how the conceptual and normative problems to which this alleged right gives rise might be dealt with, both legally and politically. The contributors to the volume are Peter Fitzpatrick, Bonnie Honig, Dora Kostakopoulou, Hans Lindahl, Valsamis Mitsilegas, Helen Oosterom-Staples, Bert van Roermund, Jo Shaw, Bernhard Waldenfels, Neil Walker and Ricard Zapata Barrero. The volume also includes a comprehensive introduction by the editor, highlighting systematic connections between the three parts and the individual essays which comprise it.

Essays in European Law: Volume 15

AF756446

A Right to Inclusion and Exclusion?

Normative Fault Lines of the EU's Area of Freedom, Security and Justice

Edited by
Hans Lindahl

·HART·
PUBLISHING
OXFORD AND PORTLAND, OREGON
2009

Published in North America (US and Canada) by
Hart Publishing
c/o International Specialized Book Services
920 NE 58th Avenue, Suite 300
Portland, OR 97213-3786
USA
Tel: +1 503 287 3093 or toll-free: (1) 800 944 6190
Fax: +1 503 280 8832
E-mail: orders@isbs.com
Website: www.isbs.com

© The editors and contributors severally 2009

The editors and contributors have asserted their right under the Copyright, Designs and Patents Act 1988, to be identified as the authors of this work.

All rights reserved. No part of this publication may be reproduced, stored in a retrieval system, or transmitted, in any form or by any means, without the prior permission of Hart Publishing, or as expressly permitted by law or under the terms agreed with the appropriate reprographic rights organisation. Enquiries concerning reproduction which may not be covered by the above should be addressed to Hart Publishing at the address below.

Hart Publishing Ltd, 16c Worcester Place, Oxford, OX1 2JW
Telephone: +44 (0)1865 517530 Fax: +44 (0)1865 510710
E-mail: mail@hartpub.co.uk
Website: http://www.hartpub.co.uk

British Library Cataloguing in Publication Data
Data Available

ISBN: 978-1-84113-949-4

Typeset by Compuscript Ltd, Shannon, Co Clare
Printed and bound in Great Britain by
CPI Antony Rowe, Chippenham, Wiltshire

ISD
SITE CW
CLASS No.
SUFFIX

Contents

Volume Contributors vii

Introduction: A Circularity and its Ramifications 1

I. Institutional Context

1. Political Discourses about Borders: On the Emergence of a European Political Community 15
RICARD ZAPATA-BARRERO

2. The Borders Paradox: The Surveillance of Movement in a Union without Internal Frontiers 33
VALSAMIS MITSILEGAS

3. Effective Rights for Third-Country Nationals? 65
HELEN OOSTEROM-STAPLES

II. Theoretical Issues

4. Phenomenology of Space: Being Here and Elsewhere 95
BERNHARD WALDENFELS

5. Finding Normativity: Immigration Policy and Normative Formation 115
PETER FITZPATRICK

6. Breaking Promises to Keep Them: Immigration and the Boundaries of Distributive Justice 137
HANS LINDAHL

7. Migrants, Humans and Human Rights: The Right to Move as the Right to Stay 161
BERT VAN ROERMUND

III. Politico-Legal Alternatives

8. The Area of Freedom, Security and Justice and the Political Morality of Migration and Integration 185
DORA KOSTAKOPOULOU

9. Proximity and Paradox: Law and Politics in the New Europe 209
BONNIE HONIG

10. **Citizenship and Electoral Rights in the Multi-Level 'Euro-Polity': The Case of The United Kingdom** 241
JO SHAW

11. **Denizenship and Deterritorialisation in the European Union** 261
NEIL WALKER

Index 275

Volume Contributors

Peter Fitzpatrick
Peter Fitzpatrick is currently Anniversary Professor of Law at Birkbeck, University of London and Honorary Professor of Law in the University of Kent. In 2007 he was given the James Boyd White Award by The Association for the Study of Law, Culture and the Humanities. He has taught at universities in Europe, North America and Papua New Guinea and published many books on legal philosophy, law and social theory, law and racism, and imperialism, the latest being *Law as Resistance: Modernism, Imperialism, Legalism* (Ashgate, 2008). Outside academia he has been in an international legal practice and was also in the Prime Minister's Office in Papua New Guinea for several years.

Bonnie Honig
Bonnie Honig, also Senior Research Fellow at the American Bar Foundation and appointed (courtesy) at Northwestern Law School, is Sarah Rebecca Roland Professor of Political Science at Northwestern University, USA. She is author of *Political Theory and the Displacement of Politics* (Cornell University Press, 1993; awarded 1994 Foundations Best First Book Prize), *Democracy and the Foreigner* (Princeton University Press, 2001), and *Emergency Politics: Paradox, Law, Democracy* (Princeton ED, 2009). Her current project on Ancient Greek tragedy is called 'Antigone, Interrupted'. She has published articles in the *American Political Science Review*, *Political Theory*, *Strategies*, *Boston Review*, *Social Text*, *Social Research*, and *Triquarterly Review*, and has edited or co-edited *Feminist Interpretations of Hannah Arendt* (Penn State 1995), *Scepticism, Individuality and Freedom: The Reluctant Liberalism of Richard Flathman* (Minnesota, 2002) and the *Oxford Handbook of Political Thought* (Oxford University Press, 2006).

Dora Kostakopoulou
Dora Kostakopoulou is Jean Monnet Professor in European Law and European Integration at the University of Manchester. Her specific research interests include European public law, free movement of persons, EU citizenship, the Area of Freedom, Security and Justice, Democracy and Legitimacy in the EU and Political Theory and Constructivism. Her work on EU migration law and policy was supported by a grant awarded by the University Association for Contemporary European Studies, for the establishment of a study group on the Evolving European Migration Law and Policy (with Andrew Geddes, University of Liverpool). Her work

on citizenship is supported by a 'Thank Offering to Britain' Fellowship awarded by the British Academy (2003–04). She has also been awarded an Innovation Award by the Arts and Humanities Research Council in order to work on the future governance of citizenship. She has published articles in such journals as *Columbia Journal of European Law*, *Oxford Journal of Legal Studies*, *Journal of Common Market Studies*, *Journal of Ethnic and Migration Studies*, *Journal of European Public Policy*, *Political Studies*, *European Journal of Migration and Law*, *Modern Law Review*, *European Law Journal* and the *Journal of Political Philosophy*. Her latest book, entitled *The Future Governance of Citizenship*, was published in 2008 by Cambridge University Press.

Hans Lindahl

Hans Lindahl is currently Professor of Legal Philosophy at Tilburg University, The Netherlands. His research focuses on issues pertaining to political representation, sovereignty and (collective) identity, in particular in the context of the EU legal order. A sub-theme within this general line of research is the structuring of politico-legal space and time from the first-person plural perspective of a 'we'. He has published articles in journals such as *Law and Philosophy*, *Ratio Juris*, *Contemporary Political Theory*, *Continental Philosophy Review*, *Oxford Journal of Legal Studies*, *Res Publica*, *Philosophy and Social Criticism*, *Archiv für Rechts- und Sozialphilosophie*, *King's College Law Journal*, *European Law Review*, *Cardozo Law Review* and *Ethics and Global Justice*, as well as chapters in, amongst others, Sacha Prechal and Bert van Roermund (eds), *The Coherence of EU Law: The Search for Unity in Divergent Concepts* (Oxford University Press, 2008) and Loughlin and Walker (eds), *The Paradox of Constitutionalism* (Oxford University Press, 2007).

Valsamis Mitsilegas

Valsamis Mitsilegas is Reader in law at Queen Mary, University of London. From 2001 to 2005 he was legal adviser to the House of Lords European Union Committee. His interests and expertise lie primarily in the area of EU law, in particular EU Justice and Home Affairs. Dr Mitsilegas is also an expert in the field of legal responses to transnational organised crime, money laundering and terrorism. His work explores the impact of measures, justified as necessary to protect internal security, on civil liberties and fundamental legal principles. He acted as Specialist Adviser to the House of Lords EU Committee for their inquiry on the European Borders Agency (FRONTEX). His publications include: *EU Criminal Law* (Hart, 2009), 'The External Dimension of EU Action in Criminal Matters' (2007) 12 *European Foreign Affairs Review*, 'Border Security in the European Union', Baldaccini, Guild and Toner (eds), *Whose Freedom, Security and Justice? EU Immigration and Asylum Law after 1999* (Hart, 2007), 'Controle des étrangers, des passagers, des citoyens: Surveillance et antiterrorisme' (2005) 58 *Cultures et Conflits* 155–82, *The EU and Internal Security* (with J Monar and W Rees) (Palgrave, 2003).

Helen Oosterom-Staples
Helen Oosterom-Staples is Assistant Professor in European Law, specialising in European Migration Law. She has taught and published extensively on the free movement rights of EU citizens and the rights of entry and residence of third-country nationals. Her PhD Thesis, *The Legal Status of Third-Country Nationals Resident* in *the European Union*, was published by Kluwer Law International (European Monographs) in 1999. Her publications include: 'Using National Security and Public Policy to Combat Terrorism; The Case of the Netherlands' (2008) 7 *EJML*; 'The Family Reunification Directive: A Tool Preserving Member State Interest or Conducive to Family Unity?' in Baldaccini, Guild and Toner (eds), *Whose Freedom, Security and Justice? EU Immigration and Asylum Law after 1999* (Hart Publishing, 2007); 'Commentaar op de vrije verkeersbepalingen in de Associatieovereenkomst EEG-Turkije ten behoeve van losbladig Commentaar op het Europese Migratierecht' (SDU, 2006); 'Case C-138/02, *Brian Francis Collins v Secretary of State for Work and Pensions*' (2005) 42 *CML Rev* 205–23; *Europeesrechtelijke grenzen aan inburgeringsverplichtingen* (Tilburg University, 2004).

Bert van Roermund
Bert van Roermund, who is professor of philosophy at Tilburg University, The Netherlands, has published extensively on various fundamental legal concepts and contemporary legal problems (constitutional review, democracy, punishment, contract law). His monograph *Law, Narrative and Reality* (Kluwer Academic Press, 1997; also in Spanish) concluded a period of research on law and language. Since then, he has focused on problems of authority and representation (sovereignty, identity, normativity, reconciliation) in supra-national contexts, inspired by Rousseau's political philosophy. With Sacha Prechal (Utrecht) he recently edited a volume with Oxford University Press, *Coherence in EU Law* (2008). He participates in a research programme on Legislation and Identity—Strategies of Authoritative Representation (2004–09) and one on Methodology and Law (2008–10). He recently (re-)turned to epistemological issues, in particular the question of what a 'model' of law would amount to.

Jo Shaw
Jo Shaw holds the Salvesen Chair of European Institutions at the University of Edinburgh. She has also worked at the Universities of Exeter, Keele, Leeds and Manchester and held visiting appointments at Harvard Law School and the Institute of Higher Studies in Vienna. Her research lies in

the field of citizenship and constitutionalism, in the context of the evolution of the European Union. Her recently published book, *The Transformation of Citizenship in the European Union* (Cambridge University Press, 2007), was awarded the UACES Book Prize in 2008 for the best book in European Studies. Further details of her research and teaching can be found on her webpage: http://www.law.ed.ac.uk/staff/joshaw/.

Bernhard Waldenfels

Bernhard Waldenfels studied philosophy, psychology, classical philology, and history inBonn, Innsbruck and Munich. He earned his PhD from the University of Munich in 1959. From 1960 to 1962 he studied modern French philosophy in Paris with Merleau-Ponty and Ricoeur. In 1967 he finished his Habilitation at Munich. He taught there until 1976, when he was appointed Professor of Philosophy at the Ruhr-Universität Bochum. Since 1999 he has been Professor Emeritus. He has been a visiting professor in Rotterdam, Paris, New York, Louvain-la-Neuve, Costa Rica, Debrecen, Prague, Rome, Vienna and Hong Kong. He is co-founder of the German Society for Phenomenological Research. He has written numerous books, including *Ordnung im Zwielicht* (Suhrkamp, 1987; translated into English as *Order in the Twilight* in 1996), *Der Stachel der Fremden* (Suhrkamp, 1990), *Antwortregister* (Suhrkamp, 1994), *Deutsch-Französische Gedankengänge* (Suhrkamp, 1995), *Studien zur Phänomenologie des Fremden* (in four volumes, Suhrkamp 1997–99), *Bruchlinien der Erfahrung* (Suhrkamp, 2002), and *Schattenrisse der Moral* (Suhrkamp, 2006), *The Question of the Other* (Chinese University Press, 2007) and *Philosophisches Tagebuch* (Fink, 2008).

Neil Walker

Neil Walker holds the Regius Chair of Public Law and the Law of Nature and Nations at the University of Edinburgh. He has published extensively on the constitutional dimension of legal order at sub-state, state, supranational and international levels, and also on the relationship between security, legal order and political community. He taught public law at Edinburgh 1986–96), was Professor of Legal and Constitutional Theory at the University of Aberdeen (1996–2000), and was Professor of European Law at the EUI in Florence (2000–08), where he was also the first Dean of Studies (2002–05). He has held various visiting appointments—including Visiting Professor, Department of Philosophy, University of Tilburg, The Netherlands (2000); Visiting Professor of Law, University of Columbia, NY (2005); Eugene Einaudi Chair of European Studies, University of Cornell (2007); and Distinguished Visiting Professor of Law, University of Toronto (2007). His books include, with Ian Loader, *Civilizing Security* (Cambridge University Press, 2007) and *Policing in a Changing Constitutional Order* (Sweet and Maxwell, 2000); his edited books include, with Martin

Loughlin, *The Paradox of Constitutionalism* (Oxford University Press 2007), *Europe's Area of Freedom, Security and Justice* (Oxford University Press, 2004) and *Sovereignty in Transition* (Hart Publishing, 2003).

Ricard Zapata-Barrero

Ricard Zapata-Barrero's main lines of research deal with contemporary problems of liberal democracy in contexts of cultural diversity, especially the relationship between democracy, citizenship and immigration. He is Director of the research group on immigration and political innovation (Grup de Recerca sobre immigració i innovació política (GRIIP)). He is currently working on different lines of research: the link between two types of cultural pluralisms, immigration and national minorities; the political theory of borders; the regional Euro-Mediterranean politics of immigration; and the political discourses of immigration. He has participated in research programmes financed by the Ministry of Education and Science and the European Union (Sixth Framework Programme). His books include: *Multiculturalidad e inmigración* (Síntesis, 2004); *Inmigración, innovación política y cultura de acomodación en España: Un análisis comparativo entre Andalucía, Cataluña, la Comunidad de Madrid y el Gobierno Central* (Cidob, 2004); *La Inmigración en naciones minoritarias: Flandes, el Québec y Cataluña en perspectiva* (Icaria, 2008); *Fundamentos de los discursos políticos sobre la inmigración* (forthcoming). His edited books include, with T Modood and A Triandafyllidou, *Multiculturalism, Muslims and Citizenship: A European Approach* (Routledge, 2006); *Conceptos Políticos en el contexto español* (Síntesis, 2007); *Immigració i autogovern* (Proa, 2007); with T Van Dijk, *Discursos sobre la inmigración en España: los medios de comunicación, los Parlamentos y las Administraciones* (Ediciones Cidob, 2007).

Introduction:

A Circularity and its Ramifications

THE SO-CALLED AREA of Freedom, Security and Justice (AFSJ), as enacted in the Treaty of Amsterdam, announces the European Union's intention to implement and enforce common policies in, amongst others, the fields of immigration and asylum. Although these policy fields are in many ways still at a relatively incipient stage of development, the avowed ambition of the AFSJ is to give fully-fledged institutional form to a *jus includendi et excludendi* for the European Union (EU), that is, a right to determine which aliens may enter, remain in, or be expelled from the EU. Yet, a closer consideration of the relevant provisions of the Amsterdam Treaty and beyond, and of all earlier treaties leading back to and including the Treaty of Rome, reveals a circularity that governs the purported *jus includendi et excludendi* to be exercised via the AFSJ: a right to inclusion and exclusion is held to be justified because the EU is the common place of its citizens; yet, to begin with, acts of inclusion (and attendant exclusion) give rise to European citizens and their allegedly common place.

This circularity, which is irreducible and inevitable, explains, first, why borders are normative *fault lines*: the closure, without which no common space could arise, excludes other possible common spaces in the very process of joining together a manifold of places into a common space. Accordingly, by referring to borders as 'normative fault lines', the title of this collection of essays seeks to draw the reader's attention to the spatiality intrinsic to normativity. It is no coincidence, in effect, that asserting that someone has been 'excluded', or that a legal act is 'inclusive', has an immediately normative resonance. It suggests that the 'metaphorical' sense of inclusiveness and exclusiveness, namely the assignment or withholding of rights and obligations, and its 'literal' sense, which evokes inside and outside as spatial categories, are mutually implicating. Border crossings by immigrants and asylum seekers, and the responses thereto by politico-legal orders, raise normative issues not only because the distribution of places in which human beings orient themselves is always already normatively charged but also, and conversely, because normativity is always, in one way or another, emplaced—and displaced.

The aforementioned circularity reveals, secondly, the intractable normative *problem* that drives the forthcoming papers: while a closure of some sort seems to be an inevitable and irreducible feature of political communities, that closure cannot, by definition, have been mandated by those who become insiders and outsiders, citizens and aliens, because it constitutes them as such, to begin with. In different ways, and from different perspectives, the contributions to this volume argue that this circularity is the *enjeu* of border crossings by immigrants and asylum seekers, on the one hand, and the legal qualification of those border crossings by European and Member State authorities, on the other. For if border crossings by immigrants and asylum seekers question, with different degrees of intensity, the right to inclusion and exclusion that the European polity claims for itself, the responses thereto by legal authorities can be seen as the ongoing endeavour to anticipate, by setting borders, the normative sense of an original closure to which the European polity has no direct access, yet whence it claims to derive its *jus includendi et excludendi*.

One way of probing this circularity is to examine how it impinges on, and destabilises, a number of the tidy disjunctions that govern European immigration and asylum policy. In effect, the papers collected in this volume can be read as critically scrutinising the following oppositions: question/response, inside/outside, norm/fact, citizen/alien, citizen/human and law/justice. In the process of examining these sets of oppositions, I will touch briefly on the institutional context, the theoretical issues and the politico-legal alternatives sketched out by the contributions to this volume.

Before beginning, however, three caveats are in order. First, although these sets of distinctions by no means exhaust the range of topics addressed in this volume, they do, nonetheless, provide a useful overview of recurrent and interconnecting themes in the chapters that compose it. Secondly, although I have distributed the chapters under three headings—institutional context, theoretical issues, and politico-legal alternatives—each of the papers impinges, to a lesser or greater extent, on the other headings as well. Thirdly, although European and Member State legislation differentiates immigrants and asylum seekers in a number of important ways, these forms of border crossings are increasingly dealt with in what has become a 'policy' continuum as much as a 'security continuum'. Accordingly, unless otherwise specified, these forms of border crossings will be dealt with jointly in this Introduction.

I. QUESTION/RESPONSE

Border crossings by immigrants and the legal qualification of those border crossings play a decisive role in understanding the genesis of politico-legal space and, more generally, the emergence of normativity. In a common sense view, collectives constitute themselves as a polity by closing themselves off as an inside against an outside. On this reading, immigration and asylum policy is part and parcel of the ongoing process by which a collective regulates for itself the terms in which it relates to its outside. Notice that this account of how boundaries arise views acts of positing boundaries as logically and chronologically *prior* to boundary crossings by immigrants: a collective must already have emplaced itself before individuals can enter its territory, whether legally or illegally. Yet, on closer consideration, the circularity that founds the EU's AFSJ irrevocably ruins this simple temporal sequence.

Zapata's and Fitzpatrick's contributions contest this 'common sense' approach to the emergence of spatial boundaries in particular, and normativity in general. Although they deploy different conceptual frameworks in making this point, both chapters obliquely point to the founding circularity of the AFSJ by reversing the relation between border crossings by immigrants and the acts of setting the borders of political communities, such that the latter appear as *responses* to the former. In his essay, Fitzpatrick notes that if borders provide a line marking apart the determinate dimension of normativity as something that is inside and separated from what is outside, the European conception of borders views bordered determinacy as *self*-constituting and *self*-sustaining, where 'ipseity' would attest to a pre-given, bounded collective subject that posits itself as a legal order. What Zapata calls the 'reactive' discourse about immigration policy prevalent in an important sector of Spanish politics shows a strong resemblance to this conception of borders and how they are posited and enforced. In effect, this discourse takes borders as already posited, as already separating political communities, such that immigration policy becomes the manifestation of collective self-rule and collective self-preservation. By contrast, Fitzpatrick points out that sustaining a border requires a constant and adaptive responsiveness to what is outside of it—an outside that cannot be comprehensively pre-determined from within. Zapata highlights a related point, when noting that immigration flows from Africa reveal that the EU has become an 'imagined community' for those who do not belong. We Europeans could not become a 'we', he notes, unless treated and addressed as such by those who 'we' then go ahead and call 'other'. Accordingly, the emergence of a European polity is not simply the outcome of a collective decision of Europeans, but rather is rendered possible by acts of immigrants, who, paradoxically, constitute the borders of the European polity in the very process of crossing them. By defending the primacy of border crossings, Fitzpatrick and Zapata can be understood as defending the radical thesis that immigrants *found* the European polity, that, paradoxically, we can only found ourselves as a community on the condition that 'we' *are founded* by those who, retrospectively, become others. For this reason, the genesis of borders and of normativity begins as an act of collective *self*-closure, not in the sense of a closure *by* a collective self but rather as a closure that gives rise *to* a collective self. It is against the background of this responsive conception of borders and border-setting that, as Fitzpatrick notes, an alternative conception of justice can come into view, an issue to which I will return at the end of this Introduction.

II. INSIDE/OUTSIDE

One of the key points Van Roermund makes in his essay, which I return to consider in a moment, is that the movement of 'migrants', whether these be refugees, economic fortune seekers, tourists, displaced persons, nomads, or whatever, only acquires its properly spatial character in terms of the inside/outside distinction, that is, in terms of border crossings whereby someone enters or leaves, *im*-migrates or *e*-migrates.

Waldenfels approaches this feature of border crossings by immigrants from the perspective of a phenomenology of space. As he points out, politico-legal space, and its constitutive distinction between inside and outside, is a particular manifestation of orientated space. In contrast with the homogenous space of modern science, in which things occupy internal positions or sites that are all relative and equivalent to each other, politico-legal space is linked to *place*, to a form of space the various aspects of which are linked to bodily involvement with the world, such as above and below, left and right, before and behind, and nearness and distance. This insight implies that the indexical 'we', by which a group of individuals refers to itself as a political community, is linked to the use of indexicals such as 'here' and 'now': part of what goes into being able to say 'we' is, precisely, also being able to say 'here'. Crucially, Waldenfels points out, human beings are never simply in or out of place; as embodied beings we are always in place *and* out of place; 'we' are always here *and* elsewhere. Drawing on Edmund Husserl's distinction between *Eigenwelt* and *Fremdwelt*, between a home world and an alien world, Waldenfels asserts that human behaviour not only has the capacity to orient itself in places but also to evince other places and other worlds, places that do not fit into the distribution of places we call 'our' world. Border crossings by immigrants are one such manifestation of this primordial 'spacing', as one might call it, which is constitutive for human behaviour. By the same token, such a splitting of the world into a home world and an alien world asks for hospitality and allows it, preparing the ground for an ethics of dwelling with others in the world. Such an ethics must resist the devitalisation of place, effected by what Waldenfels calls 'globalism', as much as the fixation thereof, in the form of 'localism'.

Mitsilegas's chapter exposes the paradox of borders that arises when the distinction between inside and outside becomes fixated through the 'securitisation' discourse. The measures of border control and surveillance put in place to secure the distinction between inside and outside to the benefit of insiders end up turning against their putative beneficiaries, to the extent that insiders no less than outsiders become the object of border control and surveillance. Mitsilegas links this paradox to the de-politicisation of European immigration policy. To the extent that immigration is viewed largely from a security/counter-terrorism perspective, border controls and surveillance are developed primarily as law enforcement/intelligence tools, subordinated to a primarily technical or managerial logic. This approach effectively de-politicises European immigration policy because it presents the need to secure a threatened political unity as the only available option. But, as Mitsilegas shows, the de-politicisation of European immigration policy has very considerable political costs for the EU. The general surveillance of border crossings by all individuals, including EU citizens, not only leads to the 'disappearance of disappearance' but also challenges the fundamental principles of privacy, equality and non-discrimination, and freedom, an issue that Kostakopoulou also explores in her chapter. The importance of the paradox of borders, as Mitsilegas describes it, consists in that holding on to the inside/outside distinction by securitising immigration policy actually undermines the European polity itself. This occurs both literally—because the cardinal distinctions between inside/outside and citizen/alien are eroded when everybody is submitted to surveillance—and foundationally—because fundamental legal distinctions and principles that underpin the idea of a common European space become compromised. Exposing this paradox and its political effects for the EU can contribute to re-politicising immigration policy and, therewith, the borders of the EU. For in a technical or managerial approach to border controls and surveillance, the question concerning the ends of political community, and this includes the questions of 'who' is a party to the community and 'what' are the terms of participation therein, are placed out of bounds. Re-politicising immigration and asylum policy would require acknowledging the constitutive character of the circularity that founds the EU as an AFSJ, hence that border crossings by immigrants are, with different levels of intensity, political events and never only events that call for the 'management' of borders.

III. NORM/FACT

If, on the one hand, a right to inclusion and exclusion is held to be justified because the EU is the own place of its citizens, an act of inclusion (and attendant exclusion), on the other, gives rise to European citizens and their own place. This circularity, as noted, tends to undermine any move by authorities to posit a simple opposition between inside and outside. It also undermines the hallowed distinction between normativity and factuality. Indeed, the circularity amounts to this: the *right* to inclusion and exclusion which the EU claims for itself rests on—and is 'contaminated' by—more or less *factual* acts of inclusion and exclusion which give rise to the EU, in the first place.

The disruption of the basic distinction between fact and norm is the underlying theme of Oosterom-Staples's contribution to this volume. She is concerned to establish whether there is a legal obligation to ensure effective legal remedies for third-country nationals in immigration and asylum cases with respect to the EU and/or its Member States, and, if this is the case, whether these polities live up to their legal obligations. Although it is tempting to view the second of these questions as a merely 'factual' question that is subordinate to the former, properly 'juridical' question, her analysis points to a deeper circularity between the factual and the juridical that is closely linked to the circularity mentioned above. Indeed, Oosterom-Staples argues, on the one hand, that access to territory is a condition for access to justice. Succeeding in entering the EU opens up the possibility for claimants of being heard in court and, thereby, of obtaining and enforcing judicial decisions concerning their requests to enter and sojourn in the EU and/or its Member States. On the other hand, the 'practice' of immigration and asylum policy shows that access to justice is a condition for access to territory. Indeed, Oosterom-Staples describes how the EU and its Member States have set up a series of three concentric circles, including the airline counters at airports and the visa counters at EU embassies or consulates, that effectively hamper judicial review of decisions that deny entry into airplanes or travel visas to the EU. (Here, 'effectively' has the double meaning of 'in fact' and 'producing an effect'.) Notice that this circularity is the inverted image of the foundational circularity noted hitherto: the factual core of the act that closes off the EU as a legal space from an outside becomes re-enacted in the form of factual acts that impede entry from the outside into the EU as a legal space. The 'effectiveness' of legal remedies in immigration and asylum cases has its inverted image in the 'effectiveness' of the concentric circles put into place by the EU. The less the EU is prepared to justify its alleged *jus includendi et excludendi* to those it has excluded, the more it must appeal to factual measures to keep them out.

Honig's chapter gives an agonistic focus to the distinction between the factual and the normative. Engaging critically with Seyla Benhabib's defence of a cosmopolitan approach to immigration policy, Honig argues that universalism posits proximity, territory and boundary as morally irrelevant terms. The mere 'fact' that individuals have entered the polity, and simply happen to be here, is purely contingent, and, as is the case for the entire realm of contingency in a universalistic frame of mind, does not possess any normative significance of its own that could galvanise political action on their behalf. By seeking to ground moral connection and obligation on universalisable norms, cosmopolitanism inures us from the call of the other that reaches us precisely from the contingent connections of geography or common cause. Appealing to Franz Rosenzweig's notion of 'neighbourliness', Honig defends an agonistic cosmopolitics in which unexpected ways of living-in-common arise from a spatial and political proximity. As she puts it, 'shared challenges make neighbours of us, putting us in common cause with those who might otherwise have been distant'. If this agonistic understanding of political action takes issue with the systematic reduction of the realm of the factual to that which has no normative significance of its own, it also takes issue with the concept of normativity enjoined by cosmopolitanism. Indeed, universalism by definition leaves no room for what gets remaindered in political action, that is, for what gets excluded in any conceivable way of living-in-common, however general. Benhabib would have it that 'democratic iterations' can accommodate the problem posed by the founding circularity of the EU's AFSJ. However, Honig points out that Derrida's notion of 'iterability' actually lies much closer to a 'politics of a double gesture', as Honig puts it, which affirms the values of universal human rights while also endorsing forms of action that seem to violate that universality in the form of political action based on solidarity with those who are near *because* they are near. Regarding immigrants, this double gesture could lead, amongst others, to political activism oriented to extending juridical institutions and safeguards for border crossers while also, say, designating some spaces as cities of refuge or advocating *droits de cité* (locational rights), whereby a variety of border crossers are extended full hospitality simply because they are here, as Derrida and Rogin have demanded.

IV. CITIZEN/ALIEN

In the same way that the circularity which gives rise to the European polity disrupts the simple oppositions between inside and outside, and norm and fact, it also disrupts the simple opposition between citizen and alien. Although European citizenship was only explicitly introduced in the Treaty of Maastricht, the Treaty of Rome paradoxically introduces the distinction between membership and non-membership by asserting that it gives institutional form to an already existent 'union among the peoples of Europe'. But as there is no direct access to the original cut between Europe and the rest of the world, and between Europeans and non-Europeans, the very conditions under which the distinction between citizen and alien are instituted render it inevitably problematic. The problematic character of this distinction is not only visible in how the European polity characterises aliens within the framework of its immigration and asylum policy, but also in how it characterises European citizenship itself. In effect, immigration and asylum policy presupposes a membership policy—and vice versa.

Kostakopoulou's contribution examines the correlation between immigration and asylum policy on the one hand, and membership policy on the other, primarily from the perspective of what she calls 'political morality'. By insisting on the notion of a *political* morality, Kostakopoulou moves away from attempts to ground a liberal European immigration and asylum policy on the basis of a universal right to migration, or concerns about distributive justice or even of charity. A properly political grounding of a liberal immigration and asylum policy rests on the political 'costs' that flow from a restrictive policy, namely, the betrayal of principles professed by the EU, and which are constitutive for its identity as a political community. Her main thesis is, therefore, that decisions taken about which immigrants are to be allowed entry, and about the conditions for their integration into the receiving society, are, first and foremost, decisions about who 'we' are as a political community. Kostakopoulou develops this general thesis in two directions. On the one hand, she traces how the enactment of European immigration and asylum policy, up to and including the European Pact on Immigration and Asylum, adopted in Brussels in October 2008, has come to set conditions for integration as a way of excluding undesirables, testing the resources and the commitment of the included, and of promoting what she calls 'identificational' integration. This approach, she argues, may compromise democratic ideals by perpetuating fictions of internal homogeneity and opening up the way for nativist narratives of belonging. On the other hand, she sketches out an alternative approach which not only pursues a more generous intake of migrants but also resolutely politicises the criteria for membership, recognising that integration is best promoted by 'citizenisation', that is, treating newcomers as stakeholders in the community and facilitating their access to citizenship.

Jo Shaw's essay approaches the citizen/alien relation by way of an analysis of citizen and electoral rights in the United Kingdom (UK). Shaw discusses how evolving policies on these issues shed light on the condition of citizenship and how citizenship can best be understood where there are multiple and often competing sites of legal, constitutional and political authority, as in both the UK and the EU. Scrutinising Lord Goldsmith's report about the current state of citizenship in the UK, Shaw dwells on the internal inconsistencies that arise as a result of the report's attempt to posit a single model of membership based on a tight connection between citizen and state. The 'messy' and 'piecemeal' franchise arrangements characteristic of the UK, which grant participation rights to groups of privileged non-nationals, are not merely suboptimal, as Goldsmith suggests, but rather the expression of another understanding of consistency in membership policy, namely one that accommodates both vertical bonds, between citizen and state, and horizontal bonds, of citizens across states, in a way that does justice to the multiple political allegiances and affiliations of individuals. Shaw brings this prism to bear on the EU, showing how the reasoning of the European Court of Justice in the *Aruba* and *Matthews* cases was driven by this transformed sense of political allegiance and affiliation. Shaw concludes by drawing the implication of this approach for non-EU nationals: precisely to the extent that political principles of participation are no longer compartimentalised on national lines, it becomes feasible to consider the possibility of extending the right to vote for the supranational European Parliament to *all residents* affected by its legislation.

V. CITIZEN/HUMAN

A further question is whether it would be possible to mitigate the implications of the founding circularity of the EU by subordinating the citizen/alien distinction to the imperatives of human rights. And, yet more radically, the question arises whether it would be at least conceivable to step out altogether from this circularity: is political community thinkable without membership? Can we make sense of a polity that would not need to appeal to the distinction between citizen and alien?

The first of these questions is at the core of Van Roermund's contribution to this volume. One of his central insights is that human rights are 'selfish' in a twofold sense. For the one, they presuppose the first person singular perspective of individual agents that engage in a reflexive relation with their surrounding world. For the other, the attribution of human rights that protect those different modalities of practical engagement presupposes the political setting of a first person plural, a 'we' that legislates in its own interest by meting out to each their own (rights). Exploiting a certain ambiguity in the notion of a 'country', as opposed to a 'state', Van Roermund asserts that the human right to move should be interpreted as a right to stay, that is, to stay rooted in the nursing and nourishing environment that 'land' or 'country' stands for in a paradigmatic way. He also points out that the necessary affirmation of a body politic, of a collective self in the attribution of human rights, renders human rights, including the right to free movement, irreducibly ambiguous in a number of ways. On the one hand, Van Roermund shows how immigration policy interprets the humanity of would-be immigrants and asylum seekers in ways that both protect them and capture them within the collective identity reflected in the parameters of what a collective counts a 'credible' story of a refugee without documents, or the circumstances deemed 'pressing' for humanitarian reasons. On the other hand, to the extent that acts of collective self-legislation claim to allot to each their own, the human right to free movement is caught up in the broader tension inherent to justice itself, namely between what counts as a distributive criterion that is binding for us, as members of the collective, and that is binding for all, irrespective of membership. Rather than attempting to overcome or elide this ambiguity, Van Roermund argues that it is necessary to reinterpret the critical potential of human rights by refusing to play the reciprocity card. Human rights are a way of allowing a divergence of interests to register without pre-figuring a political frame that overcomes and encompasses the distinction between citizen and alien.

Neil Walker's contribution on denizenship and deterritorialisation in the EU addresses the second of the aforementioned questions by probing the limits of what is conceivable with respect to political community. Walker describes the different ways in which the figure of the denizen breaks with or at least tests our traditional understanding of membership of political community. Indeed, denizenship is of great interest to those interested in the relationship between the law and the politics of migration because it is an 'in-between' concept that resists assimilation into a host of binary oppositions, including citizen/alien, insider/outsider, national/international, territorial/extraterritorial, domestic/foreign, and franchised/disenfranchised. Walker's chapter traces the variety of possible trajectories of denizenship, which includes proto-citizenship, tiered-membership, transnational membership, post-national membership and, in a more embryonic manner, post-membership. Whereas the first two varieties would tame denizenship by attempting to return it to the binary Westphalian logic, the last three mark increasingly radical steps in transcending that logic, such that, in the final trajectory, the denizen reflects and helps precipitate the marginalisation or perhaps even demise of the very idea of political membership. Or, as Walker also boldly puts it, an inversion is at least conceivable in which, rather than being a residual category with respect to citizenship, denizenship—or its functional or imaginary equivalent—might come to assert itself as the master category of association with, and investment in, political community. Drawing on these various alternative trajectories, Walker then focuses on how the strategic, ideological and generative dimensions of the denizen could contribute to reconfiguring the membership politics of the EU. In particular, he notes how the denizen provides a tangible contestation over the reflexive 'we' of the EU polity. Most fundamentally, perhaps, the denizen embodies the possibility of mitigating or even moving away from the antagonistic posing of different imaginaries of supra-national self-authorisation.

VI. LAW/JUSTICE

The circularity that founds the EU as an AFSJ not only disrupts, without effacing, the distinction between inside and outside, fact and norm, citizen and alien; it also disrupts any simple coincidence between law and justice. For, if Ulpian's formula, *suum cuique tribuere* also includes 'to each their own place', the founding act of the European polity by definition does not come about in what is this polity's *own place*. To paraphrase Waldenfels, there is a 'fissure of justice', whereby the place whence justice unfolds its possibilities does not simply coincide with the distribution of places made available by a legal order.

Lindahl's essay approaches this problem by linking the (im)possibility of distributive justice to the complex structure of legal borders. In effect, the EU's borders include by excluding, insofar as the boundaries that close off the internal market also join it to an external market, whereby inside and outside appear as places in a more encompassing whole. And they exclude by including, to the extent that the Treaty of Rome founds the European polity by including Europe and the world as a market, and excluding other understandings of what could render Europe and the world a common space. This double intertwinement, Lindahl argues, lies at the basis of two spatial thresholds of distributive justice. The first threshold marks the point at which an immigrant begins to register as having a stake in the political 'we', a person who has a de jure interest in the distribution of rights and goods by the European polity. For although distributive acts by the EU take place from the first person plural perspective of a spatially bounded 'we', acts that decide on the (il)legality of border crossings by immigrants can only claim to be just to the extent that they posit the preferential distinction between inside and outside in a way that safeguards the commonality of the world in which the EU claims to take its place. This is the threshold at which the distinction between the just and the unjust with respect to immigrants begins to take hold: 'proto-political reflexivity', as Lindahl dubs it. The second threshold marks the point beyond which claims by immigrants cease to register as claims that call for distributive acts by legal officials, because they are uttered in a place that, stripped of its normative dimension concerning immigration, has reverted to the status of a non-place that is neither inside nor outside the European polity. Italy's Lampedusa Airport Zone Holding Centre is one such non-place. In these non-places, the just/unjust distinction breaks down, marking the emergence of a 'post-reflexive politics'. These non-places, in which the immigrant finally becomes a thoroughly de facto immigrant, are also, he argues, the non-places in which the European polity ceases to claim a *right* to closure, such that its founding closure becomes nothing more than a de facto act—an act of violence.

Fitzpatrick's chapter, as anticipated at the outset of this Introduction, is concerned to link justice to the law's responsiveness and the emergence of normativity. While the Europe of the EU would lay claim to a determinate existence, as marked out, amongst others, by its borders, it also asserts a responsive range that extends beyond any determinative existence, a responsiveness without which all talk of immigration policy, in its constituent relation to polity, would make no sense. The responsiveness of the law introduces, moreover, a temporal dimension that Fitzpatrick already evokes when referring to the 'emergence' of normativity. If the law claims to be able to fix the future, by anticipating normative expectations, alterity manifests itself as what disrupts those expectations, illuminating new ways of being-in-common. The determinateness and responsive dimensions of positive law impinge directly on the problem of justice. Building on and sharpening Derrida's reflections on justice, Fitzpatrick approaches the legal response to border crossings by immigrants within the broader framework of a tension between an unlimited and a limited responsiveness to the other, a tension in which justice and positive law prove to be mutually constituent yet distinct and able to exceed each other. This tension comes to a head in the problem of the emergence of borders, which returns us to the outset of this Introduction, namely the responsive origin of borders. As Fitzpatrick points out, the border is generated *by* an outside, by a transgressive alterity, as Foucault would have it, which, in crossing and re-crossing a border, continuously makes and remakes it. That the emergence of borders and normativity has a responsive structure entails, as Derrida once put it, that foreigners pose 'the first question'.

Several of the chapters collected in this volume were first presented at a colloquium at Tilburg University, the Netherlands, hosted by the editor in May 2007. The colloquium was organised under the auspices of a research grant provided by the Netherlands Organisation for Scientific Research (NWO), to whom the editor expresses his appreciation. The editor would also like to thank the Ministry of Justice of the Netherlands, the Schoordijk Institute of the Faculty of Law of Tilburg University and the Department of Philosophy of Tilburg University for providing additional financial support, both for the colloquium and for the copy-editing of this volume. Last but not least, the volume as a whole has profited immensely from Kay Caldwell's and Jo Choulerton's expert and painstaking copy-editing of all the chapters.

Hans Lindahl
Tilburg, December 2008

I

Institutional Context

1

Political Discourses about Borders:

On the Emergence of a European Political Community*

RICARD ZAPATA-BARRERO

I. INTRODUCTION

ONE OF THE basic dimensions of migration policy is the management of borders. Migration policy is generally premised on the assumption that borders are the main expression of the existence of an independent political community unit. There cannot be a political community without borders, or so it is claimed, and there can be no borders if these cannot fulfil one of their main functions: to demarcate a political community.[1] Moreover, it is argued, borders are the main indicators of difference, are inherently exclusive, and are the main container of the sense of political community.[2] If we follow this simple logic, we can say that, strictly speaking, there are no European borders since there is no European political community. Yet, as has become particularly evident since 1989 and in the

* This chapter examines an argument that belongs to a research project financed by the Spanish Ministry of Education and Science (Ministerio de Educación y Ciencia) entitled *The politicisation of immigration: the relationship between political and social discourse in Spain and EU immigration policy* (*La politización de la inmigración: relación entre el discurso político y social en España y políticas de la UE entorno a la inmigración*) (SEJ2004-04775/CPOL, 2004–07) and sets the premises of one line of research of the current project 'Fronteras' funded by the VI National Plan of Scientifical Research, Development and Tecnological Innovation 2008–2011 Ministry of Science and Innovation, Spain (Ref: CSO2008-02181/CPOL).

[1] I follow, in the main, references on border identity related to and focusing on the constitution of political communities. Among others, see M Anderson and E Bort (eds), *The Frontiers of Europe* (London, Pinter, 1998); H Donnan and ThM Wilson, *Borders: Frontiers of Identity, Nation and State* (Oxford, Berg, 1999); M Albert, D Jacobson and Y Lapid (eds), *Identities, Borders, Orders: Rethinking International Relations Theory* (London, University of Minneapolis Press, 2001); A Buchanan and M Moore (eds), *States, Nations and Borders* (Cambridge, Cambridge University Press, 2003).

[2] Boundary as container and as excluder is described in S Wolin, 'Fugitive Democracy' in S Benhabib *Democracy and Difference* (New Jersey, Princeton University Press, 1996).

aftermath of September 11, 2001, the contemporary interaction between borders and political community challenges this traditional paradigm which can be summarised in the phrase 'One border, one political community'.

Taking this debate as the immediate context of my chapter, I would like to approach the management of borders through migration policy as building a sense of political community. In other words, and regardless of whatever else it may do, migration policy makes and re-makes the sense of political community. My main purpose is to challenge the common conservative (traditionalist) view that migration policy is grounded in a pre-existent political community, that is, that one of the foundations of an migration policy is to defend an existing political community.[3] Within the European framework there is evidence that the reverse is also true: a new sense of community emerges with the management of borders. I will explore how the European political community emerges and is being defined as a polity through the management of its borders.[4]

In this respect, Spain makes an illuminating case study. By putting pressure on the EU, Spain is effectively opening up a serious normative debate first, on who controls borders and secondly, on how it would be possible to have increased legislative intervention by the EU in a policy field that has traditionally been the sovereign realm of its Member States. A closer consideration of these issues could help us to understand how a debate on the normative foundations of a European migration policy impinges on the process of the building of a European political community.

This set of issues is approached in three steps. Section II describes empirical and theoretical questions that arise from entry by immigrants along the southern Spanish-European border. Section III analyses two main

[3] The normative discussion of this conservative and assimilationist approach as a political response to multicultural conflicts in Europe has some preliminary work in for example: C Joppke and S Lukes, *Multicultural Questions* (New York, Oxford University Press, 1999); J Levy, *The Multiculturalism of Fear* (Oxford, Oxford University Press, 2000); B Barry, *Culture and equality: an egalitarian critique of multiculturalism* (Cambridge, Polity Press, 2001); R Brubaker, 'The return of assimilation? Changing perspectives on immigration and its sequels in France, Germany, and the United Status' (2001) 24 *Ethnic and Racial Studies* 531–48; A Favell and T Modood, 'The Philosophy of Multiculturalism: The Theory and Practice of Normative Political Theory' in A Finlayson (ed), *Contemporary Political Thought: A Reader and Guide* (Edinburgh, Edinburgh University Press, 2003); C Joppke and M Morawska (eds), *Towards assimilation and citizenship. Immigrants in liberal nation-states* (Houndmills, Palgrave Macmillan, 2003); C Joppke, 'The retreat of multiculturalism in the liberal state: theory and policy' (2004) 55 *The British Journal of Sociology* 237–57); BS Turner, 'Citizenship and the Crisis of Multiculturalism' (2006) 10 *Citizenship Studies* 607–18; T Modood, A Triandafyllidou and R Zapata-Barrero (eds), *Multiculturalism, Muslims and citizenship: a European approach* (New York, Routledge, 2006); P Mouritsen and KE Jørgensen (eds), *Constituting Communities: Political Solutions to Cultural Conflict* (Hampshire, Palgrave Macmillan, 2008).

[4] See A Geddes, 'Europe's border relationships and international migration relations' (2005) 43 *Journal of Common Market Studies* 787–806 for an interesting discussion on the process of European border-building.

discourses on borders during debates about migration policy in the Spanish Parliament. One deploys a reactive logic, which defends restrictive policies and strong control; the other follows a proactive logic, which is much more concerned with human rights. These two discourses—a security-based approach and a human rights-based approach—provide us with the preliminary contours of a normative understanding of European political community, which, in turn, could ground European migration policy. Section IV draws on the findings of Sections II and III to identify and discuss several questions concerning the normative foundations of a European political community.

II. KEY EVENTS AT THE SOUTHERN BORDER AND THEIR THEORETICAL IMPLICATIONS

Although most immigrants residing in Spain originate from Latin America and Europe, for many people immigration refers to the 'invasion' of undocumented African immigrants (*los sin papeles*) who are intercepted at the Southern border. The purpose of this first section is to provide a brief overview of the current situation concerning these border crossings and of policy actions undertaken by Spain, alone or in conjunction with the other Member States of the EU, to deal with those border crossings.

Broadly speaking, immigrants enter Spain along its Southern border by way of three migratory routes: the maritime route across the Strait of Gibraltar in fishing boats called *pateras*; the route into Ceuta and Melilla, within the North African territory; and, most recently, the Canary Islands route in larger vessels called *cayucos*, which mainly carry Sub-Saharan people. The last of these began in January 2006 as a result of increased border controls in the Spanish enclaves and across the Strait of Gibraltar, coupled with improved diplomatic relations between Spain and Morocco as a result of the arrival to power of the Zapatero Administration. The arrival of *cayucos* reached a record level in August 2006, when 4,772 immigrants arrived at the Islands. From January to October 2006 some 24,000 undocumented immigrants from sub-Saharan Africa, of which 700 were minors, arrived by boat at the Canary Islands. Some 1,000 people are believed to have drowned.[5]

Brussels estimates the number of people waiting in Mauritania at that time to be shipped to the Canary Islands at some 500,000. Those who survived the dangerous crossing of the Atlantic Ocean were taken to reception centres where officials attempted to establish their nationality in order to repatriate them if repatriation agreements had been signed with the countries of origin.

[5] R Pérez Brito, 'La migración en pateras: de África a las Islas Canarias' (2006) *Canarias Semanal* (www.intermigra.info/extranjeria/archivos/revista/CanariasS.pdf).

Some 170 immigrants have been returned to Mauritania (with which there has been a Repatriation Agreement since 2003), while some 5,000 have been returned to Senegal. Meanwhile the Spanish government continues to establish repatriation agreements with other countries. Those who cannot be sent back within the repatriation agreements after having been held for 40 days in internment (which has been increased to 65 days by the Canary Islands Government) are shipped to mainland Spain and distributed territorially. Subsequently, they are released and told to leave the country within 15 days. However, most stay or travel on within the EU and get involved in black-market labour.

At the same time some 30,000 immigrants are estimated to be waiting in Morocco and Argelia to storm the fences of Ceuta and Melilla in order to cross the Spanish border by land. These Spanish enclaves in Morocco are other border sites that have received a great deal of media attention and put illegal immigration on the political agenda.

Morocco's geographically strategic location on the crossroads of Africa and Europe and its proximity to Spain make both emigration and immigration (transit) predictable issues.

Spain's response to the marked increase in immigration that reaches its Southern borders follows a strategy that combines aspects of humanitarianism with enhanced security arrangements. For example, Spain has given money to the Mauritanian government to build reception centres for immigrants and refugees.[6] But this step is coupled with the signing of an Agreement of Return with Mauritania, giving the Spanish authorities the opportunity to expel immigrants who arrive illegally on Spanish soil.[7] In addition to its own nationals Mauritania only accepts immigrants from the neighbouring countries of Senegal and Mali, which account for 90 per cent of the immigrants that arrived at the Canaries.[8] More generally, the enhanced security arrangements are reflected in Spain's move to drastically improve the control of its borders. In particular, Spain has extended the 'Integrated System of External Surveillance' (SIVE) to Fuerteventura, has sent patrol boats to Mauritania and has externalised its borders by starting a diplomatic offensive to persuade African countries to control their borders in exchange for development cooperation. After initial arrangements with Mauritania and Senegal, the minister of external affairs travelled to Gambia, Senegal, Mali, Guinea-Bissau, Nigeria, Mauritania, Ghana and Cape Verde to negotiate terms of cooperation. As there is no European

[6] RM De Rituerto, 'Bruselas asiste "muy preocupada" al desarrollo de la crisis', *El País,* 16 March 2006, 18.

[7] P Muñoz and L Ayllón, 'De La Vega afirma que Mauritania está dispuesta a aceptar las repatriaciones de inmigrantes', *El País,* 17 March 2006.

[8] P Muñoz and L Ayllón, 'Mauritania sólo acepta la devolución de "sin papeles" originarios deSenegal y Malí, El 90% de los llegados hasta ahora en patera al archipiélago son nacionales de dichos países', *El País,* 20 March 2006, 19.

framework to solve common Mediterranean problems between the South and the North, several ad hoc informal meetings have been organised, such as the EU-Africa Ministerial Conference on Migration and Development (Rabat, 10–11 July 2006)[9] and the informal meetings between the Mediterranean EU Member States (Spain, France, Italy, Portugal, Greece, Cyprus, Malta and Slovenia, held in Madrid on 29 September 2006), running in parallel to the Barcelona Process, which would have been the normal framework to govern these situations.[10]

To a certain extent, Spain has succeeded in Europeanising its Southern border. For example, the Tampere Treaty justified the building of a complex radar system to monitor entry via the Straits of Gibraltar (SIVE). The system started operating in 2002.[11] In 2003, operation 'Ulises' was launched to patrol the maritime border of the European Union, as a measure to fight illegal immigration.[12] This fight has not only been an issue on the Spanish agenda, but has also been a key topic of debate at international summits.[13] In this context special mention should be made of the Spanish presidency of the EU, where under illegal immigration was one of the main topics on the European Council meeting in Seville (June 2002). Spain proposed the deportation of illegal immigrants in military aircraft and ships, thereby criminalising immigration. The EU has also stressed the importance of the fight against illegal immigration, for example at the informal meeting of heads of state in Hampton Court, London, which took place just after the tragedies in Ceuta and Melilla[14] and at the last EU summit in Brussels, in March 2006, at the time when the Canary Islands was starting to receive so many irregular immigrants.

[9] See www.maec.gov.ma/migration/En/conference.htm.

[10] See www.europa.eu.int/comm/external_relations/euromed/meda.htm.

[11] See B Agrela, 'Spain as a Recent Country of Immigration: How immigration became a Symbolic, Political, and Cultural Problem in the "New Spain"' *Working Paper 57* (San Diego, The Center for Comparative Immigration Studies, University of California 2002).

[12] See R Sandell, '¿Saltaron o les empujaron? El aumento de la inmigración subsahariana?' Análisis del Real Instituto Elcano, de Estudios Internacionales y Estratégicos, 19 January 2006 (www.realinstitutoelcano.org/analisis), and L González-Rodríguez, 'Cambios en las Tradicionales vías de entrada de los inmigrantes clandestinos a la UE' (2004) *Geo Crítica, Scripta Nova, Revista electrónica de geografía y ciencias socials*, 1 September 2004 (www.ub.es/geocrit/sn/sn-172.htm).

[13] Examples are the last meeting between Spain and Morocco on 29 August 2005, EU Council meetings of Head of States (the last one in Brussels, March 2006), the Euro-African Summit in April 2000, the 5+5 conference of social ministers on migration (Paris, 9 and 10 November 2005), the meetings of the ten countries composing the Euro-Mediterranean Partnership (the last one in Barcelona, November 2005) and the African Union-EU Troika in December 2005.

[14] See European Commission, 'Visit to Ceuta and Melilla'—Mission report Technical mission on illegal immigration, 7–11 October 2005, Memo/05/380, Brussels (19 October); and European Commission, 'Priority actions for responding to the challenges of migration: First follow-up to Hampton Court', Communication from the Commission to the Council and the European Parliament, COM(2005)621, Brussels (30 November).

The response by Member States to Spain's attempt to Europeanise its Southern border has been uneven. Some Member States have been prepared to support the Spanish fight against illegal immigration, sending experts and donating material and money to the external border security agency, Frontex, which patrols the coast of Western Africa. Other Member States (mainly Germany, Austria, the Netherlands and France) have fiercely criticised Spanish migration policy and denied the need to support it. At the informal meeting of heads of state in Tampere, Finland, in September 2006, European politicians from Austria, Holland and Germany criticised Spain for requesting assistance in times of crisis, whereas it didn't consult with them when implementing a large-scale regularisation in 2005. The critique was headed by the (then) French Interior Minister, Nicolas Sarkozy, who blamed the large-scale arrival of immigrants to Spain on the amnesty which the Socialist government gave in 2005 to nearly 800,000 undocumented workers (most of whom were actually from Latin America). This regularisation, he argued, would not only create a 'call effect' to Spain, but also to the whole Schengen area.[15] Other vocal criticism came from a German member of the Social Democratic Party from Bavaria, who stated that 'Spain would not sink with the arrival of some 20,000 people to the Canary Islands'.

And, yet, the shift from *pateras* to *cayucos* not only highlights the innovative capacity of migrants and human traffickers to cross political borders, but also that Spain's Southern borders have become European borders, politically, technically and mentally. Indeed, for an immigrant, it doesn't matter whether the border guards wear Spanish, French, Italian or EU uniforms. Once this European border is crossed, it is easy to travel on within Schengen Europe. It became clear when a route between Barcelona and Milan was detected in October 2006 that not all immigrants arriving by *cayuco* stay in Spain. Precisely because Schengen suspends the internal borders between the states that participate therein, irregular migration within Schengen calls for the setting in place of European migration policy that defines European borders as such. I will return to this point at the end of the paper.

III. TWO DISCOURSES ABOUT BORDERS

If the foregoing section focuses primarily on empirical issues pertaining to immigration and migration policy, I will now turn to examine how these issues are approached in the two main discourses deployed in the Spanish Parliament. Whereas the previous section reveals a policy mix of security and humanitarian considerations, this section reveals a remarkable degree

[15] European states (EU and non-EU) who have implemented the Schengen Agreement of 1985, to create a territory without borders. The legal framework constituted by the Agreement and the Schengen Convention of 19 June 1990 became part of EU law with the Amsterdam Treaty, 2 October 1997.

of normative polarisation quite at odds with the realities of migration policy as enacted, and as implemented by the current Spanish government. In particular I propose to distinguish between two 'politics of discourse', namely the *reactive* (RD) and *proactive* (PD) discourses.[16] Each must be considered as an approach and an orientation that helps define migration policies. Broadly speaking, the first one follows a security-based approach, the second, a human rights-based approach. The rhetoric of the first discourse corresponds to a new conservatism; the rhetoric of the second discourse is part of a new progressivism. Exploring these two discourses becomes a way of identifying the basic issues confronting a debate about the normative foundations of a political community, insofar as each represents a distinct way of defining political community—including the EU. I will return to those issues in the following section.

Bearing this in mind, my immediate objective is to elicit the most relevant topics from the reactive and the proactive discourses. I borrow for this purpose T van Dijk's reference to a discourse as a 'semantic structure that represents what is considered to be the most relevant. It has the duty to regulate the coherence of the discourse and how the discourse itself is globally understood'.[17] In my view, the topics generate meanings and interpretations related to immigration management; they represent different ways of understanding basic issues related to the arrival of immigrants and the process through which they settle permanently. This concept of discourse allows us to identify two sets of questions that structure the normative debate about immigration and migration policy in the Spanish Parliament. The first basic question is this: How are we to interpret immigration normatively? The second is: What basic policy orientations are available to respond to border crossings by immigrants?[18]

[16] The expression *politics of discourse* is first introduced by R Zapata-Barrero in 'Policies and public opinion towards immigrants: the Spanish case' (2008) 31 *Ethnic and Racial Studies*: DOI: 10.1080/01419870802302280, URL: http://dx.doi.org/10.1080/01419870802302280. It refers to the fact that 'discourse becomes a political option, a common and deliberate practice for most traditional European political parties, especially when they have to communicate their positions on cultural diversity': R Zapata-Barrero and I Qasem, 'The politics of discourse towards Islam and muslim communities in Europe' in P Mouritsen and KE Jørgensen (eds), *Constituting communities: political solutions to cultural conflict* (Hampshire, Palgrave Macmillan, 2008) 73.

[17] T Van Dijk, 'On the analysis of parliamentary debates on immigration' in M Reisigl and R Wodak (eds), *The semiotics of racism. Approaches to critical discourse analysis* (Vienna, Passagen Verlag, 2000) 85–103 at 90; and see, amongst others, N Fairclough, *Discourse and social change* (Cambridge, Polity Press, 1992); P Chilton, *Analysing Political Discourse: Theory and Practice* (London, Routledge, 2004); DR Howarth, *Discourse* (Buckingham, Open University Press, 2000); D Tannen, D Schiffrin and H Hamilton (eds), *Handbook of Discourse analysis* (Oxford, Blackwell, 2001); T Van Dijk and I Rodrigo, *Análisis del discurso social y político* (Quito, Ecuador, Pluriminor, 1999); R Wodak and M Meyer (eds), *Métodos de análisis crítico del discurso* (Barcelona, Gedisa, 2003).

[18] I have analysed the parliamentary debates of the VIth (1996–2000), VIIth (2000–04) and VIIIth (current 2004–06) Spanish legislature.

A. Normative Interpretation of Immigration

The reactive (RD) and proactive (PD) discourses interpret immigration in quite different ways:

(i) Problem or challenge?

When defining the migratory process, the RD approaches the phenomenon as a problem that must be resolved with available legal and political means, whereas the PD approaches the issue as a challenge that needs to be managed, favouring political and legal innovation if the current means are not appropriate. From this last perspective, immigration is considered as a social phenomenon.[19] As a result, whereas the RD insists that 'it is their problem, not ours', the PD proclaims from the outset that immigration poses a challenge to *us*.[20]

(ii) Separate Communities or a Global Community?

The foregoing difference leads to very different views of community. Whereas the RD takes the view that we belong to separate political communities, and justifies borders as a barrier to free movement, the PD considers all of us as belonging to a global human community, and views borders as an opportunity for movement. It suggests, therefore, that the flow of migrants between sending and receiving countries evokes a shared challenge.[21]

(iii) Cultural or Economic Conflict?

Following this same line, the RD categorises immigration as an issue of public order and security, based on the logic of the clash of civilisations.[22] As a consequence, it argues that claims to freedom must be balanced by the need to secure a polity and its cultural substance. Ultimately, borders not only separate people but also, and most fundamentally, civilisations that adhere to incompatible religions. The PD takes a very different tack. From the outset, immigration is a process that plays a decisive role in our demographic, economic, social and cultural development.[23] Consequently, whereas the RD holds countries of emigration and the emigrants themselves as responsible,

[19] VI, 09/1999, no 261; 13916. As far as I know, there is no formal system of citing legislative initiatives in the following system: (VIII, 03/2006, no 164; 8219) meaning (Legislature, month/year, initiative number; page number in the log of the Spanish legislature's sessions).

[20] VI, 06/1996, no 166; 8841.

[21] 'One must keep in mind that Morocco also has a problem with immigrants, which is the same problem we could have' (VIII, 10/2005, no 120; 6008).

[22] VI, 06/1996, no 169; 9046.

[23] VIII, 05/2004, no 8; 289.

the PD holds the destination countries responsible for attracting the immigrants. It is clear that from the PD's point of view, borders separate people living in developing and developed countries.[24] The authentic root of conflict is poverty, not culture.

(iv) Crime or Marginalisation?

Each discourse has a 'list' of basic inadmissible dangers ensuing from bad border management. For the RD, the main negative effects of immigration are instability and crime, such that immigration can alter the peaceful coexistence of the political community.[25] For the PD, the basic danger is the creation of ghettos,[26] and matters related to racist violence, offences against workers or immigrant exploitation, legal violence, traffic of immigrants, religious intolerance, and discrimination.

(v) Xenophobia or Fragmentation?

For the RD, the massive immigrant arrival produces xenophobia, rejection or labour imbalances that justify certain reactions by citizens, while the PD argues that immigration becomes the recurring alibi for intolerance.[27] According to the PD, the arrival of immigrants becomes the pretext for forms of anti-immigrant discourse that can even become 'fascist' if they pretend 'to impose on the majority of the citizens projects of mutually exclusive or totalitarian nature'.[28] The PD is also worried by the rupture of political community, to the extent that immigration gives rise to the loss of rights.[29]

(vi) Consequences or Causes?

While the RD interprets the migratory process in terms of its negative effects on the receiving community, the PD not only emphasises the positive effects thereof but, crucially, looks to the causes of immigration: why do people come? The RD undergirds the negative consequences of immigration by employing terms such as invasion, plague, waves, avalanches. As one member of parliament put it, 'we are being flooded by the Africans'.[30] For the RD, the immigrant 'calls at the doors' of our political community; for

[24] 'The dramatic and intolerable gap of richness between the more development countries and the underdeveloped countries' (VI, 09/1999, no 261; 13912).

[25] VII, 10/2000, no 32; 1424.

[26] VII, 10/2003, no 284; 14915.

[27] VII, 05/2002, no 162; 8212.

[28] *Ibid.*

[29] 'We don't want to build a society with people from different classes, people with rights, people with rights cut in half' (VII, 10/2003, no 284; 14906).

[30] VI, 09/1999, no 261; 13914.

the PD, the act of migration is explained by the attraction of political community: the political community 'calls' the immigrant. The converse of this call is an appeal from the countries of origin: 'Africa demands our help'.[31]

(vii) Choice or Need?

Whereas the RD interprets the act of migration as a voluntary act, the PD views it as the expression of need, as an act impelled by necessity. This new analytical distinction explains why the former discourse reacts against changes to the receiving political community, whereas the latter aims to accommodate both communities. As a member of parliament put it, '[t]he immigrants of Ghana, Mr. Minister, don't read the Official Bulletin of the State, they do not read it; the immigrants of Ghana come pushed by hunger, necessity and desperation'.[32] 'Immigration is not the same in the first world, where there is freedom, as compared to immigration from the third world to the first world, to which one is forced by the attempt to escape from misery, poverty and desperation'.[33] Consolidating this same discursive logic, there are also arguments that emphasise the existing power relations in the departure countries as the cause of the act of migration: 'the citizens run from oppressors'.[34]

(viii) Receptive Political Community or Immigrants: Which Has an Obligation Toward the Other?

The fact of questioning the cause of immigration in these terms has implied fundamental rules in terms of the structural political opportunities. For the RD, the receptive political community does not have the obligation to redefine itself because the act of migration is voluntary. The whole argument is: 'if they have come voluntarily, they know they will find another political community with a different system of rules that they must accept'. The logic RD follows is that if people move into a new community, they must forget their culture and traditions and accept, without any chance of complaint, the rules of the game of the welcoming political community. From the perspective of the need paradigm, this argument forfeits its authority. In effect, the PD calls into question the assumption of the RD according to which States do not have any obligation toward immigrants, but immigrants must have the obligation to adjust themselves to the cultural guidelines of the

[31] VIII, 10/2005, no 120; 5999.
[32] VII, 10/2000, no 32; 1442.
[33] VII, 09/2001, no 102; 4971.
[34] VII, 09/1996, no 26; 1087.

welcoming political community. In line with these ideas, the PD insists that States have 'a moral obligation to receive'.[35]

B. Policy Answers to Immigration

To sum up, these two discourses have different understandings of what it is that borders separate: whereas the RD argues that borders separate civilisations, that the European border is the frontier of western civilisation, the PD stresses that borders separate rich from poor political communities. These two views provide the foundation for the two types of policy response:

(i) Security or Human Rights?

For the RD, border issues are considered as raising public order problems that require constant surveillance of containment walls with police measures and repressive policies. For the RD, to regulate is to control. To control the flow means to establish restricted rules of access. It interprets the regulation of migration flows in terms of policing, arguing that 'our reception possibilities are not unlimited',[36] that 'we can not fit all of them in here, there is limited space'.[37] The control criteria must be established basically in light of our 'capacity of reception'[38] and also with regards to the identity criteria. In this latter case, selection must be made according to national origin. The RD defends a border policy of 'national preference'. In short, border policy must follow two aims: to avoid the arrival of more immigrants ('immigration is a bad thing that should be avoided'), and to allow for the selection of these based on national origin and identity criteria. By contrast, the PD perceives the regulation of immigration in universal terms, based on the humanistic principles of non-discrimination in relation to nationality or identity criteria. It argues for the channelling of immigration through legal means: 'choose the consulates instead of small un-seaworthy boats or the stowaways'.[39] It even leads to a logic totally opposite to that of the RD: instead of reinforcing controls, it argues that these must be softened, because 'if immigrants had easier access to get in and out, a lot more of them would come as seasonal workers'.[40] It must give an incentive to a culture of canalisation of migratory flows[41] overcoming the dichotomy between 'fence' and 'solidarity'.[42]

35 VI, 04/1999, no 277; 14961.
36 VII, 07/2003, no 267; 13970.
37 VII, 07/2003, no 267; 13978.
38 Eg, VII, 04/2002, no 153; 7770.
39 VI, 04/1999, no 277; 14962.
40 VII, 10/2003, no 284; 14910. See also VII, 07/2003, no 267; 13979.
41 VII, 02/2001, no 61; 2950.
42 VIII, 10/2005, no 120; 6001.

(ii) Addressing the 'Call Effect' or the 'Exit Effect'?

According to the RD, the 'call effect' is caused by an 'open and less restrictive legislation'.[43] As a result, migration policy should be oriented towards making life more difficult for immigrants, as a way of weakening the call effect.[44] The RD even defends the need for 'taking a hard line' to avoid the call effect, arguing that 'the government cannot be weak when the time comes to defend the interests of Spain and its territorial integrity against it turning into an avalanche effect'.[45] The PD, by contrast, emphasises the existence of an 'exit effect'. In its view, the link is not between the 'call effect' and the alleged legislation/policy that may be pursued, but rather between the 'exit effect' and the characteristics of the communities of origin: higher demographic growth levels, unemployment, weak social and cultural networks, slow economic growth. 'With these problems there is no border capable of preventing people from crossing the Mediterranean Sea'.[46] Accordingly, the real task of migration policy is to address the root causes of the exit effect, tackling the gross inequalities between rich and poor countries.

(iii) Local or Global Justice?

Finally, and summarising the foregoing contrasts, these two discourses differ in their understanding of the scope of the justice which underpins migration policy. The RD moves to control the borders of the polity with a view to realising distributive justice *within* the community. It draws a sharp distinction between those inside and those outside, such that those within are viewed as the preferred recipients of rights and resources generated by the community. Justice, on this view, is a virtue of a local political community. By contrast, PD views immigration as the outcome of 'global injustice':

> Nobody migrates on a whim, thousands of human beings are forced to abandon their lands, leave their families, among other things because their towns are being pushed down by multinationals ... an economic system that sinks the majority of the planet into misery.[47]

Borders do not separate religious civilisations that are at odds with each other; instead they are the expression of socio-economical inequalities. The

[43] Eg VII, 02/2001, no 61; 2978.
[44] VII, 07/2003, no 267; 13977.
[45] VIII, 10/2005, no 120; 6001.
[46] VI, 04/1999, no 277; 14959.
[47] VII, 02/2001, no 61; 2975.

forced act of migration is looked at as one of the 'social consequences of global capitalism'.[48] From this perspective, forced migration is viewed as a systematic failure of international relations, economic and otherwise.[49]

IV. NORMATIVE CHALLENGES AND THE EMERGENCE OF A EUROPEAN POLITICAL COMMUNITY

The analysis of the political discourse on borders in the Spanish Parliament suggests the need to differentiate between two levels of normative issues posed by immigration. The first concerns competing normative dimensions of migration policy; the second, the underlying interpretation of the functions of borders and the conditions that govern the emergence of a European political community.[50]

A. Three Normative Challenges Confronting Migration Policy

The first normative challenge confronting migration policy is to what extent robust borders controls can be combined with the protection of the human rights of immigrants. Although Spain has worked hard to control its borders by extending the Integrated System of External Surveillance (SIVE) to Fuerteventura and by sending patrol boats to Mauritania, it also has (under pressure from international human rights organisations) increased its concern for human rights. This is the proactive discourse that legitimises Spanish policy. Although immigration is provoking serious problems of governance, what the current Spanish government cannot be (or does not want to be) accused of is infringing human rights while managing immigration flows. The central question confronting the Socialist government that has been in power since March 2004 is, therefore, how to balance human rights and a robust control of borders. The problem, however, is that although this new policy paradigm attaches great importance to the protection of human rights, it has not succeeded in controlling immigration flows, with adverse effects on public opinion, as numerous polls have confirmed.[51] The question that remains to be answered is whether both dimensions can be promoted or whether there is a zero-sum

48 VII, 02/2001, no 61; 2976.
49 VII, 02/2001, no 61; 2975.
50 R Zapata-Barrero and N de Witte, 'The Spanish Governance of EU borders: Normative Questions' (2007) 12 *Mediterranean Politics* 85–90.
51 Spain exemplifies there is a clear link between policies and public opinion, which is at the basis of what I call 'the ambivalence of Spanish public opinion', when border and integration issues are compared. See R Zapata-Barrero, n 16 above.

game between security and human rights, such that a robust management of borders can only be achieved by giving up the humane treatment of immigrants.

A response to this first question is no doubt related to a second normative challenge. As noted earlier, there are good reasons to believe that enormous economic inequality plays a decisive role in immigration flows from Africa to Spain and the EU. As is becoming increasingly clear, African countries have initiated an unprecedented strategic political offensive against the flagrant injustice of their economic and social situation. The only resource which they have been able to muster to this effect seems to be to promote emigration. In response, Spain has started a diplomatic offensive to persuade African countries to control their own borders in exchange for development cooperation. The background question is, however, whether these ad hoc arrangements are sufficient or whether it might not be necessary to explicitly acknowledge that migration policy and economic policy are intimately related to each other. The tension, therefore, seems to be that privileging the *local* scope of distributive justice calls forth strategic behaviour by immigrants individually, and their countries of origin collectively, while privileging the *global* scope of distributive justice tends to erode the very sense of political collectivity which fuels migration policy to begin with.

This second normative challenge leads into a third. In effect, Spain has attempted to deal with the aforementioned tension by Europeanising its borders. While in the '90s the EU pressed Spain to control its borders, today it is Spain that increasingly urges the European Union to consider border control as a European issue. Spain has raised awareness in the EU that irregular immigration is not just a Spanish but also a European problem, and that the Spanish border with Africa is also a European border. Clearly, however, success in this endeavour depends to a great extent on the readiness of the Member States to Europeanise migration policy, which has hitherto been one of the hallowed domains of state sovereignty. Moreover, to the extent that, as noted above, migration and economic policy are increasingly intertwined, Europeanising migration policy has potentially far-reaching consequences for issues of distributive justice within Spain and each of the other Member States: Europeanising Spain's Southern borders is yet a further step in Europeanising decisions concerning the distribution of political membership, resources, and rights.

B. Borders and the Emergence of a European Political Community

These normative challenges confronting migration policy allow us to conclude by briefly discussing two fundamental, 'meta-normative' issues. The first concerns the functions of borders and their relation to politics and ethics; the second concerns the relation between border crossings by immigrants and the emergence of a European political community.

As to the first of these issues, both border crossings by immigrants, and migration policy in response to those crossings bear witness to the two indissoluble functions of borders: to join and to separate. They are indissoluble because borders would cease to be such if they only joined or only separated. If borders only separated it would no longer be possible to acknowledge that there is an outside and, by implication, an inside; if they only joined, then there would be no way of differentiating between inside and outside, hence there would no longer be two regions that could be joined. Yet, although these two functions are necessarily intertwined, migration policy can privilege one or the other. This is precisely the upshot of the strong normative polarisation of the two discourses explored in Section III. In different ways, each of the contrasting terms posited by the reactive discourse (RD) in the previous section puts the predominantly separating function of borders to the fore. This is particularly clear insofar as its defence of distributive justice within discrete political communities goes hand in hand with the interpretation of illegal border crossings as a security problem that calls for strict border control. By the same token, the enforcement of political borders aims to enforce the distinction between citizen and alien. By contrast, the proactive discourse (PD) emphasises the joining function of borders. In effect, it approaches immigration from the perspective of global justice. Border crossings, in this view, highlight that borders join inside and outside, that is, that inside and outside are places within an encompassing whole—a global community. Whereas the RP emphasises that migration policy is about enforcing borders, the PD aims above all to constitute them anew, to redraw them.[52] It is not surprising, therefore, that the PD emphasises human rights, which, by definition, abstract from the distinction between citizen and alien to identify that which joins individuals as such. It would be a mistake, however, to assert that either of these discourses entirely suppresses one of the functions of borders in the process of putting the other to the fore. The RP, for example, does not renege on the human rights commitments to which Spain is bound, both constitutionally and in terms of obligations under treaties of international law. The PD, for the other, does not deny that borders separate in the very process of joining. For example, unless borders separated, it would make no sense to assert that Spain has, as cited heretofore, a 'moral obligation to receive'. Moreover, it does not aim to suppress the distinction between citizen and alien as such, but rather to redefine the terms in which this distinction is drawn.

[52] For a related discussion of the separating/joining functions of borders, and of boundary enfocement and constitution, see Hans Lindahl's contribution to this volume (ch 6).

Accordingly, if politics depends on the distinction between citizen and alien, and if ethics seeks to clarify what rights (and obligations) accrue to individuals as individuals, then we could say that the RP speaks to a politics of borders whereas the PD speaks to an ethics of borders.[53] As such, both discourses are in a certain sense complementary to each other: whereas the former shows borders to be the expression of particularity, the latter views borders as the manifestation of universality. To recognise that sheer particularity and sheer universality are unthinkable is to acknowledge that borders are more or less *porous*, ie that migration policy is always a matter of accentuating either the separating or the joining functions of borders. Migration policy, by these lights, is always a variable mix of these two functions. This is precisely what Spain's current migration policy attests to, insofar as it seeks to balance security considerations and respect for human rights.

While the analysis of Section III focuses on how these two discourses play a role in defining the normative contours of migration policy in Spain, they are also relevant to the debate about the normative contours of a European migration policy, precisely insofar as they are intimately linked to the two general functions of borders. But there is a further point which merits closer consideration. At stake here is not so much the structure but rather the genesis, the emergence of political borders and, in particular, the emergence of the EU as a political community. In effect, it is easy to overlook that European borders and a European political community arise in response to immigration flows. While European politicians are quarrelling about a common approach to immigration and the definition of EU borders, immigrants play a crucial role in constituting the EU as a political community. A certain paradox emerges here. Indeed, the EU does not manage its borders because its Member States and European citizens already view themselves as parties to a political community. In fact, and ironically, the absence of a common migration policy highlights the lack of such a vision of political community and borders within the EU itself. Whether 'we' Europeans become a political community, and what 'we' become as a political community, are not merely our decisions, which we then go ahead and implement in migration policy. Instead, immigration flows from Africa highlight that

[53] The differentiation between the politics and the ethics of borders is related to the discussion between the logic of markets and the logic of politics, which inspired J Hollifield. See J Hollifield, *Immigrants, Markets and States* (Harvard, Harvard University Press, 1992). In this case the logic of politics or the *politics of borders* wants to emphasise control as following the interests of the State, and the management of borders as a barrier to free movement. On the opposite side, the ethics of Borders is inspired by J Carens's work on the ethics of immigration admissions, and his discussion on moral constraints to control of immigration. See JH Carens, 'Who should get in? The Ethics of Immigration Admission' (2003) 17 *Ethics & International Affairs* 95–110. Compare this distinction between the politics and ethics of borders with the concept of 'political morality' developed by Dora Kostakopoulou in her contribution to this volume (ch 8).

the European Union has become an 'imagined community' for those who do not belong. Pushing this insight yet a step further, we could not become a 'we' unless treated and addressed as such by those whom 'we' can then go ahead and call 'other'.[54] In short, to the extent that the genesis of a political community is linked to the management of borders, the emergence of a European polity is not, in the first instance, the outcome of a collective decision of Europeans. Rather it is rendered possible by acts of immigrants, who paradoxically contribute to constituting the borders of the EU, and thereby the EU as a political community, in the very process of crossing them. In that case, could it not be said that in a decisive way immigrants into the EU are its founders as a political community?

[54] For a related conception of the responsive genesis of legal borders see Peter Fitzpatrick's contribution to this volume (ch 5).

2

The Borders Paradox:

The Surveillance of Movement in a Union without Internal Frontiers

VALSAMIS MITSILEGAS

I. INTRODUCTION

ONE OF THE central objectives of European integration has been the abolition of borders leading to the unhindered free movement of persons *within* the European Union (EU). This move has been combined with calls for 'compensatory' measures to strengthen the external border of the EU. This logic, which was central to the development of the Schengen project and has since permeated EU law and politics, in particular the objective of developing the Union as an 'area of freedom, security and justice', has led to the considerable strengthening and proliferation of controls at and beyond the EU external border. Efforts to that effect were marked inter alia by the *displacement* of border controls both in terms of *time* (with border controls taking place *before* departure—for instance by the introduction of visa regimes and carriers sanctions) and in terms of *space* (border controls in the territories of third countries and not at the EU external border). These measures, along with the expansion and centrality of the Schengen *acquis* in the development of EU Justice and Home Affairs law (in particular in the context of the successive EU enlargements during this decade), could lead one to believe that by strengthening the Union's external border, the goal of total freedom of movement *within the EU* for those managing to be *inside* the Union's territory could have been achieved.

The implications of this proliferation and externalisation of border controls in the EU have been well documented.[1] This chapter aims to further

[1] See in this context the seminal work of Elspeth Guild and Didier Bigo: in particular Guild's 2001 inaugural lecture at the University of Nijmegen, *Moving the Borders of Europe* (available at http//cmr.jur.ru.nl/cmr/docs/oratie.eg.pdf); and more recently the contributions in D Bigo and E Guild (eds), *Controlling Frontiers. Free Movement into and within Europe* (Aldershot, Ashgate, 2005).

the analysis on the proliferation of borders in the EU, by looking at more recent instances of imposition of controls of movement by the EU. It will be argued that these new controls differ from the earlier steps towards establishing a Schengen border management model in four main respects:

premised upon a risk-based approach, they are now explicitly linked with security and counter-terrorism;

they consist increasingly of the generalised collection and exchange of personal data (including sensitive information such as biometrics) related to different instances of movement, both within and outside the Union;

their scope extends beyond third country nationals wishing to enter the EU, to cover information on the movement of everyone, including EU citizens;

by the maximisation of such data collection and exchange, border controls are transformed into a model of generalised surveillance of movement, based on profiling, and on concepts such as the trusted or suspect passenger.

The chapter will examine the content and implications of this new model of surveillance of movement in the EU by looking at the evolution of three different strands of surveillance. The first strand involves the proliferation of controls stemming from the legal exceptions to the abolition of internal borders under Schengen. It will be demonstrated how exceptions to these rules, along with an emphasis on policing those events and individuals deemed as 'high risk' in order to maintain public order, have led to a gradual shift from border controls to surveillance of suspects. The second strand consists of developments stemming from the introduction of a logic of 'border security' into EU law. In this context, the chapter will look at the emergence of the concept of 'border security' in the Anglo-American world (emphasising its link with counter-terrorism). It will then look at its translation at the EU level via concrete measures such as the collection and exchange of passenger data, the inclusion of biometrics in identity documents and databases, and the blurring of the boundaries between immigration control and counter-terrorism in the field of information collection and exchange. The third strand, which is currently emerging, emphasises again the risk-based approach by attempting to create an automatic, high-tech system of entry and exit into the EU on the basis of biometrics and the emergence of concepts such as the trusted or bona fide traveller. These various strands of surveillance of movement in the EU will be examined in the light of their implications for both the individual (in terms of privacy, identity and non-discrimination), but also for the nature and fundamental values of a Union whose central constitutional principle has always been free movement.

II. RISK AND PUBLIC ORDER

The abolition of internal border controls under Schengen was not without exceptions. Such exceptions were introduced in the Schengen Implementing Convention in order to address the potential lack of trust between authorities in Member States as well as the destabilising feeling (at least from the point of view of these authorities) that the discontinuation of controls at the border would have. From the outset, the Schengen Implementing Convention introduced the possibility of Contracting Parties reinstating, for a limited period, national border checks on grounds of public policy or national security.[2] A study on the use of this provision pre- and post-incorporation of the Schengen *acquis* into the EC/EU legal order in Amsterdam, has demonstrated that requests by Schengen members to reintroduce border controls were in general accepted by the other members; that the events that triggered them were primarily political gatherings such as European Council and G8 meetings and Heads of State visits; and that in practice the Schengen countries have used the reintroduction of border controls to control the behaviour of those residing *inside* the EU.[3] Another Schengen exception with a similar effect has been a clause in the Schengen Implementing Convention stating that the abolition of controls in the internal border will not affect the exercise of police powers by the competent authorities of the Contracting Parties.[4] In practice this may lead to the de facto replacement of border controls by police checks near the old, abolished, border.[5]

Both these exceptions have survived the recasting of the Schengen borders provisions in the EC Schengen Borders Code.[6] The title on the abolition of internal borders includes a chapter on the temporary reintroduction of border controls at internal borders,[7] with such reintroduction being allowed exceptionally for a limited—but renewable—period of 30 days 'where there is a serious threat to public policy or internal security'.[8] The replacement of *national* by *internal* security is noteworthy in this context, not only as an indicator of the evolution of the Schengen *acquis* in Community law, but also as a term which can potentially broaden the

[2] Art 2(2) of the Schengen Implementing Convention.

[3] See K Groenendijk, 'Reinstatement of Controls at the Internal Borders of Europe: Why and Against Whom?' (2004) 10 *European Law Journal* 150–70.

[4] Art 2(3) of the Schengen Implementing Convention.

[5] For a study of the use of Art 2(3) in The Netherlands and Germany, see K Groenendijk, 'New Borders Behind Old Ones: Post-Schengen Controls Behind the Internal Borders and Inside the Netherlands and Germany' in K Groenendijk, E Guild and P Minderhoud (eds), *In Search of Europe's Borders* (The Hague, Kluwer Law International, 2003) 131–46.

[6] Reg (EC) No 562/2006 establishing a Community Code on the rules governing the movement of persons across borders (Schengen Borders Code), [2006] OJ L105/1.

[7] *Ibid*, Arts 23–31.

[8] *Ibid*, Art 25. See also Preamble, recital 16.

scope of the exception, allowing Member States to use it as a means of social control. On the other hand, the Schengen Borders Code continues to allow the exercise of police powers *within* the territory 'insofar as the exercise of those powers does not have an effect equivalent to border checks'.[9] The Schengen Borders Code also introduces the concept of 'border surveillance', whose purpose is 'to prevent unauthorised border crossings, to counter cross-border criminality and to take measures against persons who have crossed the border illegally'.[10] Immigration control and the control of criminality are thus explicitly linked, and the emphasis on the prevention of entry is notable.[11]

In practice, information available thus far indicates that reintroduction of border controls under the Schengen Borders Code has been requested during periods of political summits[12] and sports events such as the Euro 2008 in Austria and Switzerland.[13] Border controls have also been reintroduced, however, to address what was deemed 'a severe risk of public order disturbances' arising from demonstrations organised in the Basque country in Spain and Bayonne in France.[14] It is also noteworthy that, under the Schengen Implementing Convention, after the London bombings of July 2005 France reintroduced land border controls with Italy which were renewed on a monthly basis for a considerable period of time.[15] These examples confirm the earlier finding that the reintroduction of border controls is increasingly being used by Member States to monitor the activities of *EU citizens and residents*, especially those deemed to pose a risk to the State. On the other hand, it has been reported that police controls *within*

[9] See Art 21 of the Schengen Borders Code and the detailed criteria aiming to distinguish between police powers and border controls contained therein. For an analysis of the negotiation history of this provision, see E Guild, 'Danger—Borders under Construction: Assessing the First Five Years of Border Policy in an Area of Freedom, Security and Justice' in JW de Zwaan and FANJ Goudappel (eds), *Freedom, Security and Justice in the European Union. Implementing the Hague Programme* (The Hague, TMC Asser Press, 2006) 45–72 at 68–71.

[10] Schengen Borders Code, Art 12.

[11] See in this context the Commission Communication on examining the creation of a European Border Surveillance System (EUROSUR), COM(2008) 68 final, Brussels, 13 February 2008, and the work of the European Border Agency (FRONTEX). On Frontex, see V Mitsilegas, 'Border Security in the European Union. Towards Centralised Controls and Maximum Surveillance' in E Guild, H Toner and A Baldaccini (eds), *Whose Freedom, Security and Justice? EU Immigration and Asylum Law and Policy* (Oxford, Hart Publishing, 2007) 359–94 and more recently House of Lords European Union Committee, *FRONTEX: the EU External Borders Agency*, 9th Report, session 2007–08, HL Paper 60.

[12] See EC Council docs 13837/06, Brussels, 11 October 2006; 15332/06, Brussels, 15 November 2006; and 6084/07, Brussels, 7 February 2007.

[13] Council doc 10172/08, Brussels, 30 May 2008.

[14] Council doc 15933/06, Brussels, 29 November 2006. See also the reintroduction of border controls under Art 2(2) of the Schengen Implementing Convention in docs 13332/02, Brussels, 21 October 2002; and 6825/06, Brussels, 28 February 2006.

[15] See, inter alia, Council doc 5148/06, Brussels, 9 January 2006.

the territory have, de facto, replaced border controls in the aftermath of the expansion of the Schengen area to include as full members the majority of the 2004 EU newcomers.[16] The move of the EU external border eastwards at the end of 2007 has not been accompanied by a high level of trust by certain 'old' Member States (in particular Germany), something that may lead to an increased use of Article 21 of the Schengen Borders Code.[17]

Along with the shift towards control of the activities of broader categories of population—including EU nationals and residents—that they entail, the Schengen exceptions have also led to *targeted* checks on specific categories of individuals deemed by the authorities as 'high risk'.[18] This trend towards controls *within* the Schengen area (and the non-Schengen Union territory), targeted specifically against high-risk individuals which would include EU citizens and residents, has also been reflected in specific measures adopted by the Council to control the movement of individuals in relation to *events* deemed 'high risk'. In this context, the 2004 Resolution 'on security in Council meetings and other comparable events' calls on Member States to provide the Member State hosting such events with information on the movements of individuals or groups 'in respect of whom there are substantial grounds for believing that they intend to enter the Member State with the aim of disrupting public order and security at the event or committing offences relating to that event'.[19] The Resolution also addresses situations where Member States have reintroduced border controls in accordance with the Schengen Implementing Convention, stating that precedence should be given to *intelligence-led checks* focusing on individuals falling within the above category.[20] Moreover, Member States have adopted a series of measures specifically related to football matches—a Resolution on the use of bans on access to venues of football matches

[16] For an overview of recent developments, see A Faure Atger, *The Abolition of Internal Border Checks in an Enlarged Schengen Area: Freedom of Movement or a Scattered Web of Security Checks?*, CEPS Research paper No 8, March 2008 at www.ceps.be.

[17] For complaints by the German police in the light of the eastward Schengen expansion, see 'Police Protest at "Threat" of Open Borders', *The Times*, 23 November 2007. On the issue of trust and the eastward EU enlargement in the context of Justice and Home Affairs see, inter alia, N Walker, 'The Problem of Trust in an Enlarged Area of Freedom, Security and Justice: A Conceptual Analysis' in M Anderson and J Apap (eds), *Police and Justice Co-operation and the New European Borders* (The Hague, Kluwer Law International, 2002) 19–34; J Monar, *Enlargement-Related Diversity in EU Justice and Home Affairs*, WRR, Dutch Scientific Council for Government Policy, Working Document 112, The Hague, 2000; and in the context of borders specifically, V Mitsilegas, 'The Implementation of the EU Illegal Immigration *Acquis* by the Applicant Countries of Central and Eastern Europe: Challenges and Contradictions' (2002) 28 *Journal of Ethnic and Migration Studies* 665–82.

[18] On this point with regard to the reintroduction of border checks, see Groenendijk, above n 3.

[19] Council Resolution of 29 April 2004 [2004] OJ C116/18, point 1.

[20] *Ibid*, Point 3.

with an international dimension[21] and a Decision concerning access and exchange of information with regard to high-risk football supporters.[22]

Although the legal force of some of these instruments is weak, their message should not be underestimated. It demonstrates a shift from traditional border controls aimed at regulating entry into the territory to generalised surveillance aimed at preventing the movement of individuals who are deemed to pose a risk to public order. The logic of these measures—which are based upon subjective criteria and are worded broadly with regard to their scope—has since been replicated in a series of Member States' initiatives aimed at monitoring the movement of individuals deemed as 'troublesome'.[23] A web of surveillance is thus created on the basis of the concept of the 'high risk' individual. Along with the significant consequences this approach may have for fundamental rights and citizenship (for instance, the extent to which these measures will effectively shield European political elites from any kind of protest), this risk-based approach could lead to significant inroads to the very freedom of movement of EU citizens and residents *within* the Union.[24]

III. BORDER SECURITY

A. The Concept of 'Border Security'—the United States and the United Kingdom

The concept of 'border security' has appeared prominently in the United States' (US) policy discourse post 9/11. It was included within the broader

[21] Council Resolution of 23 November 2003 [2003] OJ C281/1. These bans would cover individuals previously guilty of violent conduct at football matches—point 1. See also the Council Resolution of 4 December 2006 'concerning an updated handbook with recommendations for international police co-operation' in this context [2006] OJ C322/1. In the appendix to the handbook, a 'risk' supporter is defined as 'a person, known or not, who can be regarded as posing a possible risk to public order or antisocial behaviour, whether planned or spontaneous, at or in connection with a football event' ([2006] C322/18).

[22] Council Decision 2002/348/JHA concerning security in connection with football matches with an international dimension, [2002] OJ L121/1, Art 2(1) and (2) (amended by Council Decision 2007/412/JHA, [2007] OJ L155/76). For an analysis, see A Tsoukala, *Security Policies and Human Rights in European Football Stadia*, Challenge Research Paper No 5, March 2007, at www.ceps.be.

[23] See in this context: the Dutch initiative for a Council Decision on strengthening cross-border police co-operation with regard to meetings attended by large numbers of people from more than one Member State, [2005] OJ C101/36; and recent proposals by the German Government with regard to the exchange of information on 'troublemakers'—see Council docs 15079/07, Brussels, 13 November 2007; 16585/07, Brussels, 17 December 2007; and 7544/08, Brussels, 14 March 2008. See also the relevant Statewatch Report (www.statewatch.org/news/2008/apr/04eu-troublemakers.htm).

[24] Dora Kostakopoulou makes an analogous point in her contribution to this volume (ch 8), pointing out that the securitisation of borders compromises fundamental values and principles of the European polity itself.

concept of the highly symbolic term of 'homeland security', whose use by the Bush Administration has led to the establishment of a distinct Department of 'Homeland Security' and the development of a national strategy for 'homeland security'. The latter, put forward in 2002, places great emphasis on 'border and transportation security' and on information sharing for homeland security—the ultimate aim being the establishment of a 'border of the future' (or 'smart borders') and of a so-called 'system of systems' which will provide 'the right information to the right people at all times'.[25] This strategy was translated into a series of legislative and executive measures aiming on the one hand at *monitoring the movement* of passengers into and via the US (by the establishment of pre-screening systems) and on the other at *promoting interagency co-operation and the interoperability of databases* with regard to 'homeland' and 'border' security. The latter appears as a term in the title of the 2002 Enhanced Border Security and Visa Entry Reform Act, which placed emphasis on another element of 'border security' linked to both aspects described above: the *identification of individuals* wishing to enter the US, in particular by introducing requirements that travel documents contain machine-readable data, such as fingerprints. Subsequent measures (such as the US-VISIT Programme) expressly required the taking of *biometric identifiers* from individuals entering the US.[26] Related schemes developed by the Department of Homeland Security such as the Automated Targeting System (ATS) are emblematic of this approach of collecting and comparing a wide range of data for preventive security purposes. The ATS 'compares traveller, cargo and conveyance information against intelligence and other enforcement data by incorporating risk-based targeting scenarios and assessments'.[27] It processes data stemming from passenger databases (public and private), visa databases, and also terrorist watch lists and suspect and violator indices 'to develop a risk assessment *for each traveller*' (emphasis added).[28] The centrality of profiling in this approach is evident.

A similar emphasis on 'border security' via the maximum identification of individuals *before* they reach the border can be discerned in United

[25] See in this context the—now aborted—scheme put forward by the Bush Administration for the establishment of a 'Total Information Awareness' (TIA) system. For an analysis of TIA see R Whitaker, 'A Faustian Bargain? America and the Dream of Total Information Awareness' in KD Haggerty and RV Ericson (eds), *The New Politics of Surveillance and Visibility* (Toronto, University of Toronto Press, 2006) 141–70.

[26] For a general analysis of 'border security' in the US context, see V Mitsilegas, 'Borders, Security and Transatlantic Co-operation in the 21st Century: Identity and Privacy in an Era of Globalised Surveillance' in T Givens, G Freeman and D Leal (eds), *Immigration Policy and Security: US, European and Commonwealth Perspectives* (New York, Routledge, 2009) 148–66.

[27] US Department of Homeland Security, *Privacy Impact Assessment for the Automated Targeting System*, 3 August 2007, at 2.

[28] *Ibid*, 5.

Kingdom (UK) policy, whose centre-piece has been the establishment of an 'e-borders' programme or, in Home Office jargon, of a 'joined-up, modernised and intelligence-led border control and security framework'.[29] Subsequent policy documents emphasise the priority on identifying individuals by the use of biometrics. The title and tone of the Home Office Action Plan on '*Borders, Immigration and Identity*' are indicative in this context: it is boldly stated that 'biometric technology now means that *we can link people to a unique identity*' and that biometrics are 'the most secure way of *fixing an individual to a unique identity*' (emphasis added).[30] This extraordinary use of language is repeated in the Home Office Strategy Paper entitled '*Securing the UK Border*',[31] where 'identity management' is flagged up as a key element of the Government's approach. As the Home Office proclaims,

> we want ... *to fix people's identities at the earliest point practicable*, checking them *through each stage of their journey*, identifying those presenting risk and stopping them coming to the UK. By the time a passenger has been identified at the border posing a threat, it can be too late—they have achieved their goal in reaching our shores. *Off-shoring our border control is the keystone of our border defence* (emphasis added).[32]

The key aim of such a system is the accumulation, for preventive purposes, of *knowledge* regarding individuals who move. As is explicitly stated in the same document, 'our aim is to build up *as rich a knowledge of the travelling public as possible*' (emphasis added).[33] This emphasis on (i) knowledge and identification, (ii) prior to reaching the border, (iii) primarily via biometrics is repeated in a number of subsequent UK policy documents. In 2007 alone, references to 'fixing' people's identities (or, according to the latest White Paper entitled 'Security in a Global Hub', *all individuals being 'locked into a secure biometric identity*' (emphasis added))[34] have appeared in at least three major policy initiatives on migration, borders and security.[35] Biometrics in border controls have also been used to create the concept of a 'Trusted Traveller'—under this scheme, individuals are pre-screened

[29] See Home Office, *Controlling our Borders: Making Migration Work for Britain. Five Year Strategy for Asylum and Immigration*, February 2005. For further analysis, see also V Mitsilegas, 'Human Rights, Terrorism and the Quest for Border Security' in M Pedrazzi (ed), *Individual Guarantees in the European Judicial Area in Criminal Matters* (Brussels, Bruylant, forthcoming).

[30] Home Office, *Borders, Immigration and Identity Action Plan,* December 2006, ch 2 (introduction and point 2.2 respectively).

[31] Home Office, *Securing the UK Border*, March 2007.

[32] *Ibid*, point 1.4.

[33] *Ibid*, point 4.1.

[34] Cabinet Office, *Security in a Global Hub*, November 2007, point 3.26.

[35] *Securing the UK Border*; *Security in a Global Hub*; and *Managing Global Migration* (Home Office and FCO, June 2007) in particular p 24).

and can then use fast-track access to the UK via automated gates using iris recognition.[36]

Accordingly, border security, comprising all of the elements mentioned above, has emerged as a top Government priority in the UK, inextricably linked with broader counter-terrorism purposes. This link was made crystal-clear in Gordon Brown's statement to the Commons on 'national security' in July 2007.[37] The emphasis has been on three 'lines of defence' against terrorism (before the border, at the border and in the country).[38] The use of biometrics is central in all three stages. In stage one, according to the Prime Minister,

> the way forward is electronic screening of all passengers as they check in and out of the country at ports and airports, so that terrorist suspects can be identified and stopped before they board planes, trains and boats to the United Kingdom. After a review of counter-terrorism screening ... the Home Secretary will enhance the existing e-borders programme to incorporate all passenger information to help to track and intercept terrorists and criminals as well as, of course, illegal immigrants.[39]

In both the UK and the US, 'border security' has thus emerged as part of a broader national security strategy, aiming in particular to address terrorist threats. In this context, 'border security' extends beyond border controls for the purposes of identifying those with a right to access in the territory: it extends beyond immigration control to the fight against crime and terrorism. This represents the creation of what scholars have already identified in the 1990s as the so-called '(in)security continuum' which consists of linking, in law and policy discourse, the disparate and very different aims of controlling immigration on the one hand and fighting 'security threats' such as crime and terrorism on the other.[40] Border security also extends beyond traditional border controls via its *preventative dimension*, which is leading to controls *before* travel and *before* the border. Last, but not least, the preventive dimension of border security leads to an increased focus on *knowledge* and *identification* by both the widening and (via biometrics) the deepening of information collection on individuals. While border controls focus in this context primarily on identifying third country nationals for

[36] Home Office, UK Border Agency, *A Strong New Force at the Border*, August 2008, p 17.

[37] HC Hansard vol 463, part no 130, cols 841–3, 25 July 2007.

[38] Note the similarities of this approach and the recent Commission definition of the concept of integrated border management in the EU, which involves 'measures taken at the consulates of Member States in third countries, measures at the border itself, and measures taken within the Schengen area' European Commission, *Communication on Preparing the Next Steps in Border Management in the European Union*, COM(2008) 69 final, Brussels, 13 February 2008, para 1.2.

[39] HC Hansard, above n 36, col 842.

[40] See in particular, D Bigo, *Polices en Réseaux. L'éxperience européenne* (Paris, Presses de Sciences Po, 1996).

the purposes of entry in the territory, border security extends information collection to *all passengers, everyone who is travelling*.[41] The following parts will aim to demonstrate the extent to which this concept of 'border security' has been applied at EU level.

B. Border Security through Monitoring Movement—the Emphasis on Passenger Data in the European Union

Recent years have witnessed an increased emphasis at EU level on measures requiring the collection and transmission of information with regard to air passengers. Legislation has been adopted both as a follow-up to internal EU initiatives, but also as a response to pressures to conform with external legal requirements, in particular US passenger identification standards—with similar standards recently being proposed by the Commission for flights entering the EU. While the influence of the 'border security' concept as outlined in part IIIA has been visible in the development of EU action in the field, the use of 'border security' for multiple purposes has not always led to legal solutions providing constitutional clarity.

(i) Advance Passenger Data

The 9/11 attacks have prompted an increased emphasis on collecting and monitoring passenger data in order to prevent this type of attack. The main prong of this strategy has been to require carriers to provide to the State a series of personal data related to their passengers. In the EU, such calls were made at the initiative of the Spanish Government, which in 2003 tabled a draft Directive requiring carriers flying to the EU to provide State authorities with data on all their passengers in advance of departure (the Advance Passenger Information (API) Directive).[42] The proposal was justified, and ultimately adopted, under Articles 62(2) (a) and 63(3)(b) of the EC Treaty. These serve as the legal basis for the adoption of measures relative to external border controls and illegal immigration respectively. Similarly, Article 1 of the finally adopted text states that the Directive 'aims at improving border controls and combating illegal immigration by the transmission of advance passenger data by carriers to the competent national authorities'.[43] The Directive obliges carriers to transmit a limited amount of passenger

[41] See also V Mitsilegas, 'Contrôle des étrangers, des passagers, des citoyens: Surveillance et anti-terrorisme' (2005) 58 *Cultures et Conflits* 155–82.

[42] For further details, see V Mitsilegas, 'Border Security in the European Union. Towards Centralised Controls and Maximum Surveillance', above n 11, at 359–94.

[43] Council Dir 2004/82/EC of 29 April 2004 on the obligation of carriers to communicate passenger data [2004] OJ L261/24, at 25.

data (such as names and date of birth and also the departure and arrival time of the flight) to the authorities. However, although the text of the Directive has the stated aim of combating illegal immigration, there have been attempts during negotiations to frame it also as a national security and counter-terrorism matter.[44]

The framing of the proposal as a counter-terrorism and national security measure would seem to cast doubt on the *legality* of its adoption solely under the first pillar. It could be argued that, similarly to certain Schengen-building proposals, the transmission of Advance Passenger Information (API), if justified as a border control *and* a counter-terrorism measure, would necessitate a dual legal basis in both the first and the third pillar. This would also necessitate two distinct legal instruments, a 'Title IV' (first pillar) directive and a 'Title VI' (third pillar) framework decision.[45]

The framing of the proposal as a security measure has had a considerable impact in the negotiations over the *content* of the proposal, most notably in the area of data protection. Article 6 of the Directive (on 'data processing') has been subject to long and controversial negotiations reflecting different national approaches on how far data exchanged under the Directive should be protected. Shortly before the adoption of the Directive, an agreement appeared to have been reached on strict data protection standards, including purpose limitation (transmission of data for the purpose of facilitating the performance of border checks with the objective of combating illegal immigration more effectively), limits to authorities having access to data (border authorities) and to the retention of data (which should be deleted by border authorities within 24 hours from transmission and by carriers within 24 hours from arrival). However, after pressure from the UK, two significant inroads were made to these standards:

— data would be deleted by border authorities within 24 hours from their transmission *unless* the data are needed later for the purposes of exercising the statutory functions of the authorities responsible for carrying out checks on persons at external borders in accordance with national law;
— Member States may also use personal passenger data for law enforcement purposes.[46]

It is clear that these additions render the pre-existing limits to access to, and retention of, data, as well as purpose limitation, virtually meaningless.

[44] This was undoubtedly the view of the UK Government. See their evidence in House of Lords, EU Committee, *Fighting illegal immigration: should carriers carry the burden?* 5th Report, session 2003–04, HL Paper 29.

[45] This view is reinforced by the recent ECJ ruling on the EC/US Passenger Name Data Agreement—see below.

[46] See Council doc 7595/04, 23 March 2004, where these changes were introduced.

Unsurprisingly, the insertion of these additional clauses to the text was hailed as a success by the UK government, as it would align the Directive to the UK 'multi-agency' approach, which links border checks with the fight against illegal immigration, crime and terrorism.[47] This link between immigration controls and law enforcement operations is explicitly made in Article 6 of the Directive, something that seems at odds with the justification of the proposal as a Title IV immigration and border controls measure. The link between immigration and national security is also made in the Preamble of the Directive, in a provision ironically designed to assuage data protection concerns.[48]

(ii) Passenger Name Records

(a) The EC/US Agreement While the justification of monitoring passenger data has been the subject of a debate in Europe, in the US the issue was indisputably related with counter-terrorism. Responding to the 9/11 attacks, the US passed legislation, in November 2001, requiring air carriers operating flights to, from, or through the US to provide US Customs with electronic access to data contained in their automatic reservation and departure control systems.[49] This data, known as Passenger Name Records (PNR), constitutes a record of each passenger's travel requirements and contains all the information necessary to enable reservations to be processed and controlled by the booking and participating airlines. PNR data can include a wide range of details, from the passenger's name and address to their email address, credit card details and on-flight dietary requirements. PNR is thus broader than the API data, which airlines flying to the EU were obliged to transmit under the Directive analysed above. Furthermore, US law empowered US Customs authorities to access airlines' databases (a 'pull' system), unlike the Directive, which required airlines to transmit API data by the end of check-in (a 'push' system).

The US legislation is applicable to all flights to the US, including flights from the EU. EU airlines would thus have to comply with the legislation if

[47] See the Home Office's recently published Five Year Strategy for Asylum and Immigration (Cm 6472). The UK Government states therein that it will introduce legislation to enable data exchange between the Immigration Service, HM Customs and the police (para 58). Extensive reference is made to the UK Government's e-borders programme, which will create 'a joined-up modernised intelligence-led border control and security framework' enabling inter-agency co-operation 'to maintain the integrity of our border control, target activity against those who have no right to be in the UK and assist in the fight against terrorists and criminals' (Annex 1).

[48] Recital 12 of Council Dir 2004/82/EC notes that it would be legitimate to process transmitted data for the purposes of allowing their use as evidence in proceedings aiming at the enforcement of immigration laws, 'including their provisions on the protection of public policy (*ordre public*) and national security'.

[49] Title 49, US Code, section 44909(c)(3) and Title 19, Code of Federal Regulations, section 122.49b.

they did not want to be subject to heavy fines, including the cancellation of landing rights at US airports. However, concerns were voiced in the EU that US legislation was too invasive of privacy and could be in conflict with Community and Member States' data protection standards. The Commission informed the US authorities of these concerns and this led to the entry into force of the US legislation being postponed until 5 March 2003. At the same time, the Commission began negotiations with US authorities in order to formulate standards governing the transfer of PNR data to the US, which would comply with EC data protection standards. In the course of negotiations, the European Parliament adopted a series of Resolutions urging the Commission to ensure that these standards are fully respected.[50] The US requirements were also scrutinised by the 'Article 29 Working Party' on data protection, which was highly critical of US demands.[51] Negotiations were protracted and lasted well beyond 5 March 2003, when US law formally entered into force vis-à-vis EU airlines. They resulted in an agreement between the Commission and the US authorities on 16 December 2003. Following a series of undertakings by the US authorities, the Commission accepted that US data protection standards in the context of PNR transfers were adequate.[52]

The Commission called for a global EU approach to the sharing of PNR data. On the issue of EU/US transfers, the Commission noted that the way forward was to establish a legal framework for existing PNR transfers to the US. This would consist of an 'adequacy' Decision by the Commission, certifying that the US data protection standards were adequate, followed by a 'light' bilateral international agreement between the Community and the US. Notwithstanding a series of privacy concerns by both the Article 29 Working Party on Data Protection'[53] and the European Parliament,[54] the Commission went ahead and adopted the adequacy Decision on

[50] See Resolutions P5_TA (2003) 0097 and P5_TA (2003) 0429.

[51] Opinion 4/2003 on the Level of Protection ensured in the US for the Transfer of Passengers' Data, 11070/03/EN, WP 78.

[52] Communication from the Commission to the Council and the Parliament, *Transfer of Air Passenger Name Record (PNR) Data: A Global EU Approach*, COM (2003) 826 final, 16 December 2003, p 5.

[53] In its Opinion published in January 2004, the Working Party expressly stated that 'the progress made does not allow a favourable adequacy finding to be achieved'. Opinion 2/2004 on the Adequate Protection of Personal Data contained in the PNR of Air Passengers to be transferred to the United States' Bureau of Customs and Border Protection (US CBP), adopted on 29 January 2004, doc 10019/04/EN, WP 87.

[54] The European Parliament adopted, on 30 March 2004, a Resolution calling on the Commission to withdraw the draft adequacy Decision P5_TA-PROV (2004) 0245. It also took the step of requesting an Opinion from the European Court of Justice on the compatibility with the EC Treaty of the draft PNR international agreement, which would be concluded after the adoption of the adequacy Decision. This led to a delay in the submission of the Parliament's own opinion under the consultation process of Art 300 EC Treaty. With the ECJ case pending, and the Parliament not having submitted its opinion, the Council decided to go ahead with the agreement.

14 May 2004.[55] This was followed three days later by a Council Decision authorising the President of the Council to sign, on behalf of the Community, the Agreement with the US on PNR transfers.[56] The terms of the Agreement and the US Undertakings had not changed from the draft that was so heavily criticised by the Article 29 Working Party and the European Parliament. The Agreement in essence allowed US authorities to 'pull' from the databases of carriers no less than 34 categories of passenger data. These include name, address and billing address, email address, all forms of payment information, travel itinerary, frequent flyer information, travel status of passenger, no-show information, one-way tickets, all historical changes to the PNR and 'general remarks'.

(b) The ECJ PNR Judgment[57] The Council thus prevailed and concluded an agreement in the face of strong human rights concerns in the name of co-operation in the 'war on terror'. The conclusion of the agreement meant that it was inevitable that the European Parliament withdrew its ex ante request for the European Court of Justice to issue an Opinion on the agreement. However, linking its human rights and institutional grievances, the European Parliament submitted a further challenge in the Court of Justice, asking for the annulment of the Decision authorising the Conclusion of the EC/US Agreement, on the grounds that the latter breached fundamental rights and the principle of proportionality as well as the fundamental principles of the Data Protection Directive, but also on legality grounds.

The Court of Justice addressed some of these questions in a judgment delivered in May 2006.[58] Unlike Advocate General Léger (who largely upheld the content of the agreement[59]), it is important to note that the Court did not examine the compatibility of the PNR agreement with fundamental rights. The Court focused exclusively on the legality point and found that both the adequacy decision and the agreement were adopted on the wrong legal basis and should be annulled. According to the Court, PNR data processing (envisaged by the agreement) was necessary for safeguarding public security and for law-enforcement purposes.[60] According to the Court, the

[55] Commission Decision of 14 May 2004 on the adequate protection of personal data contained in the Passenger Name Record of air passengers transferred to the United States' Bureau of Customs and Border Protection, [2004] OJ L235/11. The Undertakings of the US Homeland Security Department are annexed in pp 15–21. The list of PNR data is annexed in p 22.

[56] *Ibid.* The text of the Agreement is annexed in [2004] OJ L235/84–5. The Agreement was signed on 28 May 2004.

[57] For a detailed analysis, see V Mitsilegas, 'The External Dimension of EU Action in Criminal Matters' (2007) 12 *European Foreign Affairs Review* 457–97 at 480–84.

[58] Joined cases C-317/04 and C-318/04, *European Parliament v Council*, 30 May 2006, [2006] ECR I-4721.

[59] *Ibid*, Opinion delivered on 22 November 2005.

[60] *Ibid*, para 57.

fact that data is being transferred by private operators does not suffice to bring the activity within the first pillar—the transfer falls 'within a framework established by the public authorities that relates to public security'.[61]

The Court's approach towards the position of a measure involving the transfer of passenger data to public authorities of third countries within the EU constitutional framework (but also the earlier approach of the Council and the Commission) diverges somewhat from the position regarding the legal basis of *internal* Community measures in the same field and demonstrates the constitutional issues that may arise from the expansive—and not always clear—policy and legal use of the term 'border security'. Take the API Directive analysed above: the categories of the data transferred were much more limited to PNR and were named differently (API for Advance Passenger Information)—however, the essence of the exercise is the same—the transfer of personal passenger data to the authorities. Yet, the internal Community measure was justified, and was ultimately adopted, under Articles 62(2)(a) and 63(3)(b) of the EC Treaty. These serve as the legal basis for the adoption of measures relative to external border controls and illegal immigration respectively. It can be argued that the difference in approach is justified by the fact that, while the API transfer is necessary for immigration control purposes, PNR transfers are necessary for counter-terrorism purposes. However, as seen above, although the text of the Directive has the stated aim of combating illegal immigration, there have been attempts to frame it also as a national security and counter-terrorism matter.[62]

(c) The EU-US PNR Agreements The Court of Justice's annulment of the Agreement and Adequacy decision led to the denunciation of the Agreement by the Council[63] and the opening of negotiations for a new—albeit interim—Agreement to address the legal vacuum resulting from the Court's ruling.[64] Such an Agreement was concluded on the basis of a Decision under Articles 24 and 38 of the Treaty on European Union (TEU) in October 2006.[65] The

[61] *Ibid*, para 58.

[62] See Mitsilegas, above n 57.

[63] [2006] OJ C219/1, 12 September 2006.

[64] Mindful of such legal vacuum, the Court maintained the validity of the first pillar instruments until 30 September 2006.

[65] Council Decision 2006/729/CFSP/JHA of 16 October 2006 on the signing, on behalf of the European Union, of an Agreement between the European Union and the USA on the processing and transfer of PNR data by air carriers to the US Department of Homeland Security ([2006] OJ L298/27, the text of the Agreement is annexed to this Decision). It is noteworthy that the Decision has been classified as both a CFSP and JHA Decision. It is unclear whether this classification is there to reflect the dual legal basis only (Art 38 TEU must be used by reference to Art 24 TEU, but the Agreement is essentially a third pillar measure) or whether the Agreement is both a second and third pillar instrument. See Mitsilegas, above n 57, at 484–6.

Agreement expired in July 2007 and was replaced by a new third pillar Agreement signed on behalf of the EU on 23 July and on behalf of the US on 26 July.[66] Like the earlier texts, the agreement includes an adequacy assessment—the US is deemed to ensure an adequate level of PNR data protection for PNR data transferred from the EU—an assessment which is linked with the issue of transmission of 'EU' PNR data to third countries: the adequacy assessment means that the EU 'will not interfere with relationships between the US and third countries for the exchange of passenger information on data protection grounds'.[67] Moreover, in a statement reminiscent of the one in the EU-US Mutual Legal Assistance Agreement, the parties recognise that 'U.S. and European privacy law and policy share a common basis and that any differences in the implementation of these principles should not present an obstacle to cooperation between the U.S. and the European Union (EU)'.[68] The aim of preserving the US standards is ensured also by a provision making clear that the Agreement is not intended to derogate from, or amend, existing US (and EU) law, and expressly stating (as in earlier texts) that the Agreement 'does not create or confer any right or benefit on any other person or entity, private or public'.[69] The Agreement also seems to be creating, on the basis of reciprocity, a link between the level of data protection in the two parties. As is stated, the DHS 'expects that it is not being asked to undertake data protection measures in its PNR system that are more stringent than those applied by European authorities for their domestic PNR systems' and vice-versa.[70]

However, the text of the Agreement itself does not include details of the PNR data transfer per se. These are set out in a separate 'US letter to the EU', signed by Homeland Security Secretary, Michael Chertoff, and accompanying the Agreement.[71] The letter enumerates 19 types of PNR data covered by the Agreement (these are more or less similar to the broad categories in the earlier agreements and include data such as payment information, seat information and 'general remarks').[72] These can

[66] *Agreement between the European Union and the United States of America on the processing and transfer of Passenger Name Record (PNR) data by air carriers to the United States Department of Homeland Security (DHS)* (2007 PNR Agreement), [2007] OJ L204/18. See also Council Decision approving the signing of the Agreement on the basis of Arts 24 and 38 TEU, [2007] OJ L204/16.

[67] 2007 PNR Agreement, above n 66, para 6.

[68] *Ibid*, Preamble, recital 5. See also Mitsilegas, above n 57.

[69] Penultimate paragraph.

[70] Para 5. See also point IX of the 'US letter to the EU' accompanying the Agreement (see below, n 71).

[71] US letter to the EU, [2007] OJ L204/21. This is in turn followed by an 'EU letter to the US' confirming that, on the basis of the assurances provided in the US letter, the EU deems that the US ensure an adequate level of data protection and that, based on this finding, 'the EU will take all the necessary steps to discourage international organisations or third countries from interfering with any transfers of EU PNR data to the United States' [2007] OJ L204/25.

[72] *Ibid*, point III.

be accessed by US government authorities with law enforcement, public security or counter-terrorism functions and can also be transferred to government authorities in third countries.[73] The Agreement also contains provisions regulating the move, under certain conditions, from a 'pull' to a 'push' system for PNR data transfer[74] and provisions defining its purposes as fighting terrorism and other serious crimes, but leaves the option of the unilateral broadening of the scope by the US open.[75] The letter also extends the retention period of PNR data essentially to a minimum of 15 years—seven years in an 'active analytical database' and a further eight years in dormant status.[76] This provision has met with critical reaction from the European Parliament, which raised its concern that such databases lead to 'a significant risk of massive profiling and data mining'.[77] The European Data Protection Supervisor has also raised concerns,[78] as has the Article 29 Working Party on Data Protection.[79]

(d) The Commission Proposal for an EU PNR System Notwithstanding the sustained concerns raised by the European Parliament and specialist EU data protection bodies with regard to the compatibility of the EU-US PNR Agreements with EU privacy and data protection law, the Commission has recently tabled a proposal for a Framework Decision on a similar system of transmission of PNR data by carriers flying into the EU.[80] The Commission justifies the proposal as a result of the 'policy-learning' from the existing PNR Agreements with the US and Canada, as well as the development of pilot projects in the UK. Both these developments (involving countries, in particular the US and the UK, which as seen above have pushed forward a specific concept of 'border security' linked with technology and the fight against terrorism) have demonstrated, according to the Commission, the potential of PNR data for law enforcement purposes.[81]

However, one cannot help but notice that the EU already has established a system requiring airlines to transmit passenger data—the one put forward by the API Directive mentioned above. The API Directive is a first pillar, Title IV measure where data transfer is justified on the grounds of border and immigration control—with Member States such as the UK attempting

[73] *Ibid*, point II.
[74] *Ibid*, point VIII.
[75] By stating that 'DHS will advise the EU regarding the passage of any US legislation which materially affects the statements made in this letter' *Ibid*, point I.
[76] *Ibid*, point VII.
[77] European Parliament Resolution of 12 July 2007 on the PNR agreement with the USA, P6_TA-PROV (2007) 0347, point 20.
[78] Letter of 27 June 2007 to Wolfgang Schauble, at www.statewatch.org.
[79] See comments of 27 September 2007.
[80] *Proposal for a Council framework decision on the use of Passenger Name Record (PNR) for law enforcement purposes*, COM(2007) 654 final, Brussels, 6 November 2007.
[81] *Ibid*, 2.

however to export, as seen above, their own concept of 'border security' linking the control of movement with the control of terrorism at EC level. In the light of the API Directive, one could question the necessity and added value of an essentially similar system in the third pillar. Mindful of this criticism, the Commission attempts in the Explanatory Memorandum to the PNR proposal to distinguish between the two initiatives. The Commission notes that

> [f]or the purposes of the fight against terrorism and organised crime, the information contained in the API data would be sufficient only for identifying known terrorists and criminals by using alert systems. API data are official data, as they stem from passports, and sufficiently accurate as to the identity of a person. On the other hand, PNR data contains more data elements and are available in advance of API data. Such data elements are a very important tool for carrying out risk assessments of the persons, for obtaining intelligence and for making associations between known and unknown people.[82]

From this passage, it is clear that the Commission has adopted an intelligence-led model of border controls very similar to the 'border security' models in the US and the UK. The emphasis is on risk assessment and profiling, on the basis of the collection of a wide range of personal data at the earliest possible stage in time. From the limited categories of passport data to be transmitted prior to departure under the API Directive, we are now moving to the transfer of a wide range of information related to air passengers at a considerably earlier stage. The transfer of PNR data is viewed as necessary not only for border controls/immigration, but also for broader counter-terrorism and security purposes.[83]

This model of 'border security' legislation is confirmed when one looks at the content of the Commission proposal. It is instructive to start with the annex, containing the categories of PNR data to be transferred. These are strikingly similar to the list of PNR data contained in the latest EU-US PNR Agreement and include a wide range of data such as all forms of payment information, seat information and 'general remarks'. The text of the proposal contains similarly broad provisions. It envisages a retention period of a maximum of no less than 13 years—five initially and a further eight when data can be accessed in exceptional circumstances.[84] Transfer of PNR data to third countries is allowed, subject to a number of conditions prescribed

[82] *Ibid*, 3.

[83] In this context, see also the Explanatory Memorandum submitted by the Home Office with regard to the Commission PNR proposal, where it is stated that 'we need to allow the processing and exchange of PNR data for wider border security and crime-fighting purposes'. The UK Government further advocated a wider scope to the proposal than the one envisaged by the Commission: see House of Commons European Scrutiny Committee, Seventh Report, session 2007–08.

[84] Proposal for a Council framework decision, above n 80, Art 9.

in the proposal but also more fundamentally in the Framework Decision on data protection.[85] However, the latter text has not yet formally been adopted. Air carriers are required to send data to Passenger Information Units (PIUs) to be established under the Framework Decision[86] 24 hours before departure and immediately after flight closure—but the PIUs may require transmission prior to 24 hours from departure responding to specific threats of terrorism and organised crime.[87] Passenger data may be processed by the PIUs and the competent authorities receiving data from PIUs in Member States (these are authorities responsible for the prevention of terrorism and organised crime)[88] in order

> to identify persons who are or *may be* involved in a terrorist or organised crime offence as well as their associates,
>
> to *create and update risk indicators* for the assessment of such persons,
>
> to *provide intelligence on travel patterns* and other trends relating to terrorist offences and organised crime,
>
> and to be used in criminal investigations and prosecutions of terrorist offences and organized crime (emphasis added).[89]

The emphasis on profiling of suspect populations, regardless of their actual involvement in criminal offences, is evident in this context.

This initiative may be seen as a significant political move by EU institutions aiming to ensure real reciprocity with the US (indeed, US airlines would be subject to these standards and the adoption of EU standards in the field will trigger the application of the various reciprocity clauses in the PNR Agreement). However, what this move also means is that the EU is essentially importing the whole US (and UK) model of intelligence-led, generalised surveillance based on profiling via the gathering of a wide range of every day information on *all* passengers for 'security' purposes. While negotiations on the scope and content of the instrument are difficult and ongoing, it is noteworthy that one of the issues being discussed is extending the system to *intra-Community* flights—leading thus to the generalised surveillance of air travel also *within* the borderless Schengen area.[90] The challenges of such a model to fundamental rights—in particular privacy—as proclaimed by the EU are evident, and have been articulated in the criticism of the EU-US PNR Agreements by EU institutions and bodies.

[85] *Ibid*, Art 8. Further references to data protection standards in accordance with this Framework Decision can be found in Art 11 of the Commission proposal.
[86] *Ibid*, Art 3.
[87] *Ibid*, Art 5(3).
[88] *Ibid*, Art 4(2).
[89] *Ibid*, Art 3(5).
[90] See the Conclusions of the Justice and Home Affairs Council of 24 October 2008, Council doc 14667/08 (Presse 299) p 18.

The framing of the proposal as a counter-terrorism measure not only results into the weakening of privacy protection *inside* the EU (with the third pillar privacy and data protection framework being fragmented and limited to say the least) but also sits uneasily with the proclaimed freedom of movement within the Union.

C. Biometrics and their Spread

The use of biometrics in the field of immigration and border controls in the EU was highlighted at the Thessaloniki European Council in June 2003. Within the context of developing EU immigration databases such as the Visa Information System, EU leaders also noted that

> a coherent approach is needed in the EU on biometric identifiers or biometric data, which would result in harmonised solutions for documents for third country nationals, EU citizens' passports and information systems (VIS and SIS II).[91]

This approach—which mirrors the US emphasis on identification in 'border security' and focuses on both documents of EU citizens and third country nationals—was largely reflected soon thereafter in the EU response after the Madrid bombings. In the Declaration on combating terrorism of 25 March 2004, the European Council linked the monitoring of the movement of people with the 'war on terror' by stressing that 'improved border controls and document security play an important role in combating terrorism'. There were two elements in this approach: the inclusion of biometrics in EU visas and passports, which should be prioritised and relevant measures be adopted by the end of 2004; and the enhancement of the interoperability between EU databases and the creation of 'synergies' between existing and future information systems (such as SIS II, VIS and Eurodac) 'in order to exploit their added value within their respective legal and technical frameworks in the prevention and fight against terrorism'.[92]

Political pressure towards the insertion of biometrics into identity and travel documents in EU Member States led to the adoption in December 2004 of a Regulation introducing biometric identifiers (in the form of facial images and fingerprints) in EU passports.[93] The introduction of biometrics in EU passports was justified by the Commission as necessary to meet US requirements on document security and thus prolong the US 'visa waiver' programme that a number of EU Member States enjoy and extend it to

[91] Council doc 11638/03, Brussels, 1 October 2003, para 11.

[92] At www.consilium.europa.eu. See also Mitsilegas, above n 41.

[93] Council Reg (EC) No 2252/2004 of 13 December 2004 on standards for security features and biometrics in passports and travel docs issued by Member States, [2004] OJ L385/1, at 29.

EU Member States who are not part of the programme.[94] As in the case of the Carriers' Directive, the legal basis of the Regulation is Article 62(2)(a) EC Treaty, on external border controls, and as with the Directive, the Regulation was deemed by Member States such as the UK to be a security measure.[95] The Regulation was finally adopted notwithstanding serious objections regarding the appropriateness of the legal basis and the existence of EC competence to adopt binding legislation on the content of identity documents. These concerned the fact that existing EU measures take the form of non-legally binding Resolutions; Article 62(2)(a) refers to controls of the external border of the EU and not to the content of EU travel documents; and Article 18(3) EC Treaty explicitly states that Community action to facilitate the exercise of citizenship rights does not apply to provisions on passports, identity cards, residence permits or any such document.[96] In spite of these concerns about the legality and the proportionality of the measure,[97] negotiations on the measure went ahead and a second biometric identifier—fingerprints—was added. The Regulation was adopted swiftly thereafter in December 2004.[98] The Commission has recently tabled a proposal to amend the Regulation in order to exclude from its scope children under the age of six and persons who are physically unable to give fingerprints.[99]

Biometrics are playing an increasing role in EU immigration control both *before* and *after* the entry of *third country nationals* in EU territory.[100] In

[94] See Mitsilegas, above n 41, at 172.

[95] See letter of 15 July 2004 by the then Home Office Minister, Caroline Flint, to Lord Grenfell, Chairman of the House of Lords EU Select Committee, stating that 'our view is that the current proposal is first and foremost a security measure'.

[96] Mitsilegas, above n 11.

[97] On both concerns, see the detailed analysis by *Statewatch*, prepared by Steve Peers, *The Legality of the Regulation on EU Citizens' Passports*, 26 November 2004, available at www.statewatch.org.

[98] The need for the swift adoption of the proposal has also been justified on the grounds that the US would abandon its visa-waiver programme in respect of those EU Member States which had not introduced biometrics in their passports by a certain date. Like in the PNR case, the EU has managed to obtain an extension to the US deadline for the insertion of biometrics, but this new US deadline will not be met and it is unlikely to be extended by the US (see letter of 31 March 2005 from the Chairman of the US House Judiciary Committee to the Commission and the Council, reproduced in www.statewatch.org).

[99] COM(2007) 619 final, Brussels, 18 October 2007. It is noteworthy that an earlier Council document indicates that 'the facial changes taking place up to the age of 12 are so marked that face recognition is not possible without highly sophisticated software and the considerable expense which goes with it', doc 9403/1/06, Brussels, 26 June 2006, p 3. Yet the Commission proposal only exempts minors under the age of 6.

[100] On the use of biometrics in EU databases, with emphasis on the immigration databases, see A Baldaccini, 'Counter-terrorism and the EU Strategy for Border Security: Framing Suspects with Biometric Documents and Databases' (2008) 10 *European Journal of Migration and Law* 31–49; see also E Brouwer, 'The Use of Biometrics in EU Databases and Identity Documents' in J Lodge (ed), *Are You Who You Say You Are? The EU and Biometric Borders* (Nijmegen, Wolf Legal Publishers, 2007) 45–66.

the context of EU databases, both the emerging second generation Schengen Information System,[101] and the Visa Information System,[102] have the legal and technical capacity to include biometrics, whilst Eurodac is a database specifically designed to include the fingerprints of asylum seekers.[103] On the other hand, the Justice and Home Affairs Council agreed recently on a Regulation setting the security features and biometric identifiers to be used by Member States in a uniform format of residence permit for third country nationals.[104] The uniform format for residence permits will include a storage medium containing the facial image and two fingerprints images of the holder, both in interoperable formats.[105] The technical specifications for the capture of biometrics will be set in accordance with the requirements for the passports of EU nationals under the 2004 Regulation mentioned above.[106]

D. The Transformation of Immigration Databases

In efforts to enhance the exchange of personal data, great emphasis has been placed in the recent past on enabling the flow of data between the various EU databases and/or EU agencies and bodies, and developing legal and technological solutions to achieve this aim. Largely justified on the basis of the 'war on terror', efforts for greater synergies in data sharing have been proliferating in the recent past under the guise of two main initiatives: to enhance the 'interoperability' between EU databases; and to allow access by law enforcement authorities to immigration databases, in spite of the undoubtedly different purposes of managing migration and fighting crime—the justification put forward being that access by police authorities to immigration data is necessary for security reasons. The move towards linking databases and facilitating access to immigration data for 'security' purposes was highlighted as seen above in European Council responses after Madrid. A few months later, this priority was further confirmed

[101] The second generation Schengen Information System (SIS II) will contain photographs and fingerprints: see Art 20 of the Regulation and the Decision establishing SIS II. Council Reg (EC) 1987/2006 of 20 December 2006, [2006] OJ L381/4 and [2007] OJ L205/63 respectively. On the use of biometrics in the context of the transformation of SIS II into an investigative tool, see text to nn 135–42 below.

[102] On the Visa Information System see n 117 below.

[103] Council Reg (EC) No 2725/2000 of 11 December 2000 concerning the establishment of 'Eurodac' for the comparison of fingerprints for the effective application of the Dublin Convention, [2000] OJ L316/1.

[104] Justice and Home Affairs Council of 18 September 2007, Council doc 12604/07 (Presse 194) p 13.

[105] *Ibid.* See also Council doc 12658/07, Brussels, 6 September 2007, in particular Arts 4a and 4b.

[106] *Ibid*, Art 4b. See above n 93.

by the Hague Programme, where the perceived link between movement, migration and terrorism was clearly articulated. According to the Hague Programme,

> the management of migration flows, including the fight against illegal immigration should be strengthened by establishing *a continuum of security measures* that effectively links visa application procedures and entry and exit procedures at external border crossings. Such measures are also of importance for the prevention and control of crime, in particular terrorism. In order to achieve this, a coherent approach and harmonised solutions in the EU on biometric identifiers and data are necessary (emphasis added).[107]

This is yet another clear reflection of the concept of 'border security' as developed in the US, with controls on immigration *and movement* being prioritised and linked to the so-called 'war on terror'.[108] The collection and exchange of personal data (including biometrics) are key in this context. To boost such information exchange, the Hague Programme further places emphasis on the interoperability of databases, including in the context of migration management. It called on the Council to examine 'how to maximise the effectiveness and interoperability of EU information systems' and invited the Commission to present a Communication on the interoperability between the Schengen Information System, the Visa Information System (VIS), and Eurodac.[109] The Commission presented its Communication a year later, in November 2005.[110] The purpose of the Communication was to highlight how, beyond their present purposes, databases 'can more effectively support the policies linked to the free movement of persons and serve the objective of combating terrorism and serious crime'.[111] On the basis of this approach, the Commission argued strongly in favour of the access of authorities responsible for internal security to immigration databases such as SIS, VIS and Eurodac.[112] The Communication provided a definition of 'interoperability', which is the 'ability of IT systems and of the business processes they support to exchange data and to enable the sharing of information and knowledge'.[113]

[107] The Hague Programme, para 1.7.2.

[108] Justifying thus to a great extent the discourse on (in)security continuum, see IIIA.

[109] The Hague Programme, para 1.7.2.

[110] *Communication on Improved Effectiveness, Enhanced Interoperability and Synergies among European Databases in the Area of Justice and Home Affairs*, COM(2005) 597 final, Brussels, 24 November 2005.

[111] *Ibid*, 2.

[112] *Ibid*, 8. The Commission also took the opportunity to float proposals for longer-term developments, including the creation of a European Criminal Automated Fingerprints Identification System, the creation of an entry-exit system and introduction of a border crossing facilitation scheme for frequent border crossers, and European registers for travel documents and identity cards (pp 8–9).

[113] *Ibid*, 3.

According to the Commission, interoperability is a technical rather than a legal/political concept.[114] As I have noted elsewhere however, this attempt to treat interoperability as a merely technical concept, while at the same time using the concept to enable maximum access to databases containing a wide range of personal data (which become even more sensitive with the sustained emphasis on biometrics) is striking. It can be seen as an attempt to de-politicise an issue which may have major repercussions for the protection of fundamental rights and civil liberties, and which has the potential to shield far-reaching developments (including the blurring of the boundaries between databases established for different purposes and containing different categories of data, for the benefit of law enforcement agencies) from effective scrutiny and democratic control. The emphasis on interoperability may lead to the justification of the development of important initiatives in this context at the operational level, with the adoption of negotiated legislative standards underpinning the evolving databases (or their capacities) potentially deemed unnecessary.[115]

A key aspect of the EU strategy on databases and their interoperability is the aim to maximise *access* to personal data, including access by police authorities to immigration databases and to personal data related to identification. While not all such proposals have been accepted at the time of writing,[116] a clear example of this trend—which blurs the boundary between immigration control and police co-operation—is the development of the Visa Information System (VIS).[117] The Justice and Home Affairs Council adopted detailed conclusions on the development of VIS in February 2004, stating clearly that one of the purposes of the system would be to 'contribute towards improving the administration of the common visa policy and towards internal security and combating terrorism'.[118] It also called for access to VIS to be granted to border guards and 'other national authorities to be authorised by each Member State such as police departments, immigration departments and services responsible for internal security'.[119]

[114] *Ibid.*

[115] V Mitsilegas, 'Databases in the Area of Freedom, Security and Justice' in C Stefanou and H Xanthaki (eds), *Towards a European Criminal Record*, (Cambridge, Cambridge University Press, 2008) 311–35.

[116] See, in this context, the proposals to allow access to the Eurodac database (containing fingerprints of asylum seekers) by internal security authorities. See the Commission interoperability Communication, but also the German Presidency Programme on Police and Judicial Co-operation (Council doc 17102/06, Brussels, 22 December 2006). However, at the time of writing, it appears that such proposals are not going forward.

[117] The Visa Information System would contain data (including biometrics) on visa applicants, but also a series of data on the visa application, including details of sponsors (see Arts 3 and 6 of the draft VIS Regulation).

[118] Doc 5831/04 (Presse 37). The Council called for the inclusion in VIS of biometric data on visa applicants.

[119] *Ibid.*

In June 2004, the Council adopted a Decision forming the legal basis for the establishment of VIS,[120] and negotiations began to define its purpose and functions and formulate rules on access and exchange of data. The Commission subsequently tabled a draft Regulation aiming to take VIS further by defining its aims and rules on data access and exchange.[121] The Justice and Home Affairs Council of 24 February 2005 called for access to VIS to be given to national authorities responsible for 'internal security', when exercising their powers in investigating, preventing and detecting criminal offences, including terrorist acts or threats and invited the Commission to present a separate, third pillar proposal to this end.[122] The Commission tabled such a proposal in November 2005.[123] The two texts were linked and thus negotiated in parallel (co-decision was required formally for the first pillar Regulation, while for the third pillar Decision the European Parliament had a consultation role).[124] Agreement on both proposals was confirmed at the Justice and Home Affairs Council of 12–13 June 2007[125] and they were published in the Official Journal with considerable delay, in August 2008.[126]

Reflecting the logic of the Conclusions of the 2005 JHA Council, the VIS Regulation expressly states that one of the purposes of the Visa Information System is to contribute to the prevention of threats to internal security of the Member States.[127] The Regulation also contains a bridging clause to the third pillar Decision allowing access to VIS by Europol within the limits of its mandate and when necessary for the performance of its tasks, and by the relevant national authorities 'if there are reasonable grounds to consider that consultation of VIS data will substantially contribute' to the prevention, detection or investigation of terrorist offences and of other serious criminal offences.[128] The wording of this clause has been subject to extensive debate, with the view being put

[120] Council Decision of 8 June 2004 establishing the Visa Information System (VIS), [2004] OJ L213/5.

[121] Proposal for a Regulation of the European Parliament and of the Council concerning the VIS and the exchange of data between Member States on short-stay visas, COM(2004) 835 final, Brussels, 28 December 2004.

[122] Justice and Home Affairs Council of 24 February 2005, Council doc 6228.05 (Presse 28) pp 15–16.

[123] Commission proposal COM(2005) 600 final, 24 November 2005. See also Mitsilegas, above n 115.

[124] For details see V Mitsilegas, 'Human Rights, Terrorism and the Quest for Border Security' in M Pedrazzi (ed), *Individual Guarantees in the European Judicial Area in Criminal Matters* (Brussels, Bruylant, forthcoming, 2009).

[125] Justice and Home Affairs Council of 12–13 June 2007, Council doc 10267/07 (Presse 125).

[126] Council Reg (EC) No 767/2008, [2008] OJ L218/60; Decision 2008/633/JHA, [2008] OJ L218/129.

[127] The Regulation also enables the recording of biometric data into VIS: see Art 5(1).

[128] Council Reg (EC) No 767/2008, Art 3(1).

forward that a higher threshold is necessary for allowing access, requiring also the existence of factual indications as the basis for the reasonable grounds mentioned above.[129]

The terms of access of internal security authorities and Europol to the VIS are set out in detail in the third pillar Decision.[130] The national authorities with access to the VIS are 'authorities which are responsible for the prevention, detection or investigation of terrorist offences or of other serious criminal offences' which are designated by each Member State.[131] Member States must also designate central access points—it is through these access points that consultation of the VIS will take place.[132] Access to the VIS is thus potentially extended to a wide range of national authorities with diverse tasks.[133] It is up to the Member States to designate such authorities, and the only specification regarding their mandate is the remit of the prevention, investigation or detection of terrorism and serious crime. A wide range of agencies may be responsible for the prevention of terrorism at national level across the EU, not excluding intelligence agencies. The Decision does include further limits when specifying the conditions of access (including the requirement that access for consultation must be necessary in a specific case),[134] but the potential for access to VIS by a wide range of national agencies remains considerable.

Similar concerns with regard to access to and use of EU databases arise with regard to the Second Generation Schengen Information System (SIS II). A major change in this context involves the nature and use of personal data included in the System. Both the Regulation and the Decision provide the legal basis for the inclusion of biometrics, in the form of photographs and fingerprints, in the SIS.[135] The provisions on the use of biometrics are extremely significant in this context. In the first stage, biometrics will be used only for 'one-to-one' searches—seeking to confirm someone's identity by comparing the biometric identifiers of the person only with those existing in the SIS under this person's name—however, in the future (following the presentation by the Commission of a Report on

[129] See Council doc 5456/1/07 REV 1, Brussels, 20 February 2007.

[130] See above n 126, in particular Arts 5–7.

[131] *Ibid*, Art 2(1)(e).

[132] Art 3(3) of the Decision and Art 3(2) of the Regulation. Similarly, according to Art 7(3) of the Decision, Europol must designate a specialised unit with Europol officials acting as the central access point to the VIS. Access to the VIS only via central units seems to be a safeguard advocated by the European Parliament, see Council doc 8540/07, Brussels, 18 April 2007.

[133] Note also the possibility of transferring VIS data to third countries. For further details, see Mitsilegas, above n 124.

[134] See Decision 2008/633/JHA, [2008] OJ L218/129, Art 5, in particular Art 5(1)(b).

[135] Council Reg (EC) No 767/2008, [2008] OJ L218/60, Art 20(3)(e) and (f) and the Decision. See also their Preamble (recitals 14 in both the Regulation and the Decision).

the availability and readiness of the required technology), biometrics will also be used for 'one-to-many' searches, where biometric data of one person will be compared with the whole SIS database.[136] This development may have substantial implications for privacy, but also for the nature of the Schengen Information System, which is increasingly developing from a hit/no hit database to a general intelligence database. The fact that such an important decision to instigate one-to-many searches is essentially deemed as a technical issue and will be taken with little debate (the European Parliament being merely consulted), raises serious concerns of transparency and democratic scrutiny.

Another sign of the development of SIS into a general intelligence/investigative database is the provisions, in both the Regulation and the Decision, allowing the interlinking of alerts.[137] Such interlinking is allowed only if there is a 'clear operational need',[138] but is subject to the national law of the Member State which decides to use this option,[139] thus rendering possible the creation of significantly different systems across the EU. Interlinking of alerts is a major departure from the limited hit/no hit character of the current SIS and its potential for profiling is significant. As the European Data Protection Supervisor has noted in his Opinion on the SIS II proposals, 'the person is no longer 'assessed' on the basis of data relating only to him/her, but on the basis of his/her possible association with other persons', which may lead to their treatment with greater suspicion if they are deemed to be associated with criminals or wanted persons—moreover, the Supervisor notes, interlinking extends investigative powers because it makes possible the registration of alleged gangs or networks (eg data of illegal immigrants and data on traffickers).[140] The Supervisor noted that authorities with no right of access to certain categories of data should not even be aware of the existence of these links.[141] The Regulation and Decision seem to some extent to have taken this view on board, by stating that authorities with no right of access to certain categories of alert will not be able to *see* the link to an alert to which they do not have access.[142] However, this may not necessarily mean that these authorities will be unaware of the *existence* of a link.

[136] Art 22 of the Regulation and Decision. For further explanation of these searches, see House of Lords European Union Committee above n 11, paras 57–60.

[137] Art 37 of the Regulation and Art 52 of the Decision (see also preamble, recitals 17 in both instruments).

[138] Art 37(4) of the Regulation and Art 52(4) of the Decision.

[139] Art 37(5) of the Regulation and Art 52(5) of the Decision.

[140] European Data Protection Supervisor, Opinion of 19 October 2005, [2006] OJ C91/38. Also available at www.edps.eu.int.

[141] *Ibid.*

[142] Art 37(3) of the Regulation and Art 52(3) of the Decision.

IV. ENTRY, EXIT AND THE 'BONA FIDE' PASSENGER

Perhaps the best example of the new generalised surveillance based on monitoring movement, the creation of databases and the collection of sensitive personal data is the new move by the European Commission to propose the creation of an entry-exit system at the external borders of the EU, coupled with facilitation of border crossings for bona fide travellers and the creation of an electronic travel authorisation system.[143] The entry/exit system would be a new database, applying to third country nationals admitted for a short stay; bona fide travellers would be 'low risk' third country nationals, but also EU citizens—both would cross external borders via 'automated gates'. The Electronic Travel Authorisation System (ETA) would apply to third country nationals not subject to a visa requirement who would be required to make an electronic application in advance of travelling. Both interoperability and the use of biometrics are central to these proposals, in particular to the proposals for the establishment of a system of border crossings via automated gates. The Commission notes that

> [i]n the run-up to *full introduction of biometric passports*, the current legal framework allows for schemes based on voluntary enrolment to be deployed by Member States, under the condition that the criteria for enrolment correspond to those for minimum checks at the borders *and that the schemes are open for all persons enjoying the Community right to free movement*. Such schemes should be *interoperable* within the EU, based on common technical standards, which should be defined to support the *widespread and coherent use of automated border control systems* (emphasis added).[144]

The added value of a new database on an entry-exit system for third country nationals is not evident, especially in the light of the recent setting up of the Visa Information System. Moreover, and along with the evident proportionality concerns, there are serious legality concerns with regard to the extension of legislation on the management of the EU external border to EU citizens. There is arguably no legal basis in the EU Treaties to apply the external border controls to EU citizens, and legal basis concerns similar to those applying to the EC biometrics Regulation apply here. Notwithstanding these concerns, the momentum for the establishment of an entry-exit system along these lines is currently high. The European Council invited the Commission to present proposals for an entry/exit and registered traveller system by the beginning of 2010,[145] and more recently agreed in the European Pact on Immigration and Asylum (endorsed by

[143] Commission Communication on *Preparing the Next Steps in Border Management in the European Union*, COM(2008) 69 final, Brussels, 13 February 2008.

[144] *Ibid*, 7.

[145] Presidency Conclusions of the Brussels European Council of 19–20 June 2008, Council doc 11018/08, Brussels, 20 June 2008, para 10.

the European Council in October 2008) to deploy 'modern technological means to ensure that systems are interoperable' and stated that from 2012 the focus should be 'on establishing electronic recording of entry and exit, together with a fast-track procedure for European citizens and other travellers'.[146]

By establishing an entry-exit system—which is remarkably similar to the US VISIT Programme and UK e-border initiatives[147]—the EU introduces a system of surveillance of movement based on automaticity, interoperability, and the collection and consultation of sensitive personal data such as biometrics. Merging the logic of risk prevention with the logic of border security, this model has far-reaching consequences for the protection of fundamental rights and the relationship between the individual and the State. Movement is monitored on the basis of profiling, and the establishment of individual, subjective assessments on each traveller. Both third country nationals and EU citizens can be deemed as 'suspects' under these assessments, and their freedom of movement curtailed accordingly. The introduction of the concept of the 'bona fide' traveller is extremely worrying in this context. As the European Data Protection Supervisor has noted in his preliminary comments on the Commission proposals,

> [t]he underlying assumption in the communications (especially in the entry/exit proposal) is worrying: all travellers are put under surveillance and are considered a priori as potential law breakers. For instance in the Registered Travellers system, only the travellers taking specific steps, through ad hoc registration and provision of detailed personal information, will be considered 'bona fide' travellers. The vast amount of travellers, who do not travel frequently enough to undergo such a registration, are thus, by implication, de facto in the 'mala fide' category of those suspected of intentions of overstay.[148]

V. CONCLUSION

Public order and counter-terrorism concerns have had a profound impact on EU immigration law. The readiness of Member States—and at times EU institutions—to accommodate these concerns within the complex Union legal framework has led to a series of legal acrobatics reflected by the adoption of measures where the boundaries of legality have been seriously blurred. The attempt to do away with purpose limitation and to merge (in a manner similar to the Anglo-American model) immigration

[146] Council doc 13440/08, Brussels, 24 September 2008, point III(e).

[147] See above. For a detailed analysis of the US Visit Programme, see also C Epstein, 'Embodying Risk: Using Biometrics to Protect the Borders' in L Amoore and M de Goede (eds), *Risk and the War on Terror* (London, Routledge, 2008) 178–94.

[148] European Data Protection Supervisor, Opinion of 3 March 2008, pp 5–6.

and security in EU law has led to attempts to label measures with a clear counter-terrorism objective as immigration measures (see the passenger data example), and contaminating thus the strict guarantees of first pillar law with the broad exceptionalism of counter-terrorism law. The European Court of Justice's intervention has led in the case of PNR to a third pillar legal basis allocation which lessens considerably the legal safeguards offered to those affected—and in the case of the internal PNR measure, to less formal scrutiny and debate. On the other hand, attempts to accommodate security imperatives have also led to *EU immigration law* (addressing third country nationals with no EU links) *applying to EU citizens*—the adoption as a Title IV measure of legislation imposing biometrics on EU passports being a prime example, and future legislation on an entry-exit system on the cards.

These legality concerns are coupled with concerns of transparency, scrutiny and accountability. Along with the usual concerns with regard to third pillar law, it is noteworthy that much of the development of the EU agenda in the field takes place beyond the law, via the labelling of central elements of the system (such as interoperability of databases, or biometric requirements) as 'technical'—and not legal—issues, to be decided by expert groups or committees and thus shielded from scrutiny. The centrality of technology in the discourse of EU institutions is indicative of this trend. This technocratic approach (which is also reflected in the increased focus on agencies, such as Frontex, and databases) leads effectively to the de-politicisation of this field of EU immigration law. For, on a technical or instrumental reading of interoperability, the question concerning the ends of political community—and this means that the political questions concerning *who* is a party to relations of political reciprocity and *what* are the terms under which political reciprocity are institutionalised—is placed out of bounds. Yet, arguably, immigration evokes precisely these questions; border crossings by immigrants are, with different levels of intensity, *political* events, and never only events that call for the 'management' of borders.

In terms of substance, the move from a system of physical border controls to a system of generalised surveillance of movement is striking. Surveillance takes place on many different levels and at many different instances of movement. A wide range of personal data is collected every time an individual wishes to travel by air from the EU to a number of third countries (with PNR Agreements now being also signed with Australia and Canada) and will in the future be collected for all flights into the Union (and possibly for all flights *within* the Union). The collection of biometrics is a pre-requisite for EU citizens wishing to travel. Automaticity and perceived convenience are introduced into border controls under new entry-exit systems on the basis of the use of personal data such as biometrics, with automated gates opening if sufficient information exists for the passenger to go through.

Surveillance in all these different border points over time and space has been eloquently characterised as the pixellisation of the border.[149]

This new system of surveillance has a profound impact on individuals. It is based upon their extensive profiling. The pixellisation of the border leads to the collection of a wide range of personal data, which is collected in a wide range of databases, which become increasingly interoperable and accessible by a wide range of authorities. This leads to what has been deemed as 'the disappearance of disappearance', a process whereby 'it is increasingly difficult for individuals to maintain their anonymity or to escape the monitoring of social institutions'.[150] It also leads to the creation of individual profiles, with surveillance taking place on the basis of concepts such as the 'trusted', or the 'suspect' individual or passenger. These profiles may apply to *all* passengers. The generalised surveillance of movement in these terms poses significant challenges for the protection of individuals under European law: (i) challenges to the protection of privacy, with EU (and domestic) privacy law struggling to address legal and technological developments with profound implications for the concept of the Self and human dignity; (ii) challenges to equality and non-discrimination, with surveillance based on profiling; and (iii) last, but not least, challenges to freedom, with free movement within the EU being rendered increasingly illusory in the light of the generalised surveillance of movement of *everyone,* even *within* the EU territory.

In the light of these developments, the paradox of borders becomes especially manifest if one bears in mind that border controls are allegedly put into place to posit, regulate and enforce two basic distinctions that are deemed to be constitutive for the EU, namely the distinctions between inside and outside, and between member and non-member. First, the distinctions between inside/outside and citizen/alien are eroded when everybody is submitted to surveillance. If one of the cardinal purposes of border controls is to assure that European citizens can enjoy an area of freedom, a generalised system of surveillance undercuts this purpose to the extent that the right to privacy is an integral component of negative freedom—freedom 'from' intervention by authorities. Secondly, a general surveillance system turns against the European polity and its citizens because it compromises fundamental legal and political distinctions that underpin the idea of a common European space. We have seen in the foregoing pages that a generalised system of surveillance effectively undermines the principles of proportionality, democratic accountability, and the rule of law. There are, accordingly, excellent reasons to move away from this paradox of boundaries by (re-)politicising European immigration policy.

[149] D Bigo and E Guild, *The Transformation of European Border Controls*, paper presented at the Modern Law Review seminar on *Extraterritorial Immigration Control: Legal Challenges*, Queen Mary, June 2008.

[150] KD Haggerty and RV Ericson, 'The Surveillant Assemblage' (2000) 51 *British Journal of Sociology* 619.

3

Effective Rights for Third-Country Nationals?

HELEN OOSTEROM-STAPLES

I. INTRODUCTION

THE ENTRY INTO force of the Treaty of Amsterdam marked the transfer of competence to the European Union (EU) to regulate immigration, asylum and external borders (EIP). Since then the Community legislator has adopted a vast number of legislative acts covering all these areas. The aim of this contribution is not to discuss the contents of these acts of secondary EC law, but to argue that Member States, if not legally obliged, should at least feel politically committed to ensuring access to justice for those whom EIP claims to protect. Here, 'access to justice' means that the individual is entitled to an effective judicial remedy to enforce individual rights. Under the current status quo, this translates into an obligation for Member States—currently responsible for the processing of individual applications for entry and/or residence in accordance with the European rules—to ensure effective remedies in EIP. 'Effective' is used here in the sense that procedural rules governing access to justice allow the holder of rights to actually bring a case before a competent court of law, which then hands down a binding decision through which rights are enforced and violations of rights are prevented or redressed.[1] Effective remedies thus understood not only ensure correct application in the individual case, but are also an expression of democratic accountability.

As Community law links the obligation to ensure effective remedies to the existence of individual rights, I will first make my case that third-country nationals (TCNs) derive individual rights from EIP once they satisfy the conditions laid down in an act of secondary Community law. For reasons

[1] T Eilmansberger, 'The Relationship between Rights and Remedies in EC Law: In Search of the Missing Link' (2004) 41 *CML Rev* 1199. See also C Harlow, *Voices of Difference in a Plural Community*, Harvard Working Paper 03/00 19.

of space, my search is restricted to admission to the EU territory in general and admission/residence as asylum seeker or family member, in particular. I am fully aware that international law does not recognise a right to (seek) asylum,[2] the only express provision being the non-binding Article 14 of the Universal Declaration of Human Rights.[3] Having said this, States party to the Refugee Convention[4] are committed to respect the non-*refoulement* principle which, although open and ambiguous, bars a State 'from returning persons from its borders or territory to inhuman circumstances'.[5] Likewise, Article 3 ECHR requires Contracting Parties not to deport a person if there are substantial grounds for believing that, if deported, the person concerned faces a real risk of subjection to torture, or inhuman or degrading treatment.[6] Compliance with both obligations requires a substantive assessment of every individual case, the purpose of which is to ascertain observance of the prohibition of *refoulement* as provided for in both legislative acts.[7] As for family members, there is no such thing as a right to family reunification in international law; the obligation to respect family and private life in Article 8 ECHR does not entail a right to family reunification. More generally, there is no internationally recognised right of access to the territory of a State other than the State of nationality.[8] Let us therefore investigate whether the very nature of EC law[9] distinguishes EIP from those provisions in international law which merely recognise the right to cross-border movement without imposing an obligation on States to admit foreigners or uphold asylum rights.[10]

[2] ECtHR 25904/07 *NA v UK* (17 July 2008) para 109.

[3] Note that granting refugee status is a declaratory, rather than constitutive act (MT Gil-Bazo, 'The Protection of Refugees under the Common European Asylum System. The Establishment of a European Jurisdiction for Asylum Purposes and Compliance with International Refugee and Human Rights Law' (2007) 36 *Cuadernos Europeos de Deusto* 178).

[4] UN Convention relating to the Status of Refugees (adopted 28 July 1951, entered into force 22 April 1954) 189 *UNTS* 137.

[5] J Pirjola, 'Shadows in Paradise—Exploring Non-*Refoulement* as an Open Concept' (2008) 20 *IJRL* 640. See also A Francis, 'Bringing Protection Home' (2008) 20 *IJRL* 276.

[6] ECtHR 25904/07 *NA v UK* (17 July 2008) para 109.

[7] SH Legomsky, 'Secondary Refugee Movements and the Return of Asylum Seekers' (2003) 15 *IJRL* 629, 654 and 669–73. See also Francis, above n 5, at 278 and Council Resolution of 20 June 1995 on Minimum Guarantees for Asylum Procedures, [1995] OJ C274/13, point II, 2.

[8] Art 3(2) Fourth Protocol ECHR.

[9] Due to the principles of supremacy (ECJ Case 6/64 *Costa v ENEL* [1964] ECR 585) and direct effect (ECJ Case 26/62 *Van Gend en Loos* [1963] ECR 1).

[10] S Benhabib, *Another Cosmopolitanism* (Oxford, Oxford University Press, 2006) 30. For a broader reading of EC immigration rights see MT Bazo-Gil, 'Refugee Status and Subsidiary Protection under EC Law: The Qualification Directive and the Right to be Granted Asylum' in A Baldaccini, E Guild and H Toner (eds), *Whose Freedom, Security and Justice? EU Immigration and Asylum Law and Policy* (Oxford, Hart Publishing, 2007) 236–9. See also Conclusion of Advocate-General Poiares Maduro in Case C-465/07, *Elgafaji*, 9 September 2008, paras 18–23.

To answer the question whether there is a Community-based right to enter, to seek asylum or to family reunification, requires some understanding of the Community's notion of right. Once we have ascertained whether TCNs are bearers of rights, we will move on and consider the issue of effective remedies (section II). We will first consider whether Community law imposes a legal obligation to provide effective remedies in general and more specifically in EIP on its Member States (section III). Then we will investigate whether the very foundations of the EU—democracy, rule of law and protection of human rights—oblige it to provide effective remedies where Community rights are at stake (section IV). Section V will introduce the TCN trying to enter the EU. The purpose of this section is to pinpoint the location of TCNs when they need effective remedies to uphold their immigration and asylum rights, and to assess the success rate. Section VI will return to the question of whether Member States are obliged to ensure effective legal remedies in EIP and whether the current situation befits Europe's democratic aspirations.

II. IS THERE A COMMUNITY RIGHT TO ENTER THE EUROPEAN UNION?

A. The Notion of Rights in Community Law

Despite the fact that it plays a central role in the ECJ's case law and legal doctrine, the absence of a clear definition of 'right' leaves us with an ambiguous concept.[11] The term 'rights' is found in both primary and secondary EC law and is used by the ECJ in its case law on judicial enforceability, liability of Member States and the implementation of directives.[12] The Court's reluctance to address the issue of individual rights conclusively is explained by the main concern of the ECJ: the effectiveness of Community law. By providing individuals with a means to uphold Community law, national courts—obliged to apply the relevant rule of law—are a mechanism to ensure correct application of EC-law at the national level and the individual is the means to set this mechanism into motion.[13]

In the ECJ's early case law the existence of an individual right was a 'sort of by-product of a provision's direct applicability'.[14] The phrasing of the relevant rule (sufficiently precise and unconditional) determined whether

[11] S Prechal, *Directives in EC Law* (Oxford, Oxford University Press, 2006) 97.

[12] S Beljin, 'Rights in EU Law' in S Prechal and B van Roermund (eds), *The Coherence of EU Law; The Search for Unity in Divergent Concepts* (Oxford, Oxford University Press, 2008) 91.

[13] Eilmansberger, above n 1, at 1204–5.

[14] Eilmansberger, above n 1, at 1203 and Prechal, above n 11, at 99–106.

a right existed. If a rule satisfied the sufficiently precise and unconditional requirement, then a national judge had to apply EC law and set aside a conflicting rule of national law. In an attempt to fill this gap, various scholars have developed criteria to determine whether an individual Community right exists.

In the light of the work of Eilmansberger, Prechal and Beljin, an individual Community right exists where a provision of primary or secondary EC-law aims at granting the individual a right. Sometimes Community law is explicit in indicating that the EU-norm contains a right for the individual, but this is not a *conditio sine qua non*.[15] Where the European norm remains silent, interpreting the norm is the correct way to establish whether it contains an individual right. This is the case where the legal norm imposes 'a specific obligation on a third party towards a beneficiary to do something or abstain from doing something, to commit or abstain from committing certain acts'.[16] Obligations may be general in nature, but mostly govern specific relations. Hence the necessity to establish, through analyses of the text and purpose of the particular legal norm, whether it intends to protect the individual('s interests) and if so, to what extent.[17]

B. Is there a Community Right to Enter EU-Territory?

The three provisions that we are interested in are Article 13 Qualification Directive, Articles 4(1) and 13(1) Family Reunification Directive and Article 13 Schengen Borders Code (SBC).[18] These provisions impose an obligation ('shall') on Member States to grant refugee status, and to authorise entry and residence of family members when a TCN satisfies the conditions set out in the respective Directives, or to refuse entry permission for non-compliance with entry conditions in the SBC. Our findings in the previous section merit the conclusion that the fact that these provisions are drafted as Member State *obligations* might entail, as a corollary, individual rights. As for family reunification, on more than one occasion the Family Reunification Directive actually refers to the 'right to family reunification',

[15] Beljin, above n 12, at 113.

[16] Eilmansberger, above n 1, at 1238.

[17] Beljin, above n 12, at 110, Eilmansberger, above n 1, at 1238–42, and Prechal, above n 11, at 118–25.

[18] Council Dir 2004/83/EC of 29 April 2004 on minimum standards for the qualification and status of third country nationals or stateless persons as refugees or as persons who otherwise need international protection, [2004] OJ L304/12, Council Dir 2003/86/EC of 22 September 2003 on the right to family reunion, [2003] OJ L251/12 and Council Reg (EC) No 562/2006 of the European Parliament and of the Council of 15 March 2006 establishing a Community Code on the rules governing the movement of persons across borders (Schengen Borders Code), OJ EU 2006, L 105/1.

implying that there is actually a right to family reunification in EC law.[19] This reading is confirmed by the ECJ that found that

> Article 4(1) of the Directive imposes precise positive obligations, with corresponding clearly defined individual rights, on the Member States, since it requires them, in the cases determined by the Directive, to authorise family reunification of certain members of the sponsor's family, without being left a margin of appreciation.[20]

Having established an obligation and the individual right as its corollary, let us now consider who benefits from these obligations.

In all cases the beneficiaries are TCNs, defined as 'any person who is not a citizen of the Union within the meaning of Article 17(1) of the Treaty', that is, everyone who is not a national of a Member State.[21] The Qualification Directive also mentions the stateless, who, strictly speaking, are covered by the definition of TCN, as they have no nationality and by virtue of this lack of nationality never qualify as citizens of the Union, that status being reserved for nationals of the Member States.[22] Directive 2003/86/EC imposes the additional requirement that the sponsor (that is, the applicant) is legally resident and holds 'a residence permit issued by a Member State for a period of validity of one year or more and who has reasonable prospects of obtaining the right of permanent residence'.[23]

A further narrowing down of the beneficiaries in the two Directives is achieved by imposing conditions which must be satisfied by the individual applying for permission to enter.[24] Once these conditions are satisfied a Member State 'shall' grant refugee status[25] or authorise 'entry into and residence in a Member State by family members'.[26] In the case of the Schengen Borders Code, failure to comply with entry conditions compels the Member States to refuse entry to the territories of the Member States.[27] The conditional nature of the Member State's obligation does not merit the conclusion that the legal norm is not 'sufficiently precise and concrete' and,

[19] See recitals 6, 11, 12, Art 1 and the name assigned to the Directive as such 'on the *right* to family reunification' and Chapter IV 'Requirements for the exercise of the *right* to family reunification' (emphasis added).

[20] ECJ Case C-540/03 *European Parliament v Council* [2006] ECR I-5769, para 60. See also Report from the Commission to the European Parliament and the Council on the Application of Directive 2004/86/EC on the Right to Family Reunification, 8 October 2008, COM(2008) 610 final, 3.

[21] Arts 2(a) of Dir 2004/83/EC and Dir 2003/86/EC and Art 2(6) SBC.

[22] Art 17(1) EC.

[23] Art 3(1) Dir 2003/86/EC. Special rules apply to refugees: Arts 9–12 Dir 2003/86/EC. For the SBC see Art 5(4) SBC.

[24] See Chapters II, III and V Directive 2004/83/EC, Art 6–8 Directive 2003/86/EC and Art 5(1) SBC.

[25] Ie, to recognise a TCN or stateless person as a refugee (Art 2(d) Directive 2004/83/EC).

[26] Art 2(d) Directive 2003/86/EC.

[27] Art 13(1) SBC.

therefore, does not capture an individual right. On the contrary, time and again the ECJ has ruled that the conditional right to access to the labour market, in Articles 6 and 7 of Decision No 1/80 of the Association Council established under the EEC-Turkey Agreement, entails a right for Turkish workers and their family members who qualify under these provisions to pursue employment in a Member State. To ensure its effectiveness, the ECJ has actually read into the right to employment a right of residence in the host Member State.[28] The ECJ's reading of the EU citizen's free movement right (ex Article 18(1) EC) also confirms this reading of conditional rights.[29] Notwithstanding the reference to 'limitations and conditions' in that provision, the ECJ found that the right in Article 18(1) EC is 'conferred directly on every citizen of the Union by a clear and precise provision of the EC Treaty'.[30] Acknowledging that this right is subject to limitations and conditions, the ECJ argued that 'the application of the limitations and conditions ... in respect of the exercise of that right of residence is subject to judicial review'.[31] Along the same lines, since entry/residence of TCNs is subject to compliance with the conditions set out in the Qualification Directive, the Family Reunion Directive and the SBC, I argue that this does 'not prevent ... [Article 13 Qualification Directive, Article 4(1) Family Reunification Directive and Article 13(1) SBC] from conferring rights on individuals which are enforceable by them and which the nationals courts must protect'.[32] According to this reading, national courts protect Member States from individuals abusing Community rights. But does this reading mean that TCNs do not have a right to effective legal remedies according to Community law?

III. JUDICIAL PROTECTION OF IMMIGRATION AND ASYLUM RIGHTS

A. The Broader Context

Immigration and asylum rules are being developed in the context of the Area of Freedom, Security and Justice (AFSJ). The Tampere Council, convened in October 1999, was a first attempt to colour the notions 'freedom, security and justice'. The Council Conclusions reveal that '[t]he enjoyment

[28] ECJ Case C-192/89 *Sevince* [1990] ECR I-3461, cons 29 (Art 6) and ECJ Cases C-355/93 *Eroglu* [1994] ECR I-5113, cons. 20 and C-351/95 *Kadiman,* [1997] ECR I-2133, para 29 (Art 7).

[29] Art 18(1) EC.

[30] ECJ Case C-413/99 *Baumbast* [2002] ECR I-7091, para 84.

[31] ECJ Case C-413/99 *Baumbast* [2002] ECR I-7091, para 86. See also ECJ Case 41/74 *Van Duyn* [1974] ECR 1337, para 7.

[32] ECJ Case C-413/99 *Baumbast* [2002] ECR I-7091, para 86.

of freedom requires a genuine area of justice where people can approach courts and authorities in any Member State as easily as in their own'.[33] The link between freedom and justice begs the question of what freedom is: Are TCNs included in this notion and do they benefit from 'a genuine area of justice'?[34]

In Community law, the notions 'freedom' and 'internal market' walk hand in hand. Realisation of the internal market, that is, an area without internal frontiers, requires 'free movement of goods, persons, services and capital'.[35] Traditionally free movement of persons included workers, self-employed persons and service providers, but has since acquired the status of citizenship right.[36] Although phrased in a seemingly neutral way, free movement of persons only includes nationals of the Member State by virtue of their status as citizens of the Union. This suggests the crucial restriction that TCNs are not part of the notion of 'freedom' for the purpose of Article 14(2) EC.[37] This might have been the correct reading prior to the entry into force of the Amsterdam Treaty, but, or so I argue, this is no longer sustainable now that the Community is developing its own EIP. As the ECJ convincingly argues in its *Wijsenbeek* case,[38] free movement in Article 14(2) EC, 'presupposes harmonisation of the laws of the Member States governing the crossing of the external borders of the Community, immigration, the grant[ing] of visas, asylum and the exchange of information on those questions'.[39] What the ECJ is saying is that an EU citizen's right to freedom of movement requires Community norms regulating movement to and within the EU by TCNs; in other words a European immigration and asylum policy. Titles III and Title IV EC are thus vessels of communication. Therefore, a reading of freedom that includes everyone, irrespective of their nationality, moving to and within the EU is justified. Bearing this in mind, let us resume our investigation into what else the Tampere Conclusions say on 'freedom' and 'justice'.

The opening words of the Tampere Conclusions recognise that European integration has always 'been firmly rooted in a shared commitment to *freedom*, based on human rights, democratic institutions and the rule of law'.[40] The challenge set by the Amsterdam Treaty is 'to ensure that *freedom*,

[33] Tampere Conclusions, below n 34, point 5. Note that the Dutch, Italian and German texts use '*burgers/cittadini/Bürger*', which, correctly translated, mean citizens, not 'people', as used in the Spanish text. In the French text people translates into '*chacun*', but '*citoyen*' is also used.

[34] Presidency Conclusions, Tampere European Council, 15–16 October 1999, point 5. Retrieved from: www.europarl.europa.eu/summits/tam_en.htm.

[35] Art 14(2) EC. See also Art 3(1)(c) EC.

[36] Art 18(1) EC.

[37] Art 17(1) EC.

[38] ECJ Case C-378/97 *Wijsenbeek* [1999] ECR I-6297.

[39] *Ibid*, para 40.

[40] Tampere Conclusions, above n 34, point 1.

which includes the right to move freely throughout the Union, can be enjoyed in conditions of security and justice accessible to *all*'.[41] It is unclear what should be 'accessible to all'; but does this distract from the implication that 'freedom' in an AFSJ should include EU citizens and TCNs alike? Point 3 of the Tampere Conclusions reveals that 'freedom should not, however, be regarded as the exclusive preserve of the Union's own citizens'. Freedom, working as a magnet, includes TCNs, as a denial is 'in contradiction with Europe's tradition'. Europe's traditions—its commitment to human rights, democratic institutions and the rule of law[42]—require it 'to develop common policies on asylum and immigration, while taking into account the need for a consistent control of external borders to stop illegal immigration and to combat those who organise it and commit related international crimes'. This quote from the Tampere Conclusions corroborates my conviction that, in addition to EU citizens, TCNs, if they meet certain conditions, may benefit from this 'freedom'.

The follow-up to the Tampere Conclusions, the Hague Programme,[43] sheds no further light on the reading of the notion of freedom. However, it does include measures concerning EU citizens and TCNs alike in its section entitled 'Strengthening Freedom', thus suggesting that 'freedom' includes TCNs, who benefit from EIP-measures.[44] Article 61 EC offers further evidence that freedom includes TCNs. This provision includes free movement of persons in accordance with Article 14 EC in its list of measures that the Council must adopt in order to progressively establish an AFSJ. Therefore, at least for now, let us assume that 'freedom that requires a genuine area of justice' may include TCNs.

B. An Area of Justice; For Whom?

Having established, albeit not conclusively, that the notion of 'freedom' may include TCNs, we must consider what the notion of 'justice' entails. What we are interested in is the phrase 'where people can approach courts and authorities in any Member State as easily as in their own'.[45] In the light of our findings on the notion of 'freedom', the phrase 'as easily as in their own' is confusing. If 'own' refers to Member State, TCNs do not benefit from 'a genuine area of justice'; a reading that is also difficult to reconcile with the commitment to democracy, human rights and the rule of law in

[41] Tampere Conclusions, above n 34, point 2.

[42] See also Tampere Conclusions, above n 34, point 1.

[43] The Hague Programme, *Strengthening Freedom, Security and Justice in the European Union*; Annex to the Presidency Conclusions of the Brussels European Council, 4–5 November 2004, Doc 14292/04, 11–42.

[44] Hague Programme, above n 43, 16–27.

[45] Tampere Conclusions, above n 34, point 5.

point 1 of the Tampere Conclusions, as well as Article 6(1) EU, as we will see in section IV. As both the Tampere Conclusions and their follow-up, the Hague Programme, remain silent on 'justice' in relation to immigration and asylum issues,[46] it appears that 'justice' is understood primarily as access to justice by and for European citizens. At the very best, there is disagreement whether TCNs should have access to justice, but the more obvious conclusion is that the Member States did not intend to include TCNs in their reading of justice.

How different are the Commission's considerations on this issue, as transpires from its Communication on the 'Hague Programme' and its Communication on Title IV and the jurisdiction of the ECJ?[47] The first document reveals the goal which is to be achieved and what this entails, as the Commission makes its case for a reading of an area of justice that

> is more than an area where judgements obtained in one Member State are recognised and enforced in other Member States, but rather an area *where effective access to justice* is guaranteed in order to *obtain* and *enforce judicial decisions.* To this end the Union must envisage not only *rules on jurisdiction, recognition* and *conflict of laws*, but also measures which *build confidence and mutual trust* among Member States, creating *minimum procedural standards and ensuring high standards of quality of justice systems*, in particular as regards *fairness and respect for the rights of defence* (emphases added).[48]

In the opening sentence of its 2006 Communication, the Commission proclaims that '*[p]rivate individuals* should be able to enjoy effective judicial protection of the rights that they derive from Community law'.[49] As TCNs are undoubtedly 'private individuals' and Community law, as we saw in section II, provides individual immigration and asylum rights, at least in the opinion of the Commission, EIP is not excluded from the notion of justice. In the same document, the Commission argues for 'respect for fundamental rights, and in particular effective judicial protection for *everybody*'.[50] By using the all-inclusive notion of 'everybody' the Commission undeniably places EIP firmly in the justice discourse. Does the general principle of effective remedies and Community law reconcile these opposing opinions?

[46] In s 1, 'Strengthening Freedom', the measures to be adopted in the areas of immigration and asylum do not include effective remedies. However, on p 28 the right to seek correction of incorrect data as a means to protect the individual from abuse of data stored in automated databases, is included.

[47] Communication from the Commission, 'The Hague Programme: Ten Priorities for the Next Five Years, The Partnership for European Renewal in the Field of Freedom, Security and Justice', 10 May 2005, COM(2005) 184 final; and Communication from the Commission, 'Adaptation of the Provisions of Title IV of the Treaty Establishing the European Community Relating to the Jurisdiction of the Court of Justice with a View to Ensuring more Effective Judicial Protection', 28 June 2006, COM(2006) 346 final.

[48] COM(2005) 184 final (above n 47), at 11.

[49] COM(2006) 346 final (above n 47), at 2.

[50] *Ibid.*

C. Legal Remedies and Community Rights

The European discourse on legal remedies is extensive and complicated by the fact that the ECJ's case law develops along two lines: procedural autonomy and effective legal remedies.[51] As the essence of this section is to establish the scope of the legal obligation to provide effective legal remedies, it suffices to consider the essence of the obligation to equip individuals with tools that allow them to enforce individual Community rights.

Our starting point is Article 10 EC, which sets out the principle of Community loyalty or fidelity. Community loyalty not only entails an obligation for Member States to '*take all appropriate measures, whether general or particular, to ensure fulfilment of the obligations arising out of this Treaty or resulting from action taken by the institution of the Community*' (the so-called positive obligation), but also to '*abstain from any measure which could jeopardise the attainment of the objectives of this Treaty*'; the so-called 'negative duty'. For the purpose of protecting an individual's rights, Article 10 EC obliges Member States to implement and execute Community law in their national legal order, and obliges national courts to control the executive with a view to ensuring compliance with Community law at a national level.[52] According to Eilmansberger,

> [i]n a vertical relationship between an individual and a public authority, the right [which an individual has] that public authorities apply or execute public law provisions in a correct manner, becomes the right to be a party in administrative proceedings, i.e. standing rights, and/or the related right to appeal against administrative decisions.[53]

Where a Member State falls short of these obligations, it is ultimately the ECJ that ensures 'that in the interpretation and application of this [EC] Treaty the law is observed'.[54] This must hold true for the obligation in the legal norm and the obligation to ensure effective remedies.

[51] See eg E Brouwer, *Digital Borders and Real Rights; Effective Remedies for Third-Country Nationals in the Schengen Information System* (PhD thesis, Radboud University, Nijmegen 2007) 263–5; P Craig and G De Burca, *EU Law; Text, Cases and Materials* (Oxford, Oxford University Press 2007) 306–28; R Crumfurd Smith, 'Remedies for Breaches of EU Law in National Courts: Legal Variation and Selection' in P Craig and G DeBúrca (eds), *The Evolution of EU Law* (Oxford, Oxford University Press, 2003) 287–320; JS Delicostopoulos, 'Towards European Procedural Primacy in National Legal Systems' (2003) 9 *European Law Journal* 599–613; Eilmansberger, above n 1; FG Jacobs, 'Enforcing Community Rights and Obligations in National Courts: Striking the Balance' in J Lonbay and A Biondi, *Remedies for Breach of EC Law* (Chichester, John Wiley & Sons, 1997) 25–36; S Prechal, 'EC Requirements for an Effective Remedy' in Lonbay and Biondi (1997) 3–13 and S Prechal, 'Community Law in National Courts: The Lessons from Van Schijndel' (1998) 35 *CML Rev* 681–706.

[52] M Accetto and S Zleptnig, 'The Principle of Effectivenes: Rethinking its Role in Community Law' 11 *European Public Law* (2005–3) 375–403, at 387.

[53] Eilmansberger, above n 1, at 1242–3.

[54] Art 220 EC.

(i) Procedural Autonomy

Although the ECJ did not spell out why, ever since its landmark judgment in *Van Gend en Loos*,[55] it has maintained that national courts are entrusted with the task of protecting rights which an individual enjoys under Community law. In 1976, in the *Comet*[56] and *Rewe*[57] cases, the ECJ explicitly linked direct effect of a legal norm of Community law and the task of national courts to ensure legal protection to individuals.[58] This obligation was rephrased by the ECJ in 1991 to a more generally worded obligation to 'ensure that those [Community] rules have full effect and protect the rights which they confer on individuals'.[59] Protection of individual rights follows

> from the very fact that Community law is an integral part of the legal systems of the Member States, 'which their courts are bound to apply' in principle in exactly the same way as they are bound to apply any other rule of national law, irrespective of its 'external' origin.[60]

Where secondary Community law has not provided legal remedies, the ECJ has refrained from mingling with national rules of procedure,[61] other than through the obligation to comply with both the principles of equivalence and effectiveness.

'Equivalence' requires remedies to enforce Community law that are not less favourable, in terms of substantive and procedural conditions, than those applicable to similar actions concerning issues involving national law.[62] Equivalence is thus an expression of the principle of non-discrimination, which does not require that Community claims enjoy the most favourable national procedural rules, but merely that comparable claims are treated alike. To determine whether the principle of equivalence is infringed it is necessary to identify a similar domestic action and the applicable national rules of procedure.[63]

'Effectiveness' here means that national procedural conditions cannot make 'the exercise of Community rights virtually impossible, nor excessively difficult'.[64] In other words, national law must provide effective and adequate redress for breaches of Community law. 'Effectiveness' follows

[55] ECJ Case 26/62 *Van Gend en Loos* [1963] ECR 1.

[56] ECJ Case 45/76 *Comet BV v Produktschap voor Siergewassen* [1976] ECR 2043.

[57] ECJ Case 33/76 *Rewe-Zentralfinanz eG v Landwirtschaftskammer für das Saarland* [1976] ECR 1989.

[58] Prechal, above n 11, at 132.

[59] ECJ joined Cases C-6/90 and C-9/90 *Francovich* [1991] I-5357, para 32.

[60] Prechal, above n 11, at 133.

[61] See Prechal, above n 11, at 137 and the case law mentioned there.

[62] HG Schermers and DFW Waelbroeck, *Judicial Protection in the European Union* (The Hague, Kluwer Law International, 2001) 199.

[63] *Ibid*, 200–01.

[64] See Prechal, above n 11, at 137–8 and the case law mentioned there.

from the principle of Community loyalty and, at the same time, reflects the obligation to ensure judicial control as laid down in Articles 6 and 13 of the ECHR.[65] As we will see in the next section, the ECJ has given these provisions a broader reading than the European Court of Human Rights was prepared to do.[66]

(ii) Effective Judicial Protection

The second strand discerned in the ECJ's case law is the principle of effective judicial protection. Its origins lie in the ECJ's ruling in the *Johnston* case on the obligation to ensure judicial control contained in Directive 76/207/EEC.[67] The ECJ found that

> all persons have a right to obtain an effective remedy in a competent court against measures which they consider to be contrary to ... [Community law]. It is for the Member States to ensure effective judicial control as regards compliance with the applicable provisions of Community law and national legislation intended to give effect to the rights [Community law] provides.[68]

In reaching this conclusion the ECJ emphasised that the obligation to ensure judicial control in Directive 76/207/EEC reflects 'a general principle of law which underlies the constitutional traditions common to the Member States';[69] a principle also found in Articles 6 and 13 of the ECHR. Within months, the ECJ applied its ruling in *Johnston* to a case concerning the right to free movement of workers. It found that 'the existence of a remedy of a judicial nature against any decision of a national authority refusing the benefit of [the right to access to the labour market] is essential in order to secure for the individual effective protection of his right'.[70] By not providing appropriate judicial protection, the Member State had violated the very right the individual wished to uphold in the first place.[71]

Since its introduction in *Johnston*, the principle of judicial protection has found its way into many areas of Community law, including the so-called Europe Agreements. The obligation to provide effective remedies to TCNs who derive rights from these Agreements was spelled out in *Panayotova*.[72] The individual right at stake was the right to work as a self-employed person in a Member State, a right the ECJ had already established as having

65 Schermers and Waelbroeck, above n 62, at 202.
66 S Peers, *EU Justice and Home Affairs Law* (Oxford, Oxford University Press, 2006) 197.
67 ECJ Case 222/84 *Johnston* [1986] ECR 1651.
68 *Ibid*, para 19. See also Peers, above n 66, at 197.
69 *Ibid*, para 18.
70 ECJ Case 222/86 *Heylens* [1987] ECR 4097, para 14.
71 *Ibid*, para 17.
72 ECJ Case C-327/02 *Panayotova* [2004] ECR I-11055.

direct effect.[73] The ruling did not concern the scope of the right invoked, but rather a Member State's powers to regulate first entry/residence to its territory to prevent abuse of this right. The ECJ recognised Member State competence to install a system of checks in the country of origin to allow them to establish correct use of this right.[74] However, and this is where the case is particularly relevant,

> the immigration rules applied by the competent national authorities are appropriate for achieving the objective in view [and may not] ... constitute, in regard to that objective, measures which would strike at the very heart of the rights ... by making the exercise of those rights *impossible* or *excessively* difficult. (emphasis added)[75]

The ECJ also found that Member States must provide procedural review proceedings, that are 'easily accessible and capable of ensuring that the persons concerned will have their applications dealt with objectively and within a reasonable time, and refusals to grant a permit must be capable of being challenged in judicial or quasi-judicial proceedings'.[76] On a general note, the ECJ stated:

> Community law requires effective judicial scrutiny of the decisions of national authorities taken pursuant to the applicable provisions of Community law, and that this principle of effective judicial protection constitutes a general principle which stems from the constitutional traditions common to the Member States and is enshrined by the European Convention for the Protection of Human Rights and Fundamental Freedoms ... in Articles 6 and 13 of the Convention.[77]

For EIP three important lessons follow from *Panayotova*:

1. Exporting immigration and asylum decision-making is permitted, but may not make the exercise of individual rights 'impossible or excessively difficult'.
2. For the purpose of providing effective legal remedies, the location of an individual in need of them is immaterial.
3. The nature of a decision concerning entry/residence, administrative law *pure sang*, does not preclude application of the legal norms in Articles 6 and 13 ECHR to entry cases.[78]

[73] See ECJ Cases C-63/99 *Gloszczuk* [2001] ECR I-6369, paras 29–38; C-257/99 *Barkoci and Malik* [2001] ECR I-6557, paras 30–39; and C-235/99 *Kondova* [2001] ECR I-6427, paras 30–39.

[74] ECJ Cases C-327/02 *Panayotova* [2004] ECR I-11055, para 22; C-63/99 *Gloszczuk* [2001] ECR I-6369, para 58; C-235/99 *Kondova* [2001] ECR I-6427, para 61; and C-257/99 *Barkoci and Malik* [2001] ECR I-6557, para 62.

[75] ECJ Case C-327/02 *Panayotova* [2004] ECR I-11055, para 20. See also ECJ Cases C-63/99 *Gloszczuk* [2001] ECR I-6369, para 56 and C-235/99 *Kondova* [2001] ECR I-6427, para 59.

[76] ECJ Case C-327/02 *Panayotova* [2004] ECR I-11055, para 27.

[77] *Ibid*, with reference to ECJ Cases 222/84 *Johnston* [1986] ECR 1651, paras 18–19, and C-467/01 *Eribrand* [2003] ECR I-6471, para 61.

[78] See otherwise ECHR, *Maaouia*, 5 October 2000, No 39652/98.

D. Legal Remedies and Immigration Rights

Having established a general legal obligation for Member States to provide effective legal protection where secondary Community law remains silent, we must now consider the state of the art for EIP. Research has revealed that most of the legislative acts adopted within the framework of EIP provide for some kind of legal remedy.[79] The same research also reveals that these provisions are far from uniform. The provisions range from a loosely-worded general obligation to 'ensure that the third country national concerned may, in accordance with the enforcing Member State's legislation, bring proceedings for a remedy against any measure',[80] to the adoption of a special Directive regulating the procedure for determining and withdrawing refugee status.[81] Following extensive analysis of these provisions, Brouwer concludes that these provisions 'often lack precise and detailed procedural guarantees' and 'do not offer the same standards as those which apply to nationals of EU-Member States, or their family members, based on Directive 2004/38/EC'.[82] The latter Directive not only defines the notion of public policy and public health (two out of three legitimate reasons to withhold rights accorded by the Directive) in detail,[83] but also provides for access to judicial and administrative redress procedures allowing for

> an examination of the legality of the decision as well as of the facts and circumstances on which the proposed measure is based. They shall ensure that the decision is not disproportionate, particularly in view of the requirements laid down in Article 28.[84]

Directive 2004/38/EC also provides rules on the notification of decisions to restrict free movement rights and the duration of expulsion orders.[85] Although Member States may refuse EU citizens permission to be present in their country pending a redress procedure, it is not permitted to prevent them from submitting their defence in person, unless this is justified

[79] E Brouwer, 'Effective Remedies for Third Country Nationals in EU Law: Justice Accessible to All' (2005) 7 *EJML* 219–36 and Brouwer, above n 51, ch 9, section 3; R Byrne, 'Remedies of Limited Effect: Appeals under the Forthcoming Directive on EU Minimum Standards on Procedures' (2005) 7 *EJML* 71–86 and R Cholewinski, 'The Need for Effective Individual Protection in Immigration Matters' (2005) 7 *EJML* 240–44.

[80] Art 4 Council Dir 2001/40/EC of 28 May 2001 on the mutual recognition of decisions on the expulsion of third country nationals, [2001] OJ L /149/34.

[81] Council Dir 2005/85/EC of 1 December 2005 on minimum procedures in Member States for Granting and Withdrawing Refugee Status, [2005] OJ L /326/13.

[82] Brouwer, above n 51, at 259.

[83] Arts 27–29 Dir 2004/38/EC of the European Parliament and the Council of 29 April 2004 on the rights of citizens of the Union and their family members to move and reside freely within the territory of the Member States, [2004] OJ L /229/35.

[84] Article 31(3) Dir 2004/38/EC.

[85] Arts 30 and 32, respectively, Dir 2004/38/EC.

by public policy/national security concerns or where a redress procedure follows an entry refusal.[86]

How different is the situation for TCNs?[87] Although most acts establish an obligation to motivate and notify decisions, thus providing the person concerned and the judicial authorities with knowledge of the underlying reasons, this is not the case for suspensive effect or a right to enter the territory for the purpose of attending judicial review proceedings. Where a provision on suspensive effect is included, it is conditional[88] or subject to national discretion.[89] The situation for legal aid is not very different. Admittedly, long-term resident TCNs enjoy a right to legal aid 'on the same terms as apply to nationals of the State where they reside'.[90] As far as asylum seekers are concerned, the Procedure Directive obliges Member States to 'allow applicants for asylum the opportunity, at their cost, to consult in an effective manner a legal advisor or other counsellor, admitted or permitted as such under national law, on matters relating to their asylum application'.[91] Paragraph 2 of this provision actually provides for free legal assistance and/or representation granted on request in the event of a negative decision. The snag is paragraph 3, which allows Member States to restrict the availability of legal aid.[92] Moreover, Member States may demand reimbursement of any expenses granted 'if and when the applicant's financial situation has improved considerably'.[93] Legal aid is not included in the Family Reunion Directive or the SBC. The latter merely obliges Member States to advise a TCN who is refused permission to enter of 'representatives competent to act on behalf of the TCN in accordance with national law'.[94]

The provisions on judicial protection in the Community's immigration and asylum acts reveal the Member States' political reluctance to equip TCNs with effective judicial remedies to enforce immigration and asylum rights. However, this does not absolve Member States from ensuring effective legal protection in these policy areas as a general principle of EC law.[95] Europe's adherence to the protection of human rights and fundamental

86 Art 31(4) Dir 2004/38/EC.

87 See matrix in Brouwer, above n 51, at 275–8.

88 Art 39 Dir 2005/85/EC.

89 Art 19 Council Reg (EC) No 343/2003 of 18 February 2003 establishing the criteria and mechanisms for determining the Member State responsible for examining an asylum application lodged in one of the Member States by a third-country national, [2003] OJ L /50/1.

90 Art 12(5) Council Dir 2003/109/EC of 25 November 2003 concerning the status of third-country nationals who are long-term residents, [2004] OJ L /16/44.

91 Art 15(1) Dir 2005/85/EC.

92 Member States can choose to exclude onward appeals or review proceedings from free legal aid, to only provide legal aid to those who lack sufficient resources, to specifically designated legal advisors/counsellors, or where appeal or review is likely to succeed (where this does not restrict legal aid arbitrarily).

93 See Art 15(6) Dir 2005/85/EC.

94 Art 13(3) SBC.

95 Peers, above n 66, at 197.

freedoms sets the level of protection at that provided for by Articles 6 and 13 of the ECHR, both of which the ECJ considers to apply to immigration issues, even where the applicant is not on the territory of the Member State concerned. In sum, failure to protect immigration and asylum rights not only amounts to a violation of the obligation to provide effective legal remedies, but also to a violation of those very rights that the individual seeks to enforce.[96]

IV. FOUNDATIONAL ISSUES: DEMOCRACY AND THE RULE OF LAW

Having established a legal obligation to ensure legal remedies to TCNs claiming immigration and asylum rights, we will now consider the very foundations on which the ECJ has built this commitment—Europe's constitutional traditions.[97] At a more abstract level, effective judicial protection is part of the system of checks and balances, essential to any democracy, designed to ensure compliance by the State, as a representative of its people, with its self-imposed rules. Whatever its form, 'democracy brings together the greatest wisdom and procures policies best tailored to the common good', a process that runs the risk of degeneration if an effective system of checks and controls is missing.[98] Democracy relates to access to justice in the sense that it assigns to the judiciary the task of ensuring that everybody can enjoy the rights given to him/her by the legislator. Access to justice is thus an expression of the democratic accountability of the executive[99] and serves the dual function of guaranteeing individuals their rights *and* ensuring that rules are applied in the mode envisaged by the majority. As such, it is a form of retrospective monitoring of democratic decision-making.[100]

Addressing European law in general and EIP in particular from the perspective of democracy and the rule of law is a hazardous adventure. Europe's credentials as a democracy are highly contested. This debate is dominated by arguments relating to the absence of a *demos*, inadequate means of holding representatives accountable, the enormous empowerment of the executive and the lack of transparency.[101] To add insult to injury, immigration and asylum law hardly complies with the idea of (representative)

[96] Eilmansberger, above n 1, at 1243.

[97] See ECJ Case C-327/02 *Panayotova* [2004] ECR I-11055, para. 27. See also Tampere Conclusions, above n 34, point 3.

[98] N MacCormick, 'Democracy, Subsidiarity, and Citizenship in the "European Commonwealth"' (1997) 16 *Law and Philosophy* 344–5.

[99] *Ibid*, 344–5.

[100] MC Burkens, HRBM Kummeling, BP Vermeulen and RJGM Widdershoven, *Beginselen van de democratische rechtsstaat* (Deventer, WEJ Tjeenk Willink, 1997) 41.

[101] DM Curtin, *Postnational Democracy; The European Union in Search of a Political Philosophy* (The Hague, Kluwer Law International, 1997) ch 5.

democracy: ie rules developed by a polity in the name and to the benefit of all to whom these rules apply. Immigration and asylum law in general is, *per definitionem*, adopted unilaterally by a polity and, in providing the criteria of membership, simultaneously establishes the criteria for exclusion.[102] EIP is no exception. Like all membership norms, EIP is adopted by a 'we' that is different from the 'we' that is supposed to comply with this legislation. This situation is described as the

> paradox internal to democracies, namely, that democracies cannot choose the boundaries of their own membership democratically ... [it] can never be fully resolved [though] its impact can [however] be mitigated through the renegotiation and reiteration of the dual commitments to human rights and sovereign self-determination.[103]

Translating this into individual EIP decisions, as the closure that gives rise to the EU, turns TCNs into 'them',[104] judicial review by an independent judge is the only avenue available to 'them' to contest the validity of these EIP rules or their compatibility (for instance with human rights obligations or the Refugee Convention), either in general or in their application to their particular situation. Therefore, if we take on board, as Benhabib argues, that the human rights commitments mitigate the paradox of decisions setting the boundaries of membership, we must accept that by not providing TCNs with effective legal remedies the EU and Member States breach their international (human rights) commitments in two ways. They do so, first, because they act in violation of Article 13 ECHR (the right to effective remedy in areas covered by the Treaty) and Article 6 ECHR as interpreted by the ECJ[105] (the right to a fair and public hearing), which are both included in Article 47 of the Charter of Fundamental Rights of the European Union. And secondly, they do so because EIP is an expression of the obligations to respect family and private life (Article 8 ECHR), not to expose anyone to inhuman and degrading treatment (Article 3 ECHR) nor to return a person to the State where they risk being persecuted (Article 33 of the Refugee Convention).

Let us now consider briefly how the second foundational issue, the rule of law, affects Europe's mode of operation in EIP. There are many readings of the rule of law. The bottom line is that the rule of law is a safety net to prevent arbitrary use of powers by State organs. It is built on the assumption that the State is bound by rules which can be identified, and operates of its own accord within the boundaries set by those rules.[106] Admittedly,

[102] Benhabib, above n 10, at 19.
[103] Benhabib, above n 10, at 35.
[104] Benhabib, above n 10, at 32–6.
[105] ECJ Case C-327/02 *Panayotova* [2004] ECR I-11055, para 27.
[106] C Raat, *Mensen met macht: Rechtsstatelijkheid als organisatiedeugd voor maatschappelijke organisaties* (PhD Thesis, Tilburg University, 2007) 185–6.

this reading of the rule of law is one with which lawyers are comfortable.[107] However, I feel that here it suffices to substantiate my argument regarding Europe's obligation to ensure effective legal remedies in EIP. From this perspective, the role of the judiciary is to review decisions in individual cases. Thus the judiciary ensures that the executive's decisions are fair, not arbitrary, and in accordance with the rules adopted by the legislator as well as a Member State's international commitments. The inter-locking system of judicial control established by the EC Treaty effectively puts the national judiciary in the driver's seat.[108] So, where the Commission argues for 'an area where effective access to justice is guaranteed in order to obtain and enforce judicial decisions' (sub-section III.B), it in fact argues for a judicial system where the national judiciary are responsible not only for compliance with the norms set out by the Community legislator, but also for those found in the Refugee Convention, the ECHR and any other international agreement relevant to immigration and asylum cases. As the law currently stands, this entails an obligation for Member States to put into place a system for judicial review that takes on board the peculiarities of immigration and asylum cases. As section V will reveal, they will have to provide an adequate solution for the biggest problem in this area of law in terms of access to justice: the fact that TCNs are usually not on Member State territory when they need effective legal remedies to enforce immigration and asylum rights.

EIP, even if incipient, presupposes and impinges on democracy and the rule of law—two of Europe's very foundations listed in Article 6(1) EU. The key that leads into both democracy and the rule of law is the notion of 'access to justice' or the right to effective judicial protection where individual Community rights are at stake: a right that is presented by the ECJ as an expression of the rule of law. In sub-section III.D we argued that although the Community legislator has included provisions on legal remedies in immigration and asylum acts, this does not absolve Member States from the duty to ensure effective judicial protection as a general principle of Community law.

V. IMMIGRATION AND ASYLUM LAW IN PRACTICE

A. Introducing the Concentric Circle Model

It is time to move on and consider what is actually happening at Europe's external border. To grasp the real problems of TCNs travelling to the EU, I will use the image of concentric circles caused by a stone hitting

[107] *Ibid*, 186.
[108] Prechal, above n 11, at 133.

the water.[109] The idea underlying the concentric circle model is that the geographical border is the circle closest to the place where the stone hits the water. The location of this circle equates to the definition of external border in Article 2(2) SBC. This is Europe's *de jure* external border. Crossing the *de jure* external border, located at 'the Member States' land borders, including river and lake borders, sea borders and their airports, river ports, sea ports and lake ports, provided that they are not internal borders', is only permitted at designated border-crossing points where officials determine whether somebody satisfies the entry conditions in Article 5 SBC.[110] Everybody experiences Europe's *de jure* external border, as here checks to establish an 'individual right' to enter Europe are performed on all crossing into the middle circle.[111]

All other circles caused by the stone hitting the water represent places somewhere on this planet where a TCN travelling towards Europe's *de jure* external border is, on more and more occasions, being stopped by visa rules and by rules imposing sanctions on carriers for carrying incorrectly documented passengers to the EU. These 'borders', not rendered manifest by barriers, boards and border guards, are increasingly becoming real obstacles. They are therefore referred to as Europe's *de facto* external borders since they are the manifestation of Europe's endeavour to manage unwanted migration flows by way of mechanisms which significantly erode or compromise the possibility of effective judicial remedy.[112] Examples of measures, designed to curb the flow of unwanted migration are data exchange, visa requirements and carriers' sanctions. Research substantiates the conclusion that, together with interceptions at sea,[113] they effectively prevent TCNs from reaching Europe's *de jure* external border.[114] As the examples in this section will illustrate, *de facto* external borders, although invisible to some, are effective in terms of curbing migration flows. However, more disturbingly, effective remedies are lacking. Here 'effective'

[109] ACVZ, *Vreemdelingenbeleid en terrorismebestrijding* (The Hague, 2003) 50.

[110] Art 4(1) SBC.

[111] Art 7(2) SBC.

[112] See on shifting the external EU-border, E Guild, 'The Border Abroad—Visas and Border Controls' in K Groenendijk, E Guild and P Minderhoud (eds), *In Search of Europe's Borders, Immigration and Asylum Law and Policy in Europe, Vol 5* (The Hague, Kluwer Law International, 2002) 87–104.

[113] See ECRE, *Defending Refugees' Access to Protection in Europe* (December 2007); T Spijkerboer, 'The Human Costs of Border Control' (2007) 9 *EJML* 127–39 and R Weinzierl and U Lisson, *Border Management and Human Rights; A Study of EU Law and the Law of the Sea* (German Institute for Human Rights, December 2007).

[114] ECRE, above n 113, V Guirandon, 'Before the EU Border: Remote Control of the "Huddled Masses"' in Groenendijk, Guild and Minderhoud, above n 112, ch 10; A Hurwitz, 'The "Schengen" Practice and Case-Law in Belgium' (2000) 2 *EJML* 37–48; Spijkerboer, above n 113; H Staples, 'Adjudicating the Schengen Agreements in the Netherlands' (2001) 2 *EJML* 49–83; H Staples, 'Adjudicating the External Schengen Border' in Groenendijk, Guild and Minderhoud, above n 112, ch 11; Weinzierl and Lisson, above n 113.

means both *de facto* and producing a legal effect; *de facto* external borders increasingly and 'effectively' undermine or cancel out 'effective' legal remedies for TCNs, such that the clear cut distinction, so precious to the law, between law and fact, *de jure* and *de facto* issues, becomes thoroughly disrupted.[115]

B. Crossing Europe's External Borders

(i) Accessing the Inner Circle; Europe's de Jure *External Border*

Two examples of TCNs whose travels to Europe came to an abrupt halt at the Dutch geographical border illustrate the impact of data exchange on migration flows. Both cases concern TCNs not subject to visa requirements, and actually pre-date the entry into force of the SBC, which currently governs entry to EU territory. This, however, does not detract from their value, as the very reason for refusing entry permission was a report in the Schengen Information System (SIS), which is still a justified reason for withholding permission to enter the EU.[116] Ironically, both cases have in common the fact that the report violated the Schengen rules, but this did not prevent the Member State from refusing entry permission to a national of a State generally considered not to generate unwanted migration flows.

Let us first consider the case of Ms Mills, a citizen of New Zealand.[117] Ms Mills presented herself at the Dutch section of the external Schengen Border on 25 June 1998. Her intention was to visit Greenpeace Headquarters in Amsterdam. It was only then that she became aware of the French report in the SIS following her participation in the 1995 Greenpeace campaign against French nuclear testing in the Pacific Ocean. Reported as an 'unwanted alien', the Schengen rules compelled the Dutch authorities to refuse entry permission, albeit much to their embarrassment.[118] As France had made the report under Article 96 SIA, the Dutch authorities could not set it aside,[119] nor could they remove the report from the SIS as this is a prerogative of the reporting Party.[120] The Dutch authorities did approach their French colleagues with a view to having Ms Mills removed from the

[115] For a related discussion of the disruption of the *de facto/de jure* distinction see Hans Lindahl's contribution to this volume (ch 6).

[116] Arts 5(1)(d) and 13(1) SBC.

[117] This case was reported in the *Statewatch* bulletin (1998) 39.

[118] Currently Art 13(1) SBC.

[119] Art 94(4) SIA only allows Contracting Parties to set aside reports made under Arts 95, 97 and 99 of the Convention applying the Schengen Implementing Agreement of 14 June 1985 between the Governments of the States of the Benelux Economic Union, the Federal Republic of Germany and the French Republic, on the Gradual Abolition of Checks at their Common Borders (SIA), [2000] OJ L/239/19.

[120] Art 106(1) SIA.

SIS, but to no avail.[121] As for Ms Mills, obviously she did not make her appointment in Amsterdam!

A similar, more recent case concerns the Moon couple (US citizens). Like Ms Mills, the Moons envisaged a visit to the Netherlands in 2005, in their case to attend a meeting of the Moon movement. They knew that in 1995 Germany had reported them in the SIS because of their activities on behalf of this movement. As this had not proven problematic in 1997, 1999 and 2000—on all occasions the German report did not prevent them from entering the Netherlands—they did not envisage any problems in 2005. As they found out, this was a mistake because this time the Dutch authorities did refuse entry permission, arguing that the deterioration of international security in general (that is, the fight against terrorism) now justified strict application of the Schengen rules. For the individual this means that there is no longer an assessment of the particulars of the individual case with a view to establishing whether the reported person actually poses a threat to (inter)national security.[122] Like Ms Mills, the Moon couple did not manage to keep their appointment in the Netherlands. Unlike Ms Mills, they did instigate legal proceedings against the Dutch refusal, but with no success.

Although the SBC had not entered into force and therefore did not apply to either of these cases, for the sake of the argument I will consider, in the light of these rules, the possibility of appealing against a decision to withhold entry permission following a SIS-report. Our starting point is Article 13(1) SBC, which entails an obligation to refuse entry permission following a SIS-report; the box ticked on the standard form would be '(H) is a person for whom an alert has been issued for the purposes of refusing entry in the SIS'. Withholding entry permission obliges Member States to inform the individual of his/her right to appeal against that decision, but does not require them to suspend the effects of the decision. As the Moons experienced, the fact that the reporting Member State was Germany meant that the Dutch authorities could hide behind the incorrect German SIS-report to justify their entry refusal. So where the decision to refuse entry permission builds on a decision adopted by different Member States, this transforms the right to appeal into a theoretical rather than realistic option available to the individual. So if Ms Mills or the Moons ever want to enter the Netherlands, their first action must be to get the report removed from the SIS, for until then they are, allegedly, 'unwanted aliens' and all Member States may refuse entry permission for not satisfying entry conditions. Individuals have a right to instigate proceedings geared at removing data from the SIS in 'each Contracting Party', but no accompanying right to enter a Member State

[121] *Statewatch* bulletin (1998) 39.

[122] *Rechtbank's-Gravenhage, zittingsplaats Amsterdam*, 23 March 2007, AWB 06/37989, JV 2007/245, with commentary by E Brouwer, considerations 7.3–7.4.

for this purpose.[123] Until the report transforming them into an 'unwanted alien' is removed from the SIS,[124] Article 13(1) SBC effectively transforms Europe into an impenetrable 'fortress' for that individual.

(ii) The Middle Circle: Boarding an Aircraft to Travel to Europe

As the numbers of TCNs seeking access to Europe increased towards the close of the last century, it was felt that traditional tools regulating migration flows were inadequate to protect Europe from 'unwanted migrants ... accessing the system of legal protection and the asylum process'.[125] A solution was found in the rules on carriers' sanctions, making carriers responsible for any 'incorrectly documented alien' they transport to Europe[126] and, recently, by imposing an obligation on carriers to communicate to the authorities carrying out immigration controls at the *de jure* external border crossing point, all and sundry data on their passengers on completion of their check-in procedure.[127] Airline companies, faced with serious penalties for every incorrectly documented passenger they carry to a Member State's territory, have no choice but to comply.[128] To assist airline crew, not trained to detect false or incorrect documents, with the necessary pre-boarding checks, Member States started posting Immigration or Airport Liaison Officers (ILOs or ALOs) at high-risk international airports.[129] ILOs and ALOs *assist* airline crew in sifting the unwanted from the welcome TCNs before they board the aircraft at an international airport in a third-country.[130] The significance of this development is that the act that stops TCNs from reaching Europe's *de jure* border is not an immigration decision, but a verbal refusal to carry a person who has purchased a ticket to travel to a certain destination by air, without reimbursing costs: a breach of a civil law contract.

Recently, curbing migration flows has also become one of the activities deployed by Europe's Border Agency, FRONTEX.[131] FRONTEX operates

[123] Art 111(1) SIA.

[124] In any case, after 10 years (Art 113(1) SIA).

[125] Guirandon, above n 114, at 195.

[126] Art 26 SIA and Council Dir 2001/51/EC of 28 June 2001, Supplementing the provisions of Art 26 of the Convention Implementing the Schengen Agreement of 14 June 1985, [2001] OJ L187/45.

[127] Art 3 Council Directive 2004/82/EC of April 29, 2004 on the obligation of carriers to communicate passenger data, [2004] OJ L261/24.

[128] Art 26 SIA as supplemented by Dir 2001/51/EC.

[129] Eg Russia, Ukraine, the Balkans, Turkey, China, Pakistan and Kenya (ECRE, above n 113, at 30.

[130] ECRE, above n 113, at 30.

[131] Communication from the Commission to the European Parliament, the Council, the European Economic and Social Committee and the Committee of the Regions, Report on the Evaluation and Future Development of the FRONTEX Agency, 13 February 2008, COM(2008) 67 final.

with the Member States in the international waters surrounding Europe in an attempt to stop unwanted immigrants, who, in their desperation to reach Europe, circumvent the safety valves put into place by the Member States at international airports.[132] The 'unwanted' are intercepted *en route* and returned to the country they hoped they had left forever. At their very best, FRONTEX operations find their legal justification in the broadly-worded Article 62 EC;[133] a meagre legitimisation for operations during which 'border guards are frequently confronted with situations involving persons seeking international protection or crisis situations at sea'.[134]

What actually happens at international airports, and the same holds true for FRONTEX's operations at sea, is hard to establish as 'there is no sure way of knowing how many passengers were prevented from boarding planes and how many among them wanted to seek asylum'.[135] Both operations leave no paper trail; there are no official decisions in writing or records.

Perhaps the most cited case concerns the refusal to carry Roma following pre-clearing checks at Prague Airport by the United Kingdom (UK), in July 2001. The European Roma Rights Centre (ERRC) monitored the operation and initiated proceedings in the UK on behalf of six Roma, who after pre-clearing checks at Prague airport, were refused permission to board the aircraft they had intended to travel on. The operation was designed to reduce the number of asylum applications by Czech nationals, mainly Roma, which had risen from 515 in 1998 to 1200 in 2000. Its effect was a decline in asylum applications made by Czech nationals at entry points in the UK from 200, in the three weeks prior to the operation, to 20, in the three weeks following the instigation of pre-boarding controls. In this period, 110 passengers were unable to board an aircraft at Prague Airport, with no opportunity to contest the refusal to carry them, let alone the fact that they could not enter the UK, merely because intrusive interrogations justified the assumption that upon arrival they would apply for asylum in the UK—even if their statements indicated otherwise.[136] As for the alleged breach of the 1951 Refugee Convention, the Lords argued that as the six were still in their country of nationality the operation did not amount to a breach of the prohibition of *refoulement* in the Refugee Convention.[137] The Lords did find that the pre-clearing checks violated the principle of

[132] ECRE, above n 113, Spijkerboer, above n 113 and Weinzierl and Lisson, above n 113.
[133] Commission Staff Working Document, Accompanying the Report on the Evaluation and Future Development of the FRONTEX Agency, SEC(2008) 148, p 7.
[134] COM(2008) 67 final, above n 131, at 5.
[135] Guirandon, above n 114, at 203.
[136] Opinion Lords in *R v Immigration Officer at Prague Airport et al, ex parte ERRC et al* [2004] UKHL 55, paras 3–4.
[137] Opinions Lords Bingham of Cornhill and Hope of Craighead in the *Prague Airport Case* (above n 136).

non-discrimination, as they were designed and effectuated to target Czech Roma.[138]

(iii) The Outer Circle; Visa Regimes

Besides international airports, the Member States' diplomatic representations abroad also operate as *de facto* external borders. Here visa rules, the classical tool to regulate access to the territory, take effect as visa are issued or refused to TCNs wishing to travel to Europe. Little is known of the actual effects of visa obligations on migration flows. Research conducted in Sofia demonstrates significant differences between Member States in the application of the Schengen visa rules. Statistics published by the German Foreign Office in 2001 show that, of the 444,042 rejected visa applications, only in 167,038 cases was the refusal in writing and thus open to appeal proceedings. A further concern is that, for instance, in Algeria and Morocco, due to the limited numbers of consular posts people are paying other people to queue for them.[139] What we do know is that amongst the States whose nationals are the subject of visa obligations are 'war-torn and refugee producing countries and entities'.[140] No visa equates to non-compliance with entry conditions at the *de jure* external border.[141] No visa will certainly trigger a refusal by airline crew who, assisted by ILOs/ALOs, will refuse to carry that person to Europe's *de jure* external border, to avoid sanctions for carrying an incorrectly documented person.

A decision of the Belgium *Conseil d'Etat* sheds some light on the problems encountered by TCNs.[142] The applicant, an Albanian national, was ordered to leave Belgium, leaving his newly-wed Belgian wife behind, as he had entered the territory without a long-term visa. He argued that the absence of a Belgian Consulate in his country of nationality meant travelling to the nearest Belgian Consulate which was in Italy, and that to enter Italy lawfully he needed a Schengen visa which would have to be issued by the Italian authorities. The latter would most likely be refused, as Italy, at the time, was the favourite first port of entry for the unwanted Albanians. So here, an Italian refusal to issue a Schengen visa is the reason that Belgian immigration requirements (a long-stay visa) is not satisfied. The consequence is that a married couple cannot live together in the country of which one of them is a national. Although in this case it is unlikely that Article 8 ECHR

[138] Opinions Lord Steyn and Baroness Hale of Richmond in the *Prague Airport Case* (above n 136).

[139] Guirandon, above n 114, at 200.

[140] ECRE, above n 113, at 27. See also Art 13(1) SBC.

[141] See for exceptions Art 5(4) SBC and Art 3(b) SBC.

[142] Hurwitz, above n 114, at 45–6.

or Community law were breached,[143] Community law *would* be violated if the wife was a TCN lawfully resident in Belgium whose right to family reunificaton follows Directive 2003/86/EC.

C. Access to Justice = Access to the Territory

The erection of *de facto* external borders to curtail unwanted immigration towards EU territory means that, contrary to what the SBC would have us believe, there is no such thing as 'the' EU external border.[144] Visa procedures, exchange of data on unwanted immigrants, and carriers' sanctions in combination with the posting of ILOs/ALOs, have transformed the geographical border into no more than a last hurdle before entering the 'promised land'. The sum of measures put into place to guard Europe's *de jure* external border against unwanted TCNs has meant that on more and more occasions a TCN's first confrontation with EIP occurs in a third-country where the would-be immigrant 'stumbles on the invisible, *de facto* external border'.

What the concentric circle model reveals is that somewhere along the line an individual's right to an effective remedy got lost. Admittedly provision is made for remedies in visa cases,[145] but the question is how a TCN actually gets his/her case to the reviewing authorities, be it a judge or higher administrative body. They cannot enter EU territory to conduct legal proceedings in person and as long as they are located in a third-country, a personal consultation with a qualified lawyer competent to take their case to a Member State court is unrealistic. Likewise, the SBC provides a right to lodge an appeal and an obligation to provide information on legal aid, but omits to provide for suspensive effect. The rules on carriers' responsibility and FRONTEX operations effectively infringe immigration and asylum rights by taking the means to reach the *de jure* external border away from the would-be immigrant. Decisions not to carry TCNs are oral and taken by private actors and are therefore not open to 'immigration' review.[146]

What we are witnessing is a pernicious circularity: access to justice presupposes access to territory; in turn, access to territory presupposes access to justice. Therefore although it cannot be denied that EIP provides for remedies, what actually happens is that they are of little use as long as the

143 Community law does not provide for so-called internal situations, that is, situations where free movement rights have not been exercised by an EU-citizen. Family reunion of own nationals then remains subject of national law (ECJ Case C-127/08, *Metock*, 25 July 2008, para 76–8).

144 See Guild, above n 112; Guirandon, above n 114; and Staples, above n 114.

145 Arts 23(3) and 32(6) Draft proposal for a Regulation of the European Parliament and of the Council establishing a Community Code on Visas, 19 July 2006, COM(2006) 403.

146 See Guirandon, above n 114, at 201–6.

person who wants to use them is not in a Member State. The circularity between access to justice and access to territory means that when TCNs actually need a remedy, the current system for judicial review proceedings makes it virtually impossible to use the remedy given to them successfully. To add insult to injury, their physical location makes it impossible for them to communicate with a lawyer in person who can then act on their behalf, as lawyers are to be found in the territory that they cannot enter, not even to conduct legal proceedings. Remedies are therefore not effective in the sense of ensuring the full effect of EIP or protecting the very rights conferred on TCNs. The concentric circle approach effectively undercuts and cancels out effective legal remedies for TCNs, transforming immigration and asylum rights into paper rather than effective rights.

VI. EFFECTIVE REMEDIES TO ENSURE EFFECTIVE RIGHTS AND REQUIRED BY DEMOCRACY AND THE RULE OF LAW

In this Chapter, we have considered the right to effective legal remedies in the light of Europe's developing immigration and asylum policy. Our search for a legal obligation to ensure effective remedies in EIP was premised on the assumption that TCNs derive an individual right, albeit a conditional right to enter/reside in a Member State from the SBC, from the Family Reunification and the Qualification Directives. By considering the exact location of TCNs in need of effective remedies, we found that by 'exporting' the external border Europe has created a system characterised by a mismatch between the need for and availability of legal remedies. The concentric circles model in section V revealed a circularity between access to justice and access to territory. On the one hand, access to territory is a condition for access to justice: succeeding in entering the EU opens up the possibility for claimants to be heard in court and, thereby, of obtaining and enforcing judicial decisions concerning their applications to enter/reside in a Member State. At the same time, access to justice is a condition for access to a Member State's territory, which is precisely the right that TCNs are claiming but unsuccessful in enforcing. Contrary to the Commission's assertion,[147] what we are actually seeing is that for EIP there is no such thing as a 'full system of judicial review', as TCNs are not able to get to a court or confer with a legal representative who, acting on their behalf, can conduct legal proceedings.[148] This is especially worrying, as the Commission emphasises, in a policy area that concerns the protection of very vulnerable people and which is particularly sensitive in terms of fundamental rights.[149]

[147] COM(2006) 346 final, above n 47, at 2.
[148] *Ibid*, 6.
[149] *Ibid*, 5.

The circularity between access to justice and access to territory is also hard to reconcile with the doctrines of effective legal protection and procedural autonomy developed by the ECJ (sub-section III.C) and the Commission's reading of Justice in an AFSJ as 'an area where effective access to justice is guaranteed in order to obtain and enforce judicial decisions'.[150] The ECJ's case law on remedies reveals that the role of national courts is to 'ensure that those [Community] rules have full effect *and* protect the rights which they confer on individuals' (emphasis added).[151] This dual function assigned to national courts puts them in the driving seat as guardians of Europe's own immigration and asylum rules as well as the international obligations, in particular the Refugee Convention and the ECHR,[152] which its Member States have committed themselves to uphold. Where a system of effective legal remedies is missing, the ECJ finds a violation of the very right the individual wishes to uphold (sub-section III.C.(ii)).[153] As national courts are responsible for its enforcement, remedies are generally a matter of national rules of procedure. Although we found that provisions on procedural remedies do feature in EIP (sub-section III.D), the broad wording of many a provision leaves much discretion for Member States, discretion that is curtailed by the doctrine of procedural autonomy and the obligation to ensure effective legal remedies (sub-section III.C). Although Community law as it stands does not preclude exporting immigration and asylum decisions, this may not make the exercise of individual rights 'impossible or excessively difficult'. Irrespective of the location of the individual, Member States must provide for review proceedings that are 'easily accessible and capable of ensuring that the persons concerned will have their applications dealt with objectively and within a reasonable time, and refusals to grant a permit must be capable of being challenged in judicial or quasi-judicial proceedings'.[154] These proceedings must satisfy the standards established by Articles 6 and 13 ECHR, even though the European Court of Human Rights has found differently (sub-section III.C.(ii)).[155]

As the notion of effective legal protection has matured into a self-standing principle that finds its rationale in the rule of law, the circularity of access to justice and access to territory also undermines the EU's very foundations: democracy and the rule of law. In this context, effective legal protection operates as a guarantee against arbitrary exercise of powers as the judiciary monitors correct application of EIP by the executive and ensures that the Community legislator adopts these rules in accordance both with Europe's

[150] Sub-section IV.B.

[151] S Prechal, 'Protection of Rights: How Far?' in Prechal and Van Roermund, above n 12, at 156.

[152] Art 63(1) EC and Art 6(2) EU.

[153] ECJ Case 222/86 *Heylens* [1987] ECR 4097, para 17.

[154] ECJ Case C-327/02 *Panayotova* [2004] ECR I-11055, para 27.

[155] *Ibid.*

international commitments[156] and with the democratic decision-making procedures provided for by the EC Treaty. Access to justice as part of the system of checks and balances that forms the heart of democratic institutions gives the judiciary the job of retrospective monitoring of decision-making. As EIP, by definition, concerns legislation in which its addressees have no direct say in its enactment, the role of the judiciary is crucial in assuring compliance with international obligations designed to protect the most vulnerable. Moreover, it is the first and only institution to which TCNs, who are not members of the polity, can turn to challenge the legitimacy of EIP in general, that is, its compatibility with international law in general, or compliance with the European norm of a decision that affects them personally (section IV). By recognising the creation and existence of rights and by providing for their protection, the ECJ has given individuals a powerful tool that goes *beyond* enforcing their own rights as it simultaneously serves the purpose of controlling the legality of Member State action. Individuals are, accordingly, more than applicants, as, unknowingly, by dint of helping to ensure that Member States comply with their Community obligations and fulfil their duties, they operate as co-guardians of Community law.[157] For EIP, the role of individuals is yet larger: they also act as co-guardians of the EU's and its Member States' international law commitments under, amongst others, the Refugee Convention and the ECHR.

As the case studies in section V reveal, the true challenge for Europe is the strong relationship between access to justice and access to territory. Designing a system for judicial review which solves this problem of circularity is what Europe has to undertake if it wants to look the world straight in the face when it claims to be a Union 'founded on the principles of liberty, democracy, respect for human rights and fundamental freedoms, and the rule of law'.[158]

[156] Eg ECJ Case C-540/03 *European Parliament v Council* [2006] ECR I-5769.
[157] Prechal, above n 151, at 181.
[158] Art 6(1) EU.

II

Theoretical Issues

4

Phenomenology of Space: Being Here and Elsewhere

BERNHARD WALDENFELS

I. INTRODUCTION

CONTRACT OF CONQUEST. Questions of space and place have a political aspect in so far as there is no common life without territories and frontiers. The opening scene reminds us of the history of colonisation. It refers to the taking possession of new lands as a basic and official form of appropriation. An instruction issued by the Spanish king in 1514 describes in great detail the formal acts which have to be observed:

> The manner you must have in the taking of possession of the lands and parts which you will have discovered is to be that, being in the land or part that you shall have discovered, you shall make before a notary public and the greatest possible number of witnesses, and the best known ones, an act of possession in our name, cutting trees and boughs, and digging or making, if there be an opportunity, some small building, which should be in a part where there is some market hill or a large tree, and you shall say how many leagues it is from the sea, a little more or less, and in which part, and what signs it has, and you shall make a gallows there, and have somebody bring a complaint before you, and as our captain and judge you shall pronounce upon and determine it, so that, in all, you shall take the said possession; which is to be for that part where you shall take it, and for all its district and province or island, and you shall bring testimony thereof signed by the said notary in manner to make faith.[1]

This sophisticated procedure finds its legal basis in Roman law, according to which taking possession (*occupatio*) is legitimate insofar as there is no former owner who contradicts and registers a complaint. But in what language and in what form should the so-called natives have complained? The complaint as set forth in the instruction already presupposes a legitimate rule which

[1] Quoted from S Greenblatt, *Marvellous Possessions* (Chicago, Chicago University Press, 1991) 56, followed by the author's comment on the presuppositions and circumstances of this procedure.

prescribes how to take possession, and this rule goes back to the whole tradition of Spanish-Roman law. The rules of the game and of language are imposed, and what may well belong to the Other has already been institutionally appropriated by the conquerors before the proceedings are opened. What is to be thought of Columbus's statement in his diary that nobody had contradicted him? Is this an expression of black humour or of cynicism? And further, can we really say that questions as to who takes possession of land and in what way it is done have lost their importance in the era of global networks, or are they only complemented by other forms of space occupation?

In what follows[2] I will approach the phenomenon of otherness or alienness from the perspective of human embodiment in place or space. Our reflections will proceed in two steps and on two levels. On the first level the well-known phenomenology of body and space will be presented against the background of Western cosmology and anthropology. This rough sketch offers these achievements a certain historical depth. We will see that the order of space is not given once and for all. On the second level the phenomenological conceptions of body and space, which underlie issues such as territory, boundaries, inside/outside and immigration, will be rendered problematic in a new way. By distilling these conceptions to certain paradoxes we will raise a series of questions which all revolve around a certain non-place of the alien. We will finish with some current issues concerning the process of so-called globalisation. At this point, a phenomenology of space passes over into a politics of space.

II. THREE HISTORICAL SPACE PARADIGMS

In the course of history we can distinguish three great paradigms of space centred on the key concepts of *topos*, *spatium* and *Lebenswelt*. The variety of the corresponding terms, and the changes they have undergone, are highly significant; this aspect excludes a simple continuity of one and the same topic, and points to deep historical changes concerning our world orientation and even our dwelling in the world. Phenomenology seems to be able to cope with this multiplicity only by transforming Husserl's eidetic phenomenology, which relies on invariant basic structures, into a structural phenomenology that reckons with variable structures.[3] In addition to this,

[2] This article amplifies on ideas first espoused in my book *The Question of the Other. Tang Chun-Lectures* (Hong Kong/New York, Chinese University Press/SUNY Press, 2007).

[3] Husserl speaks of an eidetic phenomenology with reference to the Platonic concept of *eidos*, which means the essence of things grasped by intellectual intuition. Later on, Merleau-Ponty emphasises the process of structuring experience and of transforming one order into the other. Concerning the methodical background of the phenomenological approach, see ch 1 of my book, *Grenzen der Normalisierung* (Frankfurt/M, Suhrkamp, 1998) where phenomenology is considered step by step from an eidetic, a transcendental and a structural point of view, leading to a special kind of phenomenological estrangement.

it is to be expected that the multiplicity resulting from historical diachronicity finds a resonance in another multiplicity pertaining to intercultural synchronicity. To some extent, the otherness of our own past and the otherness of other cultures elucidate and reinforce each other. Whereas ethnology can be defined as research of what is culturally alien, historiography deals in part with what is temporally alien. This sort of alienness, penetrating investigations, such as scientific projects, that methodologically abstract from particular views and interests, goes back to certain places in the world and in history from which, and only from which, alienness appears as alienness. In so far as alienness pertains to the things themselves, phenomenology for its part, when trying to describe the phenomenon of alienness, takes on certain features of what may be called xenology.

Let us begin with the concept of *topos*. Understood in terms of Aristotelian physics, *topos* means that within the cosmos everything (and everybody) has its own or proper place, its *oikeios*[4] or *idios topos*, just as it has its proper time, its *kairos*. All particular places are integrated into the *koinos topos*, the common place, constituted by the order of the universe, by the *Weltall*. This totality encompasses all that exists. Things envelop each other in such a way that they are inside and outside each other like Russian dolls. Thus, the room is part of the house, the house part of the neighbourhood, the neighbourhood part of the city, the city part of the country and so on. Only the universe as a whole is something that has no outside (cf Aristotle, *Physics* III, 6, 207 a 8). The limits of the *cosmos* as a whole coincide with the limits constituted by a unique *topos*. Even human beings belong to this all-embracing order, whose members are all characterised by self-movement (*hautokinesis*) and goal-orientation (*entelecheia*). Thus it is not only living or human beings that strive for certain goals; so, too, do the physical elements: heavy bodies tend toward the centre of the earth and fire rises towards heaven, such that both tend in this way toward their natural place in the universe.

The notion of *topos* survived up to the medieval period, though re-interpreted in connection with the order of creation. But with the emergence of the modern era, and the development of physics in the Cartesian interpretation, it changes into *spatium*, a skeleton-like space which has lost its cosmic flesh. This new space looks like a container, reduced to an empty shell which is occasionally filled by something or other. All qualities that once belonged to the cosmic *topos* are now radically quantified in terms of *extension*, ascribed to each thing, and in terms of *distance*, separating one thing from another. Things, including human beings, no longer pertain to the environment they inhabit with their own space. On the contrary,

[4] It is worth mentioning that *oikeios* (= proper) has in itself a topical aspect inasmuch as it is derived from *oikos* (= house).

everything occurs *anywhere*, located in a homogeneous and isotropic space which is constituted by points, lines and dimensions. Deprived of any finality, the movements of bodies mean nothing other than the change of spatial positions, whereas for Aristotle, locomotion (*phora*) was only one form of movement (*kinesis*) among others. This has the consequence that the new space becomes, properly speaking, uninhabitable.

In our time there have been many attempts to return to what Husserl calls the *Lebenswelt*. Life-world means a world inhabited by human beings, all of them dwelling and moving bodily in the world. This far-reaching phenomenological renewal of the ancient world conception has certain affinities, amongst others, with what American pragmatists and Wittgenstein have in mind when they refer to the pragmatics of social or socialised actions. It even finds a certain resonance in post-classical physics, beginning with Maxwell's field-theory. Electromagnetic fields have configurations and structures which cannot be explained by the mere interplay of forces and counter-forces. This new orientation is notably supported by ecological tendencies which re-evoke the old concept of *oikos*, though the modern house seems to be deprived of an ever-lasting house order.

At this point another methodological remark should be made. History does not proceed on a linear path; the above-mentioned paradigms have to be read not only diachronically but also synchronically. Consequently we are faced with a set of interferences, superpositions, anticipations and revivals. New orders, established by deviation from existing orders, never completely absorb or preserve that from which they deviate. Because of their asymmetrical structure, deviations resist all kinds of 'sublation' or *Aufhebung*, in the sense of Hegel's dialectic. Where deviation happens, there is not something new opposed to something old in terms of thesis and antithesis; rather, the new only exists by deviating from something. It may suffice to mention, in this respect, the superposition of Jewish, Greek and Arabian ideas and practices in Western Culture, or the entanglement of Confucian, Taoist and Buddhist elements within the development of Chinese culture. Finally, with regard to our special topic we can discern a certain tension between the Platonic *chora*, which functions as a formless receptacle receiving every form, thereby coming close to mathematics, and the Aristotelian *topos*, which constitutes the surface or borderline of concrete things within our world of experience. This tension increased considerably in the time of Galileo, when the mathematical constructs of nature lead to a rediscovery of Plato's cosmology.

III. THE MULTIPLICITY OF THE LIFE-WORLD

Before going into the details of spatial descriptions, something general should be said about the multiple character of what Husserl introduced under the title of life-world. First, Husserl did not by any means long for some lost immediacy of simple life, but rather tried to respond to a genuine, on-going crisis, ie to the crisis of the European sciences which involved, in his view, a crisis of life. The radicality of Husserl's concept depends on the fact that in his view the life-world does not really exist as a totality of beings (*omnitudo realitatis*), and that it must also not be conceived of as a regulative idea, in the Kantian sense. The life-world is certainly given, it is given to me and to us, but in such a way that it is only co-given with whatever appears. The life-world itself has double function, as the *universal horizon* within which everything appears, and as the *universal ground* from which everything arises. I cannot speak of things within the world without speaking at once of myself and of others living with me in the world. If everything which is the case is based in the life-world, the life-world itself is not simply the case. In a certain sense we can say that the world happens as a 'worlding' (*es weltet*), and this in terms of a *uniqueness* for which the plural makes no sense.[5] Possible worlds point back to the actual world. The actual world is not merely a world among others, as conceived by the eternal thinking of Leibniz's divine mind; it is rather presupposed by all variations our world may undergo. This 'absolute fact' can neither be denied nor can it be deduced from elsewhere. It corresponds to a kind of world belief (*Weltglaube*). Linguistically, this belief could be conceived as a set of indispensable presuppositions, which include the reference to the factual world, the self-reference to me addressing others and the co-reference to the others I address and I am addressed by. Before affirming or denying anything, we presuppose that there is a world (*es gibt Welt*), and this 'there is' goes beyond universality and particularity, beyond ideality and facticity. If we take into account that the play and latitude (*Spielraum*) of our possibilities is always restricted because of factual conditions such as our corporeality and our spatial and temporal situation here and now, we must concede that this making possible means at the same time making impossible. Thus the order of the world is to some extent contingent. But to what extent? Do we simply meet with contingency within order, or is contingency inherent in order itself?

At this point some important distinctions have to be made. First, we must mention the dimension of the *concrete* and the *abstract*. This dimension points to the distinction that Husserl has in mind between a plurality of concrete life-worlds, on the one hand, and the universal structures of the one life-world to be 'distilled by abstraction',[6] on the other. Secondly, we are confronted with the dimensions of the *whole* and the *part*, due to the fact that each cultural life-world is divided into a set of particular or

[5] E Husserl, *The Crisis of European Sciences and Transcendental Phenomenology*, trans D Carr (Evanston IL, Northwestern University Press, 1970) 143.
[6] *Ibid*, 133.

professional worlds (*Sonderwelten*, *Berufswelten*). Thirdly, in addition to this intracultural articulation of the life-world, we have to take intercultural worlds into consideration, worlds that vary historically and geographically, and lead, for example, to the world of Chinese peasants that Husserl takes as an example.[7] However, nobody approaches different cultures from some random standpoint or other; rather, everybody starts from his or her own culture. So, we enter a third dimension, that is, what is one's *own* and the *alien*. Using Husserl's own terms we can say that the life-world is divided into the home-world (*Heimwelt*) and the alien world (*Fremdwelt*). This third dimension, in which the own is detached from the alien, has been especially important for us and will continue to be so.

IV. ORIENTATED VERSUS HOMOGENEOUS SPACE

Let us now turn to the special question as to how the life-world is spatially or topologically organised. Considering the fact that the rehabilitation of the life-world is invoked to overcome naturalistic trends, phenomenological descriptions of space experience usually start from a fundamental distinction, that is, from the distinction between a purely homogeneous space and an orientated type of space without which the own and the alien would be completely out of place.

Within *homogeneous* space we occupy only internal *positions* (or *sites*), and they are all relative, equivalent; something or somebody is *anywhere* or *somewhere or other*. Space schemes consist of points and lines. The void left by these schemes can be filled by anything. Nothing really 'takes place'. By contrast, things look rather different when we enter *orientated* space. This type of space originally received its name from its relation to the Orient, the region of the sunrise; but, generally speaking, it is orientated with respect to a certain 'here' (and 'now'). This 'here' may be the sun's changing position, corresponding to the habits of certain ethnic groups that prefer a strictly heliocentric orientation. In general, the particular 'here' becomes privileged among other places because it functions as a *Nullpunkt*, as the zero point from which the various dimensions originate.[8] The 'here' is neither situated on the right nor on the left, neither above nor below. In his *Theory of Language*, Karl Bühler treats the 'here' linguistically as the *origo*, that is, as the origin of a deictic field (*Zeigfeld*).[9] As is well known, the adverb 'here' belongs to the class of occasional or indexical expressions which are used to indicate the circumstances of speech, and it points to the

[7] *Ibid*, 139.

[8] E Husserl, *Ideas Pertaining to a Pure Phenomenology and to a Phenomenological Philosophy*, 2nd edn, trans R Rojewicz and A Schuwer (Dordrecht, Kluwer, 1989) 153.

[9] K Bühler, *Sprachtheorie* (Stuttgart/New York, G Fischer, 1982), trans DF Goodwin as *Theory of Language* (Amsterdam/Philadelphia, J Benjamin, 1990) 117–22.

place the actual speaker or actor occupies. Here we come across a suture between space experience and speaking, which—by the way—is neglected by many philosophers of language. Indeed, I have to be bodily involved in the situation in order to understand what the indexical expression actually means.[10] 'Here' plays a special role by marking a situation from which a world opens, and not only for me, but also for you and for others. Now, the orientation which creates such an open space is highly complex, displaying various aspects:

A. Space Dimensions

First we have to distinguish different dimensions. The dimension of *above and below* is connected with the upright position of humans which take the earth as their ground. Vertical orientation reappears in the 'statics' of buildings, which literally means an art of making stand. The rich symbolism surrounding heaven and earth entails an overdetermination of our bodily position which not only occupies a place, but also marks it. The famous free-fall studied by Galileo still alludes to this body-dependent dimension, although pure physical bodies, traversing void space in a certain direction and with a certain speed, strictly speaking do not fall at all. They move where they move without being affected by any up and down.

Moreover, the polarity of *before and behind* derives from the human face as the seat of mouth and eyes, in opposition to the back of our body, which is more exposed than posed. In the same way, houses, too, have their façade and their rear, and even the field of perception is organised by being divided into foreground and background.

Finally, we distinguish between *right and left*, ie between our right and left hand, or, nowadays, between the right and the left part of the brain. This third kind of polarity shows a greater degree of exchangeability than the two others. But it is all the more full of symbolism, even moral and political symbolism, with the right side turning to rightness, the left side to the sinister—or vice versa, according to different cultural patterns. However, how can we decide where right is and where left? Kant raises this question in his essay, *What Does it Mean to Orient Oneself in Thinking?* In his view, orientating oneself means to find the (sun) rise (*Aufgang*) from a given world region (*aus einer gegebenen Weltgegend*). The solution he proposes looks rather phenomenological: I discover the distinction between

[10] I refer to my article,'Zwischen Sagen und Zeigen' in *Idiome des Denkens* (Place, Publisher, 2005), trans as 'Between Saying and Showing' in JJ Drummond and K-Y Lau (eds), *Husserl's 'Logical Investigations' for the New Century* (Dordrecht, Springer, 2007). There I try to show how Husserl's theory of occasional expressions had a strong effect on the linguistics of Karl Bühler and Roman Jakobson.

right and left by 'feeling a distinction in my own subject', located mainly in my own hands.[11] This elementary example of corporeal thinking precedes other forms of topology, which can be qualified as geographical, as political, as mathematical, as logical or simply as literate, as in the process of writing from left to right or vice versa, or from above to below.

B. Nearness and Distance

We would completely misunderstand this highly dynamic distinction if it were taken as the distance (*Abstand*) from one thing to the other, or as a mere interval (*Zwischenraum*) separating things that exist in a pre-given space, each placed beside the other in a sort of juxtaposition. Being close by or far away presupposes somebody traversing space, such that her/his movements show a certain range (*Spielraum*) and whose tempi and rhythms differ in accordance with techniques of locomotion. Following Paul Virilio's dromology,[12] we may distinguish between immediate proximity, simply bound to the moving body; mechanical proximity, dependant on certain means of transportation; and electronic proximity, reaching the speed of light. The last step seems to announce an overwhelming tele-presence, the global neighbourhood of which would be able to create a technological version of omnipresence. We will return to this problem.

C. Inside and Outside

The difference between inside and outside looks more simple than it is. There is no inside and outside at all unless boundaries of a certain place *include* somebody and also *exclude* her/him from other places. Only living beings, qualified as inhabitants of the world, have access to inside and outside, and only human beings, living within the borders of a symbolically marked territory, are able to immigrate and to emigrate. The difference between inside and outside simply vanishes when the world is seen from a bird's-eye view, turning inclusions and exclusions into mere juxtapositions. The difference also disappears when observed from the point of view of a whole, such as the aforementioned cosmos, which has no outside. The contrast between inside and outside ensues from one's own body. Our body is simultaneously separated from and mediated with its physical and social environment by means of its skin.

[11] I Kant, 'Was heißt: sich im Denken orientieren?' ('What Does it Mean to Orient Oneself in Thinking?') in W Weischedel (ed), *Werke in sechs Bänden*, (Darmstadt, Wissenschaftliche Buchgesellschaft, 1963–64) vol III, p 308.

[12] P Virilio, *La vitesse de libération*, (Paris, Galilée, 1995) 74.

The contrast between inside and outside becomes crucial as soon as the segregation of what is one's own and what belongs to others (*Eigenes/Fremdes*) is at stake. External limits or frontiers do not exist without somebody transgressing them, being at once on this side and on the other side. There are good reasons to assume that the classical thinking of the Greeks was not really able to form a radical concept of *Fremdheit*, of alienness, because the cosmos comprehends everything in such a way that everybody can feel at home in the world. Only the chaotic seems to remain outside the well-ordered universe. And things are only reversed when Gnostics regard the universe as a bad world. In their opinion we all are strangers in the world, living in a great prison. So it looks as if we only have the alternative to live either inside the world or outside, but never both at once.[13]

D. Spatial Dispositions

Space is articulated by the disposition and composition of things and persons, all together forming a common 'roominess' or a common place. Thus, in his work *On Duties* (*De officiis*),[14] Cicero defines order as the 'composition of things at apt and appropriate places (*compositio rerum aptis et accomodatis locis*)'.[15] To some extent, order itself can be defined as a spatial order. The articulation of places and rooms oscillates between fullness and emptiness, between parsimony and abundance. Both aspects have to be understood qualitatively: rooms, towns or countries are too full or too empty. Places appear as overcrowded, like the infernal scenes of Bosch's paintings, or as empty scenarios, like the vedutas of Chirico's *pittura metafisica*. These distinctions make no sense in the void space of classical physics. In opposition to this rigid scheme, flexible orders, originating from lived space, pass through numerous variations, dependent, for example, on the distribution of people's locations in a teaching room, a factory or a restaurant. The whole arrangement may be centred or not, preferring either tables with a head or round tables. Or take the multiplicity of town plans: there are traditional European towns, surrounding a public place (*agora, forum, market* etc), centred on the parish church or the town-hall and, in contrast, non-centred towns like Kyoto, which is divided into many temple districts, or American town-landscapes, which are spread out like a carpet.

[13] More about that in my article 'The Boundaries of Order' (2004) 73 *Philosophica* (Gent) 71–86.

[14] Cicero, *De officiis*, book I, 40.

[15] B Waldenfels, *Ordnung im Zwielicht*, (Frankfurt/M, Suhrkamp, 1987), trans DJ Parent as *Order in the Twilight* (Athens, Ohio University Press, 1996).

V. REAL OR SYMBOLIC SPACE?

Is there real space, prior to symbolic representations? Is it true that symbolic space only plays a secondary role? In an attempt to answer these questions, we discover that everybody who relies on the simple distinction between 'real' and 'symbolic' would be committing a *petitio principii* and would reproduce well-known metaphysical prejudices. On this view, one simply assumes that there are things inside and things outside space, and one concludes that attributes of the former are metaphorically transferred to the latter. As a result, we would merely create, as it were, conceptual hybrids like '*high* person', '*right* reason', 'logical *exclusion*', or '*inner* world'. Instead, we should ask whether something or somebody is at all thinkable that is not, at least to some extent, previously affected by 'place identity', that is, without *its* place and *its* time. Is it possible to place 'who?' and 'what?' questions on the one side, and 'where?' questions on the other?

These general assumptions need further explanation. First, the 'here' of the speaker and the 'there' of the listener do not simply belong to what is *said*, they belong to the very process of *saying* by which speaking literally *takes place* (*findet statt, a lieu*). There always remains something as the place of speaking which cannot be reduced to the propositional content of the speech act, or to the *énoncé* realised by a certain *énonciation*. Reducing the latter to the former would ultimately abolish the speech event or the discourse practice, without which nothing would be said. Classical rhetorics had good reasons to take public speech scenes such as the political assembly, the court and the festival arena into consideration. Similarly, modern theories of law and of state refer to legal spaces and political territories which are constituted by political actions and marked by political symbols. Furthermore, as Erwin Straus clearly shows in his book, *Vom Sinn der Sinne*,[16] each sense is intrinsically determined by specific forms of spatiality. Items like localisation, direction or distance do not mean the same when we shift from one sense to the other. Sounds do not simply arise from the place where sound sources are located. We do not encounter sounds as something in front of us; rather, they surround and envelop us. We do not hear one and the same melody in the same way as we see the same tree, because repetition plays a different role in each case. Sounds happen; they are not deeply rooted, as trees are. The space of smell must be specified in a similar way, including the smoke of incense candles which passes through the temple hall, creating a particular atmosphere. Finally, whenever something is perceived, it appears *as something*, it appears *in this way and not in another*. Consequently, from the very beginning symbolic features

[16] E Straus, *Vom Sinn der Sinne* (Berlin/NewYork/Heidelberg, 1956), trans J Needleman as *The Primary World of Senses. A Vindication of Sensory Experience* (New York, Free Press of Glencoe, 1963).

inhere in the senses and in their spatial organisation, and do not only arise on a certain level of elaboration. Symbolic aspects belong to what I would call *Urdeutung* (original interpretation), a primary and productive form of interpretation which contrasts with other interpretations, not with something which is purely given. Seeing means *seeing as*, perception includes apperception, that is, taking something *as something*. Consequently the so-called sense-data are nothing other than artificial constructs. There is a history of colour and sound perception, the traces of which can be discovered down to the neuro-physiological level. As Husserl already suggests, perception, in the Greek sense of *aisthesis*, is divided into *ortho-aisthesis* and *hetero-aisthesis*. This assumption is not far removed from Foucault's reference to *heterotopics*.[17]

VI. ACTUAL, HABITUAL, AND VIRTUAL SPACE

Our body movements are not restricted to momentary situations; they are deeply embedded in time processes and in the history of our body. Our *actual* body condenses into a *habitual* body, whose limbs function as 'guardians of the past'. Proust readers will remember the initial passage of the *Recherche* where the narrator minutely describes the embarrassment of somebody who wakes up in the foreign environment of a hotel room. It would be a real disaster if absent-mindedness were doubled by an 'absent-bodyness'! Moreover, our body becomes enlarged by a *virtual* body, which opens a range of possibilities. Such time-dependent structures, pervading our bodily existence through and through, do not exclude considerable variation of the import of past and future and the roles of repetition and innovation from one situation or from one individual, one group and one culture to the other. To be as original as possible should not be taken as a universal or even categorical imperative. Normality allows for great variability. But it degenerates into pathological deformations when either the sense of reality (*Wirklichkeitssinn*) or Musil's sense of possibility (*Möglichkeitssinn*) reaches an extreme point.

Regarded from a wider perspective, we can observe that experience, when it loses balance, tends either towards *reality without open possibilities* or towards *virtuality without anchorage in reality*, and we further notice that

[17] See M Foucault, *Les mots et les choses* (Paris, Gallimard, 1966), trans A Sheridan as *The Order of Things* (London, Tavistock, 1970). As to the motives of normality and normalisation in Husserl, *cf* especially *Ideas Pertaining to a Pure Phenomenology and to a Phenomenological Philosophy*, above n 8, at para 18 and *Zur Phänomenologie der Intersubjektivität. Texte aus dem Nachlaß. Erster Teil: 1905–1920* (The Hague, Nijhoff, 1973) Text 14. But other authors such as G Canguilhem, M Foucault, A Schutz and S Freud also broach this issue. I have discussed this problem from different points of view in B Waldenfels, *Grenzen der Normalisierung* (Frankfurt/M, Suhrkamp, 1998).

our body presents itself as a scene in which such alternatives are displayed in an experimental or in a pathological manner. It seems to me that today, under the increasing influence of high technology, the process of overemphasising virtuality largely prevails against the more traditional manner of overemphasising actuality. In this respect Cervantes's famous pair, Don Quixote and Sancho Panza, is particularly apposite: the master living in the heaven of chivalrous tales, fighting windmills; the servant standing with both feet on the ground of every-day reality. The eccentricity of Don Quixote would be a striking example for the survival of a vanishing reality. Clinging to reality at any price turns into fiction, and an over-embodiment produces specific forms of disembodiment.

VII. BEING IN PLACE AND OUT OF PLACE

With regard to the selfhood and otherness of our body, we came across a strange process of self-doubling. The German language allows us to render this status with the double term *Leib-Körper*. This sort of doubling is not restricted to extraordinary events; it belongs to our precarious position in the world, including our living in space and time. Bound to my living body, I remain *here* and *now*, just at the zero point of our field of experience from which different co-ordinates rise. However, I simultaneously find myself *anywhere* in the world, due to the fact that my own 'here' and 'now', as well as your or our common 'here' and 'now', can be transformed and, to some extent, have already been transformed into local and temporal data. The basic, unreachable and immemorial fact that I was born, notwithstanding its singularity, finds its place on our geographical maps and in our calendars in terms of a certain place and date of birth. The fact that the way in which this transformation is performed differs from culture to culture, and that in this process fantastic legends or historical documents play different roles, does not exclude the fact that this singular event leaves its traces, even its statistical dry sand, in the world of facts. Or take another example, the incursion of scientific inventions into our lives. From time to time something happens which disturbs our personal or our cultural time-table, surprising us in a good or in bad manner, but even in this case something will be registered, for example, the fact that Roentgen discovered X-rays in his Würzburg laboratory on 8 November 1895. Even the protagonists of the French revolution, who were convinced that they were founding a new era, performed their work around the Louvre and the Bastille, following the rhythm of day and night, of spring and fall. Similar things hold true for making contracts; contracts happen here and now, not anywhere, and, to some extent, they always interrupt the course of things. Nevertheless they get recorded, witnessed and signed—as if, when writing one's own name, one were to look over one's own shoulder and at one's own fingers. Just as our body, assuming some features of a social body and of a physical thing, itself becomes a part of the world which it opens and articulates, in just the same way our original here and now becomes a part of the situation it inaugurates and maintains. System theorists call this re-entry: the process of drawing distinctions, by which the world becomes ordered, can itself be observed as something to be distinguished, but making distinctions and observing them never coincide. There always remains a blind spot, something invisible within the visible, which can be shown, but not abolished.[18]

In order to highlight the paradox of being in time and space, and at once being out of them, let us finally consider the zero point of traditional topologies and chronologies. Where is the so-called navel of the world? If there were something like the centre of the world we could not locate it within the world without referring to it. Or take initial events like the foundation of Rome, the destruction of the Jewish temple, the birth of Christ or Buddha and the enthronement of a new emperor. In what year did they happen? We can answer these questions only in a paradoxical or tautological way. Rome was founded in the very year in which Rome was founded, or Christ was born in the very year in which Christ was born, the emperor was enthroned in the first year of his reign, and so on. In a certain sense, all of this is very common. Where is 'here'? It is precisely where somebody who says 'here' is standing. And when is 'now'? Now is just the moment when somebody says 'now'. The rest is splitting concepts as in the chapter on 'Sensory certitude', in Hegel's *Phenomenology of the Spirit*, where indexical expressions like 'here' and 'today' are treated as predicates, with the effect that our bodily existence functions only as a springboard.

Husserl, who was no greater a friend of paradoxes than Russell was, tackles the problem in his own manner in his *Crisis*.[19] He starts from the fact that the transcendental *subject for the world* finds itself at the same time as an *object in the world*. In order to overcome the paradoxical situation that 'the subjective part of the world swallows up, so to speak, the whole and thus itself too', he claims that the subject constitutes itself as an object. This process of self-objectivation or mundanisation includes acts of self-temporisation and self-spatialisation. But we know to what extent the riddles of self-constitution—that is, the constitution of the self-object by the self-subject—pursued Husserl. The central question of otherness which he tried to solve by referring to a sort of de-presentation (*Ent-Gegenwärtigung*) and of self-alienation (*Ent-Fremdung*)[20] functions as a permanent trouble spot

[18] The insight that the eye does not see itself goes back to Schopenhauer at least. We find it in such different authors as Wittgenstein, Bataille, Merleau-Ponty, Lacan or Luhmann.

[19] Husserl, *The Crisis of European Sciences and Transcendental Phenomenology*, above n 5, at para 53 f.

[20] *Ibid*, 185.

because of the gaps permanently opening within the experience of my own self and within that of the Other. But the problem can be exposed in more general terms, close to the Cartesian counter-position based on the duality of *res cogitans* and *res extensa*. The paradox mentioned vanishes as soon as we suppose two different sorts of being: on the one hand somebody seeing from *nowhere*, as somebody who *sees without being seen*; on the other hand something located *anywhere*, as something which *is seen without seeing for its part*. By contrast, the paradox blossoms when we presuppose somebody who both *sees and is seen*, and this in terms of a self-doubling process, characterised by Merleau-Ponty[21] as a 'non-coincidence' or as a 'coincidence from afar', or by Plessner[22] as an 'eccentric positionality'. We are standing, so to speak, beside ourselves.

VIII. GLOBALISATION, LOCALISATION AND BEYOND

The original fissure which separates the self from itself continues in terms of a 'fissure of being'.[23] It encroaches on the world, on the time and the place in which we live. The place from where the whole of reality unfolds its possibilities does not find its place within the whole—unless we 'forget' what we are doing here and now, when responding to concrete situations and meeting with actual challenges. The oblivion of one's own involvement in what is going on in the world induces a *double jeu* (double game). We pretend that we could simultaneously hold our own position and draw upon the whole. Being here at a certain place, we nevertheless lay claim to divine omnipresence. In Bert van Roermund's terms (see his contribution to this volume), we confuse the first-person viewpoint with the third-person viewpoint.

This double game seems to belong to the modern Western tradition, which tries, in vain I would say, to reconcile the changing perspectives of particular subjects with the universal claim of one and the same reason. This project must fail because the point of view of universality does not allow for a universal point of view. However, what is to be found today are splinters—some call it post-modernity. Concerning our special question of being here in the world, one could speak of a quarrel between globalists and localists, which reminds us, to some extent, of the eighteenth century's *Querelles des anciens et des modernes*. As is often the case, both parties have their good points. On the one hand, globalisation opens frontiers and extends horizons. Networks multiply connections. Code switching enhances

21 M Merleau-Ponty, *Le visible et l'invisible* (Paris, Gallimard,1964) 165 f, trans A Lingis, *The Visible and the Invisible* (Evanston, Northwestern, 1968) 124 f.

22 H Plessner, *Die Stufen des Organischen und der Mensch* in Ges Schriften, vol IV (Frankfurt/M, Suhrkamp, 1981) 71.

23 Merleau-Ponty, above n 21, at 235.

flexibility. As a result of the acceleration of communication by the electronic media we are not only up-to-date, but also, so to speak, up-to-place. This process of globalisation crosses the borders of the various subsystems. It affects the economic exchange of goods, the cultural exchange of ideas, and it does not come to a stop with politics, rights and morals, thereby opening the perspective of a 'world democracy'. The electronic network makes it more difficult for dictators to keep their countries closed and to exclude the public from what they are doing. In Prague, in 1968, the Russian tanks had to advance in the light of film cameras. But on the other hand, those who defend local restrictions, as certain communitarians do, shield limited forms of life, arguing that they cannot be extended ad infinitum without loosing their contours.[24] They will insist on the fact that there is no connection (*Anschluß*) without exclusion (*Ausschluß*), that there is no information without deformation, and that, in opposition to globalistic slogans evoking a technological version of the traditional 'all together', the media fight their daily struggle for our attention, fighting against each other. So, the users of networks do not behave like mere spiders in the web, doing their peaceful work. Localists will oppose the levelling of all things, which even goes to the extent that hard cash, the *klingende Münze* (jingling coins) that can be handled, is changed into anonymous electronic processes. They can defend the meandering of sense against rash wear and tear. Should we expect the truth to lie in the middle as a golden mean, as an *aurea mediocritas*? But where could we find such a centre, such a *Mittelpunkt*?

In some respects globalisation appears to be something rather old. From Parmenides's sphere of Being to Hegel's dialectics as a circle of circles, thinking has been always tempted by figures in which every point has the same distance to the centre. And such thinking always provided for some practical orientation. The cosmic orders from which our reflections started used to have a concentric shape. By contrast, modernity stands for a certain decentring which finds its resonance in seismographic authors like Pascal, who evokes infinite spaces that ignore us, and the abyss (*gouffre*), opening under our feet, or Nietzsche and his cosmo-theological visions, where the earth errs through the universe, untied from its sun. But even a sober author like Kant, discussing the *Conjectural Beginning of Human History*, does not hesitate to depict the situation of humans as that of beings standing 'on the margin of an abyss, filled with infinite possibilities'.[25]

If we continue regarding this situation in the light of the bodily 'here', we stumble over two reactions which are diametrically opposed. They correspond to what I shall call *globalism* and *localism*, in order to suggest that

[24] In his discussion of friendship, Aristotle already remarks that friendship, like love, does not admit of extension in infinitum (see *Nicomachean Ethics*, book VIII, 7).

[25] I Kant, 'Mutmaßlicher Anfang der Menschengeschichte' ('Conjectural Beginning of Human History') in *Werke in sechs Bänden*, n 11 above, vol VI, p 89.

in both cases certain trends are forced to an extreme. There are globalists who fly forward, adhering to mere technological progress. The centre shifts into the future. This sort of globalism could be classified as an offshoot of a certain Western rationality. 'Here' manifests itself as a shifting term, oscillating between everywhere and anywhere. The technical omnipresence of a super-net, which—as Marx would have said—still has its 'theological snags', leads to the levelling of being here or there, to the devitalisation of the Here. Space approximates a sort of 'space without qualities'. The technological trend of globalisation gets reinforced by a norm-orientated process of universalisation. Legal claims, based on moral standards, are valid wherever they arise. They jump across every border. Ultimately, law is placeless and bodiless. On the other hand, localism also proves to be an offshoot. Reacting to the volatilisation of the Here, it ends with a fixation on Here. Yielding an anti-technical form of regress, one clings to what one had or, to put it in more apt terms, to what one believes one had. Space without qualities turns into a space with fixed qualities, rooted in the soil of a concrete community. Such a fixation does not seem to be innocent. If we remember ideologies such as that of blood and soil (*Blut und Boden*), we can see to what extent an excessive attachment to one's own soil contributes to transforming strangers into enemies.

Living in the world means also moving across the world. So the double orientation, favouring either the global or the local, respectively either the universal or the particular aspects of the world, has a strong influence on the phenomenon of migration, which has significantly increased since the last century. It especially influences the process of immigration, based on the difference between inside and outside. Obviously, immigration is an asymmetric process, in contrast with scientific or cultural exchange, or with the coming and going of tourists. From the viewpoint of practical norms, the opposition between globalism and localism, or between a certain liberalism and a certain communitarianism, approaches the splitting of distributive justice, analysed by Hans Lindahl (see his contribution to this volume at chapter 6) and illustrated by Walzer's position on the one hand, and Habermas's position on the other hand. Following the author, the first version leads to a bounded sort of justice, fixed on the here and now of a self-enclosed community, whereas the second version produces a boundless sort of justice, scattered about the whole of mankind.

In the first case, one draws a sharp line between inside and outside, between one's own and the alien. The threshold, separating both sides, is controlled from the inside, as if customers would survey the traffic of goods. Strictly speaking there is no immigration at all, but only an *import* of persons. Furthermore, persons are only imported as far as they are potential insiders, ready to be characterised by the same language, customs, education, and political conviction as the original insiders. No import without *assimilation*. Foreigners belong to us insofar as they cease to be strangers.

People who seem to be inadaptable are kept outside, either as displaced persons, having lost their homeland, or as hostile beings, trying to import the virus of false convictions and habits and of violence. The so-called clash of civilisations turns out to be a clash of pure in-groups or inside-cultures.

In the second case, the distance between inside and outside is bridged by establishing the universal reign of a moralised law. Immigration yields to *integration*. Strictly speaking, there is just as little immigration as in Walzer. Everybody is previously recognised as a citizen of the world, being part of the human totality which has just as little an outside as the physical totality of the cosmos—apart from the enemies of mankind, who have excluded themselves. But, unfortunately, a placeless law lacks the soil whence legal or quasi-legal claims can be made. A straight-on politics of mankind loses its political character; as Lindahl argues, the 'ought' without place is missing the 'ought-place' it needs in order to be performed. This has to do with the role of the third party.[26] Localists get in trouble when seeking a third position beyond the own and the alien, because everything is centred on the rules of one's own community. On the contrary, globalists or universalists overemphasise the role of the third; they try to settle the position of the third party by levelling down the difference between the own and the alien, and by weakening the demand of the Other. The same holds true concerning the role of the 'we', emphasised by Bert van Roermund (chapter 7). Localists or communitarians take the 'we' for granted, whereas globalists or universalists transform it into the neutral position of 'everybody' or 'anybody'. In both cases the performative 'we' fails. In practice, both positions overlap. For example, President GW Bush in his TV speech of 17 March 2003 tried to justify the fight against the enemies of his own country by identifying it with the fight against the enemies of mankind. With regard to immigration policy we should take into consideration the fact that the receiving 'we' is never homogeneous. So, in Berlin, like in other capitals, the people of Dahlem are not equally affected by the stream of immigrants as are the people of Kreuzberg or Wedding. Such differences have to do with what might be called the 'micro-politics of strangers', which shows a strong topographical aspect. We are reminded of the fact that immigration is a bodily process, touching our personal body as well as our body politic.

However, our phenomenological description of space and body leads us beyond these dubious alternatives and extremes. When we really take notice of our situation in the world, we become aware that the 'here' which marks our position has certain features of a 'not-here'. The place or *topos* of our experience shows certain aspects of a non-place, of an *atopia*. We have never been and will never be completely at home in the world, and this applies in clear opposition to traditional concentric orders, widening from

[26] See T Bedorf, *Dimensionen des Dritten* (München, Fink, 2003).

the narrowness of a home-world to a world home, for example from the *oikos* through the *polis* to a sort of *cosmopolis*. As we have shown, the life-world itself splits into *home-world* and *alien world* (*Heimwelt/Fremdwelt*). Such a splitting is nothing fatal; on the contrary, it asks for *hospitality* and allows it, preparing the ground for an ethics of dwelling with others in the world. This perspective has certain consequences, too, with regard to the problem of immigration. First, from the beginning we are *inside and outside at once*. Own and Alien are intertwined; they form a chiasm, as Merleau-Ponty puts it. Traces of Others are to be found in our own body, in our own language and in our own traditions. These are not mere facts to be registered or assessed as we like: we are provoked and challenged by Otherness when being touched by the Other's demand, and we become what we are in our inner self by responding to such demands. Secondly, our response to the Other needs a *third party* which equalises what is unequal, referring to rules and norms which are neither 'up to me' nor 'up to the Other'. The third party does not integrate the own and the alien into a whole, rather it *intervenes* in my experience of the Other, inventing and applying certain rules. Thirdly, the Other's demand can be grasped only in an indirect way, as a kind of excess or surplus, as something extra-ordinary which inspires and stimulates the search of justice within the field of law. Finally, immigration has to do with hospitality. The guest who stays at the threshold of our house or homeland calls for something like a politics of the threshold.

Let us come back to the paradox of being here and elsewhere, which determines our topography of the alien. Because the operations of our body precede and exceed their thematisation, we never totally know where we are. When we pose the question, 'Where am I? Where are we?' we start from *elsewhere*. The blind spot mentioned above does not only affect our perception and our consciousness, marking a sort of imperception in the heart of our perception, a sort of unconsciousness in the heart of our consciousness; it also affects our being here and now. There is an *alien topos* (*xenos topos*) underlying our *own* or *proper topos* (*oikeios topos*). This *atopia*, this non-place, ascribed to the Platonic Socrates, opens the door to an open series of *heterotopics*.[27] There are different ways to be here, even on the historical and cultural level. Due to these blind spots and variations, our being here and now will never be registered once and for all by a cosmological or historical world atlas and by a cosmological or historical calendar. Corresponding to the well-known time-lag (*Zeitverschiebung*) we

[27] See M Foucault, 'Des espaces autres' in *Dits et Écrits*, vol 4 (Paris, Gallimard, 1994), trans as 'Of Other Spaces' (1986) 16 *Diacritics* 22–7; as well as his preface to *Les mots et les choses* (Paris, Gallimard, 1966), trans A Sheridan as *The Order of Things* (London, Tavistock, 1970) XVIII: 'Les utopies consolent ... Les hétérotopies inquiètent'. Concerning the difference between proper and alien I refer to the last chapter of my book B Waldenfels, *Topographie des Fremden* (Frankfurt/M, Suhrkamp, 1997), called 'Fremdorte'.

experience when we fly from one continent to another, there is a specific *space-lag* (*Ortsverschiebung*). We always come back to ourselves, being at once here and elsewhere. Hence, the famous definition of the human being in terms of reason and language, the *logos*, has to be complemented and modified by certain features of *topos*. After all, we have to recognise that, owing to this self-distance, we come closer to other times and other places, and closer to the times and places of others, than we would do by clinging to fantastic and often violent ideals orientated on a universal survey or on a universal communication. Thus, our phenomenology of body and space takes on features of a sort of xenology which prevents us from simply revolving around ourselves.

5

Finding Normativity:

Immigration Policy and Normative Formation[1]

PETER FITZPATRICK

'The real constitution is accustomed to hide itself.'

Heraclitus[2]

I. PROLOGUE

THE PROLOGUE COMES out of Oujda in Morocco where Dr Liza Schuster joins a group of migrants blocked in transit and gathered now in 'a dusty café talking about their migration experiences'.[3] She strikes up a conversation with Daniel from Lagos. Daniel had, over the preceding eight years, made numerous efforts to migrate to different parts of Europe only to be deported or turned back before he had reached his destination. Dr Schuster continues her account in this way:

> [i]n the course of a long conversation to which others contributed, he told me of the money and effort and time he had expended. When I suggested that, if he had stayed at home, used that money, time and effort to create a business, he would now be a rich man, blessed with a family and children, he became angry and told me that he had a right to come to Europe and asked me by what right he was stopped. The others around the table agreed, saying that even if there were full employment and an end to poverty in Africa, they would have the right to come and see Europe for themselves—what was wrong with that?'

Although the reasons for this claim did not surface in the conversation, Dr Schuster had the impression

[1] Thanks to Hans Lindahl for much insight and to Liza Schuster for the prologue.
[2] In GS Kirk, JE Raven and M Schofield, *The Presocratic Philosophers: A Critical History with a Selection of Texts*, 2nd edn (Cambridge, Cambridge University Press, 1957) 192.
[3] That and the subsequent quotations relating to this scene come from an email correspondence with Dr Schuster in March 2007.

> that those who have experienced colonialism (personally or historically) find it difficult to understand how the colonisers have the face to refuse the ex-colonised the right to visit or travel or spend time in Europe ... Add to this those memories of mobility and the porousness of borders in regions like West Africa ... and it becomes easier to understand why people from there expect to be able to travel unimpeded even further afield.

Perhaps we could add to historical memory those histories of the pre-colonial in Africa attesting to the great mobility of peoples over vast distances. Much of that mobility had to do with trade, and this leads me to Dr Schuster's pointed observation that the difficulty people had in understanding why they could not travel to Europe was especially intense 'when they have been successful traders and businessmen—they are not coming to Europe cap-in-hand but wanting to trade as equal partners ... They are free marketeers and outraged by the "protectionism" of Europeans'. The poignancy of the contrast imported here could hardly be sharper. Perhaps also, in a post-colonial world, they were also taking seriously Europe's self-elevation as exemplifying the universal, including the 'human' of human rights for example. In responding to that point, Dr Schuster observed that 'migrants are used to hear their own governments criticised for human rights abuses, so it is unsurprising that they would assume the critics are stringent upholders of freedom and equality'.

That prologue informs the rest of this chapter. The chapter's organisation and argument are straightforward, at least in summary. Overall, the chapter follows a not unusual way of writing a three-act play. The audience is settled into the play with a first act which depicts something rather ordinary and acceptable, but which also intimates that all is not necessarily well. The second act then deeply disrupts that settled scene. Things fall apart. The third act puts them together again in a new and resolving configuration. Act 1, then, deals with normativity and the place of its conventional 'foundation' as far as immigration is concerned. In this light, normative policy is generated within a primal place. This is a place of comprehensive or near-comprehensive determination from whence the efficacy of the policy emanates. When more closely observed, however, that place becomes less determinately secure. It is 'the immigrant' who provides the telling site of such observation. Then Act 2 witnesses a dissolution of that place and of its 'norm', but this same second act also reveals how that very dissolution brings with it the incipience of a normativity that responds to the actuality of our being-in-common. Act 3 presents the composition of this normativity, including its formation as policy, both generally and in its constituent relation to immigration.

A prologue is a promise of all that is to come in the rest of the play but a prologue's connections to what follows it should not be laboured.

II. ACT 1: THE PLACE OF NORMATIVITY

The generous etymology of 'policy' would encompass 'citizenship, government, constitution, polity'.[4] That etymology, in turn, resonates with the meaning now rarely attributed to 'policy' of '[a]n organised and established system or form of government or administration (of a state or city), a constitution, polity'.[5] In its more usual or current meaning, of course, 'policy' refers to '[a] course of action adopted and pursued' by, on behalf of, or through any of these entities.[6] The connection remains constituent. There can be neither policy without a polity making it, nor polity without its expression in policy. The normative is a prescriptive formation of general policy. As such it is an orientation towards and hold on the futurity of the polity.

Let me shift focus now from that abrupt *mise en scène* to the norm as standard, normal—here the normal perception of the polity and its productions. Given the focus on Europe and immigration—and much as one would like to promote discursively the city, 'cities of refuge', and such—the normally perceived entity we are dealing with here is the nation of modern nationalism, a territorially determined land somehow demanding primal allegiance to it from entities known as its citizens, and itself providing significant existential coherence for them. The nation, its citizens, and others wishing to come to or remain in its territory are all constituted in law. Law, the law of the land, is the ultimate carrier of national policy on immigration. As the rule of law, as a normative hold on futurity, it endows the relations that constitute or could constitute nation with a necessary security and predictability. Yet law, in another standard view, is the creature of nation, of a sovereign national power that creates it and endows it with content. Other law, whether the law of units within nation or international law, is comprehensively subsidiary to the law of nation. That normal picture is complicated now by the European Union (EU). The EU in its self-presentation has transcended nation. Obviously, the EU does involve the giving of significant sovereign power to an international body. But the EU achieves its own brand of transcendence, not by becoming different from its member nations, but rather by containing them in replication of their own forms and dynamics, by taking on and vigorously promoting the attributes of nation as its own.[7] (I will use 'nation' and 'national', for some no doubt egregiously, to include the EU.)

[4] *Oxford English Dictionary*, 2nd edn, CD-ROM v 3.1 (Oxford, Oxford University Press, 2004), 'policy' n. 1 etymology.

[5] *Ibid*, at 1a.

[6] *Ibid*, at 5.

[7] P Fitzpatrick, 'New Europe and Old Stories: Mythology and Legality in the European Union' in P Fitzpatrick and JH Bergeron (eds), *Europe's Other: European Law Between Modernity and Postmodernity* (Dartmouth, Ashgate, 1998).

What both nation and the neo-nation of the EU do is mark off normatively a territory and a status, citizenship, which designate those beyond their bounds as qualitatively different and apart. Whether and how nation extends itself to these excluded is a matter that is its complete preserve, and a matter of normatively determining who ought to be included and who ought to be excluded, and a matter of determining the terms of such inclusion and exclusion—a matter, in short, of sovereign self-determination. All of which is not to deny that some balancing of this containment with the accommodation of migration is desirable, even imperative. Benhabib, for example, in *The Rights of Others* requires us, 'us' of responsible democratic nations, to operate 'our practices of democratic closure', our necessarily 'circumscribed *demos*', in calculated ways that would extend to the immigrant.[8] In the same vein, Appiah's *Cosmopolitanism: Ethics in a World of Strangers* offers us a cosmopolitanism which by way of compromise takes our relation with 'strangers' as a 'get[ting] used to each other' within the limits of what 'difference' we can tolerate.[9]

Moving well into Act 1 now, it is time to intimate some disturbance of this monadic scene. Walter Bagehot poignantly remarked of nation that '[w]e know what it is when you do not ask us, but we cannot very quickly explain or define it'.[10] That *aperçu* comes from the nineteenth century and, despite constant and numberless academic efforts there has not been anything more revealing since. In that ever-optimistic realm of academic self-reference known as 'elsewhere' I have described this intriguing failure extensively and shown that it stems from the impossibility yet necessity of combining, in and as nation, determinate existence with a responsive regard to what is beyond that existence 'for the time being'.[11] Likewise with 'Europe'. In another 'elsewhere' I have tried to show how Europe shares with nation an intriguing inability to be rendered as anything palpable at all.[12] Whilst the Europe of the EU would lay claim to a determinate existence, it would also assert a responsive range that was numinously universal, one extending integrally beyond any determinate existence. And it would do so in asserted opposition to the determinately constrained nation even as they both come to share the same characteristics. Furthermore, in this failure to provide a positively

[8] S Benhabib, *The Rights of Others: Aliens, Residents, and Citizens* (Cambridge, Cambridge University Press, 2004) 17 and 19.

[9] KA Appiah, *Cosmopolitanism: Ethics in a World of Strangers* (New York, WW Norton, 2006) 71, 76–8, 85.

[10] W Bagehot, *Physics and Politics, or Thoughts on the Application of the Principles of Natural Selection and Inheritance to Political Society* (London, Kegan Paul, Trench and Trubner, undated) 20–21.

[11] P Fitzpatrick, *Modernism and the Grounds of Law* (Cambridge, Cambridge University Press, 2001) ch 4.

[12] Fitzpatrick, above n 7.

resolved constitution, both resort to a constitute negation, to a surpassing and exemplary existence elevated in opposition to those who would come from outside of it—seekers of asylum and would-be immigrants, for example. The Maastricht Treaty, to take an instance, in Article K.1 predisposes 'asylum', 'immigration', and 'nationals of third countries' to distinctly negative connotations by dealing with all of these in conjunction with 'combating unauthorised immigration, residence and work ... terrorism, unlawful drug trafficking and other serious forms of international crime'. Thence determinacy is reconciled with the universality since negative constitution needs no compromising content—no positive content countering the claim to the universal.

There is an ensuing local difficulty, however, and one instanced by our prologue. The constituent terms of negation sustain a claim to universality, and the universal bids all to enter. Yet if all were to enter, or if all could enter, there would no longer be an intrinsic setting apart in terms of negative exclusion. Hence the mélange of 'pre-modern' expedients endowing some positivity on nation and on the Europe of the EU. One expedient would recognise the determinacy of these entities and elevate it to a transcendent universality whence the determinate becomes a situated exemplar of the universal. Then, in various myths of origin and progress, the excluded are bidden to enter this elevated domain but not quite yet, or not for so long as they remain underdeveloped, terroristic, or remain wedded to an inveterate or resurgent ethnicity. Conveniently, this conditional invitation to join the domain of the universal ensures that the excluded are held in a provocative proximity, constantly challenging the identity formed by way of their negative exclusion 'in the first place'.

'The immigrant' or the would-be immigrant poses an especially pointed challenge to this irresolute resolution. Both are endowed with a variety of rights that would question the monadic completeness of the nation or of the EU as neo-nation in solitary relation to their citizens. So, there is a variety of statuses besides citizenship enabling the legitimate and enduring presence of immigrants within the national territories. Also, the crude conception of national borders has considerably dissipated into a collection of controls on migration that are within or outside of territorial demarcation. International treaties provide incipient, if often attenuated, rights of entry and of adequate regard. All of which could be construed as not disturbing the national settlement, or the supra-national settlement that is the EU, since all of these developments could be seen as dispensational extensions of such settlement. Yet these developments are also suggestive of basic questions about the supposedly ultimate character of the national settlement.

Such questions become more insistent when extended to the illegal immigrant, so-called. Despite the illegal or transgressive presence of such immigrants within the national territory they are at times endowed by national authorities with legal rights.[13] Still, this could be construed as another benign dispensation of the polity, as its qualified extension to those who do not immediately belong to it, or construed as a compromise between 'bounded' nationality and a regard for 'human beings *simpliciter*'.[14] Yet this dispensation could be considered also as something else, as a response to a presence of illegal immigrants that is generatively constituent of the national formation. We come closest perhaps to that integrating responsiveness in the case of the United States, where a uniformly estimated presence of 12 million illegal immigrants can hold demonstrations, likewise in their millions, without any of their number being arrested because of their illegal status, and where a gathering of them can be addressed by a visiting head of state, and where the presence of illegal immigrants generally can be blessed by some presidential candidates.[15] Let us move on now, carrying these various intimations of dissolution into Act 2.

III. ACT 2: NORMATIVE DISSOLUTION

In Act 1 law was advanced as a paradigm instance of normativity, at least as far as immigration was concerned. And law will now be taken as a category of normativity which readily reveals the disruptive dynamics of normative formation. This account of law will then be segued into the formed idea of normativity generally in the third and final act.

Before embarking on what to some may be an extravagant account of law as normativity, I want to put in place matching accounts inescapable in their banality. Amplifying the conventional account of law in Act 1, we find that both academic and demotic perceptions of law, of the rule of law, would have it autonomously providing us, us moderns, with stability and predictability, with at least some certainty in an uncertain world. And whilst judges are entrusted with the task of ensuring some such enduring determinacy by 'applying' the law, those same judges increasingly affirm that law must change and adapt, receptively accommodating the protean needs of society and such. Take, for example, the quotidian task of judicial sentencing. In terms of both the rule of law and of the deterrent effect

[13] Constable's nuanced account of instances within the United States makes that account a model for considering the phenomenon generally: M Constable, 'Sovereignty and Governmentality in Modern American Immigration Law' (1993) 13 *Studies in Law, Politics, and Society* 249.

[14] Benhabib, above n 8, at 15.

[15] S Sassen, 'The Limits of Power and the Complexity of Powerlessness: The Case of Immigration' (2007) 3 *Unbound: Harvard Journal of the Legal Left* 105 at 106, 108: see http://legalleft.org/wp-content/uploads/2007/05/3unb105-sassen.pdf; B Herbert, 'Spies Like You and Me', *The New York Times*, 8 December 2007.

of penalties, sentencing must be consistent and predictable. It must, as is so often judicially intoned, resist the fickle sway of popular sentiment. Yet to have an effective general deterrence and to accommodate retributive demands, it is just as often asserted that the sentence must reflect both popular opinion and the frequency of the crime in question. So, returning to the general, even, or especially, the rule of law itself must be integrally responsive to 'social change' and such, lest it cease to rule a world that has changed around it. There is a broadly coincident divide in Jurisprudence. On the one side, there are 'positivist' theories which attempt to constitute law as what is simply 'posited' as law. These are attempts to render law as positively, completely, existently autonomous, and as having a self-determinate content. On the other side there are opposing theories that would see law as a creation of something else, as the utterly responsive instrument or effect or affect of something else—of sovereign, society, economy, class, the state of the judge's digestion, and so on.

Now to refine and amplify these dimensions of law, its determinate and responsive dimensions, as well as to heighten the potential disturbance of the 'normal scene', I will rely on various works of Derrida, mainly his 'Force of Law'.[16] In 'Force of Law' Derrida would want to 'make explicit or perhaps produce a difficult and unstable distinction between justice and *droit*, between justice (infinite, incalculable, rebellious to rule and foreign to symmetry…)' on the one hand and, on the other, 'the exercise of justice as law or right, legitimacy or legality, a … calculable apparatus … a system of regulated and coded prescriptions'.[17] This justice for Derrida imports an unlimited responsiveness to the other, an 'other' which extends in my engagement to an equally illimitable alterity. This unlimited responsiveness of justice is impossible 'in itself', always beyond attainment. To be made possible, in the sense of becoming existent, and given operative force, justice must be 'cut' into, reduced, and in a certain sense denied.[18] For Derrida the legal decision cuts into and enacts justice, even whilst denying justice as illimitably responsive. In this, 'law is the element of calculation'.[19] Law, in the legal decision, can never be 'presently and fully just'.[20] So, rather than starkly and simply attributing a dissipating 'force' to justice, Derrida would see it as dependent on the determinate presence effected by the legal decision. Derrida would go so far as to find in law, and elsewhere, some reductive ability to contain responsiveness, to ensure that 'the aleatory

[16] J Derrida, 'Force of Law: The "Mystical Foundation of Authority"', trans M Quaintance, in J Derrida, *Acts of Religion* (New York, Routledge, 2002).
[17] *Ibid*, 250.
[18] *Ibid*, 252.
[19] *Ibid*, 244.
[20] *Ibid*, 252.

margin ... remains homogenous with calculation, within the order of the calculable'.[21]

Yet, if law is necessary for justice, justice is also necessary for law. The bringing of law to bear, the legal decision, the very call for such decision, these all involve a responsiveness which cannot be contained. Not only is it a matter that 'no existing, coded rule can ... guarantee absolutely' what will be brought to bear or decided, but neither the bringing to bear nor the decision can ever fully saturate its own context, can ever 'provide itself with the infinite information and the unlimited knowledge of conditions, rules or hypothetical imperatives that could justify it'.[22] Law must ever inchoately respond to an uncontainable justice, to a justice that 'exceeds law but at the same time motivates movement, history, and becoming of juridical rationality'.[23] Yet law's rendering of justice is incipiently co-extensive with it, so much so that 'justice' cannot be peremptorily aligned with justice as virtue, as the Good, for 'justice is always very close to the bad, even to the worst, for it can always be reappropriated by the most perverse calculation'.[24] In all, although 'justice exceeds law and calculation', law has also somehow to be conceived as 'exceeding' justice.[25] We have to calculate, 'incalculable justice *commands* calculation', and for this we must 'negotiate the relation between the calculable and the incalculable': this imperative 'does not *properly* belong either to justice or law. It only belongs to either realm by exceeding each in the direction of the other'.[26] What will prove central to my argument, then, will be this negotiation and the dissonance it involves, a dissonance where law and justice are mutually constituent yet distinct and able to exceed each other. I will now, still with Derrida's help, refine this dissonance and thence the law involved.

The immediate problem becomes, then, that the negotiation between calculable law and incalculable justice as mutually constituting would seem to be of a different kind to the negotiation involved with the imperative that each be able to exceed the other. With the story so far derived mainly from 'Force of Law', law emerges as constituently pervaded by 'justice'. Yet in the same essay, and often elsewhere, Derrida sees law in positivist terms. Law, then, becomes not only a 'calculable apparatus' in its relation to justice, but also 'sometimes finds itself accounted for' by our 'placidly applying a good rule

[21] J Derrida, 'Psyche: Inventions of the Other', trans C Porter, in L Walters and W Godzich (eds), *Reading de Man Reading* (Minneapolis, University of Minnesota Press, 1989) 25.

[22] Derrida, above n 16, at 251, 255.

[23] J Derrida, *Rogues: Two Essays on Reason*, trans P-A Brault and M Naas (Stanford CA, Stanford University Press, 2005) 150.

[24] Derrida, above n 16, at 257.

[25] *Ibid.*

[26] *Ibid.*

to a particular case'; or 'if the act simply consists of applying a rule … one will perhaps say that it is legal, that it conforms to law'; or, even more strikingly, Derrida considers it a 'secure' application of the legal rule when the judge acts as a mere 'calculating machine'—'something that happens sometimes; it happens always in part'.[27] In various other pieces, Derrida seems to offer a similarly positivist notion of law or of 'juridicism'.[28] But perhaps the qualification 'in part' may be essential: '[a]s soon as there is law, there is partition'.[29] What, then, is this quality of law's being in part, of its apartness, its equation with partition?

To begin to answer that question, we have to return to what it may be to 'negotiate' not only the relation between justice and law but also, as Derrida notes in 'Force of Law', the relation involved 'in all the fields from which one cannot separate [justice], which intervene in it and are no longer simply fields: the ethical, the political, the economical, the psycho-sociological, the philosophical, the literary etc'.[30] And elsewhere, in a way that is almost mantric, Derrida directs us to 'negotiate' an enormous range of seeming antimonies such as the divide between the intrinsically 'unconditional' demands of cosmopolitanism, forgiveness or hospitality and their conditioned instantiation.[31] Given the mutual constitution of law and justice one could conceive of 'negotiate' in terms of a navigating between two dimensions which generate some tricky cross-currents between them—'negotiate' as finding a way between and accommodating the force of the antinomy. There is a striking indication that Derrida conceived, or also conceived, of 'negotiate' otherwise. In conversation with Jean-Luc Nancy, and to Nancy's evident surprise, after emphasising his use of 'négocier' Derrida proceeds to render it in terms of '*une transaction*', to render it as something that 'works' as a compromise—a compromise, it would seem, as a mutual accommodation between entities having some primal distinctness.[32]

[27] *Ibid*, 244, 251–2.

[28] Eg J Derrida, *Specters of Marx: The State of the Debt, The Work of Mourning, and The New International*, trans P Kamuf (New York, Routledge, 1994) 27, and J Derrida, *On Cosmopolitanism and Forgiveness*, trans M Dooley and M Hughes (London, Routledge, 2001) 46. Another, and perhaps the most striking, instance can be found in *Politics of Friendship* where Derrida adopts the thesis of Benjamin which he had reversed so thoroughly in bringing his whole argument in 'Force of Law' to bear in versions prior to this contrary adoption: J Derrida, *Politics of Friendship*, trans G Collins (London, Verso, 1997) 14–15.

[29] J Derrida, *Given Time: 1. Counterfeit Money*, trans P Kamuf (Chicago, The University of Chicago Press, 1992) 6. What I go on to derive from the conversation about to be invoked reveals this being 'in part' to be evanescent and suppositional. One cannot assuredly demarcate a part without an assured comprehension of the whole—a total or totalitarian comprehension.

[30] Derrida, above n 16, at 257.

[31] S Critchley and R Kearney, 'Preface' to Derrida, above n 28 (*Cosmopolitanism*) at xi.

[32] J Derrida and J-L, Nancy, 'Responsabilité—du sens à venir' in F Guibal and J-C Martin (eds), *Sens en tous sens: Autour des travaux de Jean-Luc Nancy* (Paris, Galilée, 2004) 179–80. I am grateful to Pablo Ghetti for this reference. See also the use of 'compromises' in

Limiting 'negotiate' for now to the relation between law and justice, we are left with a seeming incompatibility. For a start, and for a finish, justice for Derrida is incalculable, illimitable, and as such it cannot assume any existence capable of being compromised. And in some of Derrida's formulations, law is the same: law, for example, cannot be 'isolate[d] within sure frontiers'.[33] In its necessary responsiveness to what is ever beyond, ever 'other' to its determinate content 'for the time being', law can neither be partitioned nor can it partition in terms of any enduring existent. In its very determinateness as an enduring semblance of the self-same, law must utterly, responsively accommodate what would come to it and render it different. Law's responsiveness and its determinateness, then, cannot be separated from each other either entirely or in calculated proportions. The responsive cannot be purely beyond and thence merely inaccessible. It must be positioned in possibility, oriented towards determinacy, towards becoming present. Nor can determinateness be at all set or complete. Its assertion is always incipiently and infinitely responsive. We are left, then, with an antinomic law. It must be utterly responsive to justice yet 'positive,' posited and apart from justice.

It is in this divide that modern law's relation to sovereignty is determined. If law is to be illimitably responsive, it must be quite unrestrained, never bound to anything before it. It must, says Derrida, 'be without history, genesis, or any possible derivation'.[34] Yet law's unrestrained reponsiveness, its lack of any confining ties to the past or to anything else, its vacuity or nothingness, result in its not having any enduring content of its own. It always depends for its very content and for much of its force on some power apart from itself. 'Law itself', says Nancy, 'does not have a form for what would need to be its own sovereignty'.[35] There is point, then, to the jurisprudential perception of law's constituent dependence on such as sovereign and society. Yet, with law's refusal of any primal attachment, this dependence, this taking of content from such as sovereign or society, has always to subsist with that opposed jurisprudential tradition elevating law's autonomy. That autonomy is 'founded' in the illimitability of law, in law's insistent inability to be contained by any of the powers on which it depends for its content and for much of its force. And, no matter how seemingly

J Derrida, 'The Deaths of Roland Barthes', trans P-A Brault and M Naas, in HJ Silverman (ed), *Philosophy and Non-Philosophy Since Merleau-Ponty* (London, Routledge, 1988) 266–7; and cf J Derrida, *Negotiations: Interventions and Interviews 1971–2001*, trans E Rottenberg (Stanford CA, Stanford University Press, 2002) 12–14.

[33] Derrida, above n 16, at 257.

[34] J Derrida, 'Before the Law', trans A Ronell, in J Derrida, *Acts of Literature* (New York, Routledge, 1992) 191.

[35] J-L Nancy, *Being Singular Plural*, trans RD Richardson and AE O'Byrne (Stanford CA, Stanford University Press, 2000) 131.

abject law's borrowings, it will endow these with its own content. This content will often differ markedly from the contributed contents. Also, law will not simply absorb and re-create the contents of a given sovereignty or of a given society. It will, in its responsiveness, take on many and diverse sovereign or social configurations. And even where law determinately elevates one such configuration over another, this is neither to elevate the included pervasively nor to exclude the other finally.

IV. ACT 3: RESOLVING THE NORMATIVE

In this final act the alternation which closed the second will be brought to bear on the normative and its resolution in terms of 'policy' whilst sustaining immigration as the revelatory 'case'. There will be three quasi-scenes. In the first the alternation is extended from the dimensions of law to the constitution of normativity. In the second, normativity will be integrally related to the polity and to policy. The components of that relation will then, in the third and last scene, be extracted from it and brought into an operative combination.

A. Scene 1: The Dimensions of Normativity

To extend, then, the dimensions of law to the normative, I will resort initially and as a bridge to the meaningful generosity of 'nomos', capable as it is of accommodating both law and normativity. Running through the welter of meaning that nomos covers there is a plangent divide. On one side of the divide we find nomos not only as law but also as the very law of life, an ineffable nomos redolent with the deific or at least with the demonic, illimitable yet guiding—even if not always unambiguously so. On the other side, we find a nomos that is tied to usage and custom, a nomos that is of the earth, earthy:

> The primordial scene of the *nomos* opens with a drawing of a line in the soil. This very act initiates a specific concept of law, which derives order from the notion of space. The plough draws lines—furrows in the field—to mark the space of one's own. As such, as ownership, the demarcating plough touches the juridical sphere ... The primordial act as described here brings together land and law, cultivation and order, space and *nomos*.[36]

[36] C Vismann, 'Starting from Scratch: Concepts of Order in No Man's Land' in B Hűppauf (ed), *War, Violence and the Modern Condition* (Berlin, Walter de Gruyter, 1997) 46–7.

Notoriously, Schmitt in *Der Nomos* extracted from imperial arrogation the ground of the modern legal order in a nomos of the earth, a nomos that combined 'concrete order' with 'orientations' going beyond any contained order, a nomos providing a transcendent world-ground for the *jus publicum Europaeum*.[37] More congenially, we find on each side of the lexical divide a nomos that extends to and becomes the other. So, coming from the realm of the gods, the demon extends to and constituently incorporates earthly matters.[38] On the other side of the divide, there is the seemingly grounded 'custom', but custom is quite refractory in this respect. Doubtless, custom ceases to be custom if it ceases to correspond to the relevant usage of a people—'usage' being another strand of meaning found in 'nomos'. Yet custom is not confined to usage, to what is commonly done 'in fact'. Custom also carries with it obligation and, as such, it must extend to the limitless futurity of what ought to be.

There has been here an insinuate addition to the composition of the normative. Custom, the instance offered here, is not only a determinacy but also a normative hold on futurity, an assertion of what ought to be that channels determinacy as it goes responsively ever beyond itself. We are starting to trespass on classic concerns with normativity, concerns to do with the supposed chasm between what is and what ought to be, and these will be returned to. Before that, I will set the question of what constituent position or modality would be needed to combine the dimensions of normativity into a unit and, moving on now to the second scene of this third act, relate that position integrally to the polity and to policy.

B. Scene 2: The Polity as Normative

If immigration is taken as our case, it could be said that the defining artefact of the European national polity is the border. The border provides figuratively a line marking apart the determinate dimension of normativity as something that is inside and separated from what is outside. With the European conception of it, this bordered determinacy is self-constituting and self-sustaining. In its relation to what is outside the border, such a determinacy is ultimate. Its extension towards the outside is both surpassing and, as we saw towards the end of Act 1, universal in its range. This conjunction of the determinate and the universal ramps the determinate

[37] C Schmitt, *The Nomos of the Earth in the International Law of the Jus Publicum Europaeum*, trans GL Ulmen (New York, Telos Press, 2003) 69, 70, 82–3, 121, 127, 135.

[38] An engaging instance being Plato, *The Symposium*, trans C Gill (London, Penguin, 1999) 37–40 (201d–204b). And for law in this setting see W Benjamin, 'Fate and Character' in W Benjamin, *One-Way Street and Other Writings*, trans E Jephcott and K Shorter (London, New Left Books, 1979) 127.

up to a position of transcendence.[39] From such a position, the polity can definitively and completely determine what is inside and what is outside the border. Thence the determination of who may cross the border and come inside, and the determination of the terms of that entry and sojourn along with the normative policy enshrining these terms, all become matters emanating from the transcendent determinacy of the polity.

Such a transcendent arrogation can only be fictive, however. The very maintaining of a border requires a constant and adaptive responsiveness to what is outside of it, an outside that cannot be comprehensively pre-determined from within.[40] If it could be so pre-determined, there would be no need at all for a formed border. So we find that the border is generated by an outside, by a transgressive alterity which, in Foucault's terms, 'incessantly crosses and re-crosses' the line or limit that constitutes the border.[41] It is in that crossing and re-crossing that the formed border is continually 'made and unmade'.[42] All of which, of this 'limitless reign of the Limit', is not to deny the necessity and force of an enduring determinacy as, in Blanchot's terms now, it 'separates' itself from an insistent alterity 'via the very separation that institutes it as form'.[43]

In a similar vein of questioning addressed to the Declaration of Independence of the United States, to its assumption of the 'separate' existence and independence of 'one people', Derrida emphasises two parts of it: that invoking 'the laws of Nature and of Nature's God' as the source of entitlement being one part, and the other being the resulting declaration, made by way of an appeal 'to the Supreme Judge of the world for the rectitude of our intentions ... that these united Colonies are and of right ought to be *free and independent states*'.[44] Derrida then proceeds to bring these two parts of the Declaration together like this:

> 'Are and ought to be'; the *and* articulates and conjoins here the two discursive modalities, the *to be* and the *ought to be*, the constation [*sic*] and the prescription, the fact and the right. *And* is God: at once creator of nature and judge, supreme judge of what is (the state of the world) and of what relates to what ought to

[39] *cf* G Deleuze and F Guattari, *What is Philosophy?*, trans G Burchell and H Tomlinson (London, Verso, 1994) 45.

[40] For a related discussion of the responsive constitution of borders see Ricard Zapata-Barrero's contribution to this volume (ch 1), esp 30–31.

[41] M Foucault, 'A Preface to Transgression' in M Foucault, *Language, Counter-Memory, Practice: Selected Essays and Interviews*, trans DF Bouchard and S Simon (Ithaca, Cornell University Press, 1997) 34.

[42] *Ibid*, 32.

[43] The first quoted phrase comes from Foucault, above n 41. The other quotations are from M Blanchot, *The Infinite Conversation*, trans S Hanson (Minneapolis, University of Minnesota Press, 1993) 434. He is writing about the formation of law.

[44] As quoted by Derrida and with his emphasis: J Derrida, 'Declarations of Independence' in Derrida, above n 32 (*Negotiations*) at 51.

> be (the rectitude of our intentions). The instance of judgment, at the level of the supreme judge, is a last instance for saying the fact *and* the law.[45]

So 'after all' a transcendent is needed to unite fact and right. We could expand the conjunction and align it with the dimensions of determinacy and alterity by considering the characteristics of this God. These are the characteristics of an occidental monotheism that fuses two types of god. One is a determinate god, the god of perfect order, the god of constancy, a god caught by its own laws or by 'nature'. The other is a god of alterity, boundless, unrepresentable, an ineffable god, a god in whose presence there can only be dissolution of the existent, a god of nature confounded. The Declaration itself comes from a time when God, if not exactly dead, was nonetheless dying, and in certain ways its dependence on God was quite attenuated. Invoking 'the laws of Nature and of Nature's God' was already to align the deity with the rule of a determinacy, for this was a god subject to 'his' own determinable laws, a god forbidden by Malebranche to 'disturb the simplicity of his ways'.[46] And the Declaration presages the invention of a replacement deity, the 'new idol' of the nation-state, as Nietzsche would put it.[47]

In the Declaration itself God is definitively sidelined. The Declaration is made 'in the Name and by the authority of the good People of these Colonies', and made by their 'Representatives of the United States of America'. God then assumes a supporting role. The demotic scene can now be generalised to become one of the constitutive contributions required characteristically of 'the people' in modern political formation. Inevitably, then, we come to a classic conundrum: 'the people' create the polity, yet, as Lindahl incisively notes, 'the people' is incapable of coming together to constitute itself as a political unity and from there institute a political and legal order; rather, they come to be a people through the creation of that order.[48] So this very people, in a feat of what Derrida would call 'fabulous retroactivity',[49] is a creation of what it is taken as creating, a creature of the law, of a constitution and of laws made pursuant to it—laws to do with immigration and citizenship, electoral laws, laws to do with mental capacity, and so on. What is more, law produces the definitive processes of demotic assertion.

[45] *Ibid*, 51–2.

[46] See P Riley, *The General Will Before Rousseau: The Transformation of the Divine Into the Civil* (Princeton, Princeton University Press, 1986) 40.

[47] F Nietzsche, *Thus Spoke Zarathustra*, reprinted in *The Portable Nietzsche*, trans W Kaufmann (New York, The Viking Press, 1954) 160–61 (First Part: 'On the New Idol').

[48] H Lindahl, 'Constituent Power and Reflexive Identity: Towards an Ontology of Collective Selfhood' in M Loughlin and N Walker (eds), *The Paradox of Constitutionalism* (Oxford, Oxford University Press, 2007) 19.

[49] Derrida, above n 43, at 50.

What force, then, can 'the people' assume given its 'ungraspable' initiating quality?[50] Is the invocation of them merely 'a hypocrisy indispensable to a politico-military-economic, etc., coup of force'?[51] Or does the people have a more sinuous force of its own? It should by now occasion no surprise that I am going to argue that it does. Political appeals to the people in such as the Declaration often assume a widespread demotic purchase, yet they are not perceived as deception. And political appeals generally to 'the people' are not confined to a determinate people—to those who have the vote, for example, within a particular polity. It would not be considered an adequate or even an apt taking account of 'the people' to claim that the people were taken account of in part, that part who could vote, or that part in existence when a putative social contract was entered into centuries before, and so on. Yet 'the people' is also taken to be capable of partition and to have some correspondence to rendition in part. In short, and this interim conclusion will be elaborated on shortly—'the people' is an essentially unresolved condition mediating between 'its' determinate emplacements and 'the people' beyond such emplacement, including 'its' alterity, an alterity importing the possibility that 'its' determinacy can be ever otherwise. And, when used in situations similar to that in the Declaration, like all good origins, such as the myth of origin, 'the people' has to accommodate not just some conjunction of the determinate and what is beyond it, but it has to do so continuously. The origin has iteratively to endure as the origin of who or what 'we' are now, to this day as Derrida would have it.[52] And, further, this accommodation is something rightful, the correlate of that 'rectitude' found in the Declaration. With its irresolution and its incipience of alterity, the people cannot be rendered factually. Its composition is normative. Likewise, the composition of the polity is normative, the polity as a creation and a realisation of the people. Should the polity be confined factually to a people in some invariantly and completely realised collective enterprise, it would, in Nancy's terms, 'have as [its] truth the truth of death'.[53] In sum, the people is a normative composition and, by way of its integral reliance on the people, the polity becomes a normative composition as well, and thence also the policy which it emanates.

[50] See C Lefort, *The Political Forms of Modern Society: Bureaucracy, Democracy, Totalitarianism*, trans JB Thomson (Cambridge, Polity Press, 1984) 303; and also C Lefort, *Democracy and Political Theory*, trans D Macey (Cambridge, Polity Press, 1988) 86, 225–6. For pertinent variations on 'force' here see Derrida, above n 32 (*Negotiations*) at 35–6.

[51] See Derrida, above n 43, at 52.

[52] *Ibid*, 50 and 50–51. And see B Honig, 'Between Decision and Deliberation: Political Paradox in Democratic Theory' (2007) 101 *American Political Science Review* 3.

[53] J-L Nancy, *The Inoperative Community*, trans P Connor, L Garbus, M Holland and S Sawhney (Minneapolis, University of Minnesota Press, 1991) 12.

All of which may seem to confirm, at least for this context, the resolute dictate usually attributed to Hume, but repeated interminably since his formulation, where he observed that in accounts of 'every system of morality' of his acquaintance there is a move or a slide from 'is' to 'ought', whereas the two are 'entirely different'.[54] It would be rash to do otherwise than agree with Hume, and indeed the normativity that is the polity and the polity that is normativity cannot be rendered in terms of mere factuality. Yet, here the normativity was derived from the fact of a people being-in-common, not a static factuality but a dynamic, a continuate determinacy inexorably dependent on its responsiveness to alterity, and on the hold of right that the normative has on the futural dimension of that alterity.

C. Scene 3: Being-in-Common

Allow me now, in this third and final scene, to consider the composition of such being-in-common and its normativity, relating all of that especially to immigration. We saw in the last scene that one type of normativity, law, assumes significance in the constitution of the people, and in this present scene I will take law as my initial instance, using it as a template for the composition of other types of normativity relevant to immigration. All of which occupies about half of this comparatively lengthy scene. The remainder of the scene takes components of normativity identified in the first half and extends them to an encompassing or generalised notion of normativity, relating this notion all the while to what is necessary for being 'the people', for being-in-common.

Taking up that formidable agenda, then, we return to the two dimensions of law isolated in Act 2, dimensions perceived not only 'in theory', but perceived also as quotidian imperatives. With one of those dimensions, law assumed a determinate existence, and with the other it assumed a responsive being, a responsiveness to the demand of an illimitable alterity that was, in Derrida's terms, justice. Those dimensions of law were not only opposed but were also integral to each other, and integral not in any separable part but to the full extent of each. What this antinomy imports, to adopt now a vocabulary that will pervade the rest of this scene, is law as determinately conditioned but as (also) quite unconditional. This unconditional law cannot, to borrow from Act 2, be 'isolat[ed] within sure

[54] D Hume, A *Treatise of Human Nature* (London, Penguin, 1985) 521 (III (I)1). The idea of the normative reached here, and about to be extended factually, could also prove gregarious in accommodating, at least in part, other contested notions of normativity such as the 'voluntarist' and the 'realist': see CM Korsgaard, *The Sources of Normativity* (Cambridge, Cambridge University Press, 1996) ch 1.

frontiers'.[55] And indeed, the force of this unbounded law is 'essentially implied in the very concept of *justice as law*, of justice as it becomes law, of the law as law'.[56] That equation is rendered more directly in what Derrida takes to be an imperative 'to think the law, the law of the law, right, and justice'.[57]

Whilst Derrida would attribute an existential ultimacy to this imperative, he would find its specifically 'social' dimension in the following primal scene:

> [W]e are caught up, one and another, in a sort of heteronomic and dissymmetrical curving of social space—more precisely, a curving of the relation to the other: prior to all organised *socius*, all *políteia*, all determined 'government', *before* all 'law'. Prior to and before all law, in Kafka's sense of being 'before the law'.
>
> Let's get this right: prior to all *determined* law, *qua* natural law or positive law, but not prior to law *in general*. For the heteronomic and dissymmetrical curving of a law of originary sociability is also a law, perhaps the very essence of law.[58]

Likewise, it would seem, for Nancy. Nancy would equate 'the law of the law' with 'absolute justice' and further equate both commensurably with the 'sharing' that is our being-in-common in and as community.[59]

Even as all of that 'serves' to bolster the earlier account of the people and of its composition in terms of normativity, it still leaves us with the antinomical law arrived at in Act 2, a vacuous law, a law whose own force it seemed impossible to 'substantialise'.[60] Aptly enough, the same could be said, along with Derrida, for the commensurate social bond that is the law of the law: 'this bond ... cannot be made into a community; the promise of the bond forms neither a national, linguistic, or cultural community, nor does it anticipate a cosmopolitan constitution. It exceeds all cultures, all languages, it even exceeds the concept of humanity'.[61] Allow me now to pursue this force without force further by extending the search in terms of another antinomy advanced by Derrida, that between the unconditional and the conditioned.

This antinomy in its relevance to immigration could be instanced in a wide range of Derrida's work, but perhaps the most obvious contender is that relating to 'hospitality,' including a 'cosmopolitanism' reworked by

[55] Derrida, above n 16, at 257.
[56] *Ibid*, 233.
[57] Derrida, above n 28 (*Specters*) at 184.
[58] Derrida, above n 28 (*Politics of Friendship*) at 231.
[59] Nancy, above n 35, at 185; Nancy, above n 54, at 28. This idea of community and 'sharing' will be returned to shortly.
[60] Derrida, above n 32 (*Negotiations*) at 36.
[61] J Derrida, 'Nietzsche and the Machine' in *Negotiations*, above n 32, at 241.

Derrida in terms of this hospitality.[62] Derrida advances an unconditional 'law' of hospitality which is 'transgressive, outside the law, like a lawless law, *nomos anomos*, law above the laws and law outside the law'.[63] That is, as it were, one side of the antinomy. The other would be applied laws of hospitality, laws which 'limit and condition ... *the* law of hospitality':[64]

> [E]ven while keeping itself above the laws of hospitality, *the* unconditional law of hospitality needs the laws, it *requires* them. This demand is constitutive. It wouldn't be effectively unconditional, the law, if it didn't *have to become* effective, concrete, determined, if that were not its being as having-to-be. It would risk being abstract, utopian, illusory, and so turning over into its opposite. In order to be what it is, *the* law thus needs the laws, which, however, deny it, or at any rate threaten it, sometimes corrupt or pervert it. And must always be able to do this.
>
> For this pervertibility is essential, irreducible, necessary. The perfectibility of laws is at this cost. And therefore their historicity. And vice versa, conditional laws would cease to be laws of hospitality if they were not guided, given inspiration, given aspiration, required, even, by the law of unconditional hospitality. These two regimes of law, of *the* law and the laws, are thus both contradictory, antinomic, and inseparable. They both imply and exclude each other, simultaneously. They incorporate one another at the moment of excluding one another, they are dissociated at the moment of enveloping one another.[65]

And, aligned more to the concerns of this chapter:

> [A]n *unconditional hospitality* ... exposes itself without limit to the coming of the other, beyond rights and laws, beyond a hospitality conditioned by the right of asylum, by the right to immigration, by citizenship ... Only an unconditional hospitality can give meaning and practical rationality to a concept of hospitality. Unconditional hospitality exceeds juridical, political, or economic calculation. But no thing and no one happened or arrives without it.[66]

The gist of this chapter so far could now be concentrated in this antinomy between the unconditional and the conditioned. Derrida's equating all instances of unconditionality with 'justice' could prompt the appropriation of law in these terms, that law which was not only a conditioned determinacy but also integrally responsive to an unconditional justice.[67] These same constituent dimensions were found to characterise normativity. Then the conditioned border was found to dissipate in an unconditional

[62] J Derrida, *Of Hospitality*, trans R Bowlby (Stanford CA, Stanford University Press, 2000), and Derrida, above n 28 (*Cosmopolitanism*), Part One. *cf* on 'the unconditioned' F Nietzsche, *Twilight of the Idols* in *Twilight of the Idols/The Anti-Christ*, trans RJ Hollingdale (Harmondsworth, Penguin Books, 1968) 37 ('Reason in Philosophy' para 4).

[63] Derrida, above n 61 (*Hospitality*) at 79.

[64] Derrida, above n 28 (*Cosmopolitanism*) at 17. See Bonnie Honig's contribution to this volume (ch 9) for a related discussion of Derrida's analysis of hospitality, esp 213–15.

[65] Derrida, above n 61 (*Hospitality*) at 79 and 81.

[66] Derrida, above n 23, at 149.

[67] See Derrida, above n 23, at 135, 149–50.

and transgressive dynamic of formation, and this led to an intimation of both 'the people' and the polity as melding the unconditional and the conditioned. Next, reverting to the instance of law and justice, to the law of the law, we came in Derrida's company to 'a law of originary sociability'.[68] And it was in an effort to 'substantialise' the law and this sociability that we came finally to the antinomy between the unconditional and the conditioned and to its instances. Substance still eludes us, however, our way to it being blocked by a seeming impasse.

This impasse can be illustrated in another instance of the antinomy, that to do with forgiveness. After noting several conditioned encapsulations of forgiveness, Derrida goes on to assert that

> it must never be forgotten ... that all that refers to a certain idea of pure and unconditional forgiveness, without which this discourse [of forgiveness conditioned] would not have the least meaning. What complicates the question of 'meaning' is ... pure and unconditional forgiveness, in order to have its own meaning, must have no 'meaning', no finality, even no intelligibility.[69]

If however, and Derrida would add, 'one wants, and it is necessary, forgiveness to become effective, concrete, historic' it must become conditional and, presumably, thence have meaning; but '[t]hese two poles, *the unconditional and the conditional*, are absolutely heterogeneous, and must remain irreducible to one another. They are nonetheless indissociable'.[70] Being so indissociable, and with one of the two constituent elements having no meaning, leaves the not inconsiderable challenge of a meaning that has to have no meaning if it is to carry meaning. What is more, the absence of substantial meaning characterises all those instances of unconditionality just brought together in terms of law, justice, borders, the people, and the polity. And, in a broadly cognate context, Derrida has written of an 'impossibility of substantialising'.[71]

Staying with the cognate, Derrida can be taken as offering a lineament of substance with the invocation of 'what lets singular beings (anyone) "live together"'.[72] What this 'what' may be could then be conceived as a negative ontology—using the phrase more 'positively' than is usual. If there were no unconditionality, albeit made effective, there could be no 'living together', no being-in-common. In the absence of the 'pure' unconditional,

[68] Derrida, above n 28 (*Politics of Friendship*) at 231.

[69] Derrida, above n 28 (*Cosmopolitanism*) at 45.

[70] *Ibid*, 44–5.

[71] Derrida, above n 32 (*Negotiations*) 36; and see JD Caputo, 'Without Sovereignty, Without Being: Unconditionality, the Coming God and Derrida's Democracy to Come' (2003) 4(9) *Journal for Cultural and Religious Theory* 9, 12.

[72] J Derrida, 'Autoimmunity: Real and Symbolic Suicides—A Dialogue with Jacques Derrida' in G Borradori, *Philosophy in a Time of Terror: Dialogues with Jürgen Habermas and Jacques Derrida* (Chicago, The University of Chicago Press, 2003) 130.

along with its formative dynamic, the existence of any togetherness would be terminal. Its truth would, returning to Nancy, be 'the truth of death'.[73] It is possible also to come to the unconditional from within instances of the antinomy, conceiving it now as integrating the poles of the antinomy in a way that does not end simply as a reduction to the conditioned but, rather, as a configuration which has historical and social purchase; something that is, in Derrida's terms, a 'heritage'—a 'manner of being'.[74] This approach coming from within instances of the antinomy can be seen, retrospectively, as the way in which both the law and the normative were analysed in Act 2 and in the first scene of this Act 3. The law and the normative were mediate matters, which, even if they could not combine the poles of the antinomy deifically, could still demonically accommodate their restless resolution.[75]

If, then, the normative does subsist as mediative matter, still I have concentrated only on one side being mediated, the unconditional. '[W]hat lets singular beings (anyone) "live together"' is needful of conditioned existence, of a taking place, not just a 'manner of being' but, to use Derrida's fuller phrasing, 'one's house ... a manner of being there'.[76] And this existence has to be in constituent relation to the unconditional and, it follows, in rejection of the 'sovereign' self-elevation, the arrogated ultimacy, of such as the nation-state described in Act 1, something that the present chapter has been set against.[77] That, rather obviously, intimates a large agenda, and this third act has already broken the informal norms of dramatism by being too long, so for now I will offer an abrupt sociologic in which 'singular beings' living together impel conditioned existence.

With this sociologic, for singular beings to 'live together' there has to be a commonality. If, without more, they were simply and distinctly singular yet were still within a social bond with its necessary element of commonality, the only available commonality would be one in which they were completely the same as each other. The singularity of each depends upon a commonality which is neither reducible to its component singularities nor capable of absorbing them in some total or totalitarian comprehension. If, then, this commonality is to 'serve' as a focus for the constitution of the singular being, it must have a conditioned, a determinate and delimited presence. Yet if this commonality is to accommodate the focused infinity of ever-changing relation among singular

[73] Nancy, above n 52, at 12.

[74] J Derrida and E Roudinesco, *For What Tomorrow ... A Dialogue*, trans J Fort (Stanford CA, Stanford University Press, 2004) 160; Derrida, above n 28 (*Cosmopolitanism*) at 17.

[75] See n 38 above and the accompanying text.

[76] Derrida, above n 71, at 130; Derrida, above n 28 (*Cosmopolitanism*) at 16–17.

[77] Whether sovereignty is or can be unconditional is an issue deserving of more consideration in this setting: see generally M Naas, '*Comme si, comme ça*: Phantasms of Self, State, and a Sovereign God' (2007) 40(2) *Mosaic* 1.

beings, and if it is to provide the continuate and generative terms of their 'living together', it must as well be unconditional and thence illimitably responsive.[78]

V. EPILOGUE

That is a precipitate leave-taking, an end that is more of a beginning. My effort throughout this chapter has been to reverse the commonly perceived orientation of normative formation, the perception of the normative as the emanation of a surpassing ipseity, as the policy made by a ruling polity, and thence brought to bear on what is subjected to or apart from it. On the contrary, the constitution, the hidden constitution, of the polity was found to be dependently formed in its relation to what it would putatively rule, and that constitution rendered the polity normative 'in the first place', and it was the immigrant who opened up and sustained the question of that primacy, the immigrant who—in a final, for now, borrowing from Derrida—'puts the first question'.[79]

[78] To 'function' in this way the being-in-common must ever enable an opening onto itself. That would, in the present context, entail a normative transcendence, one which needs further consideration.

[79] Derrida, n 61 above (*Hospitality*) at 3. This is something of an adaptation: Derrida is writing of 'the foreigner' but still as a 'coming from abroad': *ibid*.

6

Breaking Promises to Keep Them:

Immigration and the Boundaries of Distributive Justice*

HANS LINDAHL

I. INTRODUCTION

ALTHOUGH IMMIGRATION IS widely recognised as raising urgent distributive issues, it has proven difficult for theories of distributive justice to conceptualise immigration in a way that does not ultimately trade politics in for morality. The temptation to move from politics to morality is great: to the extent that political boundaries entail an asymmetric relation between citizens and aliens—such that those inside decide between themselves who may or may not enter the polity from outside—morality suggests a form of reciprocity between individuals that is in principle unlimited, thereby releasing a theory of distributive justice from the constraints introduced by political asymmetry. While attractive at first sight, this move is self-defeating. For *distributive* justice requires that a political community enact a legal order that, first, identifies what rights accrue to whom, and, secondly, identifies officials who, in case of conflict, can authoritatively distribute rights among contending parties. To abandon the bounded reciprocity of political community in favour of the unbounded reciprocity of morality is to forfeit a constitutive condition of distributive justice. But simply reaffirming the asymmetry of the positions inside and outside a polity seems to collapse distributive justice into the sheer positivity of positive law, such that immigration ceases to be a problem about distributive *justice*.

* The paper which is the basis of this chapter was funded by a research grant provided by the Netherlands Organisation for Scientific Research (NWO). A preliminary version of this paper was presented at the Law Department of the London School of Economics. I greatly appreciate the in-depth comments to this preliminary version by Dora Kostakopoulou, Martin Loughlin, Damian Chalmers, and Emmanuel Melissaris.

This chapter suggests a way out of this conceptual impasse. It argues that immigration is a *political* problem from beginning to end because the boundaries of a community are posited from the first-person plural perspective of a 'we' as a unity in distributive action. Justice is spatially circumscribed because every distributive act posits, explicitly or implicitly, a boundary separating inside from outside, and claims to do so from *within* a collective's own space. The paper further argues that immigration poses a political *problem* because the conditions governing the self-closure of a polity disrupt—without effacing—the opposition between an inside and an outside. Although polities claim a right to include and exclude aliens because a territory is the 'own place' of their citizens, an act of inclusion and exclusion gives rise, in the first place, to the distinction between citizen and alien. This paper explores how this circularity renders de jure boundaries vulnerable to contestation by 'de facto immigrants', and how it also conditions the possibility of acts of distributive justice in the face of such contestation. Ultimately, it will be argued, the spatiality of distributive justice is rooted in time, in the paradoxical temporality of political judgment: as the self-closure of a polity arises through a mutual promise to which there is no direct access, immigration policy has to decide what promises have been made in the light of boundary crossings that determine what promises can be kept.

II. IMMIGRATION AND BOUNDED JUSTICE

It is important to note, at the outset, that my aim in this section is not to offer a comprehensive survey—let alone detailed analysis—of the large and ever-growing literature on the relation between migration and distributive justice.[2] My initial, more limited, aim is to understand why theories of distributive justice tend to move from a political to a moral treatment of immigration, and why we should resist this move. This is by no means to deny that immigration raises urgent moral issues. Instead, my claim is that abandoning a political approach to immigration entails forfeiting a condition of possibility of distributive justice. To make as strong a case as possible for this view, it is instructive to focus on two very different, even conflicting approaches that, on the face of them, develop explicitly *political* readings of immigration and distributive justice.

The first of these analyses is Michael Walzer's discussion of membership and immigration in his well-known book, *Spheres of Justice*. As Walzer points out, membership has become an issue of paramount importance for polities confronted with significant numbers of immigrants. Consequently,

[2] See V Bader's recent article, 'The Ethics of Immigration' (2005) 12 *Constellations* 331–61, for a systematic survey of this literature.

a theory of distributive justice must begin by scrutinising the acts by which a polity admits or turns away aliens, not only because such acts precede the distributive question concerning the conditions for naturalisation, but also because they determine all further distributive decisions in the polity. Walzer summarises his position as follows: 'The idea of distributive justice presupposes a bounded world within which distributions take place: a group of people committed to dividing, exchanging, and sharing social goods, first among themselves. That world ... is the political community'.[3] To be sure, he quickly adds that a political community is by no means a self-contained distributive unit; distribution also takes place across the boundaries that separate political communities. But, he argues, distributive decisions about cross-boundary movements, in particular about the entry of persons to a polity, are collective decisions taken from *within*. On this view, a right to inclusion and exclusion is ingredient to the very concept of distributive justice. This means that, subject to certain limitations, it is up to a political community to determine who and what may enter the community. As Walzer candidly puts it, 'no one on the outside has a right to be inside'.[4]

Walzer's defence of bounded justice is a political argument, namely an argument about collective self-determination. Indeed,

> admission and exclusion are at the core of communal independence ... without them, there could not be *communities of character*, historically stable, ongoing associations of men and women with some special commitment to one another and some special sense of their common life.[5]

Three aspects of this argument deserve mention here. First, Walzer stresses that the right to inclusion and exclusion is a collective right, a right that accrues to the members of a community acting as a *whole*. Secondly, this right is part and parcel of collective freedom because it safeguards the polity as a group of individuals committed to upholding and promoting shared values. These values lend a community its distinctiveness or 'character'. In other words, Walzer maintains that the political reciprocity of self-determination is perforce limited, for it presupposes a shared commitment to a determinate conception of the good. Accordingly, the statuses of citizen and alien are not simply interchangeable; the mutual commitment of citizens implies a *mutual preference* vis-à-vis aliens. Obviously, this preference is political, not personal. Thirdly, the argument for bounded justice and a concomitant collective right to closure ultimately rests on *collective identity*: 'the link between people and land is a crucial feature of national identity'.[6]

[3] M Walzer, *Spheres of Justice: A Defense of Pluralism and Equality* (New York, Basic Books, 1983) 31.
[4] *Ibid*, 41.
[5] *Ibid*, 62.
[6] *Ibid*, 44.

While Walzer presents a political argument in defence of the boundedness of distributive justice, his approach also requires treating immigration as a moral problem. Indeed, once it is taken for granted that communities enjoy a right to closure, the question inevitably arises whether there are *limitations* to this right. Walzer readily grants such limitations, most notably the 'principle of mutual aid'.[7] But it is also clear from his account that this principle is *moral* in character, rather than political. It speaks to a form of cross-boundary reciprocity between individuals as moral beings that suspends the constraints of intramural political reciprocity between citizens.

While there are certainly good reasons for giving serious attention to the principle of mutual aid, the prior question is whether Walzer's political argument in favour of the boundedness of distributive justice is sufficiently political. Indeed, does he go far enough when insisting that first admission is the initial—and essential—distributive act? Consider the following passage: 'We assume an established group and a fixed population', Walzer notes, 'and so we miss the first and most important distributive question: How is that group constituted?'[8] Having posed this question, one would expect him to bring the primordial distributive act—the spatial closure that constitutes a political community by separating citizen from alien—within the compass of a theory of distributive justice. For, surely, a right to inclusion and exclusion is contingent, from the point of view of a theory of distributive justice, on the conditions governing the primordial closure. Remarkably, however, Walzer arrests his questioning precisely at this point. Having raised the question, 'How is that group constituted?', he immediately qualifies its scope: 'I don't mean, How was it constituted? I am concerned here not with the historical origins of the different groups, but with the decisions they make in the present about their present and future populations'.[9] Despite having insisted that the primary distributive act concerns membership, Walzer removes from a theory of distributive justice the very closure that, dividing space into an inside and an outside, gives rise to citizens and aliens in the first place. This closure is a political, not a pre-political act, as Walzer seems to take for granted. As we shall see, immigration is a thoroughly political problem because the distinction between inside and outside is not only the presupposition of acts of distributive justice but also what boundary crossings continuously call into question as a *politico-legal* distinction.

III. IMMIGRATION AND BOUNDLESS JUSTICE

Jürgen Habermas is certainly not the only liberal thinker to challenge Walzer's thesis that distributive justice is bounded. But his position is

[7] *Ibid*, 33.
[8] *Ibid*, 31.
[9] *Ibid*, 31.

particularly apposite to our analysis because he acknowledges and attempts to overcome a political difficulty emerging from the fundamental premise shared by a wide range of defences of a right to migration. In an important article on this topic, Joseph Carens articulates the common premise underpinning Nozick, Rawls and utilitarianism. He argues that these three strands of moral thinking endorse a right to migration because all three share the conviction that moral personhood, rather than citizenship, is fundamental to a theory of distributive justice. 'Our commitment to civic equality is derived from our convictions about moral equality, not vice versa'.[10] In the context of this paper it is instructive to see how Habermas attempts to reconcile this conviction with a politico-legal approach to distributive justice. Although I cannot argue this point fully for reasons of space, the vicissitudes of Habermas's approach to immigration are exemplary for the difficulties encountered by all normative approaches that would derive political equality from moral equality.

Habermas's response to Walzer's model of bounded justice begins by pointing to an ambiguity in the concept of nation. On the one hand, a 'nation' can be construed as a community of descent with a shared historical destiny, that is, a group of individuals who are integrated geographically, and who share common traditions, language, customs, and the like. The French revolution bears witness to the emergence of a second concept of nation, namely as the holder of sovereignty. Whereas nationalism views citizenship in terms of membership of a cultural and ethnic community, republicanism does so solely in terms of participation in a political community. Although historically intertwined, these two understandings of nation are conceptually distinct. Their political dissociation is all the more necessary because the contemporary experience of social pluralism deprives a cultural interpretation of collective self-legislation of an empirical and normative foundation. Only the republican conception thereof yields a solid normative basis for addressing the issues of distributive justice arising in the context of immigration policy. As Habermas sees it, the political and social boundaries of a polity do not exhaust the responsibilities accruing to its citizens in the light of immigration.

> The moral point of view obligates us to assess this problem impartially, and thus not just from the one-sided perspective of an inhabitant of an affluent region but also from the perspective of immigrants who are seeking their well-being there.[11]

Accordingly, the distributive question, 'Who has the right to immigrate?' must be settled by identifying the apposite criteria 'from the perspective of

[10] J Carens, 'Aliens and Citizens: The Case for Open Borders' (1987) 49 *The Review of Politics* 251–73 at 256–7.

[11] J Habermas, 'Citizenship and National Identity' in Habermas, *Between Facts and Norms*, trans W Rehg (Cambridge MA, The MIT Press, 1998) 491–515 at 511.

all parties involved'.[12] Given this moral injunction, 'national governments also have to see to it that citizens fulfil their positive duties toward non-members, such as asylum seekers'.[13]

But what is the status of these 'positive duties'? This question exposes two major difficulties in Habermas's initial attempt to provide a normative grounding of immigration policy by deriving political equality from moral equality. The first concerns the hiatus separating moral from political reciprocity. Whereas morality is driven by a reciprocity that is in principle unlimited in scope, politics lives from the limitation of 'all interested parties'. Habermas obliquely recognises this, when signalling that, in processes of democratic self-legislation, 'citizens want to regulate their living together according to principles that are in the equal interest of each and thus can meet with the justified assent of all'.[14] Thus, *citizens*, as political equals, decide what counts as their shared interest. Although they can take into account the interest of aliens, and even may be prepared to accept a right to immigration as the default setting of the collective's immigration policy, this inclusiveness presupposes and confirms the asymmetry of political reciprocity. Secondly, abandoning reciprocity between citizens in favour of reciprocity between moral persons entails relinquishing a necessary condition of distributive justice: a legal order that identifies, first, what rights and goods can be attributed to whom, and, secondly, the officials that, in the face of dispute, can authoritatively establish what should be allotted to whom.

In a later essay Habermas faces up squarely to these difficulties. Rejecting the distinction between human—that is, moral—rights and fundamental—that is, legal—rights, he boldly proclaims that '[h]uman rights are juridical *by their very nature*. What lends them the appearance of moral rights is ... their mode of validity, which points beyond the legal orders of nation-states'.[15] The foundation of a world polity would secure their status as enforceable, subjective rights, and would assure all individuals of membership as free and equal citizens. Crucially, it would address

[12] J Habermas, 'Struggles for Recognition in the Democratic State' in Habermas, *The Inclusion of the Other* (Cambridge MA, The MIT Press, 1998) 203–38 at 230, 232.

[13] Habermas, 'Citizenship and National Identity', above n 11, at 511.

[14] Habermas, 'Citizenship and National Identity', above n 11, at 496.

[15] J Habermas, 'Kant's Idea of Perpetual Peace: At Two Hundred Years' Historical Remove' in Habermas, *The Inclusion of the Other*, above n 12, 165–201 at 190. In a later essay, Habermas backs off somewhat from his initial plea for a world federal state, appealing, instead, to the model of multi-level governance. It would seem, however, that Habermas locates the enactment and enforcement of human rights at the global level, such that his considerations on the juridification of human rights, as espoused in his Kant essay, remain more or less intact. See his essay, 'Does the Constitutionalisation of International Law Still Have a Chance?' in Jürgen Habermas, *The Divided West* (Cambridge, Polity Press, 2006) 115–93. For a sympathetic yet critical analysis of these essays, see N Walker, 'Making a World of Difference? Habermas, Cosmopolitanism and the Constitutionalisation of International Law' in O Shabani (ed), *The Practice of Law-Making and the Problem of Difference* (Cardiff, University of Wales Press, 2007) 219–34.

the problem of political asymmetry between citizens and aliens, for a world polity 'establishes for the first time a symmetry between the juridification of social and political relations both within and beyond the state's borders'.[16] Political reciprocity becomes co-extensive with moral reciprocity. Paradoxically, then, Habermas 'resolves' the problem of immigration by dissolving it as such; for the foundation of a world polity suppresses, at one stroke, the distinction between citizen and alien, inside and outside. He thereby lends credence to Kymlicka's wry comment that 'territorial boundaries are the source of embarrassment for liberals of all stripes'.[17] Indeed, Habermas deals with political boundaries by excising them from a theory of distributive justice. On the face of it, justice can only be *world* justice. The inversion is complete: to Walzer's bounded justice Habermas raises in opposition a justice that is boundless.

So, on closer consideration, neither Walzer nor Habermas gets around to addressing the following question: Why does immigration pose a fundamental *political problem* for a theory of distributive justice? To the extent that Walzer takes for granted the closure that gives rise to political community, only the moral limitations to an alleged right to closure, not the claimed right itself, are at issue in a theory of distributive justice. Habermas, for his part, can only rescue distributive justice by rendering political reciprocity co-extensive with moral reciprocity, thereby ridding political community of closure—and immigration. Both approaches trivialise immigration, concealing why it is a political problem that goes to the heart of distributive justice.

In the face of this impasse, it seems natural to adopt an 'intermediate' position, which attempts to reconcile the boundedness of political community with the universality of moral obligations to strangers. In one way or another, such positions call for a moral supplement to politics.[18] Although attractive at first glance, this move does not resolve the theoretical and practical problem that has emerged from the debate between Walzer and Habermas. If, on the one hand, immigration is to be dealt with as an issue of distributive justice, then it must be viewed as a politico-legal problem;

[16] Habermas, *The Inclusion of the Other*, above n 12, at 199.

[17] W Kymlicka, 'Territorial Boundaries: A Liberal Egalitarian Perspective' in D Miller and SH Hashmi (eds), *Boundaries and Justice: Diverse Ethical Perspectives*, (Princeton, Princeton University Press, 2001) 249–75 at 249. Another author indirectly voices this discomfort by claiming that all theories that are 'distributive, egalitarian, and universalistic' by temperament, including his own, 'have to conceive justice as global'. See S Gosepath, 'The Global Scope of Justice' in TW Pogge (ed), *Global Justice* (Oxford, Blackwell, 2001) 145–68 at 154.

[18] Recent examples include S Benhabib's *The Rights of Others* (Cambridge, Cambridge University Press, 2004) and *Another Cosmopolitanism* (Oxford, Oxford University Press, 2006), as well as V Bader's 'The Ethics of Immigration', above n 1, which attempts to reconcile what he calls (political) 'particularism' and (moral) 'universalism'. For an agonistic perspective on immigration to Europe that takes strong issue with Benhabib, see Bonnie Honig's contribution to this volume (ch 9).

but recognising it as such presupposes a fundamental asymmetry between citizens and aliens that is irreducible to the symmetrical relations between moral individuals. Yet, on the other hand, simply accepting political asymmetry seems to collapse distributive justice into the sheer positivity of positive law.

IV. THE STRUCTURE OF LEGAL SPACE

If we take a step back to consider the ongoing debate on immigration and distributive justice, it becomes clear that one of its fundamental shortcomings is the astounding lack of interest in an explicit and sustained inquiry into how legal space is structured, and how, if at all, boundaries might constitute that space. By and large, it is simply taken for granted that boundaries separate a domestic space from foreign countries. An inquiry into the structure of legal space is all the more urgent because Habermas's claim that distributive justice is boundless is polemically oriented against a second form of the inside/outside distinction that he views as constitutive for nationalism: the contrast between own and strange places. His distinction between an *ethnos* and a *demos* aims to liberate democratic self-legislation from 'the negative demarcation of the strange (*Fremde*) over against the own (*Eigene*)'.[19] By uncoupling the inside/outside distinction from the ethnically- and culturally-motivated distinction between the own and the strange, what remains—the distinction between domestic and foreign spaces—is the merely contingent spatial organisation of the nation-state, which can be superseded by the foundation of a world state.

To assess this thesis, we do well to accept Habermas's invitation to disencumber ourselves of a culturally loaded conception of the inside/outside distinction, and to reflect upon the most general conditions under which a world state could organise itself as a *legal* space. Our point of departure is that a legal space is a *space of action*, in contrast to, say, the space of perception. The law orders individual action by way of boundaries that establish where human behaviour ought or ought not to occur. A legal space is, minimally, a distribution of 'ought-places'; places to which individuals relate in the forms of legal emplacement or misplacement. Importantly, a legal space manifests itself as a *unity* of places—a 'territory'. Not only does every ought-place in a legal space include a reference to the totality of places in which it belongs, but it also draws its meaning *as* an ought-place from this encompassing unity of places. This entails that boundaries *join by separating*. Paradoxically, boundaries only succeed in separating places,

[19] J Habermas, 'The European Nation-State: On the Past and Future of Sovereignty and Citizenship' in Habermas, *The Inclusion of the Other*, above n 12, at 110 (trans altered).

normatively speaking, if they join these places in an encompassing whole. For example, acts that qualify a boundary crossing as illegal seek to reassert the separating function of boundaries; but, to do so, they claim that the apposite individual ought to be elsewhere, thereby joining both ought-places into a spatial unity.

How can a manifold of ought-places appear as a *unity*? Two conditions must be met: the first is that a territory be deemed a common space; the second is that a collective lay claim to a territory as its own. The first condition concerns the *binding* character of boundaries: what makes a place an *ought*-place—the place where one ought or ought not to be—is the claim that legal boundaries give spatial expression to the common interest. The second condition is, as noted, that a collective lays claim to a territory as its *own*. Crucially, the reference to 'ownership' is not juridical, as in the classical legal categories of *imperium* or *dominium*. Instead, it concerns *political reflexivity*, in a twofold sense of the term. For the one, individuals view themselves as a unity in action that posits boundaries. For the other, members of a collective view themselves as the group of individuals that has a privileged interest in the boundaries, as posited.[20]

So, the first term of the contrast between 'own' and 'strange' places is indispensable if we are at all to understand why legal space is a unity of ought-places. But need this imply that a legal space can only be structured as a unity by dint of a closure that contrasts the community's own space to *strange* places? Would not a world state preclude that possibility, to the extent that it inaugurates an all-inclusive political 'we'?

The snag is that a world state would have to determine, at its foundation, what interests unite its members in political reciprocity, by including some interests and (implicitly) excluding others as irrelevant. This inclusion and exclusion of interests would be reflected in the boundaries that determine where behaviour ought and ought not to occur. Crucially, the founding inclusion and exclusion of interests is not the outcome of a discursive process, in the Habermasian sense of the term. Someone must *seize the initiative* to establish what counts as the common interest of the polity. Moreover, whoever seizes the initiative claims to act in the name of the whole, but cannot have been mandated to this effect by interested parties, because only the initiative makes it possible to establish what counts as being an *interested* party. Political reciprocity in a world state would depend, as in any other polity, on a non-reciprocal act to get it

[20] The term 'reflexivity' is, of course, highly polysemic in the philosophical literature. I draw here on the specific sense of political reflexivity outlined in B van Roermund's powerful article, 'First-Person Plural Legislature: Political Reflexivity and Representation' (2003) 6 *Philosophical Explorations* 235–50, and to which I return in the following section.

going.[21] Certainly, there would be room for renegotiating boundaries. But instituting political equality in a world state opens up the possibility of instituting political inequality, such that world citizenship could ultimately be withdrawn from individuals who radically contest how the polity draws the boundaries defining legal emplacement and misplacement. Habermas omits mentioning in this context that securing the legal status of human rights in a world state—including a world democracy—involves introducing restrictions to their validity, the most prominent of which is the public order exception. Thus he correctly holds that 'state citizenship and world citizenship form a continuum'.[22] But the reason for this is that both forms of citizenship illustrate the asymmetry, explicit or implicit, that is constitutive for political reciprocity.

By the same token, although a world state would have no outside in the sense of foreign places, or at least not initially, the inclusion and exclusion of interests reflected in its boundaries entail that its foundation gives rise, at least latently, to strange places—places that have no place within the unity of places that constitute its territory, even though they in some sense ought to. Strange places appear abruptly, in the form of displaced behaviour, behaviour that *dis-locates* boundaries by contesting the manner in which a legal order organises the distinction between emplacement and misplacement. A good example of boundary crossings that reveal an outside in the strong sense of strange places is provided by the Brazilian *movimento sem terra*—the movement of the landless. By occupying latifundia, the dispossessed do more than trespass the boundaries of rural estates; they also challenge the terms in which Brazilian law draws the distinction between legal emplacement and misplacement, appealing to values and principles of that legal order. Hence not only do boundaries join by separating, as noted earlier, but, conversely, boundaries also *separate by joining*. The boundaries that join a manifold of legal places into a unity are also the boundaries that separate this spatial unity from strange places. Although Habermas is right to note that the domestic/foreign distinction is a contingent feature of political community, what a world state could not avoid, if it is to constitute itself as a *legal* space, is to posit boundaries that close it off as an inside over against an indeterminate outside, an outside that becomes determinate when boundary crossings that contest the claim to commonality of a legal space also intimate a different spatial ordering of human behaviour—another world. Accordingly, the distinction between

[21] 'Entry into a dialogue and exit therefrom cannot themselves be understood as dialogical without one's falling prey to a *petitio principi*': B Waldenfels, 'Vorwort: Indirekte Rede' in his *Vielstimmigkeit der Rede* (Frankfurt, Suhrkamp, 1999) 14. See also B van Roermund, *Law, Narrative and Reality: An Essay in Intercepting Politics* (Dordrecht, Kluwer Academic Publishers, 1997) 150 ff, and B Honig, 'Between Decision and Deliberation: Political Paradox in Democratic Theory' (2007) 101 *American Political Science Review* 1–17.

[22] Habermas, 'Citizenship and National Identity', above n 11, at 515.

'own' and 'strange' places is not primarily ethnic or culturally motivated, as Habermas thinks. This does not amount to making a pitch for local polities and against a global state, as Walzer does; my point is rather that a global polity would itself be local. In *this* sense, then, Habermas rightly asserts that the foundation of a world state renders possible a 'world internal politics' (*Weltinnenpolitik*).[23] The inevitability of an outside should temper enthusiasm about the vision of boundless distributive justice: the price that must be paid for abolishing immigration through the foundation of a world state is the abrogation of a right to emigration.[24]

V. TO EACH THEIR OWN PLACE

Granting that legal space requires a closure, need we conclude that *distributive justice* does, too? The key to this question, I will now argue, is collective identity. Indeed, a systematic account of the relation between boundaries and distributive justice turns on how one interprets the 'self' of collective self-legislation. Recent studies in collective intentionality cast this issue in a way that differs substantially from both Walzer and Habermas. These studies give the lie to theories of social action that view the self of collective self-legislation as a summation of individual acts, while at the same time steering clear of an ontology that postulates that collectives exist independently of individuals and their acts. As Michael Bratman puts it, 'shared intentions are intentions of the group. But … they consist in a public, interlocking web of the intentions of the individuals'.[25] Bratman is concerned to clarify the kind of unity implied in the idea of an 'interlocking web of intentions'. His central claim is that 'shared intentional activity' turns on mutual responsiveness: reciprocity of intentions, to the extent that my intention to act is co-determined by your intention to act and vice versa, and that we know this of each other; reciprocity in the meshing of our individual plans and action, in view of bringing about the shared activity. Importantly, he carefully distinguishes shared intentional activity from shared *cooperative* activity: whereas the latter rules out coercion in the

[23] Habermas, 'Kant's Idea of Perpetual Peace', above n 15, at 187–8 (trans altered).

[24] For an extended analysis of the structure and genesis of legal space, see my article, 'Give and take: Arendt and the *nomos* of political community' (2006) 32 *Philosophy and Social Criticism* 881–901.

[25] M Bratman, 'I Intend That We *J*' in Bratman, *Faces of Intention* (Cambridge, Cambridge University Press, 1999) 142–61 at 143. Similarly, Philip Pettit indicates that 'as there is a personal perspective that is available only with talk of "I", so there is a personal perspective that becomes available only with talk of "we"'. See P Pettit, *A Theory of Freedom: From the Psychology to the Politics of Agency* (Cambridge, Polity Press, 2001) 117. Both authors refer extensively to the burgeoning literature on the subject, which includes work by Margaret Gilbert, Raimo Tuomela, and John Searle.

attainment of the collective purpose or interest, the former, of which law is an instance, does not.

Although he does not distinguish them as such, Bratman's analysis reveals that shared intentional activity deploys two forms of identity. First, the purpose or interest defining what the group is doing, and what it is about, enables a collective to identify itself as the same over time, or as becoming different, to the extent that, along the way, its members confirm or readjust their understanding of what they are doing. Paul Ricœur calls this *idem*-identity, identity as sameness.[26] The second mode of identity is linked to the indexical 'we', by which individuals refer to themselves as acting together. Ricœur dubs this *ipse*-identity, the identity of selfhood. Indeed, the word 'self' is reflexive, for it denotes agents who can refer to themselves by using first-person indexicals such as 'we', 'us', and 'our'.[27] Importantly, collective self-legislation is reflexive insofar as individuals view themselves as members of the group that both intends to act and has an interest in the act. Following Van Roermund, I will speak here of *political reflexivity*.[28] Ipseity implies a form of identity because, as Ricœur notes, selfhood involves a 'permanence in time'.[29] Whereas he views character as the privileged manifestation of *idem*-identity, he sees the making and keeping of promises as emblematic for *ipse*-identity. I will return at the end of this chapter to the problem of promises and *ipse*-identity, when considering the temporal structure of boundaries.

When described in this way, the first-person plural perspective is the backbone of acts of distributive justice: acts that mete out to each their own are acts by which the members of a polity are deemed (1) to articulate a common interest, and to refer to themselves as the individuals that (2), acting jointly, ascribe rights and obligations, and that (3) have a joint interest in the acts settling what rights and obligations accrue to whom. Although Walzer does not distinguish these two modes of identity, and tends to collapse collective selfhood into sameness, he correctly asserts that 'the idea of distributive justice presupposes ... a group of people committed to dividing, exchanging, and sharing social goods, first among *themselves*' (emphasis added). For whoever cries out 'this is just!' or 'that is unjust!' already evokes the reflexive stance of a 'we' in distributive action.

Consider, now, Ulpian's famous formulation of the principle of justice—*suum cuique tribuere*, to each his own. As it stands, the principle is silent about space and legal boundaries. But the spatiality of distributive justice comes into view if one re-inscribes justice in what the legal doctrine calls the

[26] P Ricœur, *Oneself as another*, trans K Blamley (Chicago, Chicago University Press, 1992) 1–3; 115–25.

[27] Pettit, *A Theory of Freedom*, above n 25, at 116.

[28] See Van Roermund, 'First-Person Plural Legislature', above n 20.

[29] Ricœur, *Oneself as Another*, above n 26, at 118.

'spheres of validity' of legal norms.[30] The basic doctrinal intuition is that as the legal 'ought' refers to human behaviour, legal norms order behaviour in its subjective, objective, temporal, and spatial dimensions. These spheres of validity are the most general features defining the law as a normative order. Indeed, no legal order is conceivable that does not offer responses to four different questions: *Who* ought to behave in a certain way? *What* behaviour ought to come about? *When* ought behaviour to come about? *Where* ought behaviour to come about? Returning to the principle of justice, *suum cuique tribuere* evokes the material and personal scopes of legal validity, indicating who is entitled to what. Although space and time are passed over in silence, this does not mean, however, that they are only 'preconditions' of distributive justice, as though distributive acts merely come about 'in' space and time.

Turning, first, to time, notice that legal temporality is above all a subject-relative form of time, namely the historical time of a collective. As legal norms are posited from the first-person plural perspective, they situate human behaviour in the temporal arc spanning the past, present, and future of a collective. These modes of time, as Émile Benveniste, the great French linguist, has noted, are irreducible to dated time.[31] The unity of calendar time manifests itself as the continuum of a before and an after; by contrast, past, present, and future can only appear as a unity to the extent that they are the temporal modes of a 'we' (or an 'I'). Moreover, this self-attribution is linked to the commonality of historical time, in the twofold sense of a time that is shared by and distinguishes the members of a collective. These two features determine the time of law as a *limited* time. Time can only manifest itself as an *ought*-time, the time in which behaviour ought to take place, to the extent that it is deemed the common time of a collective.

Space, for its part, is a sphere of validity because law reveals space normatively, as the unity of a manifold of *ought*-places. And, as we have learned in Section IV, the unity of a manifold of ought-places depends on two conditions. The first is that a space be deemed common, that is, that its boundaries give spatial form to the public interest. The second is that a collective claim a space as its own, which presupposes the first-person plural perspective of a 'we' that constitutes itself as a legal space by closing off an inside over against an outside. The distributive question—where ought behaviour to take place?—ultimately concerns how the boundary between inside and outside should be drawn. And this amounts to a query

[30] H Kelsen, *Pure Theory of Law*, trans M Knight (Berkeley, University of California Press, 1970) 12–15; H Kelsen, *Introduction to Problems of Legal Theory*, trans SL Paulson and B Litschewski Paulson (Oxford, Clarendon Press, 1992) 12–13. For a related discussion of the principle of justice see B van Roermund's contribution to this volume (ch 7).

[31] 'As a day is identical to another day, nothing says about this or that calendar day, taken in itself, whether it is past, present, or future. It cannot be placed under one of these three categories other than by who *lives* time'. See É Benveniste, 'Le langage et l'expérience humaine' *Problèmes du langage*, ed É Benveniste *et al* (Paris, Gallimard, 1966) 3–13 at 8.

concerning the commonality of the territory a polity calls its own. The where-question can only be raised and answered against the horizon of a unity of ought-places, and as a renewed question about what constitutes a manifold of places *as* a spatial unity.

Accordingly, the four questions noted above are questions confronting a collective: they arise and are addressed from the first-person plural perspective of a 'we'. This is another way of saying that what holds together the four spheres of validity as the aspects of a *single* legal order is their subject-relatedness. Spatio-temporally speaking, this means that legal space cannot be organised according to the master distinction between inside and outside unless legal time is structured as a past, a present, and a future. Conversely, legal time cannot appear as the past, present, and future of a collective unless space is structured as an inside and an outside. Here, then, is the reason that acts of distributive justice are bounded: because such acts invoke the first-person plural perspective of a 'we', they cannot allot to each their own rights and obligations without also apportioning to each their own … place and time.

This insight also explains the link between immigration and distributive justice. The administrative or judicial act that determines whether an immigrant may enter a polity renders explicit what remains implicit and taken for granted in most acts of distributive justice: *suum cuique tribuere* is also always *suum cuique locum*. And as the question about the boundary between inside and outside calls forth the question about the sense of a collective past, present, and future, such administrative or judicial acts also distribute time, indicating which entries by immigrants can be accommodated in the temporal unity of a collective, that is, which entries or kinds of entries allow a collective to (continue) to view itself as having a shared history spanning past, present, and future: *suum cuique tempus*.

VI. THE GENESIS OF LEGAL SPACE AND THE LOGIC OF BOUNDARIES

Let me quickly take stock. An initial survey suggested that authors as different as Walzer and Habermas encounter considerable conceptual difficulties in acknowledging that immigration poses what is fundamentally a political problem for a theory of distributive justice. Focusing on Habermas, Section V showed why his move to render political reciprocity coextensive with moral reciprocity belies that distributive justice is bounded. My argument is, in a nutshell, that justice is spatially circumscribed because it is a reflexive process in the first-person plural perspective: every distributive act (1) posits, explicitly or implicitly, a boundary separating inside from outside, and (2) claims to do so from within a collective's own space. To this extent, Walzer's thesis that 'no one on the outside has a right to be inside' is plausible. Indeed, there can be no law nor politics, and a fortiori no distributive justice, without a prior closure. Yet, while it grants a certain plausibility to this claim, the argument sketched out heretofore also paves the way for a strong conceptual critique thereof.

To see why, we need to resume the debate with Walzer where it had been interrupted. While he correctly argues that membership is the primordial distributive issue, his discussion thereof begins too late: the spatial closure that founds a community, separating inside from outside and distinguishing citizen from alien, has already taken place. What is fascinating, however, is that Walzer's 'omission' cannot be corrected by bringing the foundational closure into the purview of a theory that lays out the criteria by which a distributive act can be qualified as just or unjust. We obliquely stumbled upon the reasons for this impossibility when considering Habermas' world state: the founding closure of a polity is not and cannot be the expression of political reflexivity because closure conditions the possibility of political reflexivity.

The foundation of the European (Economic) Community offers a good illustration of this quandary. The Preamble to the Treaty of Rome, enacted in 1957, states that the parties to the Treaty are 'determined to lay the foundations of an ever closer union among the peoples of Europe'. Notice, to begin with, that the enactment of the Treaty is a distributive act in the fourfold sense of the foregoing section: it indicates *who* is a party to the collective, *what* are their common interests, *where* this interest is located, and *when* this interest comes about, namely, in the course of a European history that has already commenced and which is to be safeguarded and intensified in the future through the foundation, now, of the European polity. Moreover, while the six founding Member States claimed to represent Europe as a spatial unity, they had received no legal mandate to this effect from all relevant parties, nor could they have: the founding act determines who is a relevant party by indicating *where* their interest is located—in a common market. Importantly, the European polity and its Member States not only expect individuals inside but also those *outside* to recognise and abide by the (incipient) right to closure claimed for the EC in the immigration policy provisions of the Amsterdam Treaty of 1997. Yet the preferential distinction between European and non-European arises through a closure that cannot be the outcome of a joint act by these two groups, because it gives rise to them in the first place. As a result, European immigration policy rests on a circularity that resists resolution: the European polity claims a right to include and exclude aliens because Europe is the own place of its citizens; yet, to begin with, an act of inclusion and exclusion gives rise to European citizens and their own place.[32]

[32] I develop this issue at greater length in 'Finding a Place for Freedom, Security and Justice: The European Unity and its Claim to Territorial Unity' (2004) 29 *European Law Review* 461–84. Benhabib makes a similar point in *The Rights of Others*, above n 17, at 20 ff, and in *Another Cosmopolitanism*, above n 17, at 17–20, albeit that we differ as to the normative implications that follow from this paradox. For a recent survey of transformations in European citizenship, see J Shaw, *The Transformation of Citizenship in the European*

This circularity, which is constitutive for every imaginable polity, disrupts the simple oppositions between inside and outside, and right and fact, which underpin Walzer's defence of a right to closure. Turning, first, to the opposition between inside and outside, consider, once again, the Preamble to the Treaty of Rome: 'determined to lay the foundations of an ever closer union among the peoples of Europe'. Notice that the Treaty does not only distribute space by separating and opposing an inside (Europe) and an outside (the rest of the world). In the same movement by which the Treaty closes off the European polity from the rest of the world, it includes the EC and what is excluded therefrom in an encompassing spatial unity: a world market, the denizens of which are viewed as economic actors subject to the rules of market exchange. The logic of boundaries is at work here: boundaries separate by joining. Importantly, the second leg of the logic of boundaries is also at work: the Treaty distributes space by separating Europe from *itself*: it splits Europe, including it as a common market and excluding other possible interpretations of what constitutes it as a common space, such that contestation of the common market can erupt in the name of 'another Europe'. The closure that gives rise to the common market cannot represent Europe as the common space of a community without folding a strange Europe into what is claimed to be the EC's own place. Whence the logic of boundaries: boundaries join the EC's member states into a common market by separating the latter from another Europe. Moreover, the Treaty also distributes space by separating the *world* from itself. In the same movement by which the Treaty splits Europe, it also splits the world, representing it as a market. The cry, 'Another world is possible', uttered in places such as Porto Alegre, reveals that the EC cannot take its place in a world market without folding a strange world into the world it calls its own. The logic of boundaries kicks in yet a third time: the boundaries of the internal market join it to the external market by separating the world market from other worlds.

Accordingly, the circularity governing the founding distributive act disrupts—without effacing—the opposition between inside and outside. Indeed, it ensures that a legal space is never entirely a community's own place, and this for two reasons. For the one, every community harbours strange places within what it calls its own legal space: distributive acts deploy an exclusive inclusiveness. For the other, the collective's own place can appear as elsewhere than in the legal space that claims to give it institutional form: distributive acts deploy an inclusive exclusiveness.[33] Contrary to Walzer's (and Habermas's) assumption, the distributive acts

Union: Electoral Rights and the Restructuring of Political Space (Cambridge, Cambridge University Press, 2007).

[33] For a similar argument, see B Waldenfels's contribution to this volume (ch 4).

that close a community never simply divide and oppose an inside and an outside: they bring in what they push out—and push out what they bring in. *The logic of boundaries, according to which boundaries cannot separate without joining, nor join without separating, is the obverse of the logic of distributive acts, which cannot exclude without including, nor include without excluding.*[34]

The disruption of the pat opposition between inside and outside is paired to a disruption of the simple opposition between right and fact. The circularity of the founding closure reveals an ineluctable de facto core in the alleged *jus includendi et excludendi* polities claim for themselves. This de facto core explains why, as Oosterom-Staples has perceptively indicated, the 'three concentric circles' put into place by the EU in its attempt to control entries by aliens effectively create a distinction between *de facto* and *de jure* boundaries.[35] The residual factuality of the Treaty of Rome, which posits the distinction between inside and outside, member and non-member, without being mandated to do so by all persons affected by this act, catches up with the EU from ahead as it were—from the *future*—in the form of the '*de facto*' immigrant, that is, the so-called 'economic' immigrant who seeks entry by applying for the status of political asylum seeker. As a reputed scholar puts it, '[a]lthough the EU Member States have unanimously denied that they are countries of immigration, by and large all have eventually become *de facto* immigration countries. The flow of asylum applicants has become a major source of *de facto* immigration.'[36] While he defends the 'legitimate right' of the EU and its Member States to curb such immigration, the aforementioned circularity disrupts the clean split between right and fact to which he appeals. Indeed, by including Europe and the rest of the world in an encompassing whole, the Treaty of Rome already posits a minimal reciprocity between European citizens and aliens: 'we', participants and interested parties in a world market. Boundary crossings by *de facto* immigrations point to a threshold of distributive justice that I will call 'proto-political reflexivity'. I speak of proto-*political* reflexivity, rather than of moral reflexivity, because so-called 'economic' migrants seize the initiative to implicitly evoke the first-person plural perspective of a 'we' that has a shared interest in the realisation of a world market. But I speak of *proto*-political reflexivity, instead of political reflexivity *tout court*, because the first-person plural perspective enjoined by the process of realising a world market has not obtained institutional

[34] This analysis suggests that boundaries have what Merleau-Ponty would call a 'chiasmatic' structure. See M Merleau-Ponty, *The Visible and the Invisible*, trans A Lingis (Evanston IL, Northwestern University Press, 1968) 130–55, 263–4.

[35] See Helen Oosterom-Staples's contribution to this volume (ch 3).

[36] K Hailbronner, 'Asylum Law in the Context of a European Migration Policy' in N Walker (ed), *Europe's Area of Freedom, Security and Justice* (Oxford, Oxford University Press, 2004) 41–88 at 42.

form by way of officials that, acting on behalf of a 'we', can authoritatively arbitrate about claims raised by so-called 'economic' immigrants.[37] To put it in Bratman's terms, such claims are not yet settled within the framework of an institutionalised process of shared intentional activity. In any case, *de facto* immigrants entering the EC raise an embryonic *de jure* claim as interested parties to the world market. Notice the inverted symmetry, which disrupts Walzer's pat opposition between right and fact: in the same way that there is a *de facto* core to a polity's *de jure* claim concerning its boundaries, boundary crossings by *de facto* immigrants also intimate a *de jure* claim to another way of apportioning to each their own place. To the extent that so-called 'economic' immigrants open up a possible path from proto-political to political reflexivity, they illustrate one of the central insights espoused by both Fitzpatrick and Zapata Barrero in their contributions to this volume: the immigrant as *founder* of political community.[38]

Crucially, the commonality the European polity claims for its boundaries already includes a reference to the world in which, together with other polities, it claims a place for itself: in the same movement by which a founding closure separates inside from outside, preferring the former to the latter, it includes both places within a more encompassing spatial unity (e.g. the world market), which is itself preferred to an indeterminate outside. The founding act of the European polity not only separates inside from outside but also posits the world as intersubjectively constituted. In this way, the subject-relatedness of the legal world in which the EU emplaces itself is not merely the expression of subjectivity, in the sense of arbitrariness, but also involves the claim to a standard of objectivity or justice of which it is not the sole custodian. Here, then, is the reason why immigration poses a *political* problem for a theory of distributive justice: although distributive acts take place from the first-person person plural perspective of a spatially bounded 'we', acts that decide on the legality or illegality of boundary crossings by immigrants can only claim to be just to the extent that they posit the preferential distinction between inside and outside in a way that safeguards the commonality of the world in which the European polity claims to take its place.

This insight has a number of institutional implications, some of which I would like to briefly sketch out. Most generally, acknowledging the political character of border crossings by immigrants, in particular so-called 'economic' immigrants, requires creating mechanisms that account for their interest in how the EU structures the internal market and its relation

[37] I develop this idea at further length in my article, 'In Between: Immigration, Distributive Justice, and Political Dialogue', forthcoming in *Contemporary Political Theory* (2009).

[38] For a related discussion of responsiveness see Peter Fitzpatrick's and Ricard Zapata-Barrero's and Peter Fitzpatrick's contributions to this volume (chs 1 and 5).

to the external market. At stake, then, is devising venues of institutional participation of and accountability to those whom the EU, on its own terms, views as members of the proto-political community in which it participates. This insight supports Kostakopoulou's view that there are strong democratic reasons, and not merely reasons derived from the rule of law, for a constitutional anchoring of principles of immigration policy.[39] I would add that this institutional transformation would need to go hand in hand with a substantive transformation. Indeed, the EU would also need to explicitly acknowledge that its immigration policy is inextricably bound up with its economic and commercial policy, hence that mechanisms of participation and accountability concerning immigration policy should be embedded in the institutional process of designing, enacting, and enforcing economic and commercial policy. It is significant, in this respect, that, according to Article 131 ECT, '[b]y establishing a customs union among themselves Member States aim to contribute, in the common interest, to the harmonious development of world trade, the progressive abolishment of restrictions on international trade and the lowering of customs barriers.' In the light of the foregoing analysis, the 'common interest' to which Article 131 refers is not merely the common interest of the European polity in isolation from the rest of the world; it is an enlarged sense of commonality that encompasses the proto-political community in which the EU emplaces itself. A key component of a more just European immigration policy would be, therefore, mechanisms of participation by and accountability to would-be immigrants regarding the European economic and commercial policies that articulate this enlarged common interest.

VII. IMMIGRATION POLICY AS A WAGER

These institutional considerations call forth a fundamental question: how is distributive justice possible when immigration contests the commonality of the boundaries of the polity and of the world in which it takes up its place? Rather than trying to undo, downplay, or belie the circularity that founds a community's self-closure, we must resolutely embrace it, transforming it into the touchstone of an alternative theory of the relation between immigration and distributive justice. This requires that we introduce a problem I have hitherto kept in reserve: time. Although it was asserted that *suum cuique locum* is paired to *suum cuique tempus*, a more precise formulation of this coupling is required. In effect, the aforementioned circularity attests to what might be called the 'paradox of representation': an act can only *originate* a

[39] See D Kostakopoulou, 'The Area of Freedom, Security and Justice and the Political Morality of Immigration and Integration' (ch 8) in this volume, and Kostakopoulou, 'Is there an Alternative to "Schengenland"?' (1998) 46 *Political Studies* 886–902 especially 896 ff.

community by *representing* an original community. To found a community, an act must *re*-found it, which means that the community is never directly present to itself; it must always be represented. This paradox holds, on the one hand, for the first-person plural perspective: there is no "we" in the absence of an act that seizes the political initiative to say who belongs to a collective and what goal or interest joins them together; but this act only succeeds in creating a community if 'we' retroactively identify ourselves as the individuals that had founded a political community. It holds, on the other, for legal space: an act can only inaugurate a community, closing it into a legal space, by representing a prior closure to which it has no direct access.[40]

This paradox ruins the simple opposition between an inaugural closure and subsequent acts that enforce the boundaries of a polity. If the founding closure claims to enforce and maintain boundaries that had been drawn earlier, acts that enforce and maintain boundaries always found anew the spatial unity of a polity and of the world in which a polity takes up its place—even when confirming extant boundaries. If the paradox of representation requires that distributive acts justify the qualification of a boundary crossing as legal or illegal by deriving that qualification from a prior closure, it also requires of these acts that they decide what *counts* as legal or illegal immigration, retroactively determining how the boundaries separating inside from outside had joined both the polity and what was excluded therefrom into an encompassing world. In response to an embryonic de jure claim by de facto immigrants, a distributive act can seize the initiative to redefine the boundaries of the collective, such that this de facto act retrospectively can be viewed as having been de jure. To be sure, the interaction between boundary crossings and the acts that qualify them is irreducible to the automatism of, say, 'stimulus and response'. An integral part of establishing what counts as a legal or illegal boundary crossing is determining which crossings trespass boundaries and which transgress them by calling into question the distinction between inside and outside. Immigration policy is *responsive* in a strong sense of the term, for 'that to which it responds occurs only in responding to it'.[41]

I would add that the responsiveness of immigration policy—or, as Fitzpatrick nicely puts it, the 'responsability' of law[42]—involves a political judgment about past and future that takes issue in a decisive aspect with Ricœur's discussion of collective identity. I mentioned in Section V that, according to Ricœur, the first-person perspective involves two forms of

[40] I explore the ontological implications of the paradox of representation in 'Constituent Power and Reflexive Identity: Towards an Ontology of Collective Selfhood' in Martin Loughlin and Neil Walker (eds), *The Paradox of Constitutionalism* (Oxford, Oxford University Press, 2007) 9–24.

[41] B Waldenfels, *Antwortregister* (Frankfurt, Suhrkamp, 1994) 266.

[42] P Fitzpatrick, *Modernism and the Grounds of Law* (Cambridge, Cambridge University Press, 2001) 76.

identity. *Idem*-identity, as illustrated by 'character', concerns what remains the same over time in the form of 'character'.[43] While *ipse*-identity also denotes a form of permanence in time, the example of promises makes clear that self-identity is irreducible to what remains the same over time in the form of 'character'. In effect, 'keeping one's promise ... appear[s] to stand as a challenge to time, a denial of change: even if my desire were to change, even if I were to change my opinion or my inclination, "I will hold firm"'.[44] Although Ricœur develops this idea with respect to personal identity, it also holds for the identity of a collective self. Indeed, Hannah Arendt, whose writings Ricœur no doubt had in mind, notes that 'the power generated when people gather together and "act in concert" ... is the force of mutual promise'. And she adds that the mutual promise between the members of a polity has the power to stabilise time, not because those who promise share 'an identical will which somehow magically inspires them all', but by virtue of 'an agreed purpose for which alone the promises are valid and binding'.[45] On this reading, boundaries are binding over time to the extent that political self-closure is the expression of a mutual promise.

This insight, although crucial, must be amended. For the linear temporality suggested by the notion of a promise that is first made and then kept is belied by the paradoxical temporality of political judgment. For the task of political judgment is to anticipate the meaning of the past in the future: *immigration policy has to decide what promises had been made in the light of boundary crossings that determine what promises can be kept.* As such, political judgment dislocates the simple progression of a temporal arc that begins in the past and that, passing through the present, leads into the future. To be sure, the fact that political judgment anticipates the past in the future does not mean that the past is simply at its disposition. For the past would cease to be such if it were under the control of acts that redefine its meaning as they see fit. By the same token, promises would cease to be promises unless they could be kept or broken. I submit that the political judgment deployed in immigration policy has the structure of a *wager:* it involves a reasoned initiative concerning the commonality of boundaries in the face of a past and a future that elude the collective's control.

Accordingly, the spatiality of distributive justice is rooted in *time*, in the paradoxical temporality of representation. On the one hand, there could be no distributive justice unless the exercise of political judgment in immigration

[43] Notice that it is precisely this notion of identity to which Walzer alludes when referring to polities as 'communities of character' (see Section II above).

[44] Ricœur, *Oneself as Another*, above n 25, at 124.

[45] H Arendt, *The Human Condition* (Chicago, Chicago University Press, 1958) 244–5. Identity, defined as the permanence of a collective self in time, figures discretely in Bratman's references to the 'commitment to the joint activity', and prominently in Pettit's discussion of the consistency or coherence of collective judgments over time. See Bratman, *Faces of Intention*, above n 25, at 95, and Pettit, *A Theory of Freedom*, above n 25, at 111 ff.

policy were able to *breach* the promise that had been made, by founding anew the distinction between inside and outside in response to boundary crossings that challenge the place a collective claims for itself in a larger world. This breach is *a-topic*, by dint of being neither inside nor outside the collective, and *a-chronic* because it interrupts the temporal arc spanning the past, present, and future of a collective. Not a 'dialectic of self and the other than self',[46] but rather a moment of non-identity—a suspension of collective selfhood as holding firm in time—is a necessary condition for distributive justice. On the other, there could be no distributive justice unless the breach can be viewed retrospectively as having *kept* the promise made at the foundation of a polity, as the renewal of a closure that not only separated inside from outside but also assured the community of its own place within the world it deemed common.

VIII. TWO THRESHOLDS OF DISTRIBUTIVE JUSTICE

It is becoming increasingly clear what happens when political judgment does not break promises in order to keep them. One example is Mitsilegas's analysis of the paradox of borders, whereby external controls, put in place to stave off illegal immigration, mutate into general surveillance mechanisms that encompass both aliens and European citizens.[47] A second example concerns the threshold situation confronting so-called *de facto* immigrants. For if the *de facto* immigrant attests to a first threshold of distributive justice, which I called 'proto-political reflexivity', s/he now also embodies a second threshold thereof, which might be dubbed 'post-reflexive politics'. The conditions under which asylum seekers are held at Italy's Lampedusa Airport Zone CPTA illustrate what this concretely means. According to the Italian government, CPTAs (*Centri di Permanenza Temporanea e Assistenza*) are

> the instrument selected to enable the provisions for the repatriation of aliens who have entered Italy illegally to be carried out more effectively ... they are also one of the key means of ensuring the effective functioning of expulsion procedures which ... is a pre-condition for the correct implementation of an immigration policy based on annual quotas.[48]

It is not Amnesty International's reports of allegations of 'physical assault by law enforcement officers' and other personnel of the centres, not the 'excessive and abusive administration of sedative and tranquilizing drugs', not the

[46] Ricœur, *Oneself as Another*, above n 26, at 3.
[47] See V Mitsilegas's contribution to this volume (ch 2).
[48] Cited in the Amnesty International Report, 'Italy. Temporary Stay—Permanent Rights: The treatment of foreign nationals detained in "temporary stay and assistance centres" (CPTAs)', at www.amnesty.org/en/library/asset/EUR30/004/2005/en/dom-EUR300042005en.pdf, (accessed on September 8, 2009).

'unhygienic living conditions', not the 'unsatisfactory medical care' and the like that are most fundamentally at stake in Lampedusa or other CPTAs, however horrific all of this may be. What is essential from the perspective of political reflexivity is the status of the immigrants who 'stay' at the Centre, such that expulsion can be a pre-condition for immigration policy. In this respect, Amnesty International has expressed serious reservations about the *detention* of immigrants in CPTAs, arguing that such detention is disproportionate in the face of international standards. The Italian government has countered this critique by saying that immigrants are 'held' (*trattenuti*), rather than detained, at the Lampedusa CPTA. The distinction is crucial, albeit in a way different to that intended by the Italian government. To qualify an immigrant as a detainee is to recognise that s/he is misplaced, thus that, although illegally, s/he has entered a legal space. Entry to the European legal space is precisely what the holding centre at Lampedusa is designed to avoid. Indeed, Lampedusa confronts the EC with the following paradox: the founding self-closure calls forth the possibility, held in suspense until the circumstances so require, of enforcing the borders of the polity by *dis*-owning part of Europe. This 'dis-owning' amounts to a suspension of political reflexivity as a condition for sustaining the first-person plural perspective of a 'we' as a bounded political community. This twofold movement is what makes of 'land dis-owning' a form of 'post-reflexive politics'.[49]

That distributive justice is spatially bounded means that it poses two thresholds for immigration policy. The first marks the point prior to which an immigrant is deemed to have a stake in the political 'we', hence a person who has, in one way or another, a *de jure* interest in the distribution of rights and goods by the community. This is the threshold at which the distinction between the just and the unjust begins to take hold—*proto-political reflexivity*. The second threshold marks the point beyond which claims by immigrants cease to register as claims that call for distributive acts by legal officials because they are uttered in a place that, stripped of its normative dimension with respect to immigration, has reverted to the status of a non-place that is neither inside nor outside a polity. At this point, the distinction between the just and the unjust has been obliterated—*post-reflexive politics*. These non-places, in which the immigrant finally becomes a thoroughly *de facto* immigrant, are also the non-places in which a community ceases to claim a *right* to closure, such that its founding closure becomes nothing more than a de facto act—an act of violence.

[49] By introducing this term, I am suggesting that a more complete analysis of the structure of the state of exception would need to deal with the problem of political reflexivity, a problem that obtains little or no attention in either Schmitt or Agamben. See C Schmitt, *Political Theology: Four Chapters on the Concept of Sovereignty*, trans G Schwab (Cambridge MA, The MIT Press, 1985 [1922]), and G Agamben, *State of Exception*, trans K Attell (Chicago, Chicago University Press, 2005).

7

Migrants, Humans and Human Rights: The Right to Move as the Right to Stay

BERT VAN ROERMUND

I. INTRODUCTION

CONTEMPORARY HUMAN RIGHTS discourse has it that we should attribute freedom of movement to 'migrants' as a generic set, and differentiate it according to the needs of its specific subsets: refugees, internally-displaced persons, economic fortune-seekers, nomadic tribes, academic cosmopolitans, and so on. I will argue that this discourse obscures some important features of freedom of movement as a *human* right by neutralising its political sting. First, it ignores that human rights are conceptually rooted in a first person singular point of view, that is as rights of the *individual* self. Secondly, it leaves out the fact that human rights, in order to be fully conceptualised, have to trade-in this first person singular viewpoint for a first person *plural* viewpoint. Thirdly, and as a consequence of both premises, it misses out on the *ambiguities* that come with this transformation, and that have to be sorted out in politics. Taking my cue from Arendt's diagnosis that, when it comes to human rights, 'the people, and not the individual, [is] the image of man',[1] I will detail this with regard to the actors, the authors, the representatives and the beneficiaries of the right to free movement. In the last section I will explore some normative consequences of these ideas. Throughout this chapter my claim is not that the conceptual framework of human rights with regard to free movement should be abolished, but that it should be used with much greater awareness of the political implications it brings about, and of the strategic opportunities it creates. Human rights are not 'good' by definition; rather, they are a transmission belt between good and evil that can move in either direction.

[1] Cf H Arendt, *The Origins of Totalitarianism*, New edition with added prefaces (New York, Harcourt Brace Jovanovich, 1973 [1951]) 291.

II. MIGRANTS AS A CATEGORY

A. A Growing Awareness?

In recent years a line of discourse on the right to freedom of movement seems to have emerged that is usually welcomed as a symptom of maturing politico-legal awareness, even progress. The story is this. The 1948 Universal Declaration of Human Rights was still very much rooted in the context of sovereign national states and their citizens. Article 13 proclaims that '1. Everyone has the right to freedom of movement and residence within the borders of each State. 2. Everyone has the right to leave any country, including his own, and to return to his country'. A similar passage can be found in Article 12 of the International Covenant of Civil and Political Rights (1966).[2] At the threshold of the twenty-first century, in 1999, the United Nations Human Rights Committee, acting under the same Covenant, offered a robust defence of the right to free movement. It is now able to refer to freedom of movement as a human right promulgated in a broad range of instruments of international law.[3] In Resolution 1999/44, the Committee decided to appoint[4] a Special Rapporteur on the rights of migrants, whose mandate is to 'examine ways and means to overcome the obstacles existing to the full and effective protection of the human rights of migrants, including obstacles and difficulties for the return of migrants who are undocumented or in an irregular situation'.

The wording of this mandate suggests that important things have changed with regard to the conceptualisation of the right to free movement. First, the terms of the relation have changed. Freedom of movement is now seen, at least ideally, as a relationship between an individual migrant or a group of individual migrants, on the one hand, and *a* state, not necessarily one's own, on the other. As a consequence, this individual is qualified as a migrant rather than as a citizen. Secondly, the conceptual scope of the right has widened. It is no longer only a negative freedom to render individuals independent from state intervention with regard to their residence, and comings and goings. It now also features as a positive freedom by which

[2] The European Convention on Human Rights does not grant a right of immigration into and residence for non-nationals in the territory of a state Party. Obviously, the exercise of immigration control should be in compliance with Convention standards, and there are quite a number of cases brought before the Strasbourg Court on whether the refusal to admit or the expulsion of a non-national violates certain Convention rights (mostly in view of the right to family life (Art 8 ECHR)), or on the conditions and modes of detention in cases of illegal entry, preparation of extradition, etc.

[3] See, amongst others, the Universal Declaration of Human Rights (UDHR), 10 December 1948 and the International Covenant on Economic, Social and Cultural Rights, 16 December 1966.

[4] Extended for a further three years by Resolution 2005/47.

humans can explore the ways in which they want to live their lives: 'Liberty of movement is an indispensable condition for the free development of the person'.[5]

The Office of the High Commissioner for Human Rights is still very much concerned with the pressing circumstances under which people decide 'to migrate', namely to flee from violence, oppression or poverty.[6] On the continuum between the poles of 'moving under coercion' and 'moving from choice', the High Commission views the phenomenon of migration primarily in terms of the first pole. A brief look at some relevant websites, informs us, however, that other voices tend to focus on migration primarily from the perspective of the second pole, treating migrants as a category that captures various groups of people 'on the move'. For instance, the website of the Human Rights Education Associates[7] carries the following statement:

> Who does the freedom of movement affect? This inalienable right to liberty extends to all citizens of the world. While it may seem that this right is meant to apply to immigrants, refugees and asylum seekers, it also has major ramifications concerning internally displaced persons and additionally economic migrants or even students.

Apparently, it does not occur to the authors of these lofty phrases that 'the world' neither has citizens nor attributes rights. In a similar vein, a feature article on the website of the Migration Policy Institute[8] highlights the importance of addressing migrants as 'people on the move'—neither more nor less:

> Despite the incidence of abuse, migrants' rights have remained on the margins of the international human rights agenda for several reasons. These include a lack of data; gaps between different institutional mandates; parallel systems for protecting employment rights and human rights; relatively little reporting by human rights NGOs; the dominance of refugee protection in the migration field; and the fact that, until the ICMW was drafted, human rights law only made explicit reference to migrants—as non-nationals—in the context of free movement.

Further on, the author notes:

> The ... invisibility of migrants in human rights discussion was reinforced by the way in which human rights law was written: the core treaties were drafted as rules

[5] CCPR/C/Rev 1/ Add 9, General Comment No 27 on Freedom of Movement, 2 November 1999, under para 1.

[6] *cf* High Level Dialogue on International Migration and Development, New York, 1415 September 2006, document *Migration and Development: a Human Rights Approach*, para III 19: 'The Cairo Conference identified the following factors: *(I)nternational economic imbalances, poverty and environmental degradation, combined with the absence of peace and security, human rights violations and the varying degrees of development of judicial and democratic institutions*'. (The reference is to Cairo Conference Programme of Action 1994, para 10.1).

[7] *cf* www.hrea.org/learn/guides/freedom-of-movement.html (p 1 of 8).

[8] *cf* S Grant, 'Migrants' Human Rights: From the Margins to the Mainstream'. www.migrationinformationsource.org/Feature/display.cfm?id=291.

> of universal application which do not name migrants as a specific group or make explicit provision for the protection of non-citizens except in relation to the right to leave and return to one's own country.[9]

And there is more. The right to free movement adopts a distinctly holistic ring, as it becomes a metonymy for a whole range of rights, thus encompassing—like the soul in Antiquity—'in a way everything'.[10] Human rights websites list a considerable number of rights that migrants should have, now that they are no longer cast into the mould of the refugee.[11] There is the right to education, the right to adequate housing and the right to own property, the right to family life (and providing them with means of subsistence), the right to self-employment and wage earning, the right to health (facilities and conditions), not to speak of the basic civil and political rights of free speech, access to justice and corporeal integrity. By the way, it is not uncommon to see the other rights I discussed (health, free speech) expanding in similar ways.[12] These rights, too, are said to arguably entail the right to education, freedom of movement, freedom of religion, access to justice *e tutti quanti*. Increasingly, *any* human right seems to usher in *all* human rights, at least potentially. From this metonymical switch some infer that our awareness of human rights is growing, and that growing respect for human rights is bound to follow.

Ignoring these non sequiturs and summarising the main issues, there is obviously no point in denying that the conceptual framework of freedom of movement has changed drastically over the last 50 years on at least three counts:

1. While both the Declaration and the Covenant regarded the right to free movement and residence as a negative liberty of citizens over and against their states, today we acknowledge this right as flowing from the positive liberty of individuals to use their capabilities;
2. National states are drawn into processes of re-ordering themselves in overlapping polities on both infra- and supra-national scales, sometimes begging, sometimes answering the question who is to attribute the right to free movement in the new constellations;
3. Human individuals rather than citizens emerge as subjects of free movement, and of every other human right that follows in its wake.

[9] *Ibid.*

[10] *cf* Aristotle, *De Anima*, 431 b 21.

[11] General Comment No 27, referred to in take (2), points to similar intertwinements, though with far less emphasis, as it says that liberty of movement interacts with several other rights enshrined in the Covenant [ie ICCPR], as is often shown in the Committee's practice in considering reports from States parties and communications from individuals.'

[12] See www.academic.udayton.edu/health/07HumanRights/health.htm—a website set up by Professor Vernellia R Randall.

That is to say, the standard view holds that we have made progress, as freedom of movement should be re-defined in a post-national context with regard to its content, sources and addressees.

Let me briefly comment on the development just described and cast some doubt on its received assessment. We will find sufficient reason to interpret our gains differently, to include a considerable amount of losses, and to start thinking again about freedom of movement as a human right.

B. Some Doubts

What happens when we treat migrants as a generic category? The rhetoric in the texts of the human rights websites quoted above is peculiar. They complain that the paradigm of the refugee has become too predominant in developing 'the rights of migrants', and that even the concept of 'freedom of movement' is too restrictive when it comes to understanding the situation of migrants. They mention students as typically a category of migrants falling outside the scope of the refugee paradigm: people who are moving around in the humanist tradition of academic cosmopolitanism, ignoring political borders in a pursuit of wisdom all mankind will profit from. Thus, they not only point to a problem of categorisation ('students are not a species of the genus refugees'). They also, and more importantly, suggest an alternative paradigm ('refugees are a species of the genus students'), superior in illustrating what freedom of movement is ultimately about, namely the full development of the individual person.

Adopting this paradigm shift would have dramatic consequences. It would turn migration from a political problem into a neutral phenomenon. There would be lighter and darker sides to it and we would say that these would need to be 'balanced' against each other. We would arrange all sorts of trade-offs between policies, all of which are feasible in the name of human rights but equally evasive with regard to the problem at hand. We would admit, of course, that people from state S would not ask for asylum in state T if they did not fear persecution or oppression in S. But we would agree that T would deal adequately with the rights of these asylum seekers by picking any of the following options: granting them asylum, invading S, paying for refugee relief operations in the region, or hiring them as cheap labour force, all depending on the political constellation at hand in T. But these neutralisations are not neutral; they are invariably initiated and sustained by those who already find themselves at the pole of choice rather than of coercion when it comes to migration. Instead of triggering strategies of restorative justice to the benefit of individuals lacking freedom, this paradigm shift transforms freedom of movement into just another public good that has to be dealt with in the pursuit of distributive justice.

The usual criticism has it that Article 13 of the Universal Declaration no longer identifies the right referent to warrant freedom of movement, now that the national state is withering away. What has gone largely unnoticed, however, is that the mode of reference has changed: with the national state disappearing from the scene, one seems to have lost the possibility of referring to a polity as 'one's own' by appealing to what can be called a first person viewpoint. Even though the wording of the first paragraph of Article 13 refers to 'each state', it is quite clear that what it means is freedom of movement and freedom to choose residence within the borders of *one's own* state. When the second paragraph states that 'everyone has the right to leave any country, including his own, and to return to his country', it is again obvious that it emphasises the right to leave the country one finds *oneself* in, and to return to *one's own*. This first person viewpoint seems to be lost in speaking about 'migrants'. Indeed, there are no migrants from a first person point of view. There are only *im*-migrants and *e*-migrants: people leaving 'the' country and people entering 'the' country—people coming (from outside the country) and people going (from inside the country). Note, also, that the distinction between inside and outside is always made from the inside as the preferred term of the relation; that is from an internal point of view.[13]

Practical experience in migration law only underlines the doubts just mentioned with regard to the relevance of a spectator's point of view. While international human rights law recognises the right to leave *one's* country, there is no corresponding right to enter *another* country, not even for a refugee, without that state's permission; nor is there any duty on the part of the state of destination to give that permission. It comes as no surprise, then, that the Human Rights Commission in its 1999 General Comment returns to the first person viewpoint in the effort to broaden the meaning of 'his own country':

> The scope of 'his own country' is broader than the concept 'country of his nationality'. It is not limited to nationality in the formal sense, that is, nationality acquired at birth or by conferral; it embraces, at the very least, an individual who, because of his or her special ties to or claims in relation to a given country, cannot be considered to be a mere alien.[14]

The point is well taken. What the Commission has in mind are, for instance, nationals of a country that does not recognise their 'original'

[13] *cf* B Waldenfels, *Antwortregister* (Frankfurt aM, Suhrkamp, 1994) 202ff on difference between terms made from the preferred viewpoint of one of the terms. For a related discussion of the inside/outside distinction see also Bernhard Waldenfels's contribution to this volume (ch 4).

[14] CCPR/C/Rev1/ Add 9, General Comment No 27 on Freedom of Movement, 2 November 1999, under para 20.

national background, stateless persons arbitrarily deprived of the right to acquire nationality in the country of their long-term residence, visitors with a double or triple nationality who want to return to their country of permanent residence, and so on. But from a more theoretical perspective one may well ask what this pre-condition of 'not being a mere alien' means.[15] In any case it is easy to see that the positive equivalent of 'not being alien' should be something like 'being of *one's own* kind'.[16] But which agent (if not a state) will acknowledge this kinship or membership so that it matters? This strongly suggests that even in the post-national constellation the membership issue remains crucial in human rights discourse. Thus, introducing a third person viewpoint, from which one may observe people migrating across states as if they were some species of birds, obscures the problem. The right to that kind of free movement cannot be ascribed to humans in any relevant way, as they never find themselves at that higher vantage point. Unless they identify themselves as nomads, they don't want to move; they want to settle. Their problem is that in order to settle they have to move (which, by the way, also applies to nomadism). In plain terms, they want to get *in* or they want to get *out*.

III. WHAT IS HUMAN ABOUT THE RIGHT TO FREE MOVEMENT?

These comments suffice to show that when it comes to the right to free movement there are more questions to be asked than the usual ones of legal practice: how to expand and how to restrain free movement? One may also see that these other questions are not automatically in the realm of morality; that is, the realm of assessing what is good or bad with respect to such expansions and restrictions. The primary question concerns the conceptual framework governing our thinking about the right of free movement as a

[15] HK Lindahl, 'Finding a Place for Freedom, Security and Justice: the EU's Claim to Territorial Unity (2004) 29 *European Law Review* 461–84.

[16] One is reminded of Hannah Arendt (Arendt, above n 1; with reference to Burke): 'The conception of human rights, based upon the assumed existence of a human being as such, broke down at the very moment when those who professed to believe in it were for the first time confronted with people who had indeed lost all other qualities and specific relationships—except that they were still human. The world found nothing sacred in the abstract nakedness of being human'. The context of Arendt's critical observation is that, apparently, it requires the nation state to get rights attributed, not only as the authority assigning them, but first and foremost as the whole that is determinative of the membership issue. One gets one's rights on the basis of membership in a nation, ie, more specifically, on the basis of a public realm already constituted, a realm where one has permission to appear after being properly trimmed according to the image of a human that this public sphere requires.

human right. I would like to make three points here: (A) the right to free movement can only be understood from a first person singular point of view, (B) which is linked up with the relationship between man and earth, (C) which can only be attributed in the political setting of a first person plural (a polity).

A. Human Rights and the First Person

Human rights, not just the right to free movement but *all* human rights, are irreducibly 'selfish' in a practical vein. I do not mean that they are rooted in an egoistic attitude or that they are exercised without due regard to others. I abuse the predicate 'selfish' to draw attention to the fact that they inevitably involve attribution of first person-singular references to one's self. Moreover, as is common in normative discourse, the first person position is typically determined by the parameters of agency rather than observation. An agent typically considers the question of practical thinking, 'What am I to do in the situation at hand?' rather than the question of theoretical thinking, 'What is the case in the world around me?' In asking this question the agent considers herself, that is views herself as an *object* of thinking, but precisely in her quality as the 'would-be' agent of a practical thought content, that is as a *subject*. As said, this referential structure is part and parcel of all human rights.

To illustrate this point, let me draw the parallel between freedom of movement and some other rights. Take the right to health, as distinct from the right to all sorts of conditions, facilities and services that are allegedly instrumental to 'health'.[17] Notwithstanding the importance of a just distribution of these scarce means, and notwithstanding the objective conditions that allow an organism to reproduce a threshold value of vital functions, health is primarily about how an individual relates to these functions in constituting a self. Health has to do with an individual's identity over time. She may construe this identity within a time-frame that stretches beyond either the beginning or the end of these vital functions. For instance, people with severe physical impediments have sued their parents for the tort of procreating them. They construe the life they have to live as wrongful from the moment of conception; that is before they were even born.[18] Socrates, in that most dramatic of scenes in the *Phaedo*, show us that, groping for

[17] Some authors think that the right to health should be reformulated as a 'right to health services' before we can give any theoretical account of it. *cf*, on a critical note, JP Ruger, 'Towards a Theory of a Right to Health: Capability and Incompletely Theorized Agreements' (2006) 18 *Yale Journal of Law and the Humanities* 273–326.

[18] In some jurisdictions, that is. France, for instance, has forbidden these actions by legislation.

self-hood, individuals are even able to transcend their own death and see it as a passage to health.[19] In both cases, it is reflexive rather than deictic reference that governs identity.[20] Similarly, freedom of expression is about *my* opinion, or rather about an opinion being *mine*. The right to express my opinion is crucially different from the (copy-) right to have it replicated and sold. Similarly, even the right not to be tortured is crucially 'selfish'. As we see in Orwell's *1984*, 'torture' is a predicate that cannot be applied without taking the first person point of view into account. Big Brother is able to torture people because he (that is, the system) keeps track of what frightens each and every individual person most (rats, in Winston Smith's case). It's *my* fear that is decisive of what amounts to torture, and this is exactly what is humiliating about it. The fact that *most* people fear pain does not alter that.[21]

Now if one observes (with Hannah Arendt) that freedom of movement is a right that one has as a citizen of a state, rather than as a human being, this should not necessarily be taken as a critique of nationalism, even if it was precisely that at the time of Arendt's writing. It primarily expresses the fact that claiming a human right depends on articulating selfhood, that is on being able to identify a polity as 'one's own', whatever form the polity and whatever form the reference may take.

B. Freedom of Movement as the Right to Land

Let us look once more at the wording of Article 13 UDHR. As said, reflexive references in the case of free movement are coloured not only by the phrase 'one's own state' but also by 'one's own country'. The word 'country' emerges with regard to residing, leaving and returning, as such. The word 'state' is used with regard to the permission to do these things. Apparently, what freedom of movement is about pertains to a *country* I can call 'mine', rather than a state. But it is not obvious in what sense a country could be 'mine', apart from my being authorised by a state to reside in, leave from, and return to it. The Human Rights Committee tried

[19] Socrates considered dying as cure from a disease: 'Crito, we owe a rooster to Aesclepius'. Plato, 'Phaido' in *Plato Werke in acht Bänden, Griechisch und Deutsch, Bd III*, 3, unveränd. Aufl, D Kurz (ed) (Darmstadt, Wissenschaftliche Buchgesellschaft, 1990) 118a.

[20] I use these rather technical terms in the following way. Suppose I am stopped at the border and asked: Who are you? Then I show my passport (*deixis*; from the Greek *deiknumi*) in order to prove who I happen to be. Now suppose that I am asked by my psychiatrist; Who are you? Then I tell a story about how I see *myself* (reflexively) over time in a more or less coherent picture (or fail to come up with one). A story about myself will not help me to cross the border, my passport will not help me to get rid of my multiple personality syndrome.

[21] Obviously, if this were all there is to say we would never be able to protest against torture in general. So I will return to this point, in due course.

to say something about it in terms of 'nationality', as we saw above. But this predicate is easily misunderstood as the gateway to nationalism. A more adequate understanding may be gained if we follow Arendt in her efforts to capture what she calls 'natality'—the condition of being born in the sense of making a new beginning; that is of living one's life as if it were new. 'Natality' has two sides to it, one of which illuminates, I submit, man's relation to 'country', or even more specifically, to 'land'. 'Whatever enters the human world of its own accord *or* is drawn into it by human effort becomes part of the human condition', Arendt says.[22] The two parts of this disjunction are conceptually linked to each other. They are not two alternative modes of what Arendt calls 'the human condition'; on the contrary, they mutually condition each other in constituting the human condition. Humans do not make new beginnings from nothing. They are able to act only if and when they re-engage the world they find themselves already a part of.[23] In slightly different words: One cannot be born without being borne; borne in various ways and for a considerable amount of time. Pressing Arendt a bit further on this point, I submit that there is a 'gegonic'[24] side to natality, and that life becomes impossible without it in a very basic sense indeed. The polis that is literally forced to live without land—the refugee camp, the township, the unofficial city of Um-el-Fahem in the Galilee Triangle—smells the same all over the world: it smells of humans rotting slowly.[25]

The phrase 'my country' refers to this 'gegonic' side of natality. It bears out the fact that my being 'takes place'. My country in this specific sense is the place that is part of my identity to the extent that I can

[22] Emphasis added. '[A]ction has the closest connection with the human condition of natality; the new beginning inherent in birth can make itself felt in the world only because the newcomer possesses the capacity of beginning something anew, that is, of acting. In this sense of initiative, an element of action, and therefore of natality, is inherent in all human activities. Moreover, since action is the political activity par excellence, natality, and not mortality, may be the central category of political, as distinguished from metaphysical, thought'. H Arendt, *The Human Condition* (Chicago, University of Chicago Press, 1958) 9.

[23] *cf* M Merleau-Ponty's '*j'en suis*' in M Merleau-Ponty, *Le Visible et l'Invisible*, Suivi de notes de travail. Texte établi par Claude Lefort, accompagné d'un avertissement en d'une postface (Paris, Gallimard, 1964) 178; 181 and *passim*.

[24] *cf* Plato, 'Politeia—Der Staat' in *Plato Werke in acht Bänden, Griechisch und Deutsch, Bd IV* 2, unveränd. Aufl, D Kurz (ed) (Darmstadt, Wissenschaftliche Buchgesellschaft, 1990) 414d-e, where Socrates is hesitant to share the view that the narrative underlying the polis should be that we are all '*gègenei*', ie born from the earth as *gè*. From which arises a duty of care for the earth as *chora*, ie the land. I am indebted to my Tilburg colleague, David Janssens, for bringing the richness of the terms in Plato's *Politeia* to my attention.

[25] Um El-Fahem was a village (now a densely populated town) transferred to Israel under the Rhodes Agreement with Jordan (4 April 1949). The State of Israel had promised in those agreements to honour the freedom and the property of the inhabitants. Nevertheless, all the inhabitants of Um El-Fahem became 'absent-present', and almost all their lands were confiscated. When I visited the place in 1993, there was no place for agriculture, garbage dump, sewage purification, etc. The troubles in 1998 were about more land confiscations by Israel.

acknowledge it as the place *from* where *I* enter the world, that is, the place where I was born/borne. It is without borders as far as I am concerned. There is, thus, an important sense in which I relate to a country as 'mine' by virtue of it being 'my land'—land as the sum-total of the conditions of my being in a permanent metabolism (as Marx would say[26]) with the world around me. It certainly includes the mere continuation of biological functions or the satisfaction of vital needs that happen to be mine. But it also goes beyond that. It conditions *self*-preservation rather than subsistence. Indeed, to some extent one's country is like one's skin, only thicker: the 'interface' between what is surrounded and surrounding. It is part of my inside rather than my outside. Prior to becoming a *kosmos*, the earth is *gè* for each of us. In that way, a country is not 'my land' in the trivial sense of some place that I, like others, can identify by a set of co-ordinates or other definite descriptions. As long as we do not understand this, and do not take it into account in our politico-legal institutions, we will continue to ignore—to our detriment, no doubt—the passions raised by land issues.[27]

The initial, reflexive mode of the right to free movement should therefore be interpreted, paradoxically enough, as a right *to stay* rather than to move, namely to stay rooted in a nursing and nourishing environment that 'land' or (more broadly) 'country' stands for in a paradigmatic way. Hence, the cosmopolitan academic is not the right role-model for freedom of movement. For the academic, 'shifting grounds' is certainly an enriching and nourishing experience. But these *ex*-plorations presuppose a 'homeland' from which one may set forth to other regions, and to which one can always return. It is an utterly romantic idea to suggest that every individual is keen on being an explorer. For most people, freedom of movement is a right they would prefer not to exercise, as it alludes to a very different role-model: the model of the vulnerable vagrant rather than the self-assured savant. I will come back to this in the section on representatives. Let me just say, at this stage, that I am not advocating *Blut und Boden* ideology.

[26] 'Die Natur ist der *unorganische Leib* des Menschen, nämlich die Natur, soweit sie nicht selbst menschlicher Körper ist. Der Mensch *lebt* von der Natur, heißt: Die Natur ist sein *Leib*, mit dem er in beständigen Prozeß bleiben muß, um nicht zu sterben. Daß das physische und geistige Leben des Menschen mit der Natur zusammenhängt, hat keinen anderen Sinn, als daß die Natur mit sich selbst zusammenhängt, denn der Mensch ist ein Teil der Natur'. K Marx, 'Zur Kritik der Nationalökonomie—ökonomisch-philosophische Manuskripte' in H-J Lieber and P Furth (eds), *Karl Marx Frühe Schriften, Bd I* (Darmstadt, Wissenschaftliche Buchgesellschaft, 1971 [1844]) 506–665 at 566. [Nature is the non-organic body of man, to wit nature in so far as it is not human body itself. 'Man *lives* from nature' means: nature is his body, with which he has to stay intertwined in order not to die. That the physical and psychic life of man is linked up with nature only means that nature is linked up with itself, for man is part of nature. (*My trans*, BvR)]

[27] Note that often enough reconciliation after political oppression is predicated on 'the land issue'.

To the contrary, one has to understand which truth it exploits if one wishes to remain critical of such an ideology.[28]

C. From the First Person Singular to the First Person Plural

That human rights are reflexive in the sense described above draws them into ambiguous perspectives. These ambiguities arise because the first person *singular* viewpoint inherent in human rights cannot be deployed conceptually without seeking recourse to a first person *plural* viewpoint. I have to summarise an argument here which I have presented in more detail elsewhere.[29] The core of it is this. A person in search of herself has reasons to frame her identity by putting its consecutive versions to the test of what is most certainly not herself, that is, to what is irreducibly 'other' than herself or, indeed, alien. The most powerful reason for putting myself to the test of 'the other' is probably that it is the best strategy for self-preservation.[30] It is not just that I have to take the other into account in order to successfully pursue my acts of will.[31] The point is that my volitions will remain volatile and self-destructive as long as I do not make an effort to learn what I *really* need, or want, or aspire to, in the first place. Making this effort presupposes that I refrain, as much as I can afford to, from defining the world beforehand as a function of my needs and beliefs. I have to give the other its due, a fortiori if this other is the Other par excellence, who not only resists but downright opposes my definition of the world—another 'I'. Thus, being drawn into the realm of otherness raises the problem of justice in its primordial form. For 'to give (every instance of) the other her or his due' is a canonical formula of justice.

Now, suppose that 'giving'[32] in this context has the minimal sense of re-allocating something scarce. In effect, providing someone with something

[28] Hans Haacke made the point very well in a reply to Martin Warnke, who had criticised his installation in the Reichstag of the sculpture 'Der Bevölkerung', for reminding the people of '*Blut und Boden*' ideology: 'that one should not grant a second victory to National Socialism by granting it semantic sovereignty on the matter 'earth'". ('dass man dem Nationalsozialismus nicht einen zweiten Sieg feiern lassen dürfe, indem man ihm die Bedeutungshoheit über das Material Erde überliesse'.) *cf* H Haacke, 'Der Bevölkerung: Ein Faxinterview von Astrid Wege mit Hans Haacke' (April 2000) in (2002) 10 *Texte zur Kunst* 38–49 (accessed through www.bundestag.de/bau_kunst/kunst/kuenstler/haacke/derbevoelkerung/projekt/interview01.html on 6 December 2008).

[29] See B van Roermund, *Themis' terzijde. Omtrekken van rechtsfilosofie* (Nijmegen, Ars Aequi Libri, 1990) ch 2.

[30] On the intricacies of self-preservation, *cf* HK Lindahl, *Welfare and Enlightenment. An Enquiry into the Rational Foundations of the Welfare State* (Leuven, Leuven University Press, 1995) 155ff. Here I only aim at subsistence.

[31] *cf* R Bacon's 'Nonnisi obedienda natura vincitur' [Nature is only to be conquered by obeying it. (*My translation*, BvR)]

[32] Also in the sense of 'recognition' (*Anerkennung*).

abundantly available is not considered to be 'giving'. Then, precisely because it is a formula that should be fleshed out from a first person singular perspective, 'giving the other her or his due' can only yield directives for action if and when it is cast in the mould of a first person plural: the question of acknowledging otherness becomes the question how *we* are going to deal with what is due to *each of us*. Thus, hiding deep inside the principle of justice, '*suum cuique tribuere*', prior even to its dovetailing into distributive and corrective justice, is a first person plural. No agent could ever claim to distribute or attribute to everyone her or his due, and thus no one would ever acknowledge receiving it, unless he imagines himself to be included in a set of co-agents (call them subjects, citizens, constituents, neighbours, fellowmen or contracting parties) who, in turn, include themselves in the same set as him.[33] In order to distribute the relative scarcity of living conditions favourable for human flourishing, we have to know how many we are. And if the answer is that we cannot count because there are no borders, distribution becomes random. From the agents' point of view, some set of properties should constrain[34] the formal quantor 'everyone', so that they can establish the circle of those among whom distribution or compensation is going to take place. Only then can one proceed to determine what is 'due' to everyone, to determine, in particular, what is equal to what and how it should be treated. To the extent, then, that administering *justice* requires setting, acknowledging and defending the boundaries of a domain of 'agents involved', or 'co-agents', generating a body politic is part and parcel of its very principle.[35]

IV. AMBIGUITIES IN MIGRATION LAW[36]

A. The Actors and the Authors of Freedom of Movement

Ambiguity emerges with this affirmation of the body politic. No sooner are we ready to acknowledge its pertinence and accept the discourse of *commonwealth*, *public* interest, *national* security and their ilk, than we find ourselves pushed back into what this public sphere calls the private sphere.

[33] The parable of the Good Samaritan (Luke ch 10, v 25ff) is the *locus classicus*: before you can live according to the law, you have to answer the question: who is my neighbour?

[34] This is not to say that the properties cannot be taken for granted, revisited and revised.

[35] For a related discussion of the principle of justice and the first person plural see Hans Lindahl's contribution to this volume (ch 6).

[36] The model that is in the background of the following section is a formal account of legislation [LEX], which harbours four logically different places for the first person plural to emerge. However, my argument will be largely independent of these intricacies. For those who are interested in [LEX], see B van Roermund, 'First person Plural Legislature: Political Reflexivity and Representation' (2003) 6 *Philosophical Explorations* 3, 235–50.

The private sphere is ambiguous as it consists, on the one hand, of the leftovers of the public sphere, while, on the other, it remains the breeding place of disorderly elements from which the public sphere has to emerge, if it is to exist at all. Here, once again, Arendt's warning is apposite:

> Since the Greeks, we have known that highly developed political life breeds a deep-rooted suspicion of this private sphere, a deep resentment against the disturbing miracle contained in the fact that each of us is made as he is—single, unique, unchangeable. This whole sphere of the merely given, relegated to private life in civilized society, is a permanent threat to the public sphere, because the public sphere is based on the law of universal difference and differentiation. Equality, in contrast to all that is involved in mere existence, is not given us, but is the result of human organization insofar as it is guided by the principle of justice. We are not born equal; we become equal as members of a group on the strength of our decision to guarantee ourselves mutually equal rights.[37]

It is difficult to overestimate the disturbing relevance of these observations. Contrary to what one might think, Arendt's claim is precisely that mutuality cannot be primordial when it comes to law and politics. Whatever the importance of the principle of mutuality in explaining what is today called 'shared intentional action',[38] it always comes too late. Like social contract theory in general, it ignores the bases on which the terms of these reciprocal relationships are selected. Indeed, there is a problem at the very heart of reciprocity: prior to reciprocal acknowledgement, a decision has already been taken concerning who is to be involved in the set of individuals between whom reciprocity will reign. And, by necessity, this decision cannot be taken reciprocally, without seriously begging the question.

So, the gist of Arendt's critical observation is that, apparently, a pre-reciprocal account of the polity[39] is required to respond to the membership issue. In effect, one gets one's rights on the basis of membership in a polity, or more accurately, from a public realm already constituted. Thus one gets them on the conditions of that realm as already established. One is invited to appear in that realm, provided that one is trimmed in accordance with the image of a human being that this public sphere requires. The typical parameters of the 'national' public sphere are just one example, but nothing in the 'logic' of the polity changes when these parameters are replaced by others. This is why Arendt can say that, since the French Revolution, it has become gradually clear 'that the people, and not the individual, was the image of man'.[40] Note that the term 'people' has to be

[37] Arendt, above n 1, at 301.

[38] ME Bratman, *Faces of Intention. Selected Essays on Intention and Agency* (Cambridge, Cambridge University Press, 1999) 1515.

[39] Arendt would say 'the nation state'. But not much depends on that.

[40] *cf* Arendt, above n 1, at 291. Further on in the text (*ibid*, 299), Arendt makes it clear that even if one expands 'the people' to 'mankind', the problems return: 'For it is quite

taken here as a name (rather than a predicate), that is as a dummy for a first person plural position, a 'we' or—slightly more precisely—the plural 'self' of this 'we'.

This pre-reciprocal composition of a plural self is decisive for restricting, furthering, qualifying, conditioning, and so on, immigration and emigration.[41] As Spijkerboer[42] has shown on the basis of extensive empirical research in the Dutch context, the set of shared values that compose a collective identity within the constraints of a specific political situation is reflected in the parameters of what a state counts as a 'credible' story of a refugee without documents, or what circumstances it finds 'pressing' for 'humanitarian' reasons. It allows this state to say, in point of fact, that some humans are more human than others. It is the ground for making a distinction between refugees and fortune-hunters, often politely rephrased as that between political and economic refugees or 'migrants'. Last but not least, it marks the gap between welcome (well-educated) and unwelcome (poorly educated) immigrants.

But let us make no mistake. Arendt's analysis does not imply an immediate moral appeal to downplay everything that has to do with the public realm. It does not prompt us to reverse the charges and turn things around in the name of an alternative right-wrong distinction. Arendt's account remains deeply 'agonistic'.[43] What it shows, as said, is the ambiguity of the public realm, but only after it has acknowledged its necessity. Moral appeals can make sense only within this ambiguous framework. Human rights are the positive counterpart of the insight that the public sphere cannot articulate its own ambiguity or opacity. This is why human rights are rooted in the same sphere which they are supposed to protect people from: the political sphere. It does not make them 'nonsense upon stilts', as Bentham would have it;[44] it makes them part and parcel of that form of politics that acknowledges, on its own account, that something must be allowed to count against a specific polis. That is to say, it makes them part

conceivable, and even within the realm of practical political possibilities, that one fine day a highly organized and mechanized humanity will conclude quite democratically—namely by majority decision—that for humanity as a whole it would be better to liquidate certain parts thereof'.

[41] *cf* the crime of *Republikflucht* in the former DDR or the former Albania.

[42] T Spijkerboer, *Gender and Refugee Status* (Nijmegen, Gerard Noodt Instituut, 1999) and 'Asielbeleid bevestigt ons zelfbeeld', *De Volkskrant*, 16 oktober 1999.

[43] For an incisive analysis of Arendt's conception of politics see HK Lindahl, 'Give and Take. Arendt and the Nomos of Political Community' (2006) 32 *Philosophy and Social Criticism* 881–901. The phrase 'agonistic' democracy is proposed by in C Mouffe, 'Deliberative democracy or agonistic pluralism?' (1999) 66 *Social Research* 745–58. See also A Schaap, *Political Reconciliation* (London/New York, Routledge, 2005).

[44] *cf* J Bentham, 'Rights, Representation, and Reform: Nonsense Upon Stilts and Other Writings on the French Revolution' (1795) in P Schofield, C Pease-Watkin and C Blamires (eds), *The Collected Works of Jeremy Bentham* (Oxford, Clarendon Press, 2002).

and parcel of law. By claiming freedom of movement we assert that, in the final analysis, it should not be left to the state to decide whether or not there is a country I can call 'mine'.

B. Spokesmen and Beneficiaries

I would now like to detail how the ambiguities of the plural self spill over into two other directions: its representatives and its beneficiaries, and how that again affects human rights discourse, in particular with regard to freedom of movement. Let me take beneficiaries first. As Arendt reminds us,[45] the *demos* in Modernity is not only the reflexive form of those who rule,[46] it is also the set of those who are supposed to profit from their *own* ruling. Although this may seem pretty obvious, it is in fact a separate conceptual turn, marking a separate mode of the act of self-inclusion, for the simple reason that agents do not by necessity act in their own interest. Since interests are mixtures of needs and desires, and since agents (collective agents included) have limited insight into what they really need and want, their ruling themselves does not logically entail that they will rule in their own interests. This is why we have to add this dimension of the political self in an analysis of democratic law-making (be it in legislation, administration or adjudication): the people rule themselves *in their own (that is, common) interests*. Indeed, it is part and parcel of a democracy that nothing is considered to be right apart from the common good.

But this tenet is precisely the source of further ambiguities, as Arendt reveals. If law is exhausted by this notion of the common good, one has to admit that good is what is good for the people, good for (an) 'us', even if this 'us' is 'as large as mankind itself'.[47] And Arendt adds (half a decade after the end of the Second World War):

> Hitler's motto that 'Right is what is good for the German people'[48] is only the vulgarized form of a conception of law which can be found everywhere and which in practice will remain ineffectual only so long as older traditions that are still effective in the constitutions prevent this.[49]

[45] Arendt, above n 1, at 299.

[46] Let alone the common referent of 'the people who rule' and 'the people who are ruled', as if democracy would settle for these two being 'the same' (*idem*) from some third-person point of view. The core point is, rather, that the people rule themselves (*ipse*). (See Van Roermund, 'First person Plural Legislature: Political Reflexivity and Representation' (2003) 6 *Philosophical Explorations* 3, 235–50).

[47] Arendt, above n 1.

[48] Recht ist was dem deutschen Volke nützt [*my addition*, BvR].

[49] Arendt, above n 1.

The central ambiguity is this: on the one hand, within a society there is no appeal to justice that would override the common good. Indeed, what could be more just than what is good for 'all of us'? Justice is what is good for all of us in our social relationships. But, on the other hand, that is exactly the problem for those who are not within that society, for instance those who are involved in the processes of im-migration or e-migration. They either do not count yet, or don't count anymore. In either case they will not be regarded as belonging to the beneficiaries of democratic law-making. If law really boiled down to nothing other than the common good, it would basically boil down to an economy of values, that is, of more or less shared preferences. If we believe that to be a dangerous bet, we will have to concede that democracy is not able to cater to everything law stands for. In other words, if human rights are part of the rule of law, this is not by dint of democracy. This certainly deepens the ambiguity of human rights: on the one hand, we cannot escape from defining them as 'good for us'; but, on the other hand, if we do, we will never be farther away from justice as a *norm*. Or, to put it the other way round, democracy is more inclusive, and *therefore* more exclusive, than any other political system. Its main advantage seems to be that boundaries can be changed more quickly.

Another layer of ambiguity concerns the representation of the *demos* as the plural self of the 'we'. There is no *we* that is able to say 'we', as Waldenfels (following Benveniste) observes.[50] The 'we' is always said by spokesmen and mouth-pieces; that is, by representatives. Or again, with Rousseau, we may ask not only how the people will know what they really want, but also how they will speak with one voice.[51] Thus, the voice of the 'we' heard in democratic law-making is construed by virtue of their representative actions. It does not precede these. A fortiori, the self of that 'we'—the *demos* said to govern itself—remains absent from the scene where it is construed. It will never be present, in spite of the fact that its presence has to be made felt if the presentation is to succeed as re-presentation. In this respect 'the people', as Rosanvallon wrote, will remain '*introuvable*'.[52]

As an abstract neutrum between emigrants and immigrants, the predicate 'migrants' is particularly apt to frustrate any attempt to be convincing as far as representation of the *demos* is concerned. Reflecting a third person viewpoint beyond the first person idiolect of in-clusion and ex-clusion, migrants do not register on the radar of a polity other than as free-movers. They are nowhere in political space and they 'evaporate into the eternity of a now

[50] B Waldenfels, *Verfremdung der Moderne. Phänomenologische Grenzgänge* (Göttingen, Wallstein Verlag, 2001) 139–40.

[51] J-J Rousseau, *Du contract social; ou principes du droit politique* (Paris, Gallimard, 1964 [1762]) vol I, ch 7.

[52] Cf P Rosanvallon, *Le peuple introuvable. Histoire de la représentation démocratique en France* (Paris, Gallimard, 1998).

without a future'.[53] To acknowledge their 'right' to free movement makes no sense, in terms of representational practices. It is as if we would ascribe the right to walk on two feet to those who are defined by walking on two feet. Or, to revert to a discussion that took place during the last decades of the *Ancien Régime*: it makes no sense to ban migrants from the polity because the life of a migrant is a voluntary ban. From the perspective of political representatives, it is the connotation of migrants' 'indifference' to the polity inherent in their being 'passers-by' which makes them unfit to be represented. It therefore does not increase one's credibility as a politician to claim that one is representing them. They have the status that Rousseau, in the chapter on civil religion,[54] ascribes to the migrants par excellence: the Christians. As migrants on earth, always on their way to a somewhere and a sometime beyond the polity, they are profoundly unreliable. They embody anti-patriotism,[55] indeed they embody anti-*Verfassungspatriotismus* (*pace* Habermas). Oh yes, many a political representative will note, they make good mercenaries, because they are indifferent to the question for whom they fight as long as they can earn a living.[56] Basically they are the ones who a priori withdraw from the social contract, first because they cannot be expected to deliver according to the economic precondition of the social contract (appearing at the market place where everything will be shared), and secondly because they cannot be judged by the rules that will give form and content to the social contract.[57]

In closing this section, let me add a caveat pertaining to the whole of it: I was not stating my view on how migrants ought to be regarded. I was explaining some consequences of an ambiguous logic of political representation in a democracy under the rule of law—a logic to which migrants fall victim. If this logic is not perceived—and leftist political parties especially tend to ignore it—then all one has to offer to migrants is one's moral indignation. That, I think, is an immoral attitude in times of reviving political nationalism and economic protectionism.

V. TOWARDS SOME NORMATIVE ANCHOR-POINTS

Where do we find some normative anchor-points amidst this four-fold ambiguity in freedom of movement: ambiguities with regard to its agents,

[53] F Tanghe, *Sociale grondrechten tussen armoede en mensenrechten. Deel I: Van de middeleeuwen tot de Franse Revolutie. Deel II: Recht op leven* (Antwerpen, Kluwer rechtswetenschappen, 1998) 294.

[54] *cf* Rousseau, above n 51, vol IV, ch 9.

[55] Tanghe, above n 53, Deel II, 290.

[56] Tanghe observes (*ibid*, 287) that for centuries, army, vagrancy and mercenaries have been communicating vessels.

[57] Under the *Ancien Régime*, a major problem was that one could never establish whether a crime committed by a migrant was a second offence. *cf* Tanghe, above n 53, Deel II, 316 fn 8.

its authors, its advocates and its beneficiaries? To answer the question it is common to call on moral theory and wage a battle between the good of morality and the evil of politics. Let me try to steer away from this philosophical Manicheism, and keep to the track followed thus far: an analysis of the political stage on which freedom of movement has to perform. I would like to demonstrate that the logic of 'the political' has to be developed a few steps further in order to perceive the possibilities opened up by the public realm, such that we can mitigate its verdicts, despite their pertinence. I will venture that freedom of movement has an important role to play in bringing these possibilities into sight. In other words, I will show that the plural self of the public realm leaves some conceptual gaps that can be used for countervailing tactics.

An appropriate starting point would be a largely ignored footnote in Rousseau's *Du contrat social*, where he quotes the Marquis d'Argenson:[58] 'the convergence between two private interests is formed only in virtue of their opposition to a third'. Rousseau comments by adding that the convergence of all interests will be formed by their opposition to that of each. 'If there were no divergent interests, one would not notice the common interest as it would not encounter any obstacle: everything would go on of its own accord and politics would cease to be a craft'.[59] Rousseau emphasises that divergence between interests needs to be shown and articulated before converging steps can be taken. His gloss intimates the conceptual gap at the heart of his own model: that 'the disclosure of commonness depends on plurality'.[60] He seems to suggest, paradoxically, that refusing to play the reciprocity card too quickly is, in the end, a pre-condition of the reciprocity that the social contract seeks to establish. Though he could not accommodate this intuition in his model, perhaps this is why human rights make sense. Human rights format the refusal to swallow reciprocity as a point of departure for power to be legitimate. That is why, from their inception, they have taken the form of privileges, that is, of rights snatched away from the law before duties could be linked up with them. This makes their conceptual place less 'co-original' with public autonomy than Habermas (or even Lefort) submits.[61]

[58] Cf Rousseau, above n 51, vol II, ch 3.

[59] [*My translation*, BvR]. With due apologies for being picky when it comes to translations of the *Social Contract*. The point being here, that 'divergent interests' is definitely better than 'different interests', which is used in most official English translations of the text.

[60] *cf* A Schaap, *Political Reconciliation* (London, Routledge, 2005) 83, which leads us to Arendt's famous phrase that plurality is the keyword of politics. See H Arendt, *Was ist Politik? Fragmente aus dem Nachlass*, U Ludz (ed), Vorwort K Sontheimer (München/Zürich, Piper, 2003 [1993]) 9.

[61] *cf* J Habermas, 'On the Internal Relation between the Rule of Law and Democracy' in J Habermas, *The Inclusion of the Other* trans C Cronin and P de Greiff (Cambridge, MA, The MIT Press, 1998) 253–64, C Lefort, *L'invention democratique. Les limites de la domination totalitaire* (Paris, Fayard, 1981) 45–86 ('Droits de l'homme et politique'); C Lefort, *Essais sur le politique (XIXe–XXe siècles)* (Paris, Du Seuil, 1986) 31–58 ('Les droits de l'homme et l'état providence').

I propose to see freedom of movement as the legally warranted opportunity to literally run away from forms of reciprocity by which one feels politically excluded. The criterion of 'having land' in the paradigmatic sense explained above will be decisive here. In many cases there will be no 'land' because oppression continues, or continues with reversed charges (when former victims become oppressors and vice versa). In other cases it will be because after oppression the trauma cannot be healed, or resources are not redistributed, or criminality takes over from oppression. But whatever the specific case may be, sometimes the only possibility a person has to refuse what is, for her, forced or false reciprocity is to turn her back on it and run. Making use of this right does not necessarily imply that the refugee is 'good' or 'worthy of respect'. Some migrants have reason to flee from the domination of a new regime, because they were protagonists or beneficiaries of the old one. Being the antipode of the sovereign, the refugee has nothing to show, other than the singularity of her existence—which is what Arendt meant when she wrote that human rights mean nothing if the only quality one can appeal to is one's humanness. The problem is not only that humanness just does not register. The problem is also that, in a sense, humanness is not *supposed* to register, namely in so far as it expresses the singularity of every form of existence we call 'human'. As soon as it registers, general categories and common frameworks take over. Of course this is what the refugee hopes for; otherwise, she will not enter a new country. But she cannot appeal to it. When we talk of freedom of movement as a human right, this possibility is what we aim to protect. Therefore, I propose that the refugee remain our paradigm throughout when we conceive of freedom of movement as a human right.

But although we do not have reason to change our paradigm of the migrant we do have reason to change our paradigm of oppression, so as to undercut the idea that only oppression by the use of violence counts. Oppression can be defined as a sequel to Weber's definition of power. According to Weber, power is the chance to pursue one's will notwithstanding resistance, on whatever basis this chance may rest. Oppression, I propose, is the exercise of power squared: it is the chance of pursuing one's efforts to destroy resistance to power, whatever way they may take. One will appreciate that there are more subtle and more efficient ways to increase this chance than the use of violence, in particular in the sphere of the economy, and that they are increasingly dependent on access to technology. Humans should be able to appeal to freedom of movement whenever they feel victim to such efforts of domination. This is, once more, what their right to stay, that is, their right to 'land', entails.

What we could also do is to reorganise the ways in which states can exercise discretion to address migration as a legal problem rather than a natural phenomenon. Conceding that they have the right to draw the distinction between refugees and 'fortune-seekers', one could agree on other parameters to draw it, for instance by ranking emigration-generating states on a scale of economic growth. People have better reasons to leave countries involved in a race to the bottom than those which are booming, even if on average their standards of living are comparable. One could also agree on differentiated percentages of GDP that receiving 'rich' countries should spend annually on the admission of refugees, with G8-countries as first compliers. The more refugees a rich country has to take in yearly, the more reason it has to fight the causes of the refugee fluxes, in particular, poverty.

Although the WTO may be an increasingly important forum to decide on these strategies in the future, it should not be regarded as the only possible or even the privileged one. Where effects are global, initiatives can often be local. It seems more important to judge strategies on their merits in terms of the equal opportunities parameter. The neutral term 'migration' is often used to evade this parameter. For instance, we are led to believe that free movement of people can be mutually beneficial to both migrant-sending and migrant-receiving countries, provided that labour flows are effectively managed. One points to the liberalisation of visa policies by receiving countries, advocating that at the same time high-skilled and/or low-skilled labour capacity in (low-income) sending countries should be mobilised by development aid. The idea is that migration management will ultimately enhance employment and income opportunities for migrants and non-migrants alike in sending countries. It is also expected to diminish labour-market tensions in high-income, industrialised countries. The extension of the provisions governing freedom of movement of people may thus result in a win-win game for poorer sending countries, as well as for richer receiving countries. This is an example of a strategy that should be judged critically on the basis of the above. While it may well be implemented as an effective instrument, its merits very much depend on how it takes into account what I called 'the land issue' and everything the latter stands for. If freedom of movement merely amounts to global permission to 'follow money', instead of the freedom to re-create one's existence from the place where one is born(e), migration management will soon turn out to be the newest fashion in colonialism.

Similar things can be said with regard to the plea that we should consider migration policies and trade policies jointly. Here it is often argued that migration and trade are complements rather than substitutes. Not only does the management of migration flows require some form of multilateral regulation, but multilateral agreements need to encompass all flows if the full developmental benefits of trade liberalisation in goods and services are to be realised, and if the commitment to greater policy coherence for development is to be implemented. Migration is only one of these. This is of course true, and it may be a good idea to make use of these obvious interrelationships. But here again, if there is no recognition of the crucial point that 'development' is about redistribution of resources in the name of equality of opportunities, are we not just promoting neo-colonialism and preparing the ground for more failed WTO rounds and more stalled multilateral negotiations on trade?[62]

[62] I owe thanks to Hans Lindahl, Neil Walker, David Janssens and Nanda Oudejans for their comments on an earlier version of this text. I would also like to thank Mrs Phyllis Lewis for correcting many linguistic errors.

III

Politico-Legal Alternatives

8

The Area of Freedom, Security and Justice and the Political Morality of Migration and Integration

DORA KOSTAKOPOULOU

I. INTRODUCTION

NOTWITHSTANDING THE UNCERTAINTY surrounding the process of ratification of the Treaty of Lisbon, and the echo of the Constitutional Treaty and constitutional debates,[1] the European Council adopted the European Pact on Immigration and Asylum in Brussels on 16 October 2008. In this, European leaders undertake to implement five political commitments, thereby laying down the foundations of a common European migration and asylum policy. Although the rationale of the Pact is to institutionalise a better—in the sense of more efficient—management of (selective) migration, it reflects the legacy of 'Schengenland' and the prevailing definition of migration as a security threat and a problem. There exists little reflection on the connections between principled policies and practices in the domain, robust democracy and harmonious community relations and healthy civil societies, and the much broader socio-economic and political canvas that the Commission has sought to paint over the last five years is missing. In this chapter, I review the institutional development of justice and home affairs co-operation in the European Union (EU) and the evolving doctrine of migration control. I argue that the paradigm of the securitisation of migration is tired and unlikely to be beneficial in the short or long term. I seek to make the case for rethinking migration and integration at the EU and national levels and for the articulation of a principled and non-restrictive migration paradigm which promotes peoples' engagement in co-operative practices, embraces the idea of open and relaxed communities, provides

[1] On the importance of constitutional symbolism, see N Walker, *After the Constitutional Moment* (2003) Federal Trust Online Constitutional Essay.

opportunities and promotes inclusion. Although liberal democratic theory by and large accommodates restrictive migration policies and upholds states' sovereign power to exclude, I argue that democracy works best if it is accompanied not only by flexible membership[2] and a constructive model of citizenship,[3] but also by porous boundaries and a more liberal migration policy.[4]

By the latter, I do not mean one which simply complies with international law norms by admitting all those having rights of admission under bilateral agreements concluded by the Member States and third states, or by the Community and third states. Nor do I mean simply a liberal migration policy which includes refraining from introducing arbitrary distinctions, respecting the right to family life, defending the humanitarian admission of displaced persons and refugees as an integral part of constitutional traditions and democratic political cultures, or providing a system of effective appeal remedies and procedural safeguards against arbitrary expulsions. For such norms are deeply embedded in international law and national constitutional traditions—notwithstanding the Member States' deficient implementation records. What is more difficult to establish is how the vast majority of applicants who have no prima facie right to be admitted into a country because they do not belong in any of the above categories should be treated.

I argue that the EU and European polities have a positive obligation to design a liberal migration policy and to refrain from imposing hurdles on their entry, residence, settlement and, eventually, naturalisation by imposing integration tests. This duty arises not out of a universal right to migration nor from concerns about distributive justice[5] nor even charity. They have a duty to admit out of concern about the 'costs of restriction', that is, about the profound effects that closure and the present law-enforcement migration regime have upon admission applicants, the principles on which they profess to be based, and upon the identity of European citizens. After all, admission and belonging are issues relating to 'what kind of polity we wish to have' and 'who we choose to become'—not simple correlatives of the state's power to exclude. In this sense, migration and integration confront the EU with questions of what I will call political morality.

[2] R Rubio-Marin, *Immigration as a Democratic Challenge* (Cambridge, Cambridge University Press, 2000).

[3] T Kostakopoulou, 'Towards a theory of Constructive Citizenship in Europe' (1996) 4 *Journal of Political Philosophy* 337–58.

[4] The argument here draws on ch 6 of my book, *Citizenship, Identity and Immigration in the EU: Between Past and Future* (Manchester, Manchester University Press, 2001).

[5] For an excellent discussion on this, see V Bader, 'The Ethics of Immigration' (2005) 12 *Constellations* 331–61.

II. MIGRATION AND INTEGRATION WITHIN THE INSTITUTIONAL ARCHITECTURE OF THE AREA OF FREEDOM, SECURITY AND JUSTICE

Justice and Home Affairs, which is now known as the Area of Freedom, Security and Justice (AFSJ), has developed in an incremental, and not always predictable, way. Ad hoc and loose intergovernmental co-operation in order to tackle terrorism, drug trafficking and organised crime in the 1970s precipitated a more advanced intergovernmental co-operation in the mid-1980s which culminated in the Schengen project. France, Germany and the Benelux countries signed the Schengen agreement on the abolition of border controls in 1985 and agreed its implementing measures in 1990. These included an external frontiers policy, the harmonisation of visa policies, common rules on asylum and migration-related issues, forms of operational co-operation by police and customs authorities and the establishment of a central information database which would allow national law-enforcement officers to obtain, and to exchange, data on people and stolen objects. The Treaty on European Union (in force in November 1993) brought nine areas of justice and home affairs co-operation, including rules on the crossing of external borders, asylum, migration and the policy regarding nationals of third countries, within the Community's formal structure, by designing a separate intergovernmental pillar (the so-called third pillar). Participation in such a framework of 'diluted' intergovernmentalism prompted national executives to reflect upon larger contexts and transnational challenges—be they terrorism, drugs trafficking, international crime and human mobility—to interrogate the doctrine of sovereignty, to learn to trust each other and to search for improved institutional arrangements. Consequently, they agreed to the partial Communitarisation of the third pillar at the 1996 Intergovernmental Conference, that is, to the transfer of migration related issues and judicial civil cooperation from the third pillar into the EC Treaty.[6]

At Amsterdam, justice and home affairs co-operation was also replaced by the notion of 'an area of freedom, security and justice'. This is defined as an area 'in which the free movement of persons is assured in conjunction with appropriate measures with respect to external border controls, asylum, immigration and the prevention and combating of crime'. Article 29 of the Treaty on European Union (TEU) further elaborates on this objective by stating that the Union's objective is to provide citizens with a high level of safety within an area of freedom, security and justice by developing common action among the Member States in the fields of police and judicial co-operation in criminal matters and by preventing and combating racism and xenophobia. This objective is to be achieved by preventing and combating crime, organised or otherwise, in particular terrorism, trafficking in

[6] The Amsterdam Treaty entered into force on 1 May 1999.

persons and offences against children, illicit drug trafficking and illicit arms trafficking, corruption and fraud.

The association of the concept of freedom with security and justice was neither accidental nor purely conjunctive. Since the 1980s, official discourses had constructed a chain of equivalence between the single market project, free movement of persons and security—thereby creating the assumption that a security problem exists in a Europe without internal border controls—which was well-embedded within policy circles.[7] The area of freedom, security and justice reflected the securitisation ethos[8] that characterised justice and home affairs co-operation since the 1970s and gave police and customs agencies the opportunity to craft a new role for themselves within an enlarged Europe, by identifying specific categories of security risk.[9] As the Council and the Commission's Action Plan on how best to implement these provisions of the Amsterdam Treaty stated,[10]

> [f]reedom loses much of its meaning if it cannot be enjoyed in a secure environment and with the full backing of a system of justice in which all Union citizens and residents can have confidence. These three inseparable concepts have one common denominator—people—and one cannot be achieved in full without the other two. Maintaining the right balance between them must be the guiding thread for Union action. It should be noted in this context that the treaty instituting the European Communities (article 61 ex article 73I a), makes a direct link between measures establishing freedom of movement of persons and the specific measures seeking to combat and prevent crime (article 31 e EU), thus creating a conditional link between the two areas.

Although the 'freedom, security and justice' configuration creates the impression that 'security' and 'justice' are mere complements to 'freedom', in reality the triad led to important transmutations of meaning. First,

[7] S Lavenex, 'The Europeanisation of Refugee Policies: Normative Challenges and Institutional Legacies' (2002) 39 *Journal of Common Market Studies* 851; P Boeles, 'Introduction: Freedom, Security and Justice for All' in E Guild and C Harlow (eds), *Implementing Amsterdam: Immigration and Asylum Rights in EC Law* (Oxford, Hart Publishing, 2001); A Geddes, *Immigration and European Integration: Towards Fortress Europe* (Manchester, Manchester University Press, 2000).

[8] The term securitisation refers to the removal of an issue from the normal political arena and to its articulation as an issue of national security and/or as an existential threat justifying measures outside the normal bounds of political procedure. On this, see B Buzan, O Weaver and J de Wilde, *Security. A New Framework for Analysis* (London/Boulder CO, Lynne Rienner, 1998); O Waever, Securitisation and Desecuritisation, Working Paper 5/1993, Centre for Peace and Conflict Research. Also published in Lipschutz (ed), *On Security* (New York, Columbia University Press, 1995). When the agenda is dominated by security concerns, then the range of policy options becomes quite narrow.

[9] Risk analysis found a clear expression in the Presidency conclusions of the Seville European Council in June 2002. On this, and on the subsequent project on Common Integrated Risk Analysis model (CIRAM), see E Guild, *The Legal Elements of a European Identity; EU Citizenship and Migration Law* (The Hague, Kluwer Law International, 2004) 179.

[10] European Council and European Commission, *Action Plan on how best to implement the provisions of the Treaty of Amsterdam establishing an area of freedom, security and justice*, 12 July 2008 at 1–2.

security obtained an individual dimension: Union citizens were seen to be vulnerable to threats and should be protected from risk, danger, anxiety or fear. Secondly the meaning of freedom widened. It was no longer associated with free mobility, but it took on the meaning of freedom from fear, violence and deception. And although the Action Plan referred to the maintenance of the right balance between the two, in reality security was promoted at the expense of freedom.[11] As Mrs Anita Gradin, former Commissioner, stated,

> liberty signifies a lot more than freedom of movement. It also implies the right to live in a society which takes effective action against those who place themselves above the law. The concept of Europe therefore requires that all MS have confidence in each other's ability to deal with serious organised crime.[12]

A value-laden hierarchy was thus created, whereby security was seen to be a prerequisite of free movement.[13] But as Huysmans has argued,

> security policy is not simply a practice of protecting and/or limiting a pre-given freedom. It is a governmental practice that translates the abstract notion of freedom into a concrete practice through shaping and moulding practical modalities of the legitimate and optimal conduct of freedom within a society.[14]

The primacy and centrality attributed to security signalled not only the sedimentation of the securitisation ethos in discourse and policy, but also the framing of security as the condition of possibility for freedom of movement and liberty, in general.

Previously, competing organisational actors, such as the Council and the Commission, jointly took part in the institutional dynamics of shaping a new form of political order in post-Amsterdam Europe. The area of freedom, security and justice aims at creating a European public space in which citizens feel that 'a proper sense of "European Public Order" has taken shape and is actually visible today in their daily lives'.[15] In December 1998, the Vienna European Council adopted the 'Action Plan on how best to implement the provisions of the Treaty of Amsterdam on an area of freedom, security and

[11] H Lindahl has explored the constitutive relation between security and freedom in 'Finding a Place for Freedom, Security and Justice: The European Union's Claim to Territorial Unity' (2004) 29 *European Law Review* 461–84. Compare also his article on 'Give and take: Arendt and the nomos of political community' (2006) 32 *Philosophy and Social Criticism* 881–901.

[12] *Liberty, Security and Justice: an Agenda for Europe*, PE168.396, 14–15.

[13] On this, see J Huysmans, 'Security! What do you Mean? From Concept to thick Signifier' (1998) 4 *European Journal of International Relations* 226; J Huysmans, 'The European Union and the Securitisation of Migration' (2002) 38 *Journal of Common Market Studies* 751; D Kostakopoulou, The 'Protective Union: Change and Continuity in Migration Law and Policy in Post-Amsterdam Europe' (2000) 38 *Journal of Common Market Studies* 497; D Bigo, 'Criminalisation of "Migrants": the Side Effect of the Will to Control the Frontiers and the Sovereign Illusion' in B Bogusz, R Cholewinski, A Cygan and E Szyszczak (eds), *Irregular Migration and Human Rights: Theoretical, European and International Perspectives* (Leiden, Martinus Nijhoff, 2004).

[14] J Huysmans, *Security and* Freedom, Paper presented at the UACES Workshop on the Evolving European Migration Law and Policy, University of Manchester (2002).

[15] Working Group X, Freedom, Security and Justice Final Report WD 18 REV.

justice', which entailed a list of measures which had to be adopted within a time-frame of two years and five years, respectively.[16] These included the adoption of a European migration strategy based on the reduction of migration pressure at the source, the combatting of undocumented migration and the control of legal entry of people.

The Tampere European Council (15 and 16 October 1999) diluted the restrictive character of the above objectives and set out a number of policy orientations and priorities which would make the AFSJ a reality. A scoreboard was set up to monitor progress towards its implementation. The common priorities were: a) partnership with the countries of origin; b) a common European asylum policy; c) the fair treatment of third-country nationals (TCNs); and d) the fair management of migration flows.[17] The fair treatment of resident TCNs entailed a vigorous integration policy and the grant of rights and obligations comparable to those of EU citizens. Perhaps the most visible manifestations of the influence exerted by the rights-based template of integration advanced at Tampere were the Commission's proposed directives on family reunification (1999) and on the status of long-term resident third country nationals (2001), respectively. The former Directive[18] was based on Article 63(3)(a) EC and sought to harmonise national legislation in this area by granting the right to family reunification to all third country nationals—including refugees under the Geneva Convention of 1951 and persons enjoying temporary protection who reside lawfully in a Member State and hold a residence permit for at least a year regardless of the purpose of their residence. It also covered Union citizens who had not exercised their right to free movement whose situation has hitherto been subject solely to national rules. The draft Directive on the status of third-country nationals who are long-term residents was based on Articles 63(3)(a) and 63(4) EC and was designed to harmonise national laws governing the conditions for the acquisition and the scope of long-term resident status, and to grant long-term resident third country nationals the right of residence in the other Member States.[19]

Both draft Directives mirrored the regime pertaining to mobile Community nationals and, predictably, failed to meet the Member States' approval. The Netherlands, Denmark, Austria and Germany insisted on uploading

[16] *Action Plan of the Council and the Commission on how best to implement the provisions of the Treaty of Amsterdam on an area of freedom, security and justice* [1999] OJ C19/1.

[17] Tampere Presidency Conclusions, European Council 15–16 October 1999, SN 200/99 Brussels.

[18] European Commission, *Proposal for a Council Directive on the right to family reunification*, COM(1999) 638 final, 1 December 1999, CNS 1999/0258; Amended Commission Proposal COM(2000) 624 final.

[19] European Commission, *Proposal for a Council Directive concerning the status of third-country nationals who are long-term residents*, COM(2001) 127 final, Brussels 13 March 2001.

national approaches to integration at the European level, thereby diluting the Commission's proposed provisions in order to make them fit with their own migration rules.[20] Accordingly, provisions on integration conditions and measures were added to both Directives.[21]

By that time, integration had become a prominent theme in certain national arenas and a convenient means of restricting naturalisation and permanent residence. The Justice and Home Affairs Council in 2002 called for the establishment of National Contact Points on Integration, that is, national experts in this area who would meet in order to exchange information, monitor progress and co-ordinate their actions at national and European levels,[22] while the European Council meeting in 2003, in Thessaloniki, set the foundations for the development of an integration policy for migrants based on a set of common basic principles and invited the Commission to present annual reports on migration and integration.[23]

The Commission responded to the JHA Council's call for a common policy framework by issuing a Communication on *Immigration, Integration and Employment*.[24] The Communication was a joint product of the DG Employment and Social Affairs and DG Justice and Home Affairs, and although it made reference to the Member States' security concerns, the Tampere discourse on the fair treatment of TCNs was prominent. Integration was framed as a challenge which could be met by the development of 'a holistic approach' that takes into account the socio-economic aspects of integration as well as other issues, such as cultural diversity, citizenship, participation and political rights. Tackling racism, strengthening anti-discrimination and promoting family reunification[25] were deemed to be crucial axes for such an integration policy. The Communication also highlighted the need for a closer dialogue with third countries concerning the 'mutual recognition of professional qualifications acquired by [TCNs]

[20] S Carrera, 'Integration as a process of inclusion for migrants? The case of long-term residents in the EU' in H Schneider (ed), *Migration, Integration and Citizenship: A Challenge for Europe's Future* (Maastricht, Forum Maastricht, 2005) 699–721.

[21] See Arts 4 and 7 of Council Dir 2003/86, [2003] OJ L251/12 and Arts 5 and 15 of Council Directive 2003/109, [2004] OJ L16/44. Compare also Directive 2004/114 on the conditions of admission of third country nationals for the purposes of studies, pupil exchange, unremunerated training or voluntary service, [2004] OJ L375 and Dir 2005/71 on a specific procedure for admitting third country nationals for the purpose of scientific research, [2005] OJ L289/15.

[22] Council Meeting 2455, Luxembourg, 14–15 October 2002. The NCPs have contributed to the compilation of the first edition of the *Handbook on Integration for Policy-Makers and Practitioners*. The second edition (2007) focused on the issues derived from the Common Basic Principles and a third edition is forthcoming.

[23] Thessaloniki European Council, 19–20 June 2003. Presidency Conclusions 11638/03. The first report was published in 2004: COM(2004) 508.

[24] European Commission, *Communication on immigration, integration and employment*, COM(2003) 336 final, 3 June 2003.

[25] *Ibid*, 25.

prior to their arrival in the EU based on the principle of reciprocity'.[26] Taking an overall view, the Commission's communication embraced the positive aspects of migration and highlighted its future role in sustaining productivity and economic growth in Europe.[27]

Reflecting the 2003 Communication on Immigration and Integration, the Commission's First Annual Report on Migration and Integration in Europe called for the development of comprehensive integration policies and the mainstreaming of immigration concerns in all relevant policy fields.[28] Migration was framed in positive terms in light of its fiscal impact and the prospect of an ageing and shrinking working-age population in the EU. The Report also created a conceptual link between migration and integration by stating that '[a]dmission and integration policies are inseparable and should mutually reinforce each other'.[29] It restated national concerns about the migrant duty to 'understand and respect the fundamental norms and values of the host society' and to speak the language of the host state, thereby overcoming 'major barriers to integration'.[30]

The Hague Programme, the successor to the Tampere programme, which outlined the policy priorities for the development of the Area of Freedom, Security and Justice in the period between 2005 and 2010 and was agreed by the European Council on 4 and 5 November 2004,[31] reiterated the need for greater co-ordination of national integration policies and EU initiatives and for the development of a clear framework on integration based on a set of common basic principles (CBPs). It is worth noting here that the programme's priorities concerning the strengthening of 'freedom' were modest in comparison with those surrounding the objectives of strengthening security and justice, and there was very little commitment to propose or adopt legislation in the area of legal

[26] *Ibid*, 34.

[27] Having said this, irregular migration is the subject of a law-enforcement approach; 'the only coherent approach to dealing with illegal residents is to ensure that they return to their country of origin'.

[28] European Commission, *First Annual Report on Migration and Integration*, COM(2004) 508 final, Brussels, 16 July 2004, p 5.

[29] *Ibid*, 9.

[30] *Ibid*, 9.

[31] On 4 November 2004, the European Council adopted the Hague Programme, which set the objectives to be implemented in the area of freedom, security and justice for the period 2005–2010. This was followed by the Commission's Action Plan (May 2005), which outlined ten priorities for action, a set of implementing measures and a timetable for their adoption. The priorities cover fundamental rights and citizenship, counter-terrorism, a common asylum area, migration management, integration, internal borders, external borders and visas, privacy and security, organised crime, civil and criminal justice, sharing responsibility and solidarity. The Commission's effort to strike a better balance between freedom and security is evident in the Action Plan, which was approved by the Council on 2 June 2005. See European Commission Communication to the Council and the European Parliament, *The Hague Programme: Ten Priorities for the next five years—the Partnership for European Renewal in the filed of Freedom, Security and Justice*, COM(2005) 184 final, Brussels 10 May 2005.

migration.[32] The JHA Council of 19 November 2004[33] adopted the CBPs. The principles reflect national priorities and conceptions and incorporate the discursive shift of emphasis to migrants' responsibilities to integrate (CBP 1), to respect the basic values of the EU (CBP 2), learn the language, history and institutions of the host society (CBP 4.1), be active societal participants (CBP 5) and the possibility of conflict of cultural and religious practices with European rights or national law (CBP 8.2). The Hague Programme also invited the Commission to present a policy plan on economic migration, which materialised with the publication of a Green Paper on an EU approach to managing economic migration in 2004.[34] The Green Paper highlighted the link between migration and integration by stating that strong integration policies should accompany admission measures and reflected the increasing salience of demographic pressures and the need to maintain Europe's competitiveness in light of the Lisbon objectives.[35] The Commission drew attention to the impact of demographic decline and the ageing population on the economies of the Member States and highlighted the important role of economic migration for the socio-economic development of the Union and for the development of a common migration policy. By so doing, it redressed the security-oriented and utilitarian perspective on migration entailed in the Hague Programme and counterbalanced the emphasis on external border controls and the combating of irregular migration that had prevailed since the Seville European Council meeting in June 2002.[36]

The Commission sought to put flesh on the common basic principles by publishing a Communication on a Common Agenda for a Framework for the Integration of TCNs in the EU in 2005.[37] The Communication contained more explicit ideas for the development of a framework on integration based on a set of suggested actions at both the national and EU levels with the view of implementing the common basic principles. It also highlighted the need for a more coherent approach to integration at EU level and contained a visible external dimension. Little reflection, however, was given to the conceptual underpinnings of such a policy and the need for an external dimension to integration. Whereas the implementing measures relating to

[32] The Commission published a Green Paper on managing economic migration in January 2005, below n 34.

[33] Justice and Home Affairs Council Meeting 2618, 14615/04 of 19 November 2004.

[34] European Commission, *Green Paper on an EU approach to managing economic migration*, COM(2004) 811 final, Brussels, 11 January 2005.

[35] This refers to the target of making the EU the most competitive and dynamic knowledge-based economy in the world, capable of sustainable economic growth with more and better jobs and greater social cohesion.

[36] Presidency Conclusions, Seville European Council, 21–22 June 2002, Bulletin EU 6-2002.

[37] European Commission, *A Common Agenda for Integration. Framework for the Integration of Third-Country Nationals in the European Union*, COM(2005) 389 final, Brussels, 1 September 2005.

CBP 2 on respect for the basic values of the EU centred on newly-arrived migrants, the implementation of CBP 4—that is, 'basic knowledge of the host society's language, history and institutions is indispensable to integration; enabling immigrants to acquire this basic knowledge is essential to successful integration'—referred to the strengthening of 'the integration component of admissions procedures, for example through pre-departure measures such as information packages and language and civic orientation courses in the countries of origin'. And according to the Annex,

> as managed migration schemes are established, and within the context of developing a European approach to the admission of labour migrants there is scope for paying more attention to pre-departure measures which can improve the integration process on arrival. Such measures can be part of comprehensive migration and development strategies.

In its Second Annual Report, the Commission provided an overview of migration trends and mapped the actions taken by the Member States regarding the admission and integration of migrants at national and European levels. It noted that 'there is a new emphasis on obligatory integration courses, containing both language instruction and civic orientation'.[38] It also mentioned plans in the Netherlands to introduce pre-departure integration conditions for migrants coming to the Netherlands for family formation or reunification and for refugees.[39] And with reference to integration in the labour market, the Commission pointed out that fixed and measurable national targets should be adopted in order to reduce the unemployment gaps between EU and non-EU nationals. The Third Annual Report highlighted the need for the continual reinforcement of legal migration policies and integration strategies.[40] It also announced that greater emphasis would be placed on exploring various concepts of citizenship participation and 'the added value of common European modules for migrant integration'.[41] In the same year, the European Integration Fund was established,[42] having a budget of 825 million Euros, and with the view to promote actions in the field of integration of newly-arrived third country nationals and those who seek to comply with pre-departure integration measures in a third country. The absence of serious reflection on the conceptual coherence and justifiability of 'integration abroad' as well as its impact on integration processes and family reunification is puzzling. One discerns here the conceptual

[38] European Commission, *Second Annual Report on Migration and Integration*, SEC (2006) 892, Brussels, 30 June 2006, at p 5.

[39] *Ibid*, 10.

[40] European Commission, *Third Annual Report on Migration and Integration*, COM(2007) 512 final, Brussels, 11 September 2007.

[41] *Ibid*, 10. Compare the Commission's Communication, *The Global Approach to Migration one year on: Towards a comprehensive European migration policy*, COM(2006) 735 final, Brussels, 30 November 2006.

[42] Council Decision 2007/435/EC, 27 June 2007.

widening of integration owing to its closer association with migration and the uncritical acceptance on the part of the Community of the notion of de-territorialised integration. Little attention was given to the fact that, by its very definition, integration, as both a process and outcome, makes little sense outside the whole (social group, polity etc) of which you wish to become part. Physical presence in a country is, in my opinion, a sine qua non for integration; one cannot integrate into a society by being abroad, in the same way that a family cannot be considered to be integrated by virtue of its members being apart. Similarly, the nexus between migration and integration has not been adequately theorised.[43] The balance has been tipped in favour of a restrictive approach that uses integration conditions as a means of filtering the population seeking entry, keeping the undesirables out, testing the resources and the commitment of the included, and of promoting 'identificational' integration. For migrants do not only have to learn the language of the host society and its history, but they also have to internalise its values and ways of life and to develop a disposition, containing emotional, rational and behavioural elements, which qualifies them for admission into the collective body of national citizens.

Indeed, the Global Approach to migration adopted by the European Council in 2005[44] and the ensuing Communication bearing the same title, which was adopted by the Commission in 2006, confirm the grafting of the Member States' security-based agenda on migration onto the EU, by announcing that the EU is taking a 'two-track approach' based on facilitating 'the admission of certain categories of migrants on a needs-based approach and to provide a secure legal status to all legal migrant workers' and the launch of the FRONTEX agency with a view to co-ordinating joint maritime operations in the Atlantic and Mediterranean regions, thereby disrupting, and preventing, irregular migration.[45] The Commission's Communication on 'Towards a Common Immigration Policy' clearly associated the EU's economic interest in migration (the resource perspective) with a policy on integration, 'which has been the subject of a pragmatic approach sustained by strong political demand',[46] security, dialogue and cooperation with migrants' countries of origin, and the alleged need to combat irregular migration. It stated that migration presents both a challenge and an opportunity for the EU and that a common policy on immigration would have to be based on: legal migration (and integration policy); Schengen; visas; management of external

[43] See the Commission's Communication on the Global Approach to Migration, above, n 41.

[44] Presidency Conclusions of the European Council meeting in Brussels, 15–16 December 2005, SN 15914/01/05.

[45] See above n 34.

[46] European Commission, *Towards a Common Immigration Policy*, COM(2007) 780 final, SEC(2007) 1632, Brussels, 5 December 2007, p 4.

borders; new technologies (biometrics); combating illegal immigration and the external dimension.[47]

Following the 2007 Communication and the European Council's meetings in December 2007 and spring 2008[48] which underlined the need for the development of a comprehensive and coherent European migration policy and of the next multi-annual programme on an AFSJ, the Commission issued a Communication on 'A Common Immigration Policy in Europe: Principles, Actions and Tools'.[49] In this, the Commission stated that immigration is a reality that needs to be managed effectively[50] and proceeded to outline the (10 common) principles upon which a future common immigration policy would have to be based. These are grouped under three main strands of European policy, namely, prosperity, solidarity (burden-sharing, funding for border management control and integration, and co-operation with third countries) and security (striking the balance between individual integrity and collective security concerns). Each of these principles is to be complemented by concrete actions at multiple levels. Although 'freedom' is not mentioned in the Communication, it was made explicit that the common migration policy should 'build on the universal values of human dignity, freedom, equality and solidarity espoused by the EU', including the EU Charter of Fundamental Rights and the ECHR. But the new triad, prosperity, solidarity and security, showed that migration-related issues continue to be addressed through the lens of security and migration control and that the Member States' migration agenda had become hegemonic.

The Communication stated explicitly that a common immigration policy should promote legal migration and there should be a correlation between skills and labour market needs. Integration was placed under 'Prosperity' and was pronounced to be 'the key to successful immigration'.[51]

> The positive potential of immigration can only be realised if integration into host societies is successful. This requires an approach that does not only look at the benefit for the host society but also takes account of the interests of the immigrants: Europe is and shall continue to be a welcoming environment for those who have been granted the right to stay, be they labour immigrants,[52] family members, students or persons in need of international protection'.[53]

[47] *Ibid*, para 2, pp 4–6.

[48] Presidency Conclusions, Brussels 13–14 March 2008, point 14

[49] European Commission, *A Common Immigration Policy in Europe: Principles, Actions and Tools*, COM(2008) 359 final, SEC(2008) 2026, Sec(2008) 2027, 17 June 2008.

[50] *Ibid*, 2.

[51] *Ibid*, 7.

[52] See the Commission's *Proposal for a Council Directive on the conditions of entry and residence of third country nationals for the purposes of highly qualified employment* (COM(2007) 637 final, 23 October 2007) and the *Proposed Directive on a single application procedure for issuing a single permit for third country nationals to reside and work in the territory of a Member State* (COM(2007) 638 final, 23 October 2007).

[53] COM(2008) 359 final, above n 49, at 3.

Interestingly, the notion of 'integration abroad' did not feature at all in the Communication, which, among other suggestions, included an assessment of 'the implementation and the need for modification of the Council Directive 2003/86/EC on the right to family reunification'. However, principle three, on 'prosperity and integration', bestowed legitimacy on integration tests and programmes by stating that 'immigrants should be provided with opportunities to participate and develop their full potential. European societies should enhance their capacity to manage immigration-related diversity and enhance social cohesion'. Little attention has thus been given to the fact that national programmes aiming at enhancing social cohesion might in effect prevent the realisation of migrants' full potential and participation by denying them entry, permanent residence, naturalisation and family reunification. In addition, diversity was portrayed as an exogenous feature which is brought about by migration, and not as an intrinsic characteristic of European societies. The strand on security and immigration included four principles: 'a visa policy that serves the interests of Europe', 'the integrated management of external borders', 'stepping up the fight against illegal immigration and zero tolerance for trafficking in human beings' and 'sustainable and effective return policies'. A number of traditional—and new—preventative measures, law-enforcement actions and sanctions were envisaged under those headings. The third section of the Communication, entitled 'governance of immigration', invited the European Council to endorse these principles[54] and called for the development of new tools to strengthen the monitoring and evaluation of their implementation.

The French Presidency of the European Council seized the momentum by calling for a 'renewed political commitment on asylum and immigration' in the form of adopting a European Pact on Immigration and Asylum, which would entail the foundations of a common migration and asylum policy. Following several drafts,[55] agreement on the text of the European Pact was reached at the JHA Council on 25 September 2008. This was adopted by the European Council on 16 October 2008 in Brussels.[56] The Pact endorsed the Global Approach to migration, which was adopted in 2005, and the Commission's Communication on a Common Migration Policy, and proposed the implementation of five political commitments which would have to be implemented by national and European measures: the organisation

[54] The Lisbon Treaty, which was agreed on 13 December 2007, will facilitate the development of a common migration policy by abolishing the third pillar, extending the application of the co-decision procedure to the areas which were governed by unanimity, such as regular migration, and by furnishing new legal bases for regular migration and coordinating action in the domain of integration.

[55] See Version II of the European Pact on Immigration and Asylum, 4 July 2008. Available at www.libertysecurity.org.

[56] The final text is more conservative in both tone and content than the draft dated 4 July 2008.

of legal migration to take into account the priorities, needs and reception capabilities determined by each Member State and to encourage integration; to control illegal immigration by ensuring the return of illegal migrants to their country of origin or a country of transit; the reinforcement of external border controls; to construct a Europe of asylum; and comprehensive partnership with the countries of origin and transit to encourage synergy between migration and development. Obviously, none of these principles is new. Although it is stated that 'rejecting both closed door and open door policies, the Pact strikes the right balance Europe needs' and 'demonstrates that Europe is able to protect its citizens, honour its traditions and develop partnerships', the five commitments reflect the Member States' restrictive migration agenda and their preference for according priority to security and control over the fair treatment of migrants and refugees. In comparison to the Commission's Communications discussed above, the Pact encapsulates a more conservative and law-enforcement approach which appears to legitimise the Member States' restrictive stance:

> legal immigration policy must be selective and concerted'; 'family immigration must be more effectively organized … must be in accordance with the acceptance capabilities of the Member States and the integration capabilities of migrants;[57]
>
> foreign persons who are in countries illegally must leave territories, preferably of their own free will. Deportation decisions taken by a Member State will be recognized by all Member States. Measures of assistance for voluntary repatriation will be recommended and must be extended across all Member States. Member States must cooperate with each other more effectively and take joint measures to ensure the repatriation of illegal immigrants. Member States must limit themselves to regularization on a case-by-case basis for humanitarian or economic reasons;
>
> the issue of visas containing biometric identification will be extended across all Member States from January 2012. A Visa Information System electronically connecting all consulates and central government departments will be set up;
>
> Whenever it proves necessary, coordination for the control of the external borders of the EU will be provided by the FRONTEX agency. The Agency's resources must be strengthened to deal with crisis situations.

Clearly, in the evolving area of freedom, security and justice the paradigm of migration control and law-enforcement continues to be dominant. Governments will define who is deemed to be worthy of entry and will keep out the unwanted and undesirable. Selective migration will thus take place within the limits established by national regulatory regimes, the circulation of temporary workers will be encouraged and irregular migration will be combated. Indeed, notwithstanding the deployment of the notion of a 'pact', if one compares the French Presidency's inventory of migration control with the one

[57] The draft dated 4 July defined integration capabilities on the basis of a) families' resources and accommodation in the host country and b) knowledge of that country's language.

presented by the Austrian Presidency a decade ago[58] very little seems to have changed. The policy agenda continues to be dominated by security concerns, thereby resulting in a rather narrow, and predictable, range of policy options.

III. THE AREA OF FREEDOM, SECURITY AND JUSTICE AND BELONGING: THE CONTINUING SPECTRE OF SECURITY AND CONTROL

Despite the Commission's efforts to highlight the positive impact of migration and the demographic and social pressures facing Europe in the future, migration issues continue to be approached through the traditional perspectives of security, control and restrictiveness. Echoing the fashionable discourse on contractual relations, the European Pact on Immigration and Asylum illustrates the Member States' hegemony over the framing of migration-related issues and their resurgent power to control legal entry, combat irregular migration and dictate the terms of migrants' integration. There is little reflection on normative considerations and on the negative impact of restrictive and law-enforcement approaches on the formation of a European identity and the values underpinning the European project. National executives have shown their preference for traditional frames and old tools, and the similarities between the French Presidency's European Pact and the 1998 Strategy Paper adopted by the European Council attest to this.[59] The only difference is that, due to demographic pressures, the Member States would be prepared to admit certain categories of migrants because they need them. Yet, in so doing, they will continue to place hurdles in their path to temporary or permanent residence and to citizenship, which is now framed as a privilege or a status that has to be earned.

An alternative approach to migration governance would have to reflect critically on the concepts, legal initiatives and policies that have characterised the last 30 years of Member State co-operation in this area and to rethink, and reframe, the area of freedom, security and justice. Reframing the area of freedom, security and justice requires, among other things, the de-legitimation of the present law-enforcement approach and the de-securitisation of migration; that is, its removal from the conceptual realm of security and sovereignty and its designation as a 'normal' issue to be dealt with through political processes.[60] This is required in order to undercut the prevailing definition of migration as a threat and/or a problem and to

[58] European Council, 'Strategy Paper on Immigration and Asylum policy', 9809/98, 1 July 1998, Brussels.

[59] *Ibid.*

[60] B Buzan, O Weaver and J de Wilde, *Security. A New Framework for Analysis*, above n 8. For a related defence of the 'politicisation' of immigration and asylum policy see Valsamis Mitsilegas's contribution to this volume (ch 2 pp 61–63), especially.

disentangle migration from integration issues. In the subsequent discussion I defend the merits of such a de-securitised and liberal approach and of establishing a disjunction between migration and integration with a view to realigning the latter with domicile and citizenship.

It is true that liberal theories of justice have been elaborated against the background of bounded communities with given membership and fixed borders.[61] The question that escaped attention until the late 1990s[62] is whether porous boundaries and liberal admission policies can be defended on the basis of democracy itself. Making the states' right to admit and exclude aliens an issue of democratic self-determination has probably been the most credible justification of the states' right to exclude. Walzer has addressed the question of immigration from the standpoint of membership in a political community: 'the primary good that we distribute to one another is membership in some human community'.[63] Accordingly, Walzer's defence of the right of a sovereign state or a political community to restrict the entry of foreigners ('legitimate' closure) is that democracy entails the right of the community to determine its membership and to maintain its distinct identity and the integrity of 'shared understandings'. However, implicit in this argument is a differentiation between internal and external membership decisions that is not accounted for. It is difficult to imagine a democratic polity that creates, and maintains, various classes of citizenship, for it has been well established that internal membership decisions are subject to principled constraints. If internal membership decisions are subject to normative constraints, it is not at all clear why external membership decisions should be exempt from any normative test and why the existing citizens' alleged power to make admission decisions should be unconditional. It seems to me that what has escaped Walzer's notice is that commitment to democratic ideals may require the subjection of a community's competence in the migration field to principled thinking and to the same constitutional constraints that limit the exercise of other political competences. In designing migration law and policy, communities must give due regard to constitutional, international and supranational law principles in the fields of human rights protection, asylum provision, the rights of the child, family reunification, protection of migrant workers, equal treatment and non-discrimination with respect to gender, race, nationality,

[61] The argument here draws on ch 6 of my book, *Citizenship, Identity and Immigration in the EU: Between Past and Future* (Manchester, Manchester University Press, 2001).

[62] *Ibid*; D Kostakopoulou, 'Is there an alternative to Schengenland?' (1998) 46 *Political Studies* 639–56; S Benhabib, *The Rights of Others* (Cambridge, Cambridge University Press, 2004); *Another Cosmopolitanism* (Oxford, Oxford University Press, 2006); B Honig, *Democracy and the Foreigner* (Princeton NJ, Princeton University Press, 2001); A Honneth, 'Democracy as Reflexive Cooperation: John Dewey and the Theory of Democracy Today' (1998) 26 *Political Theory* 763–83; L Bosniak, 'Universal citizenship and the Problem of Alienage' (2002) 94 *Northwestern University Law Review* 963–82; 'Citizenship Denationalised' (2000) 7 *Indiana Journal of Global Legal Studies* 447–518.

[63] M Walzer, *Spheres of Justice* (New York, Basic Books, 1983) 31.

ethnic origin, religion and so on. For a failure to abide by, and honour, such commitments cannot but compromise the democratic culture of communities and the principles upon which they are founded.

A few decades ago, it would have been futile to attempt to establish clear limits on the discretionary power of states to admit and exclude, beyond those entailed by international law instruments. National statism projected communities as particularistic entities possessing a distinctive and, paradoxically enough, fragile culture, and state borders as barriers (stopping points)—not as permeable membranes (meeting points). Internal freedom of movement was seen to depend on some form of external closure, since the latter would ensure the protection of the way of life of the community and guarantee the distinctiveness of its culture.[64] But the world has changed considerably over the last 30 years, and the project of European unification has demonstrated that the value and the significance attached to borders can be altered and made subordinate to other political objectives, such as creating an internal market and a Union of peoples. This contrasts sharply with the nationalist strategy of transforming territory and borders from a mere 'geographical expression of cultural identity into a fundamental basis for defining groups and individual identities'.[65] In addition, the reality of globalisation and the constant perforation of boundaries by messages, cultural images, money, and people have made cultures more visibly fluid, overlapping and interwoven. Within such a 'floating world', distinctiveness and vitality in cultures and societies, more often than not, are the by-product of contact, communication, the flow of ideas, cultural exchanges and cultural collisions. True, certain theorists, such as Kymlicka, could still defend cultural interchange to the extent that it does not threaten the survival of a culturally distinct society. According to Kymlicka, changes in the character of a culture must be the result of the choices of its members, and must not threaten the existence of a culture 'as an intelligible context of choice'.[66] Whilst it is true that an individual's pursuit of worthwhile life plans takes place only within a cultural-societal context, Kymlicka has not been able to show that the narratives and resources needed for making meaningful choices must come from a single, unified, fully-constituted and secure cultural matrix. Nor is the congruence between society and culture so unproblematic as Kymlicka himself assumes, as arguments about cultural survival, fears of 'being swamped by alien cultures' and the absorptive or assimilative capacity of a country often entail a way of thinking which unavoidably slips back to essential national identities, unified cultures and communities and to fear of difference and change.

[64] *Ibid*, 38–9.

[65] J Penrose, 'Nations, states and homelands: territory and territoriality in nationalist thought' (2002) 8 *Nations and Nationalism* 277–97 at 283.

[66] W Kymlicka, *Multicultural Citizenship* (Oxford, Clarendon Press, 1995).

Perspectives which take membership as 'given' and community as a unified, cultural entity have not examined whether restrictive immigration policies may compromise democratic ideals by perpetuating fictions of internal homogeneity and promoting nativist narratives of belonging. It has been assumed that polities are empowered to restrict immigration without compromising their internal process of democracy and that exclusionary migration policies have no significant bearing upon the nature of the polity ('the no-effect assumption'), even though constructions of 'the other' or of 'them' are closely linked to internal definitions of membership, the quality of community relationships and the recognition accorded to diversity. Strangers are perceived as a 'threat' to the liberty, welfare or culture of the host community only in relation to certain ideological conceptions as to what constitutes a member, and these conceptions almost invariably tend to be inflexible and unresponsive to diversity. Admittedly, one of the most important yardsticks by which to judge the quality of democracy is inclusion,[67] and adherence to supposedly unified, single and homogeneous nation-states or cultural frameworks gives rise to closure and impairs the cultivation of an ethic of the Other. It also precludes a deeper understanding of the 'dynamics of distancing and relating' in contemporary societies; that is, the possibility of togetherness in apartness (the creation of border-transcending communities) and apartness in togetherness (the various forms of diversity existing even within the most supposedly homogeneous group).

Migration may be a 'blessing', precisely because it forces a rethinking of existing conceptions of community, a periodic review of the meaning and terms of membership and the recognition of the artificiality of binary oppositions between 'us' and 'them', since strangers eventually become associates in a collective experience and members of the *demos*.[68] After all, democracy

[67] J Carens, 'Aliens and Citizens: the Case for Open Borders' (1987) 49 *Review of Politics* 251; J Carens, 'Membership and Morality: Admission to Citizenship in Liberal Democratic States' in R Brubaker (ed), *Immigration and the Politics of Citizenship in Europe and North America* (New York, University Press of America, 1998); J Careens, 'Why Naturalisation Should Be Easy: A Response to Noah Pickus' in N Pickus (ed), *Immigration and Citizenship in the Twenty-First Century* (Boulder, Rowman and Littlefield, 1998) 141–8; R Dahl, *Democracy and Its Critics* (New Haven, Yale University Press, 1998); R Goodin, 'Enfranchising all Affected Interests, and Its Alternatives'(2007) 35 *Philosophy and Public Affairs* 40–68.

[68] My argument should not be taken to imply that I am advocating open borders and universal free movement. The closed/open borders dualism is quite misleading, since it forecloses various possibilities for in-between positions. It also reinforces the traditional view of upholding the state's right to exclude since, in the absence of a realistic alternative, theorists are persuaded to turn their attention to the ethics of restricting migratory flows or to articulate standards of decision-making in local contexts that are fair from the perspective of society members only. Given that the present European migration regime is about letting a few in, but keeping most out, a principled and non-restrictive immigration policy which circumscribes admissions decisions within definite legal bounds and extends the obligations that polities may have to individuals beyond the confines of national borders would entail a much more generous intake of migrants. For a related discussion see Neil Walker's contribution to this volume (ch 11 266–268) especially.

does not necessarily presuppose nationality as the qualifying criterion for the participation of all those subject to the jurisdiction of a country and affected by its laws in the decision-making process. Nor do individuals' interests as homeowners, parents, employees, neighbours, local participants and consumers differ in accordance with their 'citizen', 'resident' or 'illegal alien' status. Irregular migration amplifies the artificiality of these categories, because the absence of state authorisation of migrants' entry and/or residence makes them offenders of migration laws, 'illegals' and 'outsiders who have no right to be here'.[69] Accordingly, states have the power to order the removal of undocumented migrants, and the weight attributed to states' consent (or the lack of it) subdues considerations related to individuals' de facto social membership. Settlement, employment, contributions to the commonwealth are not seen to be normatively relevant under the paradigm of migration control and governmental restraint. But by stepping up identity checks in order to identify the undocumented migrants, using biometric technology, excluding them from social rights, discouraging their regularisation and imposing sanctions on those who hire them, states assign migrants to a subordinate status and undermine principled commitments. Apprehension and removal in turn emits powerful signals about the undesirability of migrants, thereby fuelling intolerance and xenophobia. Migration rules thus convey important messages about the nature and quality of the polity and, in turn, affect perceptions about membership and shape attitudes toward democratic citizenship.[70]

[69] B Bogusz, R Cholewinski, A Cygan and E Szyszczak (eds), *Irregular Migration and Human Rights: Theoretical, European and International Perspectives* (Leiden, Martinus Nijhoff Publishers, 2004).

[70] On the argument that a liberal migration policy would clash with other principles, particularly those underpinning the welfare system, see D Miller, *On Nationality* (Oxford, Oxford University Press, 1996); D Miller, 'Immigration: The Case for Limits' in A Cohen and C Heath Wellman (eds), *Contemporary Debates in Applied Ethics* (Oxford, Blackwell, 2005); R Baubock, 'Legitimate Immigration control' in H Adelman (ed), *Legitimate and Illegitimate Discrimination: New Issues in Migration* (Geneva, UNESCO, York Lanes Press, 1995) 3–40. There are two major weaknesses in this argument. The first major weakness in the 'social rights protectionist' or 'social trust' argument, in its various forms, is that it assumes that there is some correlation between national homogeneity and robust redistributive programmes. By so doing, it fails to account for the facts that non-national residents, who are normally excluded from political membership in the host society, at least in the first few years of their residence, and do not share a sense of common identity with nationals, may be willing tax payers, whereas one may find a large number of co-nationals willing to block redistributive programmes for ideological or purely selfish reasons. Secondly, it tends to misdiagnose the status and aspirations of migrants; the latter are seen as poor, unskilled and vulnerable. This view is incorrect. Similarly, refugees are not just scarred people and vulnerable dependants. They are people with talents, skills, energy and determination to build a better life and contribute to economic growth. Many migrants are entrepreneurs, ready to start their businesses. And although the effect of immigration on entrepreneurship in the host country has not been the focus of systematic research, most studies confirm that migrants are more likely to be self-employed, or employers, than autochthonous citizens. In addition, all are consumers creating a greater demand for manufactured goods and investors.

In the 1980s and 1990s, Western European governments designed their migration policies by separating migration from integration. The main argument put forward was that integration could only work if migration were restricted; by building petty-fortresses to filter out the movement of people, migrants' settlement, citizenship-building and race relations would be enhanced. Liberal citizenship laws were thus seen to require tighter border controls. In the new millennium, however, we have been witnessing a deliberate alignment of migration and integration in official discourses and policies, despite the problems associated with such an alignment. True, migration brings in the people who need to 'be integrated', but it is not a sufficient condition for integration to occur. Otherwise put, migration does not promote integration. But 'citizenisation', that is, treating people as stakeholders and facilitating their access to citizenship, does precisely this. What is also noticeable in the new framing of the nexus between integration and migration is that restrictiveness now extends to both. By imposing mandatory integration conditions abroad or as a condition for the grant of a temporary or a permanent resident permit, governments place the entry and residence of migrants under tighter control.

This may not be apparent at first sight owing to the framing of integration as 'a two-way process' or as 'a contract' between the state and the migrant. However, one has to bear in mind that this conceptual frame has been state-led, too. Civic integration initiatives have been neither the product of societal consensus nor the outcome of a far-reaching public debate on the strengths and weaknesses of multiculturalism. On the contrary, governments took the lead in defining national belonging and refashioning national identity in response to conservative reactions and right-wing extremism in the Netherlands, Denmark, the United Kingdom and elsewhere in the 1990s and the new millennium.

It is quite perplexing that governmental elites believe that a sense of 'shared belonging' can emerge by testing one's fluency in the host language and requiring the accumulation of factual information about life in the host state, or about its history and traditions. After all, most of the information one accumulates in this way is bound to be forgotten a few months after the written or oral examination. It is equally puzzling that the European Commission has not called this view into question. Certainly, one cannot

For a fuller exposition of these criticisms, see Kostakopoulou, 1998, above, n 62 and 2001, above, n 61. Compare also, Smith and Edmonston (eds), *The New Americans: Economic, Demographic and Fiscal Effects of Immigration* (Oxford, National Academy Press, 1998); H Kurthe, 'Immigration and the Welfare State in Comparison: Differences in the Incorporation of Immigrant Minorities in Germany and the United States' (1997) *International Migration Review* 721–31; see G Freeman and J Jupps (eds), *Nations of Immigrants: Australia, the United States and International Migration* (Melbourne, Oxford University Press, 1992); and N Harris, *The New Untouchables: Immigration and the New World Worker* (Harmondsworth, Penguin, 1996) 172.

disregard the Member States' agenda-setting power in this field as well as the underlying ideological premises of their positions. Ideology is crucial, because if communities are perceived to be organic entities, unified on the basis of a shared language, unique historical experiences and a shared culture—as ethno-nationalist and cultural nationalist narratives postulate—membership would have to be conditioned on linguistic assimilation, knowledge of history and the acceptance of national conventions. In civic nationalist narratives of community, on the other hand, emphasis would have to be put on the acceptance of the values of the country and one's understanding of the historical context which has given rise to those values. Although much depends on the various conceptions of the nation and understandings of national identity pertaining in the Member States, it is, nevertheless, the case that by framing community membership along nationalist lines, governments ultimately succeed in creating the nation and writing its identity. As Smith has observed,[71] 'creating nations is a recurrent activity which has to be renewed periodically'. The role of nationalist ideology in this conceptual shift of integration from a citizenship effect to a condition of migration is also attested by the fact that integration programmes entail not only devotion to one's values, language and culture, and a commitment towards their preservation, but also an implicit or explicit assignment of greater value to one's particular traditions and the stereotyping of other traditions.[72] Programmes of civic integration and social cohesion are thus allegedly justified on the basis of the need to correct the deficiencies of migrants by encouraging competence in the host language, imparting skills, preparing people for citizenship and re-educating them to respect the national values—and not on the basis of national definitions of community, the prevalence of certain conceptions of the nation among elites and their advisers, anxieties about national identity and the desire to make the state (and the party in power) relevant.

If, on the other hand, community is conceived of in political terms (and the European Community cannot be conceived of otherwise), then its membership rules would have to reflect people's sharing of common experiences and their willingness to work together to solve common problems and to contribute to the welfare of the commonwealth. In such a political community, qualities such as a desire to succeed and carve out a space for yourself and your family, to create a home and a better future on foreign lands, a higher motivation to work hard, to persevere, to solve problems, and to display economic creativity and entrepreneurship would be given more weight than the acceptance of traditional markers of national identity,

[71] Anthony Smith, *The Ethnic Origins of Nations* (Oxford, Blackwell, 1986) 206.

[72] This applies to national integration programmes and to the Common Basic Principles discussed above, such as CBP2 (respect for the basis values of the EU), CBP4 (basic knowledge of the receiving society's language, history and institutions) and CBP 8.2 (the practice of diverse cultures and religions must not conflict with other inviolable European rights or national law).

such as knowledge of the language, the civics and internalisation of national (and European) values.

It is, indeed, unfortunate that the political understanding of community and the outward-looking and dynamic notion of society which was dominant in the 1990s is under retreat. Much of the present policy is firmly embedded in a present that not only draws on a nationalist and misremembered past, but it also disregards the long-term point of view. Security concerns and discussion about the role of Islam in western societies might make provincialism an attractive position for some, but one must bear in mind that globalisation cannot be not reversed and that even a world in financial crisis is pushed closer together. In addition, multilingualism and diversity are no longer optional extras and the demographic picture makes it quite likely that the future well-being of western societies might well depend on the sacrifices and labour of the very persons they seek to exclude from membership. The migration pact discussed above does not take this into account. Nor does the EU framework on integration reflect the process-like nature of adaptation and settlement and prioritise interaction, mutual learning and co-operative association between newcomers and existing citizens. Interculturalism and pluralism continue to remain credible alternatives for they put emphasis on what really matters; namely, on developing partnerships, cultivating mutual respect, fostering interactions and dynamic learning in action among majority and migrant communities.

A pluralist approach would recognise that whether newcomers will develop feelings of belonging and a sense of identification depends as much on the kind of institutions and practices of membership that will regulate their lives, as on the way they will be treated by the host country. It is hard to imagine, for example, an organisation that, as part of its admissions policy, chooses to impress markers of difference upon new recruits, stressing continually that they are unlike the existing members and that they need to overcome their alleged deficiencies in order to become part of it. Even if such an organisation existed, it would be neither well functioning nor successful. It has been well established that the key to creating a collegiate environment within which individuals are given the opportunity to thrive and to contribute to the success of the organisation, is the provision of support to newcomers, parity of treatment and giving them a sense of being stakeholders. Any other approach simply would not work. By analogy, if the aim is to encourage social co-operation and a sense of shared belonging in European polities and the EU, governments would have to refrain from adopting neo-national narratives of fear and division; instead, emphasis should be put on the things that people can do together and on what can be done to improve the conditions and experience of social membership and citizenship for everybody. Institutionalising indirect discrimination based on nationality erodes the credibility of admissions policies and placing multiple hurdles on the path to citizenship or putting people on probation undermines the credibility of naturalisation policy.

Given the European institutions' interest in devising a coherent framework of migration governance, it seems to me that both European polities and the EU need to rethink the framing of migration and integration and to redesign their migration and integration policies. Neither the area of freedom, security and justice, nor the suggested new triad of prosperity, solidarity and security de-securitises migration and integration. A principled, coherent and pragmatic approach would view migration as a resource and integration as matter of developing partnerships, fostering mutual respect and dynamic learning among residents and newcomers. The contrasting templates of internal mobility in the EU and the rights and equal opportunities that flow from it, on the one hand, and of migration, on the other, shed ample light on the benefits of inclusiveness, equal treatment and openness and polities' capacities to take risks. A new deal can be struck in this domain by adopting a common sense and rights-based approach, which sees little difference between internal mobility and migration. After all, it is an integral part of democracy for a political community to be willing to put its self-understanding and definition of membership to a normative test—that is, to examine whether both conform to its underlying principles, avoid nationalist ideology and ethnocentrism, observe human rights standards and international law norms and foster respect for people—and to review them periodically in line with changes in the external environment and new developments. Bearing in mind the profound effects of restrictiveness, migration control, national mobilisation around closure and traditional boundaries, and of the close intertwining of race and nation[73] upon democratic principles and citizens' identities, a positive commitment to inclusiveness in the EU is needed. In such a schema, the goals, interests and aspirations of non-members are neither disregarded nor superseded by the needs of insiders and/or the relevant duties towards one's community. For any damage or hardship inflicted upon outsiders due to the restrictive and law-enforcement character of immigration policy is a cost, since it impacts negatively upon the scope and nature of the principles underpinning a polity. These normative reductions do not only inflict undue damage and hardship on outsiders, but they also compromise the fundamental values underpinning democratic political communities. Shifting the focus from the migrant to the host community and defending inclusiveness as a principle of *political morality* in the Member States and the EU is thus necessary.

[73] A Rattansi, *Racism* (Oxford, Oxford University Press, 2007) 167.

9

Proximity and Paradox: Law and Politics in the New Europe[1]

BONNIE HONIG

'If a "not yet" is written above all redemptive union, the only result can be that, ..., it is, at least to begin with ... the neighbor [the well-nigh nighest] who is precisely there ... [W]here someone or something has become the neighbor of the soul, a part of the world becomes what it was not before: soul'.

Franz Rosenzweig

I. INTRODUCTION

IN *ANOTHER COSMOPOLITANISM*, Seyla Benhabib promotes the idea that recent developments in international institutionalism evidence the growth of what she calls cosmopolitan norms. She turns to an emergency to set the stage: genocide serves as her synecdoche for several new legislative and normative trends in human rights, especially in Europe. Noting the lack of appropriate institutions with which to try Adolf Eichmann in 1961, Benhabib presses upon her readers the need to support international tribunals now. But the lens and mood set by Eichmann and genocide set us up to relate in a certain way—in a mode of dependence and felt need of rescue—to the project of interstate law and cosmopolitan norms that Benhabib here seeks to promote. It is problematic in a way that recalls the question posed by Bernard Shaw to Mike Dukakis in the 1988 American presidential election campaign, (something like) 'What would you want done to the perpetrator, if your wife was raped and murdered?'[2] Dukakis's dispassionate response, in which he said he would want

[1] This essay is a much-revised version of my response to Seyla Benhabib, first published as 'Another Cosmopolitanism? Law and Politics in the New Europe' in R Post (ed), *Another Cosmopolitanism. The Tanner Lectures* (New York, Oxford University Press, 2006).

[2] 1988 Presidential Debates, CNN.com. www.cnn.com/ELECTION/2000/debates/history.story/1988.html (accessed 25 August 2008).

the perpetrator to be tried, underscored for the electorate what was seen as his passionless bureaucratic character. But the problem was with the question, not the answer. One is thrust by the spectres of genocide, rape and murder into extremes of (il)legality: passionate vendetta or sober, fair judicial process.

If Benhabib begins and ends *Another Cosmopolitanism* with the concern about genocide and the need for institutional accountability for it, that may be because she senses greater consensus on that particular issue than on some of the more intractable issues of multicultural politics which she discusses in the pages in between. She hopes the divisions of multicultural politics may become less intractable if they are adjudicated by way of the universal norms that condemn genocide and to which, on Benhabib's account, the new International Criminal Court gives expression. In short, Benhabib's intention is to enable widespread acceptance of new developments in EU law that she sees as expressing moral condemnation of intolerance from genocide to multicultural politics. But, although universal outrage against genocide may seem a promising ground for a new cosmopolitanism, Benhabib's universal norms also insulate us from the urgencies of contingency and contiguity out of which solidaristic progressive politics often arise. If we focus on the fact that those who happen to be here have no more claim on us than those far away, or if their being here can only 'count' once it has passed a test of universalisability, then the impulse to act in concert with them simply because they are here is attenuated and indeed de-legitimated. The same goes for those who are distant, physically, but with whom we might feel neighbourly in the sense of sharing a common cause. Here, Franz Rosenzweig's idea that in 'the just present moment, the universal and highest [is represented] by the approximately proximate' is potentially very powerful, as I will suggest below.

The politics of genocide has not, in any case, always produced the unanimity Benhabib seeks. Benhabib opens and closes *Another Cosmopolitanism* by invoking Hannah Arendt, the democratic theorist to whom she and I are in different ways indebted. The Hannah Arendt with whom she opens is in dialogue with Jaspers in 1960 regarding the need (shared by Jaspers and Arendt but felt more keenly by him) for international institutions to try Eichmann for war crimes. Arendt expressed hesitations about the 'impaired' quality of the justice meted out at Nuremberg and then at the Eichmann trial in Jerusalem. Her hesitations are overcome by Benhabib, who casts the establishment of the new International Criminal Court in 2002 as itself a fulfillment of the promise of those initial, partial efforts and as an instance of the sort of inaugural action that Arendt theorised and praised in *The Human Condition*, *On Revolution* and elsewhere. This is the second Arendt, the Arendt with whom Benhabib closes *Another Cosmopolitanism*, the theorist of revolutionary beginnings who sees politics as an opportunity for actors to inaugurate a '*novo ordo saeclorum*'.[3]

But would the Arendt who expressed concerns about the impaired quality of the Eichmann trial have agreed with Benhabib's endorsement of a new normative and juridical universalism? True, Arendt bemoaned the absence of appropriate institutions with which to try Eichmann. And she did criticise the Israeli court for trying Eichmann on the wrong charge—crimes against the Jewish people rather than crimes against humanity. This may be why Benhabib believes that the new international court along with the new moral fact—prohibiting crimes against humanity—together answer Arendt's earlier concerns. But Arendt's analysis of the Eichmann trial did not stop there. These two criticisms are part and parcel of a third, in which Arendt not only noted the imperfections of the trial, but also tracked the trial's political impact or effects. She asked not only 'How are they trying Eichmann?' but also always: 'What are they doing by trying Eichmann? What political ends is this trial serving?' The urgency of the moment, the need to do justice in response to the Holocaust, did not obviate these political concerns. For this Arendt was seen, perhaps predictably, as insensitive or even treasonous. And in some ways, she was. Her portrait of the Eichmann trial is unforgiving in its detail, and the acidity of her judgements is to this day still sharp.

Her readers were offended by many things, especially by her suggestions that Jewish complicity was an issue in the genocide. This seemed to undermine Nazi culpability while also manifesting a deep failure to understand what people do when pressed to focus in the barest possible terms on survival. Many readers were also offended by Arendt's relentless insistence on the politicality of the trial. For Arendt, the Eichmann trial, in spite of the fact that it was needed and not completely invalid but only impaired, nonetheless was a way also for the still new Israeli state to establish its own legitimacy as a nation state by casting itself as protector of international Jewry and seeker of justice for the crimes of the Holocaust. It is in this context that Arendt's other two criticisms—wrong charges (crimes against the Jewish people), and wrong setting (Israeli court in Jerusalem)—are significant. The trial provided the State of Israel with an opportunity further

[3] Arendt did, Benhabib acknowledges, write in the Postscript to *Eichmann in Jerusalem* that it 'is inconceivable … that [an international] court would be a criminal tribunal which pronounces on the guilt or innocence of individuals' *Eichmann in Jerusalem: A Report on the Banality of Evil* (New York, Penguin Books, 1994) 298, quoted in *Another Cosmopolitanism* (above n 1), 15), but Benhabib pronounces this statement 'baffling' and explains that it is symptomatic of Arendt's 'civic republican vision of political determination' (*Another Cosmopolitanism* (above n 1), 15), a vision in need of mediation or overcoming. Benhabib's lectures, positioned as they are, as an effort to mediate between cosmopolitan norms and republican self-determination in part by way of practices of democratic iteration, might well be seen as Benhabib's own iterative effort to offer Arendt the middle way she did not see or might have refused. (But which is it?).

to nationalise itself as a state and this dealt yet another blow to Arendt's already dashed dream of a bi-national state of Israel in which Palestinians and Jews would share power. This is the reason for Arendt's scathing criticisms of Gideon Hausner in the early pages of *Eichmann in Jerusalem*. Indeed, her half-hearted wish for an international criminal court, expressed in the form of a lamentation of its impossibility, was not simply a wish to escape from politics as such into a really neutral or just realm of law.[4] Or that's not all it was. It was (whatever else it was) a way to highlight and criticise the part played by the Eichmann trial in a larger politics of state-building to which she was opposed.

So the question is: Would Hannah Arendt—if she were writing now—have any less political an analysis of the formation of the European Union and the use therein of law, courts, and bureaucracy to promote and consolidate a particular conception of Europe as a political form? Would she be any less likely now than then to ask not just 'What can we accomplish through law on behalf of human rights?' but also 'What new political formations are advantaged and legitimated thereby?' Her example suggests not. It suggests that she would assess new international norms, laws, and institutions on their own terms but *also* always as political manoeuvres in their own right. In this particular instance, I imagine she might see the developments tracked by Benhabib as signs of welcome developments in human rights. But Arendt would not stop there. She would also, I believe, ask whether these developments might not also be part of an effort to consolidate a certain conception of Europe and promote it over other contenders. Thus, rather than treat the Arendt who wished for appropriate international institutions to judge Eichmann as if she were fulfilled or satisfied by the inauguration of today's new norms and institutions, we might do better to see in Arendt's example a demand that we assess emerging new orders in the most relentlessly political and critical terms. Arendt offers a valuable example of the double gesture often called for in political engagement when she criticises the politicality of the Eichmann trial while nonetheless affirming its imperfect justice.

Working from a perspective that owes much to Arendt's political analysis in *Eichmann* and is indebted as well to the work of Jacques Derrida, I look at recent developments in Europe focused on by Benhabib. Benhabib works her views out by way of Kant's idea of a right to hospitality. I begin with Derrida's own reading of that right, for it motivates an alternative to Benhabib's neo-Kantian cosmopolitanism. That alternative is often termed

[4] For an insightful account of Arendt's *Eichmann in Jerusalem* as a critical engagement with, rather than an endorsement of, neutral legal proceduralism, see Lida Maxwell, 'The Demands of Justice: Courts and Publics in Hannah Arendt's *Eichmann in Jerusalem*'. Presented at the annual meeting of the American Political Science Association, Chicago IL, September 2007.

cosmopolitics and, as I argue here, it is better served by Rosenzweig's idea of neighbourliness than by neo-Kantian universals over which the neighbour, as such, famously has little claim.[5]

II. HOSPITALITY AND RIGHTS

As with many of the concepts he deconstructs, including the gift, justice, forgiveness, and democracy, Derrida casts hospitality as belonging to two, discontinuous and radically heterogeneous orders, conditional and unconditional, whose conflict and asymmetrical necessity render ethical-political life (im)possible.[6] There is no question of a choice that must be made between one order and the other, between the conditional and the unconditional. Nor is there a fundamental compatibility between the two such that, for example, one is legal and one is moral or one is specific and the other generic, in which case the latter could subsume the former and make sense of it or complete it. Rather, the two orders or concepts co-exist in 'paradoxical or aporetic relations ... that are at once heterogeneous and inseparable'.[7]

Unconditional hospitality postulates a giving without limit to the other, an infinite openness that both enables and jeopardises one's capacity to

[5] I have in mind here Kant's famous discussion of the absolutism of the prohibition against lying, even to save the life of someone who has sought sanctuary with you, a topic attended to in some detail by Derrida, who casts it as a violation of hospitality. Kant, 'On a Supposed Right to Lie because of Philanthropic Concerns' in *Grounding of the Metaphysics of Morals, with On a Supposed Right to Lie Because of Philanthropic Concerns*, (trans) JW Ellington (Indianapolis, Hackett, 1993); Derrida, *Of Hospitality*, (trans) R Bowlby (Stanford CA, Stanford University Press, 2000) 65–73.

Cosmopolitics is the term under which Pheng Cheah and Bruce Robbins gather a collection of essays exploring themes of hospitality, transnational debt, and international engagement. *Cosmopolitics: Thinking and Feeling Beyond the Nation*, Pheng Cheah and Bruce Robbins (eds) (Minneapolis, University of Minnesota Press 1998). Derrida identifies Kant with a mere *cosmopolitics* and notes that Levinas never used that term, nor the more usual *cosmopolitanism*, preferring instead*: universalism*. Derrida suggests that Levinas abjured the term cosmopolitanism or cosmopolitics (Derrida does not here distinguish the two) for two reasons: 'first, because this sort of political thought refers pure hospitality and this peace to an indefinite progress [which also always "retains the trace of a natural hostility" which is its point of departure in Kant]; second, because of the well-known ideological connotations with which modern anti-Semitism saddled the great tradition of a cosmopolitanism passed down from Stoicism or Pauline Christianity to the Enlightenment and to Kant'. J Derrida, *Adieu to Emmanuel Levinas*, (trans) P-A Brault and MB Naas (Stanford CA, Stanford University Press, 1999) 88.

[6] J Derrida, *Rogues: Two Essays on Reason* (trans) P-A Brault and MB Naas (Stanford CA, Stanford University Press, 2005) 145. For a complementary reading of Derrida on this and related issues, especially of the foreigner in relationship to democracy, see Peter Fitzpatrick, esp 128–30.

[7] *Ibid*, 173 fn 12, citing *Of Hospitality* (above n 5), *On Cosmopolitanism and Forgiveness* (New York, Routledge, 2001), and *Adieu* (above n 5).

host another.[8] Conditional hospitality, by contrast, postulates a finite set of resources and calculable claims. It is 'the only one ... that belongs to the order of laws, rules, and norms—whether ethical, juridical, or political—at a national or international level'.[9] In this second order of hospitality, distinctions must be made and limits set, lest hospitality be extended to or demanded by everyone and encompass everything to a point at which the would-be host would be dispossessed of the very property and scope that enable him to offer hospitality to the dispossessed other.[10]

Kant delimited hospitality (to the right of those washed ashore to be permitted visitation or offered refuge) precisely in order to avert this risk of dispossession and thereby secure, by limiting it, the duty of (conditional) hospitality. Derrida, by contrast, insists we see what the averted risk itself intimates, that against which we cannot inoculate ourselves: that those who claim a right to hospitality are positioned inevitably in an ambiguous and undecidable terrain marked by both hospitality and hostility. (Elsewhere he also notes that the French term for hosts [*hôtes*] is the same as the term for guests, denoting another register of undecidability).[11] The undecidability of host/hostility and its ethico-political implications are erased, not expressed, by an analysis like Benhabib's that identifies *hostility* with one singular principle—*ethnos*, or republican self-determination, or state nationalism—and *hospitality* with another that is distinct and apart—Enlightenment universalism. The division of host/hostility into two distinct and opposed binary options cleanses hospitality of its fundamental undecidability and misleadingly casts the threat to universal hospitality as something that always comes to it from some distinct and unrelated outside source.[12] The mutual implication of host/hostility, by contrast, illustrates the persistent trace even in our own most cherished ideals of that which we seek to overcome.[13]

[8] Derrida, *Adieu* (above n 5), 47; *Of Hospitality* (above n 5), 25–7.

[9] Derrida, *Rogues* (above n 6), 173 fn 12.

[10] In a way, this is analogous to or even a version of the domain problem explored by David Miller in 'Democracy's Domain,' manuscript on file with the author.

[11] See J Derrida, 'Hostipitality' in G Anidjar (ed), *Acts of Religion* (New York, Routledge, 2001).

[12] This is reminiscent of Rogers Smith's effort to identify ascriptive moments in United States history not with the liberal tradition but with alternative ascriptive rivals to that tradition. RM Smith, 'Beyond Tocqueville, Myrdal, and Hartz: The Multiple Traditions in America' (1993) 87 *American Political Science Review* 549–66. On Smith, see Jacqueline Stevens, 'Beyond Tocqueville, Please!' (1995) 89 *American Political Science Review* 987–95 and my *Democracy and the Foreigner* (Princeton NJ, Princeton University Press 2001) chs 1 and 5.

[13] As Derrida puts the point in the 'Force of Law': 'The undecidable remains caught, lodged, as a ghost at least, but an essential ghost, in every decision, in every event of decision. Its ghostliness deconstructs from within all assurance of presence, all certainty or all alleged criteriology assuring us of the justice of a decision'. J Derrida, 'Force of Law: "The Mystical Foundation of Authority"' in Gil Anidjar (ed), *Acts of Religion* (New York, Routledge, 2001) 253.

Any right to hospitality is caught in the aporia signaled by the two orders, the one heterogeneous to the other, and yet necessary in some way to it. And, Derrida points out, although '*unconditional* hospitality [is] impossible ... heterogeneous to the political, the juridical, and even the ethical ... the impossible is not nothing. It is even that which happens, which comes, by definition'.[14] One way to think (part of) this thought might be as follows: any particular right to hospitality takes its motivation, its energy and animation, not just from a finite economy of right, a moral law, universal human rights or a particularist ethics, but also and problematically from the infinitude of the unconditional hospitality that is both expressed and betrayed by any proclaimed table of values or by any enacted right to, or gift of, hospitality as such.

The distinction between the unconditional and the conditional might illuminate from a new angle Arendt's famous call for *the right to have rights*.[15] This is a call in the name of an unconditional order of rights, something that is quite distinct, as she herself makes clear in her reading of *Billy Budd* and elsewhere, from such tables of rights as universal human rights, the Rights of Man, or EU charters.[16] The right to have rights is itself a double gesture: it is a reproach to any particular order of rights (albeit certainly to some more than others) *and* a demand that everyone should belong to one such order.[17] A double gesture is necessary because, paradoxically, we need rights because we cannot trust the political communities to which we belong to treat us with dignity and respect; however we depend for our rights upon those very same political communities.[18] Are we helped out of the paradox by locating the ground of rights in a different, higher order of belonging, such as international institutions? Yes and no. Having another place to go to appeal when you lose in one venue is a good thing. But being able to so appeal still presupposes a belonging against whose fragility those very same rights are supposed to protect us. In the international arena no less than in the national, rights still presuppose belonging, now not only

[14] Derrida, *Rogues* (above n 6), 172 fn 12.

[15] Arendt, *The Origins of Totalitarianism* (New York, Harcourt, 1985) 296.

[16] Arendt, *On Revolution* (New York, Penguin Books, 1963) 82–7.

[17] A similar point is made by Etienne Balibar, who says that Arendt's '"right to have rights" does not feature a *minimal* remainder of the political, made of juridical and moral claims to be protected by a constitution; it is much more the idea of a *maximum*. Or, better said, it refers to the continuous process in which a minimal recognition of the belonging of human beings to the "common" sphere of existence (and therefore also work, culture, public and private speech) *already* involves—and makes possible—a totality of rights. I call this the "insurrectional" element of democracy, which plays a determinant role in every constitution of a democratic or republican state'. *We, the People of Europe?* (trans) J Swenson (Princeton NJ, Princeton University Press, 2003) 120. (Note that democracy, quite properly, is not here cast as insurrectional, but as having an 'insurrectional element'.)

[18] For another take on the paradox of rights, to which I refer elsewhere in this book, see W Brown, 'Suffering the Paradoxes of Rights' in W Brown and J Halley (eds), *Left Legalism/Left Critique* (Durham NC, Duke University Press, 2002).

to states but (as in Benhabib's depiction) also to a legal, bureaucratic and administrative order or to the European Union.

The unconditional—such as Arendt's right to have rights—is a way of marking the fact that no venue and no armoury of rights (conditional, contingent), no matter how broad or developed or secure, can represent the subject's absolute value in economies of rights-adjudication that are at once contingent, communal, legal, judicial, bureaucratic, moral, administrative, governmental, and discretionary. And there is no way out of the paradox of rights, though awareness of it can inflect our politics in useful ways. Indeed, Arendt's right to have rights—a polemical, political call—directs our attention repeatedly to the need for a *politics* whereby to express and address the paradox as it is experienced by minorities, the stateless, the powerless, and the hapless.

Benhabib too wants to endorse a politics in response to a paradox that she wants *not* to resolve but to ease. For this she turns to what she calls 'democratic iterations', particular culturally or politically inflected enactments of universal or cosmopolitan norms. One way to assess the differences between her approach and that developed here is by comparing each one's distinct diagnoses of the current situation, and the paradoxes on which we focus. From a vantage point shaped by awareness of the conditional/unconditional and modelled on Arendt's own call for the right to have rights things look more ambiguous than on Benhabib's account.

For example, although Benhabib is right to point out the great promise for democratic citizens in the development of Europe's newly porous borders, in new recognitions of extra-citizen human rights and alien (but still membership-based) suffrage, and in extra-state fora in which state-based injustices can be appealed against, it is also the case that a focus on these developments misleads, as does the casting of these developments as signs of an increasingly capacious normative universalism.[19] The new porousness of territorial borders among EU countries has been accompanied in recent years by the erection of new, not-at-all porous borders inside the European Union. The hosts are not only welcoming; they are also hostile.

And this is no accident. In France, for example, as post-colonial immigrants exercise their option in recent years for French citizenship or legal residency, those who do not fit the profile of the proper citizen are subjected by formal and informal state agents to police or administrative control and

[19] Indeed, Benhabib herself confesses in the final version of the lectures that she may have been, with regard to the French headscarf case, overly optimistic, given events in the year since (*Another Cosmopolitanism* (above n 1), 75 fn 8). Etienne Balibar, by contrast, is not less optimistic. He is cutting: the Maastricht definition of European citizenship that awards EU citizenship to nationals of any constituent national state, he says, 'immediately transforms a project of inclusion into a program of exclusion,' given the size of the resident alien population in Europe at the time and given the dependence of Europe on that population's labour. *We, the People of Europe?* 122.

informal intimidation. When policed post-colonial subjects—only some of them *sans papiers*—are constantly asked for their papers, this renders fraught and fragile the place of all post-colonial immigrants, residents and ethnic minorities on the territory to which some of them are now said to belong, in some sense, under French and EU law. Is it not significant that at a time of new economic pressures a new class of worker is created, an always already criminalised population that is unable to access the resources of law and rights that are at that moment expanded? Criminalised populations are often quiescent. But they sometimes take the risk (riskier for them than most) of politics, as the *sans papiers* movement has demonstrated. What that movement also demonstrated is that in practice if not in law, French residents are now repartitioned not along the formal juridical line—undocumented/documented—but along racial lines. Many are moved by the situation to joke cynically that their *cartes d'identités* are their faces, their skin-colour. Etienne Balibar names the new racialised political order 'apartheid in Europe'.[20]

In this Europe, formal law lives side by side with, but is also both aided and undercut by, an administrative police-state apparatus and a xenophobic public that legalists disavow at their peril. (These points may ring familiar to readers of Arendt's insightful analysis of the situation in inter-war Europe.[21]) Benhabib, however, in the second lecture of *Another Cosmopolitanism*, 'Democratic Iterations: The Local, the National and the Global', focuses for the most part on formal law—state and regional powers, commissions' rulings and court decisions.[22] She has a formalist's understanding of law as independent of, and prior to, politics:

> The law provides the framework within which the work of culture and politics go on. The laws, as the ancients knew, are the walls of the city, but the art and

[20] Balibar, *We, the People of Europe?* 122, 162 and passim. For example, 'European citizenship, within the limits of the currently existing union, is not conceived of as a recognition of the rights and contributions of *all* the communities present upon European soil, but as a postcolonial isolation of "native" and "nonnative" populations' (*ibid*, 170).

[21] I am thinking here of Arendt's discussion of the Dreyfus case as well as of her argument that police powers developed to deal with the stateless after World War II would, if left unchecked, soon be used against the general population. Arendt, *Origins of Totalitarianism*, pt I ch 4; pt II, ch 9.

[22] In her discussion of the French Marianne (*Another Cosmopolitanism* (above n 1), 59–61), Benhabib leaves the terrain of law altogether to mark out the importance of cultural politics, with which I agree. In only one instance does Benhabib leave the terrain staked out by the binary of formal law versus democratic contestation to acknowledge the abundant powers of administrative discretion, and the example she mentions is a positive one of discretionary power used to the good: 'Although officially the wearing of the "turban" (a form of headscarf worn by observant Muslim women) is banned [in Turkey], many faculty members as well as administrators tolerate it when they can' (*ibid*, 79). On discretion and the rule of law, see ch 3 of my *Emergency Politics: Paradox, Law, Democracy* (Princeton NJ, Princeton University Press, 2009).

> passions of politics occur within those walls and very often politics leads to the breaking down of those barriers or at least to assuring their permeability.[23]

Although Benhabib's call to break down the barriers between law and politics by way of politics seems to attenuate law's autonomy, it actually does the opposite. It posits a chronology in which law is, first, prior to politics and capable therefore of providing a framework for it; then, secondly, law is corrupted by politics; and finally law is brought into the political arena in order to wrest from law (in its limited democratic or republican form) payment on its universal (context-transcendent, that is extra-political) promise:

> It is only when new groups claim that they belong within the circle of addressees of a right from which they have been excluded in its initial articulation that we come to understand the fundamental limitedness of every rights claim within a constitutional tradition as well as its context-transcending validity.[24]

A view of rights as always pointing beyond themselves is deeply attractive. But to what do they point? Benhabib assesses new rights in terms of their fit with moulds and models already in place; incomplete, but definitive in their contours. Notwithstanding her commitments to reflexivity and revisability written about in detail elsewhere, what changes in Benhabib's practices of democratic iteration is the subject's relation to universalistic categories, not the categories themselves: the universal stays universal, the particular stays particular. Benhabib notes:

> it is clear that all future struggles with respect to the rights of Muslim and other immigrants will be fought within the framework created by the universalistic principles of Europe's commitments to human rights, on the one hand [but what evidence could put their universality in doubt? What principle?], and the exigencies of democratic self-determination on the other.[25]

Although she treats the universal and the particular as two moments in a dialectic, the two are not equal. One overcomes the other: Universality represents a *principle*; democratic self-determination an *exigency*.

With Europe's commitments cast as universalistic (in theory if not in practice, Benhabib might concede; but then something in her theory prevents the practice—racial stratification, police-state style policing, and so on—from being seen as significant evidence regarding the theory), there is little room to take seriously the sort of concern aired by Derrida in *Of Hospitality*:

> the foreigner who, inept at speaking the language, always risks being without defense before the law of the country [or region] that welcomes or expels him; the

[23] *Another Cosmopolitanism* (above n 1), 60.

[24] *Ibid*.

[25] *Ibid*, 61. Here she seems almost to echo Julia Kristeva, whose (more) French universalism I criticised in detail in *Democracy and the Foreigner*, ch 3.

foreigner is first of all foreign to the legal language in which the duty of hospitality is formulated, the right to asylum, its limits, norms, policing, etc.

Here the paradox of politics re-emerges, for 'he has to ask for hospitality in a language which by definition is not his own'.[26] For that request to be heard, for it to be audible, the hospitality in question has to always already have been extended to the speaker. It has to be given before it is asked for, or in spite of the fact that (and, indeed precisely *because*) the request for hospitality is incomprehensible, or dangerous. This is hospitality's unconditionality. It is risky. That is why it is always partnered with its conditional, risk-assessing partner: conditional hospitality.

The unconditional makes no promise about our future, and it inspires and haunts every conditional order of rights. From its vantage point, we wager that every political-legal settlement generates remainders, no matter how progressive or expansive that settlement aims to be. This is in no way to suggest that all orders are equal from this perspective; only to suggest that even those that are better than others still depend upon the supplement of a politics that is different from Benhabib's dialectically iterative politics. From the vantage point of the unconditional but not from that of Benhabib's universal, for example, even a full realisation of universal human rights on earth would necessitate further political work, generating new claims, each of which would make its own universal appeal, perhaps on behalf of those forms of life remaindered by the order of universal human rights, which would itself be in its instantiation a conditional order.[27] Benhabib by contrast would see such further claims as coming from a particularity in need of education or adjustment, one in want of appreciation for that full achievement of universality. Put a different way: if we expect hospitality always to harbour a trace of its double-hostility-then proponents of hospitality will always be on the lookout for that trace and its remainders. The same goes for universalism or cosmopolitanism. And that wariness will surface in our politics, often in the form of a double gesture in which the promises *and* risks of a particular conditional order of hospitality (and universalism or cosmopolitanism) are named and confronted.

III. THE DOUBLE GESTURE'S PARADOX

Benhabib's idea of democratic iterations is her response to paradoxes that afflict her cosmopolitanism. The paradox of democratic legitimation, which

[26] Derrida, *Of Hospitality* (above n 5), 15.

[27] This claim is one I defend at length vis-à-vis Rawls and Sandel in *Political Theory and the Displacement of Politics* (Ithaca, Cornell University Press, 1993) ch 5. In this context, here, it makes sense to note also that such political claim-making would be undercut and not just aided by the successes of universalism since such successes may attenuate lines of accountability and participation, privileging courts as venues of adjudication over popular participation.

Benhabib and I have written about in detail elsewhere (what happens when the majority whose will legitimates a democracy *itself* favours undemocratic actions?), reappears in her later work on cosmopolitanism, but it shifts.[28] The paradox of democratic legitimacy slips into the paradox of bounded communities when Benhabib says the paradox of democratic legitimacy is 'the necessary and inevitable limitation of democratic forms of representation and accountability in terms of the formal distinction between members and nonmembers'.[29] In fact there are two paradoxes or, as Benhabib puts it in her first lecture, 'The Philosophical Foundations of Cosmopolitan Norms', '[o]n close examination, we are dealing with a dual paradoxical structure'.[30] She restates the paradox of democratic legitimacy so that it again highlights the troublesomeness of mere majoritarianism (as opposed to a more normative variety): 'that the republican sovereign should undertake to bind its will by a series of precommitments to a set of formal and substantive norms, usually referred to as "human rights"'. This is a paradox between liberalism (universal human rights) and democracy (republican sovereign). The problem of membership is now cast as a different distinct problem, not between democracy and its others but rather 'internal to democracy, namely that democracies cannot choose the boundaries of their own membership democratically'.[31] This 'paradox of bounded communities' is an 'anxiety that must be faced by any serious deliberative democrat', she says.[32]

The paradox of bounded communities is actually a product of the deliberativist commitment to a certain universalism, though Benhabib would not put it that way. 'Because the discourse theory of ethics articulates a universalist moral standpoint, it cannot limit the scope of the moral conversation only to those who reside within nationally recognised boundaries;

[28] See my 'Between Decision and Deliberation: Political Paradox in Democratic Theory' (2007) 101 *American Political Science Review* 1–16 (revised as ch 1, *Emergency Politics*) and the citations to Benhabib therein. See also responses to that essay and my 'An Agonist's Reply' in the Dutch journal of legal philosophy, (2008) 2 *Rechtsfilosofie en Rechtstheorie*, edited by Sanne Taekema and Hans Lindahl.

[29] *Another Cosmopolitanism* (above n 1), 17. Compare with her earlier casting of the paradox: 'Rousseau's distinction between the "will of all" and "the general will", between what specific individuals under concrete circumstances believe to be in their best interest and what they would believe to be in their collective interest if they were properly enlightened, expresses the paradox of democratic legitimacy. Democratic rule, which views the will of the people as sovereign, is based upon the regulative fiction that the exercise of such sovereignty is legitimate, ie can be normatively justified, only insofar as such exercise of power also expresses a "general will", that is, a collective good that is said to be equally in the interests of all'. Benhabib, 'Deliberative Rationality and Models of Democratic Legitimacy' (1994) 1 *Constellations* 26–52, 28–9.

[30] *Another Cosmopolitanism* (above n 1), 35.

[31] *Ibid*.

[32] *Ibid*, 18. For a powerful critique of this claim, from Dahl to the present, see David Miller, 'Democracy's Domain'.

it views the moral conversation as potentially including all of *humanity*'.[33] Boundaries themselves require moral justification, since 'membership norms impact those who are not members precisely by distinguishing insiders from outsiders, citizens from non citizens'.[34] The problem is:

> either a discourse theory is simply irrelevant to membership practices in bounded communities in that it cannot articulate any justifiable criteria of exclusion, or it simply *accepts* existing practices of exclusions as *morally neutral* historical contingencies that require no further validation.[35]

The second paradox captures a somewhat different problem from the first. The first worried that a majority could betray its legitimacy by willing the wrong thing, that democracy could be immoral by failing to will only universalisable legislation. In the second, the concern is that those defined as the majority by the happenstance of boundaries are arbitrarily relevant from a moral point of view. The focus here is not on what is decided but rather on who is doing the deciding. This shift in focus is welcome because it calls us to consider, more centrally than did the paradox of democratic legitimation, the politics of membership and solidarity. It also calls attention to a problem with universalism. In the first paradox, universalism solves the problem (or tries to) by insisting that the people's will must be universalisable. Here in this second (version of the) paradox, universalism is *causing* the problem: it is from the perspective of universalism that proximity, community, territory and boundary are morally *ir*relevant. So a world in which these contingencies still define life chances, as indeed they do in our world, is subject to the paradox of bounded communities if we take a universalist perspective: How can a people morally constrained to will universalisably premise that willing on non-universalisable contingencies of membership? The answer, Benhabib says, is that the conflict between particularity and universality, between membership and cosmopolitan norms must be mediated by democratic iterations and by international and national law, with the aim, she says, not of exiting the paradox but rather of relaxing it. As sovereign states adopt increasingly cosmopolitan constitutions, and citizens internalise cosmopolitan norms, the paradox will, she wagers, be further eased.[36]

I favour a different, two-pronged strategy that does not draw for its solution on the very thing—universalism—that is causing the problem. First a democratic politics should be committed to diminishing international inequalities

[33] *Ibid.*
[34] *Ibid*, 19.
[35] *Ibid.*
[36] Another response might stress the importance of diminishing international inequalities such that it would matter less from a moral and material point of view where one was born. Such a response would highlight the power relations and inequalities that govern the international sphere and subject some nations and nationals to the will of others.

so that it would matter less from a moral and material point of view where one was born. Such a response highlights the power relations that govern the international sphere and subject some nations and nationals to the will of others. But since this first strategy can never be entirely successful and there will always be differences of power and privilege associated with different locations, a second strategy is needed to respond to that inevitability. The second strategy seeks not to ease but rather to embrace the paradox of bounded communities by supporting action on behalf of those contingent neighbours who just happen to be here for no good universalisable reason (though they are often 'here' for known reasons of political history—as the slogan goes: they came here because we went there.). At the same time, of course, we must realise that proximity and neighbourliness are no longer dictated alone by spatial nearness. We have global neighbours as well. Democratic activists enter into coalition with those near and far. Some become our neighbours as a result of the way pollution, consumerism, violence and capital cross borders. Shared challenges make neighbours out of us, putting us into common cause with those who might otherwise have been distant. I have noted elsewhere how before the American revolution the American colonists and revolutionaries cannily *expanded* the distance between themselves and the king by pretending never to have received sovereign instructions sent from England.[37] Here, too, we see that distance is not a fact, as it were. It can, conversely, be shortened by way of political work as well.

It matters whether we relate to those near or distant under the sign of universality or under the sign of the neighbour. Indeed, I suggest, those who move to universalisable norms to ground a sense of moral connection and obligation may find that the promise of contingent connections of geography or common cause are undone, not solidified, by a universalist morality and politics. Universalism attenuates such connections and insulates us from the call of the other. Universalism may seek to ground human rights, but human rights also postulate the very memberships and proximities with which universalism is ill at ease, as Hannah Arendt knew.[38] Thus my preferred two-pronged strategy points to the need for a 'double gesture' that both affirms the values of universal human rights (the equal dignity of persons) while calling for forms of action that may seem to violate that universality at the same time, as when we act on the basis of geographic or political proximity in solidarity with those who are near just for that reason—because they are near.

[37] See my 'Between Decision and Deliberation'.

[38] On this point, see also Simon Critchley who says: '[I]t sometimes seems to me that the only thing in which American leftists believe … is law, particularly international law. International law is a very nice thing, but if it fails to have an anchor in everyday social practices then it leads to a politics of abstraction'. *Infinitely Demanding: Ethics of Commitment, Politics of Resistance* (London, Verso, 2007) 144.

Such double gestures are necessary because, in any case, rights are not enough. When Benhabib points out that over time second-class members of democratic regimes like women and African-Americans have been brought into full possession of formal rights, she does not note that these subjects have still never come to bear those rights in the same way as their original bearers. Her optimism is supplemented by her assumption of progressive, evolutionary time, as when she characterises the second-class status of colonial American Jews as 'transitional' (en route to what?).[39] This is a tempting narration, and a familiar one, in which supposed systems of rights are (to borrow Habermas's term) 'tapped', as liberal democracies take the protections and privileges they first limited to propertied white males and then spread them outward to encompass all classes, races and genders. It is from this perspective that the status of colonial Jews looks transitional. But that is not how colonial Jews would have described their status. The speaker here, unlike those in the moment, speaks as if she already knows that the human rights side of the democratic legitimation paradox will, in the end, win, even though we are not yet at the end of the story, nor could we ever be, and so cannot ever know who or what wins in the end. In Benhabib's text, the constitutive tension central to her argument is a bit more past than present, with universality positioned toward a (cosmopolitan) future and particularity toward a (Westphalian) past. Discussing the French veiling controversy, for example, Benhabib says of the girls who stood up for their 'cultural rights' that having learned to 'talk back to the state', they will likely one day learn as well to 'talk back to Islam'.[40] Here Benhabib's cosmopolitanism seems to both presuppose and promise citizens who do not yet exist. These citizens negotiate state and cultural powers on behalf of universal human rights which are themselves (again) both the condition and the goal of liberal democratic statehood in a cosmopolitan setting. So far, so good. But Benhabib breaks the vicious circle, first by staging it as a conflict between universality and particularity (returning us to the paradox of democratic legitimation as she recasts it in *Another Cosmopolitanism*) rather than between or within democratic freedom and democratic (self-)sovereignty, and then by inserting the amended paradox into a time sequence. She wagers that these young women will likely talk back to Islam too one day and thereby show in the course of historical time that they have learned democratic and cosmopolitan citizenship. The prediction of eventual Islamic cultural self-overcoming confines the paradox of politics to a particular historical moment, to a present pre-cosmopolitan moment whose eventual, promised, overcoming is what underwrites *our* affirmation of *their* culturalism now.

[39] *Another Cosmopolitanism* (above n 1), 34.

[40] *Ibid*, 67. Benhabib finds it likely that the experience of standing up to the state will provide the girls with the resources to 'engage and contest the very meaning of the Islamic traditions that they are now fighting to uphold'.

Whether or not this wager is right (a great deal depends upon domestic and international political and economic developments in France, Europe, and the Middle East, not simply on the trajectory of rights) is less important than the work the wager does. The wager privileges the backward-looking gaze of a still-future cosmopolitanism. We assess the present from the perspective of a posited future in which the particularities of the present are overcome. That temporality anchors what I have elsewhere called chrono-logic of rights, the quasi-logical unfolding of rights in accordance with the sequencing demands of linear, normative progress—*Die Weltgeschichte ist das Weltgericht* (world history is the world's verdict)—and it also occludes from view impositional and violent processes that help secure such developments when they do occur.[41] Benhabib is aware of current xenophobic policies but she does not worry that any coming cosmopolitanism may be not just obstructed by them but itself partly *produced* by them. She does not worry that cosmopolitanism might carry the traces of the beliefs and practices it is said to oppose. That is, she does not ask whether such policies might both violate and also help to produce the projected coming of a (post-)cultural cosmopolitanism.

From the perspective of Benhabib's history of democratic (trans-)statism as a history of expansion and increasing universalisation, we simply do not see that which does not fit its linear time trajectory: for example, the history of disenfranchisement. In the Jim Crow South, newly won juridical rights were rendered nugatory by local political intimidation and a failure to secure and enforce the political and material conditions of rights-taking. In the United States and Canada resident alien voting was once an uncontroversial practice, but it was ended by the xenophobia of the World War I era. Historically, it is worth noting, alien suffrage occurred without all the things that Benhabib sets up as necessitating it now: border attenuation, pressures on state sovereignty and extra-national institutions.[42] Faced with the prior practice of alien suffrage, it is hard to think of recent EU gains

[41] On the chrono-logic of rights, see my 'The Time of Rights: Emergent Thoughts in an Emergency Setting' in M Shapiro and D Campbell (eds), *The New Pluralism: Essays for William Connolly* (Durham NC, Duke University Press, 2007), revised and republished as ch 2, *Emergency Politics*.

[42] In Canada, alien suffrage was ended at the same time as some women (military wives), were first given the vote (1917–18). Until then co-residents were assumed to share a fate, a shared future, if not a past. This is different from the German court's invocation of 'fate' in its decision on alien suffrage, in which, it seems, the fact that people moved once (in a cross-border migration; presumably other residents had moved too but not across national borders), was taken as licence to script those people as *always* about to leave. (This, it seems to me, is the real offence, insofar as it bespeaks the unimaginability of real immigration. They may have come here but they are never really here because, having come from elsewhere, they will certainly leave; they will be called home? Or expelled, deported?). In other words, the fact of proximity, so important in this chapter, is radically undone by a symbolic politics that scripts the immigrant not as one who is here but rather as one who is always on his way out (evidence for which, as it were, is that he came here in the first place).

in alien suffrage as the latest in a line of serial expansions earned by our progressive tapping of the system of rights.[43]

For example, it is surely not insignificant that the idea of alien suffrage appealed to the province of Schleswig-Holstein in 1989 when the aliens to be empowered to vote were all citizens of Northern European countries, while the new minorities putting the most pressure on traditional German conceptions of citizenship at the time were from the more liminal borderland of Turkey. And it is surely not insignificant that recent debates in Europe about the social rights of aliens, specifically about whether 'we' should share our social welfare with 'them', have occurred in the last two decades at the very moment at which European social welfare rights have been downsized. Depictions of foreigners as those who want to come 'here' to take 'our' welfare have worked to reassure western Europeans that they still have social welfare worth taking (which they may, by comparison with others, but which they do not, by comparison with themselves 30 years ago). This is one of the ways in which xenophobic politics are not just negative but also productive.

Benhabib knows that at the very moment in which 'the entitlement to rights' is expanded, 'the condition of undocumented aliens, as well as of refugees and asylum seekers ... remains in that murky domain between legality and illegality', but she does not read this remnant as a *remainder produced in part by* the conditional order of universal hospitality (as I myself have been suggesting, though other forces are at work too).[44] Instead, her language suggests, the problem is that some people have been left passively behind by an imperfect but still progressive cosmopolitan law, in which case appeals to human rights commissions and exercises of cultural political interventions may correct the wrong and result in a truer universalism. She subtly puts us onto a temporal register in which this limit is always already about to be overcome. From that register, we are in no position to ask whether these remainders are the direct products of the political project of Europe-formation—which is, we might note, not only a way to transcend national belonging, but also a way to re-secure national belonging. In a time when claims to national belonging, say, in France, are being made by non-Europeans, the political (re)formation of Europe as a site of belonging is surely a way to re-secure and not just attenuate or transcend national

[43] At the lectures Benhabib responded, as Habermas also has to objections similar to this one, by acknowledging the fact of the regress, saying 'OK, "one step forwards two steps back"'. This response is different from the double gesture called for here insofar as it rescues progress from any evidence against it, and preserves the linearity of its timeline: progress and regress are two sides of the same coin and regress is here suffered due to the promise of progress. Thus, the alternative to progressive time is not regress but rather plural temporalities, an idea developed by William Connolly (along with some useful thoughts on cosmopolitanism) in his recent work, *Pluralism* (Durham NC, Duke University Press, 2005) and commented upon by me in *Emergency Politics*, ch 2.

[44] *Another Cosmopolitanism* (above n 1), 46.

belonging. As Derrida points out in *The Other Heading*: 'I am (we are) all the more national for being European, all the more European for being trans-European, and international'.[45]

The challenge, then, is to see the situation in all its ambiguity and from that vantage point to intervene in ways that claim Europe for a different present, for different futures, for different constituencies, for a different politics. The challenge is to open up room for the much-needed double gesture: for example, one might oppose the constitutionalisation of the European Union in the name of an alternative locatable and accountable rule of law, to counter that future with another in the name of the very democratic and human rights that constitutionalisation has historically *claimed* to entrench, and to do all this without being cast as a mere agonist or defender of national particularity, or as a member of the National Front, as if these were the only options (naysayer versus lawgiver, National Front or European Union).[46] Or one might argue in favour of such constitutionalisation, while seeking to embed within it some counters to its own gravitational pull to centralised sovereignty, as some US founders sought to, and thought they had. We know however, from the US example, that no charter can deliver on its promises of stability and accountability without an activist politics to risk and secure them.

The same challenge of the double gesture is incited by Benhabib's treatment of sovereignty. Here the very same evidence that allows her to speculate hopefully but cautiously that 'the conflict between *sovereignty* and *hospitality* has weakened in intensity' could also suggest that sovereignty is, on the contrary, in the process of being shored up, transformed into something altogether new.[47] The new openness Benhabib endorses can just as well be a sign of sovereignty's adjustments, accommodations, and relocations—from visible peripheral borders to less visible internal ones (city/suburbs, French/Algerian, Catholic/Moslem/Jewish/secular), from states to regions or from states weakened by globalisation to states re-empowered by their new, sometimes fraught, membership in regional associations such as Europe, which restore nationalist fervour or salvage it while also perhaps attenuating or redirecting it, and working to secure the continent's peripheral borders in ways that mime old state sovereignties.[48] Just as the problem of refugees to which Benhabib briefly alludes may not be (just) a *problem* for state sovereignty but rather *or also*, as Nevzat Soguk argues, an *occasion*

[45] J Derrida, *The Other Heading: Reflections on Today's Europe* (trans) P-A Brault and MB Naas (Bloomington, Indiana University Press, 1992) 48.

[46] I take Wendy Brown to have something like this approach in mind when she talks about 'suffering the paradoxes of rights', in *Left Legalism, Left Critique*.

[47] *Another Cosmopolitanism* (above n 1), 47.

[48] The same might be said as well for the new human rights regime itself, which as Derrida points out, is a new site of sovereignty and counters sovereignty with sovereignty, not with non-sovereignty.

for the refinement and enhancement of state power, so too the problem of refugeeism in Europe, testified to by the many refugee camps lined up on both sides of Europe's old and new borders, may serve as a sign of the new continental sovereignty of the European Union.[49] Here, Giorgio Agamben's suggestion regarding state sovereignty may motivate a new analysis also of the European Union: What if refugees, rather than (or in addition to) being the exceptions of the juridical state (or continental) system, are metaphorically its norm, the exemplary objects of the sort of power that the state system and its sovereign legalism represent but hide—bio-power and its rule over all as bare life?[50] The risk of such an analysis is its disempowering interpellation of citizens into the (for many of them, imagined or exaggerated) subjection of emergency sovereignty. But there is also a gain to be had. Agamben does not allow camp existence to be dismissed as an exception to the human rights rule but rather insists on the disturbing possibility that in the camps we find what Hannah Arendt said was perversely postulated by universal human rights as such: the bio-politics of, in Agamben's language, bare life or, in my language, the mere survival of mere life.[51]

IV. NEW FACTS, OLD NORMS

Benhabib says she is led to cosmopolitanism by the new empirical facts of state sovereignty attenuation in the late twentieth century. A lot *has* changed in recent years. But the 'facts' are not univocal; they are subject to widely varying interpretation, as I have demonstrated here. Indeed, Benhabib's turn to cosmopolitanism seems to me to have been in some sense over-determined by other factors. Long before cosmopolitan norms were on their agenda, Habermas and his followers sought a solution to the paradox of democratic legitimation (what happens when the people, on whose will the legitimacy of a regime rests, will the wrong thing?), another version of which serves as Benhabib's point of departure. They found that solution in various forms of statism (including the rule of law), which they relied upon to preserve deliberative democratic norms and procedures from the caprice of the people, or local majorities. Concerns about the undemocratic nature of the statist solution got vented in the 1990s by way of analyses of the paradox of constitutional democracy, a paradox that in failing to

[49] N Soguk, *States and Strangers: Refugees and Displacements of Statecraft* (Minneapolis, University of Minnesota Press, 1990). On the camps, see Etienne Balibar, 'Europe as Borderland', paper presented as The Alexander von Humboldt Lecture in Human Geography, University of Nijmegen, 10 November 2004. (www.ru.nl/socgeo/n/colloquium/Europe%20as%20Borderland.pdf).

[50] G Agamben, *Homo Sacer: Sovereign Power and Bare Life*, (trans) D Heller-Roazen (Stanford CA, Stanford University Press, 1998).

[51] For a discussion of the distinction between mere and more life see my 'Surviving: Mere Life or More Life?' Introduction, *Emergency Politics*.

name the state, as such, as a problem for democracy, covered over the real concern while also giving some vent to it.[52] Because there are now concerns about the state's caprice—most especially about state-sponsored violence and injustice—a new paradox of democratic legitimation, one which pits cosmopolitanism norms against republican self-determination, surfaces as the problem that has to be solved in Benhabib's lectures. (All of Benhabib's examples in her second lecture, 'Democratic Iterations: The Local, the National and the Global', are of state-based injustices agitated against by local and transnational agents and agencies.) But although it surfaces as a problem, the new paradox of democratic legitimation is really also working as a solution, the solution to the last paradox's now problematic solution: statism. In short, at each register, universalism seeks a new harbour: liberalism, constitutionalism, state institutions, and now—cosmopolitanism. But no harbour is safe. (Sound familiar? It is the story Hegel tells in the *Philosophy of Right*.) That is, of course, because the universal is never really as we imagine it to be: truly unconditional, context-transcending and unmarked by particularity and politics.

In the end, statism is not really overcome. Benhabib applauds three girls from Creil for having learned to 'talk back to the state' but the applause is to some extent contingent on the likelihood that they will therefore also learn one day to 'talk back to Islam' and thereby affiliate better with the proper universalism of the French state and the European Union.[53] But those three girls from Creil did not act alone; they were fronts for an organisation, a social movement represented in Benhabib's text by Monsieur Daniel Youssef Leclerq, head of Integrité and former President of the National Federation of Muslims in France. This is, for Benhabib, an indication that the girls' gesture was a 'conscious political' one.[54] That may be. But it also indicates something else: the girls appeared in the public realm as the effects of a social movement no less than Rosa Parks did when she supposedly spontaneously one day, out of the blue, simply refused to move to the back of the bus. It is a trick and a victory of statist law and politics in liberal democracies to ascribe to individuals those significant actions that are products of a concerted politics. Rival sovereignties, oppositional movements, and political dissidence are thereby erased from view and we

[52] Here Benhabib provides a minor amendment to Habermas who treats constitutionalism as if it were merely the rule of law. He does not attend to constitutions as expressions of particularity. (I myself criticise him on this point, as does Alessandro Ferrara. See our replies to Habermas: Honig, 'Dead Rights, Live Futures: A Reply to Habermas's "Constitutional Democracy"' (2001) 29 *Political Theory* 792–805; Ferrara, 'On Boats and Principles: Reflections on Habermas's "Constitutional Democracy"' (*ibid*, 782–91). Benhabib, by contrast, does emphasise the character of the act of political self-legislation as an act of self-constitution in which the 'we' defines itself as a 'we' in relation to a territorialised setting.

[53] *Another Cosmopolitanism* (above n 1), 67.

[54] *Ibid*, 53.

are left only with small individuals (three girls) or large phantoms (Islam, radical particularism, etc).

Benhabib does not dwell on the role of social movements in these cases of 'democratic iteration' and so it is hard to tell what's democratic about them. It is also hard to tell what's 'iterative' about them. The term, in the hands of Derrida, whom Benhabib cites here, signifies a drift and residue, a ruptural quality of language as such; hence 'iteratibility' (not iteration) is his term, connoting something different from the subject-centred practice suggested by Benhabib's term 'democratic iterations'. Derrida meant to call attention by way of iterability to a quality of language and practice that pushes terms and concepts always to exceed and undo the intentions and aims of any particular speaker in time; this would include the languages of law and even universality itself.[55]

Iterability, as Derrida theorises it, is not inconsistent with the notion that the women in the French veiling controversy should have been 'given more of a public say in the interpretation of their own actions'.[56] This is Benhabib's suggestion in response to the concern that 'the meaning of [the girls'] actions [was] dictated to these girls by their school authorities'.[57] I do not disagree. But the suggestion does highlight the agent-centred quality of Benhabib's view of political action and performativity. For, unlike iteration, iterability presses upon us awareness that such public say cannot control the semantic field. If the veil looks 'backward' to some French citizens, appears offensive to others, and legitimate to still others, that is the shape of the political battle, a battle in which the girls should of course take part. By privileging the girls' interpretation of their actions because the actions were 'their own', Benhabib rightly seeks to enhance their agency and correct their exclusion from the interpretative field. What Benhabib does not note is that such inclusion, while necessary and perhaps promising, is also fated to replay the conflict.

Indeed, one of the issues for the school authorities was precisely whether the girls' action was 'their own'. This concern cannot be allayed by moving from action to justification; it will rather almost certainly be replayed. The same questions that were posed about the false consciousness of the girls' action will now be posed about their post hoc account of themselves: Is their explanation their own? Is their interpretation authentic? This is one of the key points in dispute for the players, after all: Were the girls pawns or were they autonomous actors?[58] Benhabib herself slips into the morass when in order to argue that the girls' act was a 'conscious political' one and not a manifestation of false consciousness, she points out that they were working with the head of

55 Derrida, *Of Hospitality* (above n 5), 65.
56 *Another Cosmopolitanism* (above n 1), 57.
57 *Ibid.*
58 See my *Democracy and the Foreigner*, ch 3 for a detailed discussion of this issue.

Integrité, Monsieur Youssef Leclerq. She infers from their involvement with Integrité that the girls' actions were consciously political and autonomous. But this fact also licenses the opposite conclusion, that the girls' actions manifest not autonomy but heteronomy, because their association with Leclerq can be seen to implicate the girls in his agency and agenda, not their own. This is a problem for a politics of democratic *iterations* but less so for an analysis focused on iterability. Iterability has us focus not on the autonomy of the players but on the play of meanings and dissemination. That the girls should have a voice in that and that they can and should *claim* their actions as their own is indisputably clear. But agonistic political theorists, more focused on diagnosing the 'stuckness' of such situations than in generating norms to govern them, see that something more than the equal inclusion of all players is needed—movement politics, action in concert, new coalitions and pressure groups—if we are to move beyond this conflict and its eternal return.

V. AGONISTIC COSMOPOLITICS

An alternative cosmopolitics, oriented by the unconditional order of hospitality, prizes proximity and might join Benhabib on several fronts, including her endorsement of the reinhabitation of the French Marianne by post-colonial (*im*)migrants. But a cosmopolitics might also unsettle elements of her universal human rights agenda. For example, it might adopt a hyperlegalist critique of state violence in the name of the rule of law while also resisting the legalists' project of constitutionalising the European Union. These seemingly contradictory moves would be made in the name of those human rights more likely to be attenuated than secured by the European Union's constitutional order, and in the name of a more engaged, accountable democratic politics than that thus far identified with the European Union, a politics hampered until now by the famous 'democratic deficit' that is unmentioned by Benhabib.[59] Such a double gesture is characteristic of an 'agonistic

[59] Most of the arguments relevant here are well summarised by Anand Bertrand Commissiong in the review of David Held's 'Global Covenant: The Social Democratic Alternative to the Washington Consensus' (2005) 4 *Logos* (2) www.logosjournal.com/issue_4.2/commissiong.htm (accessed 29 August 2008).

'The challenges the authority and execution of international legal regimes face in controlling these [ie anti-modern] forces [both of Bush's messianism and of Islamic extremists] illustrate further the complexities of the stalemate. As Tocqueville noted, courts in a democracy represent an un-democratic strain essential to the system's proper functioning. The relation between natural law and democratic will, a key component of modernity, was accomplished over several hundred years partly through the compromise of political negotiation in successful national formation processes in Europe and North America. But this process in many cases also violently ruled out effectively dissolutionary elements that sought to establish smaller, autonomous units. (Tilly) Even in some Western countries these forces were not entirely pacified and still simmer ... [Held's] vision can only be realized if some sense of world-wide solidarity, or covenant if you will, develops to take shared control of these networks'.

cosmopolitics' by contrast with Benhabib's normative cosmopolitanism. An example of this might be the battle by Slow Food, an activist food politics group that ably plays the globalisation game, to support sustainable food production by creating global markets for local producers. With that same goal in mind, Slow Food also resists EU standardisations, which harm local food producers and privilege the largest players in the mass food and agriculture industries. Slow Food never loses sight of questions like Arendt's: What interests are advanced or advantaged by certain institutional innovations? And, more broadly, what new worlds are brought into being thereby? What will we lose if we win?

Arendt's unconditional right to have rights is as good a motto as any for the project of an agonistic cosmopolitics, as long as we understand rights to imply a world-building that is not incompatible with the project of building juridical institutions and safeguards, but also reaches beyond that project because it is wary of how power and discretion accrete in such institutional contexts. In the name of such a right to have rights, and motivated by the doubly-gestured diagnoses developed here of in/formal law and politics as they are operating in early twenty first century Europe, an agonistic cosmopolitics might call for the enactment of underground railroads devoted to the remainders of the state system, such as refugees (Michael Rogin); or the designation of some spaces as cities of refuge (but not camps) such as Jacques Derrida called for (following the recovery of them by Immanuel Levinas, who commented on the Biblical injunction to establish six of these in Ancient Israel); or we might stand up for *droits de cité*, a demand to extend full hospitality to refugees and other non-immigrant border crossers simply because they are here.[60]

The phrase 'Simply because they are here' rejects the legitimationist demand that some justification be given for privileging those who are proximate. The Habermasian concern on this front is with 'the paradox of bounded communities', which Benhabib says must be attended to by any 'serious' deliberative democrat. The worry encapsulated in this paradox is: it is an arbitrary matter who is in, and who is out of, this particular community which now has to hold itself responsible for universalisable legislation. But that legislation will, however, only apply to this contingently bounded community. There is in fact no problem of logic here, however; only a political problem introduced by the particular form of the demand for universality made by Habermas and his followers. Another way of thinking of universality might see proximity not as a problem but as an opportunity, not as an artifact of the contingency of boundaries, but as a device for their attenuation. This, or something like it, is what Franz Rosenzweig is after when he thematises neighbour-love which he characterises, in Eric Santner's

[60] M Rogin, *Ronald Reagan, the Movie*. (Berkeley, University of California Press, 1987); J Derrida, *On Cosmopolitanism and Forgiveness* (above n 7).

parsing, as a process of 'ensoulment' in which we 'by acts of neighbour-love—small miracles, as it were, performed *one by one*, mov[e] from one neighbour to the next (rather than by way of a love directed immediately to *all* humankind)'.[61]

In a passage quoted at the head of this essay, Rosenzweig himself richly puts the point:

> If a 'not yet' is written above all redemptive union, the only result can be that, it is, at least to begin with ... the neighbor [the well-nigh nighest] who is precisely there ... [W]here someone or something has become the neighbor of the soul, a part of the world becomes what it was not before: soul.[62]

Here the neighbour presents not a moral problem to be solved (why him and not someone else? What justifies that?), but an ethical and political opportunity to be acted upon. The former justifies, as Bernard Williams points out, or it paralyses, as does all philosophy on Rosenzweig's account (as on Wittgenstein's), but the latter propels.

Qua acts of neighbour love, we can enact *droits de cite*—by taking people in, harbouring them, offering them shelter, finding sympathetic agents of discretionary power who are willing to look the other way—while also risking the re-authorisation of law's authoritative institutions by working through them to win papers or amnesty for those who are here simply because they *are* here. Under these circumstances the poor migrants and refugees living in that murky space mentioned by Benhabib will not be so dependent on law to position them with more clarity in its network. Then they will not have to wait for their time to come, and a good thing too—because it won't. For even when our time seems to have come, time can nonetheless still subject us to its trickery.

'*This is a story about the trickery of time*', is the first line of an article about Ibrahim Parlak, a Kurd from Turkey and a would-be immigrant to the United States who was held for almost a year in detention and was almost deported to no-country as a result of the recasting of his past by post 9/11 politics and by likely abuses of discretionary power that post-dated his previously approved applications for asylum in the United States. Post hoc, Parlak was cast as a terrorist but this has not yet erased from his neighbours' memories (not yet!) his decade-long membership in a Michigan community.[63] The activism of his many friends and supporters—his Michigan neighbours—prevented him from becoming one of the disappeared, a

[61] Santner, *On Creaturely Life: Rilke, Benjamin, Sebald* (Chicago, University of Chicago Press, 2006) 207.

[62] Franz Rosenzweig, *The Star of Redemption*, (trans) BE Galli, (Madison WN, University of Wisconsin Press 2005), 252; see also Santner, *Creaturely Life*, 207.

[63] A Kotlowitz, 'The Politics of Ibrahim Parlak: How did a political refugee who became a popular café owner in a small Michigan town suddenly become a terrorist in the eyes of the government? A post 9/11 story', *New York Times Magazine*, 20 March 2005.

casualty of policing and immigration policies that we now think of as post 9/11, even though they were also pre 9/11. The Antiterrorism and Effective Death Penalty Act of 1996 played a role in his recasting, though again, due to time's trickery, even that legislation—a response to the Oklahoma City bombing—is now often assumed to be part of our post 9/11 landscape in which the emergency is *foreign* terrorists, not domestic ones. A Federal Court ordered Parlak set free on bond on 20 May 2005. Two years later, as Parlak was preparing to appeal against his deportation by the Department of Homeland Security's Immigration and Customs Enforcement Office, the Department of Homeland Security had appealed against the federal court's decision to free Parlak on bail, and lost, and was filing a motion to vacate the judge's order on a technicality.[64] Meanwhile a group called 'Free Ibrahim' formed. Their slogan? 'Ibrahim for Citizen'. They succeeded in getting Senator Carl Levin and two representatives to introduce two bills in the House and Senate to make Parlak a permanent resident should he fail to prevail in the courts.[65]

In this set of events, I discern a connection hinted at by Rosenzweig 100 years ago. In his remarks on neighbour love quoted above, Rosenzweig took advantage of a pun in German in order to put proximity and urgency into connection. As Santner points out: the German for neighbour, *der Nächste*, is shifted in the passage from Rosenzweig's *Star* to *das Nächste*, as in the well-nigh *nighest*, a term which connotes now not proximity but urgency. The pun is apt, not because urgency is never distant but because when it is proximate, we often find ways to render it less so, to reason our way out of action. The need is greater elsewhere; what justifies my actions here? Or: their proximity to me here is illegitimate and illegal. Why should they gain from breaking the immigration queue when others wait legally? Or: we must work through the proper channels. These concerns are not wrong. These worries about consistency and principle are important. But they undo the compelling call of the neighbour. That is their troubling remainder.

An agonistic cosmopolitics would approve of movements like Free Ibrahim and of those that demand alien suffrage for co-residents—'because they are here'. They made their own 'lucky break' (language I borrow from Jonathon Lear) and can serve as ours and we as theirs. But an agonistic cosmopolitics

[64] US District Judge Avern Cohn on 21 May 2005 set bail at US$50,000 for Parlak, deciding that he should be freed while he appealed against his deportation. As the *Chicago Sun-Times* reported, Judge Cohn reasoned that otherwise Parlak 'was likely to be held for an unreasonable time period, given the complexity of his deportation case'. Released on bond on 3 June, Parlak was back in Harbert, Michigan for the time being while his lawyers prepared his appeal. *Ibrahim Parlak v Robin Baker* (Detroit Field Office Director, US Immigration and Customs), US District Court for the Eastern District of Michigan Case No 05-70826. See also M Thomas, 'Jailed Immigrant to Get out on Bond', *Chicago Sun-Times*, 21 May 2005; J Romig, 'Family, Friends Embrace Parlak', *South Bend Tribune*, 4 June 2005; www.harborcountry-news.com/articles/2006/03/23/news/story2.txt.

[65] www.freeibrahim.com.

requires also that we at the same time work to prevent the energies of our political movements from being lost once our state-centred and state-affirming goals are won: thus, such a politics postulates ongoing activisms. We might join with those working to diminish the desperate global inequalities that are among the reasons people are set in motion; we might work globally to sustain local economies that can thrive, a goal also set by the food politics group Slow Food. Or we might declare our cities to be sister cities in solidarity with cities from other nation states, thus inaugurating all sorts of extra-statist relief, aid, trade, and learning between us.[66] Or within the juridical domain, we might see more citizens of privileged nations marrying, instrumentally, those who seek to live among them in order thereby to enable their fellow world-dwellers to stay on as their neighbours: as a nice by-product we would be de-romanticising *two* institutions insistently romanticised and still claimed by most states as their monopoly, both marriage and citizenship.[67] Practices such as these and others are designated by Étienne Balibar, drawing on Bodin, as 'marks of sovereignty', in a move meant to take Bodin and democratic sovereignty back from the state sovereigntists.[68] Such practices are jurisgenerative in Robert Cover's sense perhaps more than in Benhabib's because, although she does not mention it, the jurisgenerative in Cover's account is always partnered with the jurispathic.[69] Generativity without destruction is no more possible for Cover than is hospitality without hostility for Derrida.

Were all this to happen and to be visible to us (for it does happen but it is often not visible), through lenses that do not *privilege* (although they do take note of and seek to engage, improve and democratise) formal legal, state, state-like, and interstate institutions, then we might see more worldliness, in Hannah Arendt's sense of care for the world. For, contra Benhabib, Arendt is no 'Kantian in moral theory'.[70] Arendt's Kant is that of the Third Critique,

[66] On sister cities, see ch 3, *Democracy and the Foreigner* and the several sources cited therein. Derrida also looks to cities as a source of promise for a new cosmopolitanism: see *On Cosmopolitanism and Forgiveness* (above n 7).

[67] Entry into citizenship and entry into marriage (at least normalised, permitted marriage) are two of those moments (paradoxically permanent moments) at which the state's role as authoriser empowers it over those who seek its recognition and rewards. States, the US in particular, insist that we treat both institutions romantically, not instrumentally. Both are contracts that we must enter into with the least contractual motives, out of a non-instrumental desire to belong, or to share, or to contribute but never out of a desire to profit in any way from the relationship. This indeed is the quandary faced by those who seek refuge in states like France and the United States. Neediness marks the would-be immigrant as an undesirable. But, as Etienne Balibar points out in *We, the People of Europe?*, who but the needy would come? I discuss the connections between marriage and citizenship in 'Foreign Brides, Family Ties, and New World Masculinity,' in ch 4 of *Democracy and the Foreigner*.

[68] Balibar calls also for works of citizenship that engage economic power and religious knowledge in comparative perspective in 'Difficult Europe', in *We, the People of Europe?*, 173 and *passim*.

[69] RM Cover, 'The Supreme Court, 1982 Term, Foreword: Nomos and Narrative' (1983) 97(4) *Harvard Law Review* 4–69.

[70] Benhabib, *Another Cosmopolitanism* (above n 1), 15.

not the Second. Moreover, Arendt is not, nor are (so-called) postmodernists '*skeptical* that political norms can ever be judged in the light of moral ones'.[71] Arendt has a critique of that.[72] Arendt did have a juridical moment in relation to Eichmann; who wouldn't? Benhabib is not wrong to suggest that there is in Arendt a persistent legalism that is on display in her *Eichmann in Jerusalem*.[73] But the *limits* of that trait in Arendt's thinking are also on display in *Eichmann in Jerusalem*, perhaps most when Arendt derisively dismisses the survivor, K-Zetnik, for his inability to testify coherently before the Israeli court. In Arendt's cutting portrayal of this man's failure, the ruthlessness of her legalism is as apparent as its tone deafness, its inalertness to context.[74]

For Arendt, the chief political virtues are worldliness and care for the world; and these are in danger of being sidelined by versions of cosmopolitanism in which law, states, state-like and inter-state institutions are our principal addressees (in all of Benhabib's examples), our guardians, ventriloquists, impersonators, shapers and censors of our voice, our desires, our aspirations, our solidarities. Under the sign of worldliness, however, and in the name of neighbourliness, potential commonalities might emerge between a normative cosmopolitanism like Benhabib's and an agonistic cosmopolitics. They may share a common motivation and a common cause: to combat the abundant forces of inequality in our world. But, committed to the view that all institutional settlements generate remainders, an agonistic cosmopolitics is committed to the perpetual generation of new sites of action in concert on behalf of worlds not yet built or on behalf of those still emergent and in need of activist support and sustenance.

Thus, some differences remain even when the differences between Benhabib's position and my own seem to disappear:

> The democratic dialogue, and also the legal hermeneutic one, are enhanced through the repositioning and rearticulation of rights in the public spheres of liberal democracies. The law sometimes can guide this process, in that legal reform may run ahead of popular consciousness, and may raise popular consciousness to the level of the constitution; the law may also lag behind popular consciousness and may need to be prodded along to adjust itself to it. In a vibrant liberal multicultural democracy, cultural-political conflict and learning through conflict should not be stifled through legal maneuvers. The democratic citizens themselves have to learn the art of separation by testing the limits of their overlapping consensus.[75]

[71] *Ibid*, 19.

[72] For an analysis of Arendt's critique of moralised politics and of the Kantian injunction that politics should bend its knee to morality, see my *Political Theory and the Displacement of Politics*, ch 4.

[73] But Arendt's legalism is different from Benhabib's. On this see Lida Maxwell, 'The Demands of Justice'.

[74] *Eichmann in Jerusalem*, 223–4. For an alternative, more empathic and insightful treatment of the K-Zetnick episode, see S Felman, *The Juridical Unconscious: Trials and Traumas of the Twentieth Century* (Cambridge MA, Harvard University Press, 2002).

[75] Benhabib, *Another Cosmopolitanism* (above n 1), 60–61.

These are Benhabib's words. To 'the art of separation' I would marry '*the craft of recombination*'. Against and together with the idea of raising popular consciousness to the level of the constitution, I would promote the need for an a-constitutional politics as well, to raise constitutions to a new consciousness. What each of us might mean by re-articulation of rights surely differs, as I have argued in detail here.

VI. POSTSCRIPT

In a response to my response to her Tanner Lectures, Benhabib attributed to me an anti-statist governmentality-centered Foucaultianism: 'For Honig, neither the state and its institutions nor the law and its apparatus can be sites of democratic iteration and emancipatory politics'.[76] I am said to endorse 'movement politics' and to manifest 'hostility toward institutions'.[77] The charge of anti-statism is also a charge of non-seriousness.[78] The latter charge is made explicit later—'political struggles which address the state and its institutions ... mean *getting serious* about the political by engaging with it at all levels of state, law and civil society'.[79] To ignore the state is, perforce, to be 'lite', marginal. It goes to the heart of what we think we are doing as political theorists. Do we aspire to write constitutions for emerging democracies, influence sitting judges with amicus briefs, map out agendas, be part of the action, point the way forward? Or will we editorialise from the sidelines, write critiques, diagnose our 'stuckness', and call for double gestures to engage the complexities of the current situation?[80]

The precise phrasings in my original reply to Benhabib belie the charge of anti-statism.[81] The state and its institutions are always our addressees. They

[76] *Ibid*, 161.

[77] *Ibid*, 163.

[78] On the politics of (non)seriousness see chs 1 and 2 of my *Emergency Politics*, with regard to Stephen Holmes and Slow Food. See also Simon Critchley, who knows that 'comical tactics can hide a serious political intent' (though, I would add, sometimes the tactic IS the intent). Critchley, *Infinitely Demanding*, 124.

[79] Benhabib, *Another Cosmopolitanism* (above n 1), 164.

[80] For a brief in favour of irrelevance see my 'Against Relevance' Paper presented at the Perestroika Reception during the annual meeting of the American Political Science Association, Boston, MA, September 2002.

[81] Here are some quotations from my original reply that evidence a more nuanced position ('Another Cosmopolitanism' (above n 1)102–27):

— Arendt's unconditional right to have rights is as good a motto as any for that project, as long as we understand rights to imply a world-building that is not incompatible with the project of building juridical institutions and safeguards, but also reaches beyond that project because it is wary of the sedimentations of power and discretion that accrete in such institutional contexts.

— we can enact *droits de cité*—by taking people in, harbouring them, offering them shelter, finding sympathetic agents of discretionary power who are willing to look the other

wouldn't have it any other way. But when they are our addressees, when they self-privilege as our most important addressees, we are called—indeed interpellated—into and by their perspective and we lose hold of our capacity to imagine politics otherwise. There is nothing 'holier than thou' about pointing this out, surely.[82] It is one of the many double binds of political action in the contemporary world.

To use the term interpellation is risky. It is, Benhabib says, 'old Althusserian language'.[83] But for me, it continues to capture something no newer term does: the ways in which our entire being is swept up in the address of the state and its agents, even in anticipation of such address. Not just that of the police, though they are pretty good at it, but also immigration agents, passport control, transportation safety employees, the revenue service, health insurance agents, and so on. One of the things progressive democratic activists must do is to join those swept up in those interpellations and help engage these institutions: elect different representatives, protest institutional injustices, educate members and aliens, demand accountability, strive for better legislation and demand better court appointments.

Engaging the state is a feature, but not the essence, of democratic politics. The choice between social movements and a more juridical politics focused on state and transnational institutions is a false one. To focus on institutions of governance without a foot in movement politics and critique is, perforce, to perform juridical politics without the balancing perspective of a life lived otherwise. It is to be left vulnerable to the self-privileging perspective of statism and its formalisms.

Juridical politics is always in need of the support and orientation of life lived in political movement. In addition to engaging state and transnational institutions directly, democratic actors must also, and not as a secondary matter, in some ways begin living now as if we had already succeeded in that first endeavour. Otherwise we get locked into the eternal agon of small

way—while also risking the re-authorisation of law's authoritative institutions by working through them to win papers or amnesty for those who are here.

— Meanwhile a group called Free Ibrahim has formed. Their slogan is 'Ibrahim for Citizen' and they have succeeded in getting Senator Carl Levin and two representatives to introduce two bills in the House and Senate to make Parlak a permanent resident should he fail to prevail in the courts.

— We should 'approve of movements like Free Ibrahim, and of those that demand alien suffrage for co-residents—"because they are here". But advocates of an agonistic cosmopolitics would work at the same time to prevent the energies of those movements from being lost once their state-centered and state-affirming goals are won'.

— Were all this to happen and to be visible to us, (for it does happen, but it is often not visible) through lenses that do not *privilege* (although they do take note of and seek to engage, improve, and democratise) formal legal, state, state-like, and interstate institutions, then we might see more worldliness, in Hannah Arendt's sense of care for the world.

[82] Benhabib, *Another Cosmopolitanism* (above n 1), 164.
[83] *Ibid*, 163.

(or even large) institutional victories and never actually do what we want those institutional changes for—that is, to live otherwise. And this could and should happen, even in advance of those victories. Better to get on with the business of what Franz Rosenweig might have called neighbourliness and what Hannah Arendt called action in concert. In so doing, we do not ignore or sideline the state. But we insist—and we remind the state and ourselves—that it does not exhaust life.

On Hannah Arendt's account, the most revolutionary thing that the American revolutionaries did was done long before the revolution occurred. More important than their protests and challenges to the King, more weighty than any tea party, was the experiment in living which they undertook alongside sovereigntist politics. This was an experiment, the reverberations of which moved from the margins to the centre of an empire. It succeeded in becoming an institutional revolution because the form of life it presupposed had somehow, through the daily work of life, been magically brought into being, *avant la lettre*. Some changes do need to be argued and fought for on judicial or formal institutional terrains. But they also need to be lived. From a democratic theory perspective, neither tactic is more serious, nor more central, nor more important than the other and both carry risks. The work of institution-building simply cannot succeed without the support and perspective of life lived otherwise.

Benhabib, in her reply to me, claims Derrida for her argument:

> ironically, Derrida himself is far from splitting the political into the unholy realm of the state and its institutions and the angelic realm of social movements. He states:
>
> '[T]he political task remains to find the best "legislative" transaction, the best "juridical" conditions to ensure that, in any given situation, the ethics of hospitality is not violated ... To that end, one has to change laws, habits, phantasms, a whole "culture"'.

Benhabib concludes: 'Changing "laws, habits, phantasms and a whole culture" is not contradictory to seeking the best legislative and juridical practices'.[84] She is right; there is no contradiction here and I have nothing against seeking the best legislative and juridical practices nor do I think social movements are 'angelic'. A lot of them scare me. But in seeking the best legislative and juridical practices, we must be mindful of how such endeavours press us to make our cases and envision ourselves and our political futures in terms quite different from those we might otherwise imagine and seek to vouchsafe. That is a concern that Benhabib simply does not share. She sees law as regulative not productive. I note here that Derrida, but not Benhabib, places the terms culture, legislative, and juridical all in scare quotes. Why? Perhaps it is the 'phantasms'.[85]

[84] *Ibid*, 164.

[85] On one impact of those phantasms, see Penelope Deutscher's contrast of Derrida and Blackstone on the decision: Derrida, she says, 'emphasizes ... the importance of recognizing

Still skeptical of Althusser, Benhabib says, 'Honig practises the method of ideology critique and shows that every universality is afflicted by particularity and difference which, in turn, it must repress. But if this is an ideological truism, how does its repeated deployment help?'[86] It is not an ideological truism, however. Rather it is a conclusion drawn again and again from the study of particular would-be universals in action. As we track the work of Benhabib's universals in her neo-universalist cosmopolitanism, we can see through a close reading of her work how the universal operates in a way that does not simply mediate the political[87] but also triumphs over it in ways she seems to approve. However, more importantly, I mean to be arguing *in favour* of something like the repeated deployments dismissed here. The repetition of critique could be a symptom of repetition compulsion, which is what Benhabib implies with her criticism. But it could also be a sign that the critique bears repetition, that in spite of the claim that we have moved on, we in fact continue to repeat our old errors or remain stuck in our old habits, a point made by Nietzsche who mourned the fact that although we have killed god we continue to dwell in his old houses. What choice do we have, in such instances, but to repeat and re-deploy our critiques? Besides, we need not assume that repetition is like dead ritual. If we repeat our criticisms and engagements as Rosenzweig counsels us to repeat daily liturgy, we may find that, as Rosenzweig predicted, we ourselves are reshaped by the exercise. If we repeat our concerns always in new ways with new resources in relation to new texts or new political events, we do so not in order to win the argument but rather in order to illustrate again and again the stakes of winning or losing it.[88] In other words, one way to assess the merits of a political theoretic position is by inhabiting it for long enough to see the world through its perspective and assess that world. That is what I have tried to do here.

the incalculability and "undecidability" of law. Compare with Blackstone, for example, whose aim is to make the law as calculable and predictable as possible. Though this is what we most often expect from the law, Derrida nonetheless emphasizes the simultaneous importance of the undecidable factor in legal decision-making'. Deutscher, *How to Read Derrida* (New York, WW Norton, 2006) 97.

86 *Another Cosmopolitanism* (above n 1), 162.

87 *Ibid*, 159.

88 For an account of Rosenzweig and Derrida on the generative possibilities of repetition, see Zachary Braiterman, 'Cyclical Motions and the Force of Repetition in the Thought of Franz Rosenzweig' in A Cohen and S Magid (eds), *Beginning/Again* (New York, Seven Bridges Press, 2005). See also Arendt: 'Experiences and even the stories which grow out of what men do and endure, of happenings and events, sink back into the futility inherent in the living word and the living deed unless they are talked about over and over again' (*On Revolution*, 222). On the need to inhabit and not just argue for a position, I recur to another passage from Rosenzweig: 'Everyone should philosophize at some time in his life, and look around from his own vantage point. But such a survey is not an end in itself. The book is no goal, even a provisional one. Rather than sustaining itself, or being sustained by others of its kind, it must itself be "verified". This verification takes place in the course of everyday life'. Democratic theory and politics would be well served by replacing discourse theory's validation with Rosenzweigian 'verification'. Rosenzweig quoted in NN Glatzer (ed), Introduction to *Franz Rosenzweig: His Life and Thought* (Indianapolis, Hackett, 1998).

10

Citizenship and Electoral Rights in the Multi-Level 'Euro-Polity':

The Case of The United Kingdom

JO SHAW*

I. INTRODUCTION

OF THE MANY languages of citizenship, perhaps the one most frequently used is that of citizenship as a democratic ideal. This relates to the perfection of the link between the people and the exercise of political power: government for the people, by the people. This formulation demands that critical attention be paid to the question: 'Who are the people?'[1] For in a world where nation states are challenged from above by integration and globalisation processes such as the European Union (EU) or global migration, and from below by autonomy claims from sub-state regions and nations, that question can rarely be answered simply by pointing to the historically hegemonic claims of the boundaries of the Westphalian 'nation state' as the sole legitimate democratic reference point. The 'national' people may be simpler to recognise than any other more cosmopolitan variant of the notion, because it offers something more certain and rooted as a baseline. It may also be a simpler concept to define than the 'people' of a sub-national unit, not least because it relies upon a well-established body of (international) law regulating acquisition and loss of nationality, and setting the parameters of physical frontiers across land and water. However, the claims of the national 'people' are not universally recognised as the sole legitimate carrier of democratic aspirations.[2]

* I would like to thank Anja Lansbergen, PhD candidate at the University of Edinburgh, for provoking my interest in membership models.

[1] J Shaw, *The Transformation of Citizenship in the European Union* (Cambridge, Cambridge University Press, 2007) 20.

[2] See R Rubio-Marín, *Immigration as a Democratic Challenge* (Cambridge, Cambridge University Press, 2000); D Kostakopoulou, *The Future Governance of Citizenship* (Cambridge, Cambridge University Press, 2008).

Yet in the overwhelming majority of the world's states, the right to vote in national elections (and in 'regional' elections within federal states) is restricted to those who have acquired, whether by birth, registration, naturalisation or other legal process, the status of national citizen.[3] More often than not, states also allow *non-resident* national citizens to vote, although expatriate or external voting is not universal by any means.[4] Other non-national residents are excluded. Moreover, despite exhortations to be found within some international legal instruments such as the Council of Europe Convention on the Participation of Foreigners in Public Life at Local Level,[5] which are intended to promote the integration of migrant non-nationals into the host state through political participation, most states still restrict the right to vote in local elections to national citizens only. The major exception to this is, of course, the situation of citizens of the EU (under Article 17 EC), when resident in a Member State other than the one of which they are a national. EU citizens have the right to vote in local (and European Parliamentary) elections in the state in which they reside, under the same conditions as nationals (that is, an equal treatment right) (Article 19 EC).[6] But equally, while a number of Member States of the EU extend the right to vote in local elections to all resident third country nationals,[7] the majority of third country nationals resident in EU Member States do not have the local franchise under national law,[8] not least because the states with the largest populations of third country nationals such as France, Germany, Italy and Spain do not give voting rights to resident non-nationals other than under EU law.[9] The United Kingdom's (UK)

[3] H Waldrauch, 'Electoral Rights for foreign nationals: a comparative overview', Paper prepared for the ESF/LESC-SCSS Exploratory Workshop: *Citizens, non citizens and voting rights in Europe*, Edinburgh, 2–5 June 2005.

[4] *Voting from Abroad*, The International IDEA Handbook, 2007, available at www.idea.int/publications/voting_from_abroad/upload/Voting_from_abroad.pdf; R Bauböck, 'Stakeholder Citizenship and Transnational Political Participation: A normative evaluation of external voting' (2007) 75 *Fordham Law Review* 2393–447.

[5] ETS No 144; opened for signature on 5 February 1992; entered into force 1 May 1997; www.conventions.coe.int. This has been signed by ten Member States, but only five of those states have ratified it.

[6] Shaw, above n 1, especially ch 5. Implementation of Art 19 is regulated by Council Dir 93/109/EC, OJ 1993 L329/34 (European Parliament elections) and Council Dir 94/80/EC, OJ 1994 L368/38 (local elections).

[7] Belgium, Denmark, Estonia, Finland, Hungary, Ireland, Lithuania, Luxembourg, the Netherlands, Slovenia, Slovakia. Not all give the right to stand as well as the right to vote. See Shaw, above n 1 , at 78 and 80, and *Trends in the EU-27 regarding participation of third-country nationals in the host country's political life*, Briefing Paper prepared for the European Parliament LIBE Committee by the Centre for European Policy Studies, Brussels, 2007.

[8] *Ibid.*

[9] Voting in local elections by third country nationals is possible in principle in Spain under conditions of reciprocity, but in reality it is restricted to citizens of Norway. This excludes Spain's large population of Moroccan and Latin American immigrants (although some of the latter have either Spanish citizenship by descent or, more often, Italian citizenship by descent).

voting rights for third country nationals are also patchy, being confined to Commonwealth citizens, thus excluding many recent immigrants who are not of Commonwealth origin. At present, there is nothing in EU law which requires Member States to extend the right to vote in local elections beyond EU citizens to include third country nationals as well.[10] Thus, understanding the pattern of political participation rights in the context of the EU and its Member States (understood here as a composite 'Euro-polity') requires the study of both national and EU law side by side.

While the position of the majority of states worldwide on electoral rights for non-nationals is still relatively restrictive, it is clear that the existence of entities such as the EU which mandate the extension of certain national political participation rights to groups of *privileged* non-nationals (ie EU citizens), combined with the inclusive national policies followed in a number of states in the EU, as well as elsewhere in Europe and the world,[11] have blurred, at least partially, the allegedly sharp boundaries between citizens and non-citizens.[12] This seems to suggest that empirically speaking the distribution of the rights of citizenship may be a little messier than the democratic ideal might at first blush demand. But this mismatch of theory and practice does not necessarily act as a direct challenge to *normative* arguments that citizenship *should* continue to be seen as a democratic ideal, although it does raise many questions about what the reference point for the notion of democracy should be in the future. Should it be defined as operating within each individual state or by reference to a wider cosmopolitan political community, which would demand rights across state borders? What is the specific role of both the EU as a polity, and of the relationships horizontally between the various Member States in the wider euro-polity, in the context of trying to work out the appropriate reference point for assessing the scope of democratic participation?

The difficulties inherent in matching the democratic ideal with the messy political reality are well illustrated by the case of citizenship and voting rights in the United Kingdom, which will be the empirical focus of this paper. The UK has a complex and variegated system of political participation rights, which need to be studied in the context of the wider structures of European integration as well as the UK's own history and contemporary politics. Studying UK political participation rights means exploring the nature of citizenship in a multi-level and highly internally differentiated polity. In other words, while the focus of this chapter may seem parochial

[10] Shaw, above n 1, especially ch 7.

[11] Norway, some Swiss cantons and municipalities, Venezuela and South Korea are examples of the diverse range of states which offer votes in local elections; Uruguay and New Zealand are two of the rather fewer examples of states which allow non-nationals to vote in national elections.

[12] For a related discussion of 'denizenship' and the transformations of membership see Neil Walker's contribution to this volume (ch 11).

in the context of a volume focusing on the EU's Area of Freedom, Security and Justice, the intention is emphatically to use this case study in order to make a number of more general points about the condition of citizenship and how citizenship can best be understood wherever there are multiple and often competing sites of legal, constitutional and political authority. For the UK, like the EU itself, is a multi-level polity, where the exercise of power is increasingly contested. Like the EU it also has a framework of electoral entitlements which is both geographically differentiated and partially inclusionary, in the sense that certain groups of people are treated as privileged non-nationals (that is, Commonwealth citizens as well as EU citizens). The entry point for the discussion is offered by debates about citizenship in the UK, which have become more prominent since the mid-2000s than they have been for several decades, but it is possible to build outwards from this in order reflect more generally upon the nature of inclusion and exclusion in a wider European context. Through an assessment of these debates we can start to see some of the challenges of constructing a coherent membership principle for those citizenship rights, such as the right to vote, existing in a state such as the UK, which is a member of the EU, a member of the Commonwealth, and a union state marked by close historic ties with another state with which it shares these islands off the north west coast of continental Europe, the Republic of Ireland.

II. CITIZENSHIP DEBATES IN THE UNITED KINGDOM

Debates about citizenship in the UK have been given a prominent role within a wider national debate about the notion of 'Britishness' which was promoted by Gordon Brown when he became Prime Minister in the middle of 2007. As part of the Britishness debate, Brown commissioned the former Attorney General, Lord Peter Goldsmith, to deliver a report which would provide a fuller picture of the current state of citizenship in the United Kingdom, whilst at the same time providing some suggested recommendations on how the allocation of citizenship rights could be used in order to foster a stronger and more cohesive sense of (national) citizenship. Goldsmith's report, delivered in March 2008,[13] suggests that there is a need to 'make proposals for how to introduce greater clarity to the "citizenship settlement" between citizens and the state'. The Report intimates that this lack of clarity is a historical relic, which can be corrected for the future.

Both the debate more generally and the specific recommendations made by Goldsmith have to be viewed against the background of the contemporary challenges posed to notions of British citizenship by a number of factors.

[13] Lord Goldsmith QC, *Citizenship: Our Common Bond*, Citizenship Review, March 2008; available from www.justice.gov.uk/reviews/citizenship.htm ('Goldsmith') 12.

These include very high levels of inward (and outward) migration since the 1990s (some temporary, some permanent); the realisation that some British citizens could take up political violence against civilians in general and especially against their fellow citizens, in the name of and in support of radical Islamic sentiments; and the continuing uncertainties about the long-term political and territorial settlement within the UK in the wake of the election of a Scottish National Party government in Scotland in 2007, not to mention the complexities of Northern Irish politics since the peace settlement and the introduction of power-sharing between the Nationalist and Unionist communities. As regards the immigration-related dimensions of these challenges, Goldsmith's has not been the only recent contribution to the debate: in February 2008, the Home Office produced a report called *The Path to Citizenship: Next Steps in Reforming the Immigration System*, which explicitly linked the process of accessing national citizenship to the proposition that a person must display certain features and must 'deserve' to access British citizenship. In other words, it is not just about long-term residence, the acquisition of English language skills, the absence of criminal convictions or other signals of delinquency, and the passing of a citizenship test, but also potentially about the pursuit of 'active' citizenship through contributions which are not required of those who acquire citizenship by descent or birth. This paper highlights that Goldsmith's more informal review of the state of British citizenship is rooted within a more general debate in government circles about integration and citizenship.[14]

It is interesting to note that Goldsmith's Report is entitled *Citizenship: Our Common Bond*. This bond is indeed the focus of the recommendations, many of which have proved to be controversial; none, so far, have been implemented. For example, the report suggests that there should be citizenship ceremonies for all young people, rather than just for 'newcomers' going through the naturalisation process, as has been the case since 2004 by virtue of provisions contained in the Nationality, Immigration and Asylum Act 2002.[15] The idea of ceremonies for all, likely to coincide with a young person reaching the minimum school-leaving age, is intended to promote a stronger sense of common belonging, and indeed to mark a rite of passage. The suggestion received a good deal of mixed comment; in particular, outside England, most of the comment was rather negative because of the difficulties of reconciling the conscious affirmation of a single common national citizenship (with the apparently inevitable connotation of pledging allegiance to the Crown) with the complex national identities

[14] For a related discussion of integration see Dora Kostakopoulou's contribution to this volume (ch 8).

[15] See M Rimmer, 'The Future of Citizenship Ceremonies', paper prepared as part of the Goldsmith Citizenship Review, October 2007, available from www.justice.gov.uk/reviews/citizenship.htm.

which are especially common amongst those resident in Northern Ireland, Scotland and Wales.[16]

Less attention was paid by commentators to those sections of the report which addressed the current mélange of electoral rights for citizens and non-citizens which exists in the UK. These are as much the result of the UK's earlier imperial history and its ongoing relationships with Commonwealth states and with the Republic of Ireland, as they are the result of the contemporary impact of EU law. Thus, not only EU citizens but also Commonwealth and Irish citizens are privileged non-nationals in a UK electoral context. Irish, Maltese and Cypriot citizens fall into two categories of privilege, and—unlike other EU citizens—they can vote and stand for election in all elections in the UK, including elections to the UK parliament in Westminster. The Representation of the People Act 1918 established the first truly modern franchise for the Westminster parliament, abolishing property qualifications for men and introducing the franchise for (some) women for the first time. The franchise was, at the time, given to 'British subjects', there being then no modern conception of British citizenship. When Ireland and what are now the countries of the Commonwealth became independent states at various points during the twentieth century, the franchise arrangements were preserved and updated.[17] The relevant consolidating legislation laying down the general entitlement to vote is the Representation of the People Act 1983, as amended.[18] In this political sense, neither Irish nor Commonwealth citizens are treated as 'aliens', although in the case of the latter group the right to vote and to stand[19] in any elections in the UK is subject to immigration status. Only persons who are 'qualifying', in the sense of not requiring leave to enter or remain, or having been granted it, are able to vote and to stand. For Maltese and Cypriot citizens, who are both Commonwealth citizens and EU citizens, this qualification does not apply, as indeed it does not for Irish citizens.

It is worth mentioning that some degree of reciprocity exists between the voting rights of Irish citizens in the UK and those of UK citizens in Ireland. In 1985, after a Supreme Court case[20] which required this matter to be put before a referendum in order to effect a constitutional change,

[16] See eg, 'Salmond slates "Pythonesque" UK citizenship plan', *The Herald*, 12 March 2008.

[17] See eg the Ireland Act 1949.

[18] For more details on all UK elections see House of Commons Library Standard Note, 'Electoral Franchise: Who Can Vote?', SN/PC/2005, 1 March 2005.

[19] The right to stand for election is covered by the Act of Settlement 1700, although the issue of immigration status is dealt with by the Electoral Administration Act 2006 s 18. See House of Commons Library Standard, 'The Franchise and Immigration Status', SN/PC/419, 11 October 2005, House of Commons Library Research Paper 05/65, 'The Electoral Administration Bill 2005', October 2005.

[20] *In the Matter of Article 26 of the Constitution and in the Matter of the Electoral (Amendment) Bill, 1983 [SC No. 373 of 1983]* [1984] IR 268.

legislation was introduced to allow UK citizens to vote in *Dáil* (ie, lower house) elections, although not to stand.[21] This was done in the name of reciprocity by the Irish Parliament. Bearing in mind that there are no elections to the upper house of Parliament in the UK, nor for the Head of State, it is understandable that voting rights were not given in elections for the *Seanad Éireann* and the President of Ireland to UK citizens. There is also a lack of parallelism in relation to referendums. Irish citizens may be able to vote in referendums in the UK, depending upon the legislation establishing both the question and the franchise,[22] but given the specific constitutional status and function of referendums in Ireland, where popular consent for constitutional change is formally built into the system, it is not surprising that UK citizens again are not permitted to vote. Goldsmith mentions these rights very briefly,[23] but does not discuss the broader issues in the context of European integration as well as the UK-Irish relations which lie behind these developments.

The other novelty of UK political participation rights is that they display some degree of internal variation and geographical differentiation. This stems partly from the fact that certain types of elections (notably those for the devolved bodies of Scotland, Northern Ireland and Wales, as well as the Mayor and Assembly of London) simply do not exist in some parts of the UK, so that voters in the UK have different political rights depending upon where they are resident. But the real curiosity stems from the decision to give EU citizens the right to vote and to stand in these categories of elections.[24] It is entirely a matter of internal choice for the UK to extend the local electoral rights mandated by the EC Treaty to the 'regional' level, where such elections exist in the UK, and indeed the UK is the only EU Member State to do so. Votes in elections to the sub-national units of federal or quasi-federal states such as Austria, Belgium, Germany and Spain are not included in the scheme of EU law rights in those states, which extend only to the lowest level of municipal democracy. While electoral rights for EU citizens to vote in 'county-level' elections are extended alongside municipal electoral rights voluntarily by a number of Member States which have such elections, such

[21] Electoral (Amendment) Act 1985.

[22] Eg the Government's European Union Bill, introduced into the House of Commons in 2005 and providing for a referendum on the Constitutional Treaty, was based on, but went somewhat beyond, the Westminster franchise, as the basis for giving a right to vote (cl 7).

[23] Goldsmith, above n 13, at 49.

[24] Section 3(1) of the Local Government Elections Regulations 1995 (SI 1995/1948) provides the basic amendments to the local electorate to incorporate the requirements of EU law; in relation to the inclusion of EU citizens in the 'regional' franchise see s 17 of the Greater London Authority Act 1999; s 11 of the Scotland Act 1998; s 10 of Schedule 1 of the Government of Wales Act 1998; s 2(2) of the Northern Ireland (Elections) Act 1998. For further discussion, see J Shaw, 'Political Rights and Multilevel Citizenship in Europe' in E Guild and S Carrera (eds), *Integration of Third Country Nationals and Illiberal Practices in the EU* (Ashgate, Houndsmills, forthcoming).

as Hungary and Sweden (and indeed the UK, where such entities exist), these levels of government represent more accurately an expression of local self-government than they do the exercise of legislative sovereignty. The UK devolution scheme is different, with a territorially-differentiated scheme for internal governance which some would call quasi-federal in nature.[25] The Scottish Parliament, in particular, which has the power to pass primary legislation under the Scotland Act 1998, has significantly greater powers which cut directly into the legislative sovereignty of the UK as a whole. Moreover, since the passing of the Government of Wales Act 2006, considerably more power actually and potentially is also conferred upon the Welsh Assembly to pass measures which are definitely more substantial than 'simple' delegated legislation. Likewise in relation to Northern Ireland, ever more substantial areas of competence, along with the power to take relevant measures, are likely to be passed to the Assembly and to the Northern Irish ministers in the future.

It is worth noting that the UK has gone even further than giving the right to vote and to stand to EU citizens; with the exception of the devolution referendum in Northern Ireland which was conducted on the basis of the Westminster franchise, EU citizens were able to vote in all of the referendums which have preceded the establishment of the various devolved elected bodies throughout the UK, on the basis of residence in the relevant part of the UK. Ascertaining why the UK should proceed in this manner is a little tricky, especially since the previous round of devolution referendums held in early 1979, when the proposals for both Scottish and Welsh assemblies were rejected (in the former case because, although there was a majority, it was not a sufficiently large one), used the Westminster franchise as the basis for determining who should vote in the referendums. It seems most plausible to suggest that the decision to use the local government franchise and electoral register as the basis for determining who could vote and stand for election expressed an intuition that devolution marks the extension of what constitutes 'the local' within UK constitutional politics.[26] It is not, on this reading, the revised expression of the notion of constituent power within a quasi-federal state. However, while the notion of 'the local' may have been the aspiration of those in union-supporting parties who drove the devolution agenda from the early 1990s onwards, and who brought it to formal fruition after the election of the Labour Government in May 1997, a different constitutional reality has emerged since then. In this context, devolution is more a process than a 'thing', demonstrating the capacity to result in changes

[25] See eg A Gamble, 'The constitutional revolution in the United Kingdom' (2006) 36 *Publius: The Journal of Federalism* 19–35.

[26] It also avoids the question of expatriate voting, which was introduced for the first time into UK law after the election of the Conservative Government in 1979, which followed the first round of failed devolution referendums.

in the UK's fundamental territorial settlement. This has become all the more striking, especially since the election of governments in Northern Ireland, Scotland and Wales, where nationalist parties which did not necessarily participate fully in the 'devolution' agenda now share or hold power.

Lord Goldsmith's arguments when discussing the right to vote and to stand for election in his Report were somewhat perfunctory. He focused on the external exclusivity of national citizenship, arguing that

> [v]oting in all elections, along with holding a passport, is the ultimate badge of citizenship. That view is reflected in the rules of most other countries around the world which do not permit anyone but citizens to participate—or to stand—in national or often even local elections. Clearly in the UK we do not have the same clarity around the significance of citizenship.[27]

He went on to propose

> that the government gives consideration to making a clear connection between citizenship and the right to vote *by limiting in principle the right to vote in Westminster elections to UK citizens*. This would recognise that the right to vote is one of the hallmarks of the political status of citizens; it is not a means of expressing *closeness between countries*. Ultimately, it is not right to give the right to vote to citizens of other countries living in the UK until they become UK citizens' (emphasis added).[28]

It is not explicit in the discussion in the body of the report, but is made clear in the executive summary,[29] that Goldsmith would propose narrowing UK voting rights down just to what is *required by* EU law, and no more. Hence he does not touch European Parliament electoral rights at all, even though the precise nature of the right to vote in European Parliament elections and consequently the implications of such a right for elections and democratic participation at the national level remains somewhat uncertain. All Commonwealth voting rights (apart from Maltese and Cypriot citizens' EU rights) and Irish voting rights (apart from EU rights) would go, since by Goldsmith's argument the historical or contemporary closeness between the relevant countries is not sufficient to outweigh the need to link the gold standard of political participation with the formal membership of the polity. This includes removing voting rights in devolved and local elections from almost all Commonwealth citizens. It is therefore anomalous that Goldsmith does not question the voting rights for EU citizens (including Irish, Maltese and Cypriot citizens) in the devolved elections. Given the increasingly powerful nature of those bodies, a consistent approach to citizenship in accordance with the principles articulated by Goldsmith would surely demand the inclusion of these elections in list of those confined to

27 Goldsmith, above n 13, at 75.
28 Goldsmith, above n 13, at 75–6.
29 Goldsmith, above n 13, at 6.

UK citizens. Moreover, it is clear that these rights are *not required* by EU law and yet accommodating the strict requirements of EU law does seems to be the test which Goldsmith has applied, when allowing departures from the national principle. Accordingly, it would seem that failing to address this question is inconsistent in the light of his predominant theme.

It is also interesting that Goldsmith himself recognises that apart from EU law there are at least two other important constraints upon the extent to which UK voting rights can be 'tidied up' along the statist lines suggested in the report. First, he accepts that those Commonwealth and Irish citizens who have already acquired rights to vote in Westminster elections should not lose them so long as they remain resident in the UK. His proposals are merely aimed at newcomers. Secondly, there is the 'problem' of the Good Friday Agreement, signed in April 1998 by the UK and Irish Governments and explicitly endorsed by most of the Northern Irish political parties.[30] In addition to settling the details of the power sharing and devolved government in Northern Ireland, this document recognises and guarantees that the people of Northern Ireland are free to take either British or Irish citizenship (or both), and identify themselves as British or Irish as they wish. Goldsmith thus recognised that his neat scheme based on UK citizens voting in UK elections must cede in the face of the complexities of the peace process in Northern Ireland. Ever hopeful, he suggested that distinguishing between Irish citizens in the UK who are not connected to Northern Ireland and those who are was merely a practical problem which could be overcome, so that only the former would be denied the right to vote in Westminster elections. Beyond this concession, it is interesting that Goldsmith does not seem to think that the case of Northern Ireland poses more than practical difficulties. The irony of this conclusion—quite apart from potentially trivialising the serious practical obstacles to drawing the distinctions suggested, given the possibilities for mobility between Ireland, Northern Ireland and Great Britain—is that as an outcome it would suggest that any rearrangement of UK citizenship rights must necessarily continue to respond to complex political and historical reality, rather than simply reflecting some single model of (exclusive) membership based on the tightness of the connection between citizen and state. This is precisely the opposite principle to that which Goldsmith intends to defend. Not seeing that irony, Goldsmith consequently fails to engage with the argument that such an 'anomaly' in practice undermines the very cleavage he wishes to highlight between the vertical state-citizen relationship on the one hand, and the horizontal relationships between states, on the other.

Indeed, the biggest challenge to Goldsmith's scheme for citizenship rights does not concern his attempt to distinguish between democratic principle

[30] For the text of the Agreement see www.nio.gov.uk/agreement.pdf.

and messy political practice, but instead attacks the very nature of the principle which he seeks to defend. For Goldsmith rejects the proposition that the notion of citizenship which operates in the context of a Member State of the EU could, or should, have a horizontal dimension other than in relation to the obligations explicitly required by the EC Treaty. On the contrary, in Goldsmith's worldview, it is the vertical relationship which matters and, despite plenty of discussion of the rights (and very limited duties) flowing from EU law in the report, it is also clear that in the context of voting rights he accords privilege to the (national) state above all other sites of political and legal authority. This is the ultimate legitimate reference point for determining questions of political community, regardless of the existence of the EU.

Now at one level it is quite easy to dismiss the UK's messy and piecemeal franchise arrangements as lacking a single organising and consistent principle of membership, making it practically impossible to reform one part of them without this impacting upon another part. But a different way of looking at the problem is to see it as the search to elaborate a more consistent principle of membership in a complex multi-levelled polity (the UK) nested in another complex multi-levelled polity (the EU). Such a principle should ideally both explain existing patterns of rights, and also provide predictions as to future developments. Goldsmith has proffered what he suggests is a fundamentally 'national' perspective upon reforming UK voting rights. This is certainly a principle which has been defended quite staunchly by some theorists and commentators.[31] But another perspective could focus instead on what may be seen as the inextricable links between the vertical and the horizontal bonds which make up the complex figure of citizenship in the multi-level Euro-polity. It is not, on this view, about forcing a choice between fostering close polity/citizen links and sustaining the 'closeness between countries', which Goldsmith mentions rather dismissively. Both these principles may operate side by side in a transformed political space. This approach, it could be argued, offers a better basis for building a dynamic model of membership, one which could even—for example—survive a fundamental change in the basis of the UK polity, such as the ending of the historical union between England and Scotland, and all that follows from this. Above all, it would do more than merely assign a negative (constraining) meaning to developments within EU law, so far as they impact upon electoral sovereignty in the UK. In other words, EU law should not just be seen as something which constrains the expression

[31] See in particular D Goodhart, *Progressive Nationalism. Citizenship and the Left* (London, DEMOS, 2006) who defends a more tightly bound national concept as the best way of defending ideals about collective welfare and security which are generally associated with the left of the political spectrum. For a more academically constructed defence, see also D Miller, *On Nationality* (Oxford, Oxford University Press, 2005).

of sovereignty in the UK, but as having its own constitutive force, often in combination with national constitutional law.[32] To this end, we need to figure out in more detail the contemporary meaning of citizenship and to identify relevant transformatory processes by focusing on the dynamic interactions between different elements of membership within a multi-level and highly differentiated Euro-polity, deploying a focus on recent case law of the European Court of Justice on political rights.

III. WHAT IS 'CITIZENSHIP' IN THE CONTEXT OF THE EURO-POLITY?

Since 1993 and the inception of the Treaty of Maastricht, commentators have reflected in detail upon the nature of citizenship of the Union.[33] Many have concluded—to use the terminology applied by Paul Magnette—that the horizontal 'isopolity' element—comprising the principles of non-discrimination and free movement which protect the transnational migrating EU citizen—is much more developed than the vertical 'sympolity' element, based on the constitution of a (political) relationship between the citizen and the Union. Yet, the latter—if developed—would also have the potential to affect the status of all EU citizens, including the non-migrating ones.[34] To put it another way, the market citizen dominates the political one, with the latter predominantly a thing of potential, rather than a current reality. This point was well expressed by Ulrich Preuss in an early commentary:[35]

> European citizenship does not mean membership in a European nation, nor does it convey any kind of national identity of 'Europeanness'. Much less, of course, does it signify the legal status of nationality in a European state. Rather, by creating the opportunity for the citizens of the Member States of the European Union to engage in manifold economic, social, cultural, scholarly, and even political activities irrespective of the traditional territorial boundaries of the European nation-states, European citizenship helps to abolish the hierarchy between the different loyalties ... and to allow the individuals a multiplicity of associative relations without binding them to a specific nationality. In this sense, European citizenship is more an amplified bundle of options within a physically broadened and functionally more differentiated space than a definitive legal status.

[32] For a more extended articulation of this position, see the work of Leonard Besselink, in particular L Besselink, 'The Notion and Nature of the European Constitution after the Reform Treaty' (ms, January 18 2008, http://ssrn.com/abstract=1086189) and L Besselink, *A Composite European Constitution* (Groningen, Europa Law Publishing, 2007).

[33] For a review of the debates and of the relevant legal developments, see Shaw, above n 1, especially ch 2.

[34] P Magnette, *Citizenship: The History of an Idea* (London, ECPR, 2005) 177.

[35] U Preuss, 'Problems of a Concept of European Citizenship' (1995) 1 *European Law Journal* 267–81 at 280.

As this suggests, it may in fact be both artificial and misleading to reflect—whether negatively or positively—upon Union citizenship as a discrete concept, which can be studied in isolation, without taking into account the reconstructive potential of the complex multi-level nature of the Euro-polity itself, with its multiple sites of legal, political and constitutional authority. In this polity, impacts and effects occur across both the (vertical) levels between the EU, the Member States and the sub-state regions and nations, as well as horizontally between states and regions, as the regulatory practices adopted and the choices made in one state increasingly impact upon the others. Translating this into the citizenship domain, Samantha Besson and André Utzinger[36] suggest the use of a composite figure of 'European citizenship', as the means of reflecting how citizenship is now firmly rooted in *both* the EU *and* the national levels (and, one might add, the sub-national level). While Union citizenship is parasitic upon the definition of national citizenship,[37] so that only nationals of the Member States may be citizens of the Union, and the Union is not capable of determining autonomously the outer normative limits of its own citizenship, it is equally true to say that the national level of citizenship is itself increasingly contingent in nature. It is affected first by transnational ties and links based on factor and commodity mobility and on political, socio-economic and even cultural integration between states and peoples and secondly, in both direct and indirect ways, by directly applicable EU Treaties and laws which cut into the fabric of national sovereignty. Besson and Utzinger express it thus:[38]

> First, citizenship in Europe has become multileveled as European citizens are members of different polities both horizontally across Europe (other Member States) and vertically (European transnational, international, and supranational institutions). Second, national citizenship in and of itself has changed in quality and has been made more inclusive in its scope and mode of functioning. Union citizenship adds a European dimension to each national *demos* and, to a certain extent, alters national citizenship in reconceiving it in a complementary relation to other Member States' citizenships.

They see this as a transformation of *national* citizenship, with the reconfigured notion being best expressed through a concept of 'European' citizenship; this concept escapes the narrower classification of 'Union citizenship', which refers to the EU alone and excludes the national but increasingly

[36] S Besson and A Utzinger, 'Toward European Citizenship' (2008) 39 *Journal of Social Philosophy* 185–208; see also L Besselink, Case Notes on *Gibraltar*, *Aruba*, and *Sevinger and Eman v The Netherlands* (2008) 45 *CMLRev* 787–813 at 801, arguing that the composite constitutional arrangement underpinning the Euro-polity is not a 'monolithic European concept of citizenship'.

[37] Art 17 EC: 'Citizenship of the Union is hereby established. Every person holding the nationality of a Member State shall be a citizen of the Union. Citizenship of the Union shall complement and not replace national citizenship'.

[38] Besson and Utzinger, above n 36, at 196.

europeanised dimension. It is an explicitly plural concept. Politically speaking, this expresses how the various national *demoi* come together across national boundaries and in national and supranational fora to constitute a functional (but not ideational) European *demos* (a *demoi-cracy*, not a *democracy*[39]). But this contributes not only to the transformation of *national* citizenship, but also to the transformation of *Union* citizenship. Each level and each site of membership rights in a multi-level and territorially and politically differentiated polity contributes to polity-building, and is transformed through the iterative relations with other levels and concepts of membership.[40] Because of the market-dominated nature of Union citizenship in the early years, this process of transformation has been slower to take root in relation to the EU itself. But while the dramatic developments in the European Court of Justice in relation to the concept of Union citizenship since the Court first tested out of the concept in the *Martínez Sala* case in 1998[41] have focused above all on the trans-border rights of mobile Union citizens, some limited signs are now becoming visible of Union citizenship itself transforming into a more distinctively political entity, where the cross-border element is no longer the key to triggering the relevance of Article 17 EC on EU citizenship or bringing about linkage between Article 17 and other fundamental principles of EU law such as equality.

Of particular significance in this context is the *Aruba* case concerning the right to vote in European Parliament elections of Netherlands nationals resident in Aruba.[42] This territory is a semi-autonomous part of the Kingdom of the Netherlands, and it is not part of the EU. This small group of EU citizens resident on a Caribbean island were able to establish that they had been discriminated against as a result of a Dutch legislative scheme which did not give them the right to vote in European Parliament elections so long as they were resident in Aruba, but did give it to them if they moved to a third country, where they would be covered by the normal expatriate voting rules under Dutch law. These gave all Netherlands nationals the right to vote in European Parliament elections without distinguishing as between whether they had previously been resident in Aruba or in the European part of the Netherlands. Effectively, the Arubans established that the Dutch legislative scheme was irrational, and needed to be revised, even though ostensibly Article 1(2) of the European Parliament Elections

[39] See S Besson, 'Deliberative demoi-cracy in the European Union: Towards the Deterritorialization of Democracy' in S Besson and JL Marti (eds), *Deliberative Democracy and its Discontents: National and Post-National Challenges* (Aldershot, Ashgate, 2006) 181–214; K Nicolaïdes, 'We, the Peoples of Europe ...' (2004) 83 *Foreign Affairs* 97–110.

[40] See generally S Benhabib, *The Rights of Others* (Cambridge, Cambridge University Press, 2004).

[41] Case C-85/96 *Martínez Sala v Freistadt Berlin* [1998] ECR-I 2691.

[42] Case C-300/04 *Eman and Sevinger v College van burgemeester en wethouders van Den Haag (Aruba)* [2006] ECR I-8055.

Directive seems to preclude EU law interference into national discretion in relation to expatriate and or external voting by nationals.[43] Thus, Member States are not free to leave in place schemes which discriminate against EU citizens by treating different categories of nationals differently, even where they have not moved from one Member State to another.

What is interesting about the *Aruba* case is that the express provisions of the EC Treaty on electoral rights are, as noted above, limited to an equal treatment right under Article 19, giving EU citizens the right to vote and stand in European Parliament elections under the same conditions as nationals when resident in *another* Member State. There are no provisions of the EC or EU Treaty either in their present versions, or indeed in their putative post-Lisbon versions, which state—in terms—that EU citizens have the right to vote in European Parliament elections (that is, the right to vote for 'their' Parliament). Indeed, most aspects of European Parliament elections are still dealt with under national law including, for example, the question whether it is permissible for Member States to include third country nationals amongst the electorate for these elections within their territory.[44] What the *Aruba* case has done is to bring a degree of Court of Justice control over national legislative restrictions on the right to vote in European Parliament elections, preventing a Member State keeping in place an irrational legislative scheme, such as that described above, whereby EU citizens gain the right to vote by leaving a part of the national territory, albeit one which is not part of the EU.[45] It can now be argued that the Court implied, but did not make explicit, that the right to vote in European Parliament elections is a Union citizenship right. In contrast, Advocate General Tizzano in his April 2006 Opinion was much more explicit. Drawing on a range of material from the Treaty and from the European Convention on Human Rights and Fundamental Freedoms, which guarantees free and fair elections as well as universal suffrage, he concluded that it was indeed such a right, and moreover that it was *the most important* of the EU citizen's rights.[46]

Aruba has not been the only case in which the Court of Justice has looked at the conditions under which Member States regulate voting in European Parliament elections. In a case decided by the Court on the same day,[47] it was required to resolve a dispute between Spain and the UK about the precise terms under which the UK had responded to the requirements imposed

43 See above n 6.

44 See Case C-145/04 *Spain v United Kingdom (Gibraltar)* [2006] ECR I-7917.

45 For a more extended discussion see J Shaw, 'The political representation of Europe's citizens: Developments' (2008) 4 *European Constitutional Law Review* 162–86.

46 Opinion of AG Tizzano of 6 April 2006, para 67: '[I]t can be directly inferred from Community principles and legislation as a whole, thus overriding any indications to the contrary within national legislation, that there is an obligation to grant the voting rights [in European elections] to citizens of the Member States and, consequently, to citizens of the Union'.

47 Case C-145/04, above n 44.

upon it by the European Court of Human Rights case of *Matthews v United Kingdom*. In a judgment of 18 February 1999,[48] the Court found that the UK had violated Article 3 of Protocol No 1 of the ECHR—which obliges states to hold free and fair elections ensuring the free expression of the people in the choice of the legislature—because it caused to be included in the original Act on Direct Elections to the European Parliament an annex limiting those elections to the UK territory alone, thus excluding Gibraltar. Gibraltarians objected to their exclusion, and successfully established before the Court of Human Rights that although Gibraltar is not part of the EU as such, it is affected by sufficiently large portions of EU law that it is possible to say that vis-à-vis this territory the European Parliament constitutes a legislature, and thus Gibraltarians have a right to a say in the composition of this body once it became directly elected. In extending UK electoral law to Gibraltar, which was incorporated into one of the UK's multi-member constituencies for the purposes of the 2004 European Parliament elections, the UK also granted the same rights to vote in European Parliament elections as apply in the UK. In other words, Commonwealth citizens resident in Gibraltar (some 100–200 persons) were allowed to vote in the elections organised in that territory.

Spain has used the prism of EU law as the basis for giving expression to its sovereignty claims vis-à-vis Gibraltar on a number of occasions, and it was therefore unsurprising that it chose to object to a number of the steps which the UK took to implement the *Matthews* judgment, including the extension to Commonwealth citizens of the right to vote. Of course, it is true that strictly speaking these arrangements do represent a violation of primary EU law in the form of the still unamended Annex to the Act on Direct Elections. However, the Act on Direct Elections was not amended because UK attempts in the wake of the *Matthews* judgment to remove the offending statement about only organising elections to the European Parliament in the UK were vetoed by Spain. Hence the UK had to choose the route of unilateral action.

After seeking in vain to persuade the Commission to bring an enforcement action against the UK under Article 226 EC, Spain itself brought an action against the UK in the Court of Justice seeking a declaration that it was acting in violation of its obligations under EU law, notably by allowing Commonwealth citizens to vote in European Parliament elections in Gibraltar. However, in its pleadings, Spain sought to distinguish the case of Commonwealth citizens voting in the rest of the UK, arguing that its points arose only in relation to Gibraltar. In practice, it is impossible to see how, if it were not permissible under EU law for the UK to extend the franchise to Commonwealth citizens in Gibraltar, it could be permissible in the UK.

[48] *Matthews v United Kingdom* no 24833/94, ECHR 1999-I.

Consequently, in defending the action in the Court of Justice, the UK was not only defending the sovereignty issue in Gibraltar, but it was also defending what the Court of Justice itself called in its judgment one of the 'constitutional traditions' of the UK,[49] namely the pattern of Commonwealth citizen voting rights discussed in the previous section and under apparent threat in Goldsmith's citizenship report. Passing over the apparent irony that—as Attorney General from 2001 to 2007—Goldsmith ultimately sanctioned the use of a defence of Commonwealth citizen voting rights by the UK in the *Gibraltar* case in terms of a 'constitutional tradition' (language which is likely to be have been fed to the Court of Justice in the submissions of the defending party), it is interesting to see that whatever weight Goldsmith might place upon such constitutional tradition in his report *Our Common Bond*, it is not sufficient to outweigh his more pressing concerns about reinforcing the national exclusivity of core citizenship rights, such as the right to vote. To repeat the point made earlier, it is clear from the report taken as a whole that Goldsmith suggested reducing electoral rights in the UK down to the minimum mandated by EU law or necessitated by the difficulties discerned in relation to the Good Friday Agreement. If implemented, this would signal, presumably, a belated victory for Spain, because in the *Gibraltar* case the Court of Justice found for the UK, concluding that there was nothing in EU law as it stands which requires that the right to vote in European Parliament elections has to be limited to EU citizens alone.

While the Court's judgment might be thought to have little wider resonance beyond the specific, rather sui generis case—not least because unlike the *Aruba* case it is not framed in terms of the legal coordinates of EU citizenship—it is none the less interesting to see how easily and fluidly the Courts slips, in its reasoning, between the different constitutional orders. This is not—to reverse a criticism which Besselink makes of the European Court of Human Rights in relation to a case on Netherlands national voting rights in *Aruba* which came before it in 2007[50]—an instance of 'compartmentalized reasoning',[51] in which the constitutional orders of the EU and the UK are seen as separate and unrelated to each other. Quite the contrary. The Court works constructively with the approach taken by a state such as the UK to categories such as Commonwealth citizens even though this clearly has spillover effects vis-à-vis the EU itself as well as the other Member States. For this approach effectively mandates an inclusive approach at the outer borders of the EU in relation to this particular EU citizenship right, the right to vote in European Parliamentary elections. Some states, such as Spain in this particular case, have clearly reacted negatively

[49] Case C-145/04, above n 44, paras 78 and 79 of the judgment.

[50] *Sevinger and Eman v The Netherlands*, Applications 17173/07 and 18180/07, judgment of 6 September 2007 declaring the applications manifestly inadmissible.

[51] Besselink, Case Notes, above n 36, at 802.

to the impact of these spillovers. But sometimes states react positively to spillovers or externalities resulting from the citizenship laws of the other states. This is the case with Ireland. It reacted, after some time, to the existence of voting rights for its citizens in the UK by instituting some reciprocal rights. Obviously, it is not directly a concern of Goldsmith—or indeed the UK if it chose to enact the measures necessary to repeal Irish voting rights in Westminster elections—how Ireland would react to such a step. If one refutes *closeness between countries* as a relevant measure of constitutional action, then certain perspectives on what other states do necessarily flow from that. However, given the links which Ireland chose to make between its present reciprocal arrangements with the UK (albeit it partial in nature) and the wider question of its relations with other EU Member States, it is clear that answering the question about how Ireland might react does have a European (citizenship) dimension.

For it is interesting to note that when it changed its constitution and adopted the necessary primary legislation, Ireland set in place an enabling mechanism whereby—if conditions of reciprocity apply—the Minister can designate the citizens of *any* Member State as able to vote in *Dáil* elections. No further legislation is required. All that is required is that the other Member State should enfranchise Irish citizens. This might be, as I have argued elsewhere,[52] a trigger for *national* developments which effectively enrich the concept of EU citizenship, by relying precisely on ties of closeness, trust and reciprocity between states to extend voting rights in national elections to migrant EU citizens. But such initiatives would also enrich the composite notion of European citizenship sketched in this chapter, not least because this would be an example of a set of national reforms effectively strengthening the supranational constitutional regime, and breaking down the barriers between the *demoi* as they currently exist.

IV. CONCLUSION

This chapter has outlined an argument why a national principle alone is insufficient as the basis for modelling membership rights within a complex polity such as the EU, at least where these take the form of voting rights. It has shown that EU law has developed substantially in relation to the constitutionalisation and concretisation of a set of political rights for EU citizens. But more importantly the chapter has identified the many iterative relations which are evolving between the various EU law rights under the Treaty, the specific interpretations which the UK (for example) chooses to place on these EU law rights by extending them to include the elections to the devolved bodies in the UK, and the UK's historical constitutional

[52] Shaw, above n 1, at 202–6.

traditions so far as these extend to including certain privileged groups including third country nationals (Commonwealth citizens) within the franchise for national elections. At the very least, even without having regard to particularities such as the impact of the Good Friday Agreement, it is impossible not to conclude that any reform of UK voting rights would be a very complex process indeed. But more positively, one can draw an interim conclusion that it might not be impossible to discern the basis for a consistent model of membership. This derives its force from viewing the overall constitutional framework for the Euro-polity as a plural evolving framework in which there is constant spillover vertically from one level to another, and horizontally across the politically and territorially differentiated space. Further work is needed to identify more precisely what might be the precise contours of such a model, and in particular how it would model not only the relationships existing for the nationals of the Member States between their *national* citizenship and their *Union* citizenship, but also the outer contours of both national and EU citizenship, and the position of third country nationals. For in a polity where political principles of participation eschew compartmentalisation on national lines, it is not necessarily obvious why, for example, the right to vote for the supranational European Parliament should not extend to *all residents* affected by its legislation. Such an argument, however, would require space beyond the scope of this chapter for it to be developed in full; it must, at this stage, be left to one side.

11

Denizenship and Deterritorialisation in the European Union

NEIL WALKER

I. LOCATING THE DENIZEN

THE CONCEPTS OF *denization* and *denizenship* find their legal origins in a process of the English common law dating from the thirteenth century by which a foreigner could gain some of the privileges of an English subject through the operation of the royal prerogative, including the right to hold land. Common law denization fell into disuse when statutory mechanisms began to develop for the naturalisation of putative subjects who were born neither within national territory nor to parents who were already full subjects, although at the same time denizenship acquired new statutory meanings complementary to the naturalisation process. For example, in the English Settlement Act of 1701 the term denizenship was used to describe naturalised foreigners who remained excluded from appointment to certain public offices.

From the beginning, therefore, the idea of a denizen, like the *metic* of the classical Greek city state, was intended to capture the situation and status of someone who was neither citizen nor non-citizen. For the most part, the idea developed within a context of migration and residence, and indeed the broader non-legal meaning of denizen remains that of resident or dweller. Yet the term has also from time to time been used of other 'half-way' situations where socially accredited position and the entitlements associated with that position are neither fully present nor entirely absent, such as that of free blacks prior to the abolition of slavery in the United States.

The residence-based meaning is the one that has dominated in current academic, legal and political discourse. When the Swedish political scientist Thomas Hammar reintroduced the term in the context of contemporary Europe,[1] he was referring to the situation of migrant workers who came

[1] T Hammar, 'Legal Time of Residence and the Status of Immigrants' in R Baubock (ed), *From Aliens to Citizens. Redefining the Status of Immigrants in Europe* (Vienna, European Centre, 1994) 187–98.

to Western and Northern Europe from the 1960s onwards in order to find employment or protection and who stayed to become long-term residents. These immigrants typically came to enjoy a full set of negative freedoms, including free access to the labour market, and they also gradually acquired a reasonable level of positive social security rights, limited political participation rights, and protection against sudden expulsion from the country. Yet, crucially, the development from the mid-twentieth century onwards of this catalogue of rights in the states of Western Europe, and increasingly through international organisations such as the Council of Europe and supranational organisations such as the EU, was not and has never since become conceptually linked to the acquisition of citizenship through any of the obvious avenues, of which we may identify four. In brief, denizenship has been understood and treated (i) neither as an *incident* of citizenship, (ii) nor as fully *constitutive* of citizenship, (iii) nor as *tantamount* to citizenship, (iv) nor even as having the acquisition of citizenship as its designated or probable *terminus*.

The purpose of the present paper is to explain and pursue why this renewed understanding of denizenship—as something proximate to but stubbornly irreducible to our conventional understandings of citizenship—is such a suggestive concept both for those interested in the relationship between the law and politics of migration (at a point when the categorical background against which we understand the movement of populations is in flux), and more generally, for those concerned with the making and sustaining of a democratically warranted political community in the context of a contemporary multi-tiered Europe. The basic answer is a simple one, even if it soon becomes more complicated. The idea of denizenship, of a form of stable association with the polity other than through the medium of citizenship, breaks or at least tests the frame of our traditional understanding of membership of political community, with all that that implies in terms of rights and obligations, participation and belonging. It is an 'in-between' concept,[2] one that challenges the series of binary oppositions—not just citizen/alien but also insider/outsider, national/international, territorial/extraterritorial, domestic/foreign, franchised/disenfranchised—that organise and reflect the political imaginary of the Westphalian system of states. In particular, it disturbs the classical idea of statehood and national citizenship as involving a form of political organisation based on certain exclusive and exclusionary, and so also mutually exclusive and mutually exclusionary properties—namely membership, territorial jurisdiction and political authority.

What is more, denizenship has various advantages over other 'in-between' putatively frame-breaking concepts. It speaks, like the concept of citizenship

[2] H Oger, '"Residence" as the new additional inclusive criterion for citizenship' (2003) 5 *Web Journal of Current Legal Issues*.

itself, in three registers, objectively, subjectively and inter-subjectively. It refers, objectively, to a bundle of rights and correlative obligations; subjectively, to a form of self-identification; and inter-subjectively, to a mark of social recognition. It also speaks to the inter-relationship between these three registers, and so in the round to a *social status*. It thus holds an explanatory and performative edge over other concepts which lack this particular and comprehensive combination of references and resonances. Unlike more abstract or more general terms like 'cosmopolitan' or 'migrant' it is grounded, through its articulation of an objective bundle of rights and obligations, in practical reason—it has immediate action-consequences. Unlike institutional terms such as 'post-sovereignty' or 'supranationalism', it speaks directly to the subject and to the transformative potential inherent in the 'double shift' in her self-recognition and recognition by others.

In turn, the combination of practical significance and the potential for altered self- and other-recognition, together with its basic transgressive 'in-betweenness,' helps account for the open-ended social and political potential of denizenship. It cannot readily be assigned to any teleological chapter within the Westphalian narrative—to any familiar story of means and ends. By the same token, however, it inhabits the same ideological and authoritative spaces as more traditional Westphalian narratives and power structures, and both competes and mingles with them. Accordingly, denizenship has an indeterminate and potentially deeply contested significance. One set of tensions and contestations concerns the perennial pressure to reduce and return it to the binary Westphalian logic—either to fast-forward denizenship to citizenship or to rewind it to alienship. Another, though closely intersecting set of tensions and contestations concerns the elusive terms of any possible transcendence of the Westphalian frame. In what follows, I will try to demonstrate how this compound set of tensions unfolds by mapping the variety of possible trajectories of denizenship. Thereafter, the problems and opportunities that flow from this are resituated in the volatile polity-constitutive politics of today's EU.

II. TRAJECTORIES OF DENIZENSHIP

In seeking to grasp the referential range of the denizenship idea we can make a useful preliminary distinction between those conceptions of denizenship that are reducible to the basic paradigm of the nation state and those that seek a new political imaginary which goes beyond that paradigm. Here, we may draw upon Will Kymlicka's distinction between 'taming' and 'transcending' liberal nationalism.[3] According to Kymlicka, recent developments

[3] See, eg, W Kymlicka, 'Liberal Nationalism and Cosmopolitan Justice' in R Post (ed), *Another Cosmopolitanism* (Oxford, Oxford University Press, 2006) 128–46.

in the law and politics of membership in the EU can be read in different ways, but for him the key battleground remains within the framework of the liberal national project. He points to the fact that many rights which we typically understand as part and parcel of national citizenship—including residence rights, liberal freedoms and some social rights and political rights, have become gradually 'unbundled'[4] from citizenship. He then draws a distinction between what we might call a 'tiered membership' model and a 'proto-citizenship' or 'emergent citizenship' model for understanding the position of the denizen as holder of these unbundled rights. Under the first model, unbundling is the cue for vertically differentiated (that is, more or less, unqualified or qualified) membership of the polity, while under the second, which he favours over the first, unbundling is just a phase in a process which—to return to an earlier formulation—has as its *terminus* the 'rebundling' of these rights 'in the form of full and equal citizenship within the framework of liberal nationhood'.[5]

On the other 'transcending' side of Kymlicka's divide, we can begin to trace a variety of alternative trajectories of denizenship. We can do so by parsing the Westphalian frame of national citizenship into its various components, and asking which element or combination of elements of the frame is the focus of challenge. To recall, the Westphalian model of citizenship is premised on three different aspects of exclusivity and mutual exclusivity, and thus of exclusion and mutual exclusion—namely of membership, of territorial jurisdiction and of political authority. Adapting a distinction drawn by Dora Kostakopolou,[6] we may differentiate between 'transnational membership' and 'post-national membership' models depending on whether just the first or all three of these elements of exclusivity is challenged.

According to the 'transnational membership' model developed by writers such as Rainer Baubock,[7] intensified transnational migratory movement and greater interaction between national societies creates more porously bordered societies. An increasing number of individuals develop attachments and make investments in more than one national society, whether simultaneously or consecutively. It follows that, however gradually and unevenly, these societies, while retaining exclusive or dominant political authority and jurisdiction over persons within their territory, become more receptive to the idea of those mobile individuals possessing and acquiring

[4] *Ibid*, 138.
[5] *Ibid*, 139.
[6] D Kostakopoulou, 'Thick, Thin and Thinner Patriotisms: Is This All There Is?' (2006) 26 *OJLS* 73–106 at 83.
[7] See, eg, R Baubock, *Transnational Citizenship* (Aldershot, Edward Elgar, 1994). The direction of Baubock's subsequent work is very much towards the 'postnational membership' model discussed in the text below. See, eg, R Baubock, 'Political boundaries in a multilevel democracy' in S Benhabib and I Shapiro (eds), *Identities, Affiliations and Allegiances* (Cambridge, Cambridge University Press, 2007).

membership rights and status in more than one polity. At one pole lies the status of 'dual citizenship', but short of that high-point of plural recognition we can observe all sorts of positions and combinations of positions on the denizenship continuum.

According to the 'post-national membership' model developed by writers such as Yasemin Soysal,[8] not only is membership no longer mutually exclusive, but the exclusivity of territorial jurisdiction and political authority is also increasingly challenged. In particular, the EU offers a model of supranational authority and jurisdiction, as well as a model of membership, which speaks to a more general de-territorialisation of political community. What is more, other and sub-state rather than super-state levels of local membership, territory and authority (ie city, regional or national) are also relevant here in eroding the state-centred structures of mutual exclusivity. Indeed, in the EU context the sub-state and supra-state level may be understood not merely as complementary but also as mutually reinforcing challenges to the citadels of exclusive state prerogative.[9]

Ideas of post-national *citizenship*—and in particular EU citizenship with its necessary and sufficient grounding in national citizenship[10] and its address to a supranational polity with territorial jurisdiction and authority that overlaps that of the member states—also attract much academic and political attention here.[11] Again, however, citizenship provides only one model, and an extreme one, with a whole range of other positions on the denizenship continuum also available. Indeed, it is arguable that, particularly through Directive 2003/109/EC,[12] the most significant developments in the membership politics of the EU in recent years have been as regards long-term third country residents with neither Member State national nor (it follows) European supranational citizenship—a category which clearly falls within the denizenship definition. The grant of long-term resident status to third-country nationals with five years of lawful residence in a Member State, together with a whole range of other rights and protections more or less equivalent to those of national citizens (including the right to work and to study), marks a significant if still limited watershed in a protracted politics of recognition. In this regard, it arguably outstrips anything achieved in the same period at the level of European supranational citizenship.

[8] Y Soysal, 'Changing Parameters of Citizenship and Claims-Making: Organised Islam in European Public Spheres' (1997) 26 *Theory and Society* 509–27. For a related discussion of transformations of the concept of citizenship in multi-level polities, see Jo Shaw's contribution to this volume (ch 10).

[9] See, eg, S Tierney, 'Reframing Sovereignty: Sub-State National Societies and Contemporary Challenges to the Nation-State' (2005) 54 *International and Comparative Law Quarterly* 161–83.

[10] Art 17 EC Treaty.

[11] The literature is massive. For a recent overview, see the Special Issue of the *European Law Journal* on *EU Citizenship*: vol 13(5) 2007, edited by Samantha Besson.

[12] Dir 2003/109/EC, OJ 2004 L16/44.

The European citizenship term was coined in the Maastricht Treaty in 1992 (and modestly refined in the 1997 Amsterdam Treaty) to formalise existing mobility rights and to supplement these with a menu of political rights including the right to stand and vote in local and European (but not national) elections. Since then, with the exception of an incremental ECJ-inspired strengthening of the scope and financial security of mobility and residence rights,[13] little more has been achieved by way of systematic improvement of the membership rights of EU supranational citizens living or travelling in EU countries other than those in which they are national citizens.[14] What is more, quite apart from the sharper transformative edge of legal developments within the third-country denizen category, demographic factors mean that the net impact of changes in the standing of denizens is greater than that of the changes affecting the second-country European citizen category. In the EU of today, after all, it is estimated that of the five per cent or so of residents who do not possess citizenship of the state in which they live, more than twice as many (68 per cent) have third-country denizen status than possess EU citizen status (32 per cent).

Beyond transnational and post-national membership models of the relationship between denizenship and political community we can, finally, also locate on the liberal nationalist-transcending side of the divide a host of positions tending towards what we might, somewhat provocatively, call a 'post-membership' model.[15] The key to this is not the redundancy of territorially located and enduringly authorised political communities. Short of a comprehensive cosmopolitan vision, distinct if increasingly overlapping political communities will remain situated in a particular space and in a particular time. Rather, it involves the decreasing salience of the very idea of membership of a political community. That is to say, if we think of the three factors which make up the social status (citizen, denizen or alien) which marks the relationship with political community within the current political imaginary, namely the bundle of rights and obligations, the self-understanding, and the recognition by others, under the post-membership model these are, or should be, decreasingly mediated through an idea of membership. The rights (and obligations) associated with presence and

[13] For a discussion of recent case-law, see F Jacobs, 'Citizenship of the European Union—A Legal Analysis' (2007) 13 *European Law Journal* 591–610.

[14] On the highly uneven record of the EU member states in implementing or extending the Treaty voting rights, see J Shaw, *The Transformation of Citizenship in the European Union: Electoral Rights and the Restructuring of Political Space* (Cambridge, Cambridge University Press, 2007).

[15] Authors I would locate here in terms of their general focus, though they themselves might well not endorse the 'post-membership' label, include Kostakopoulou, n 6 above, as well as her contribution to this volume (ch 8); see also her 'European Union Citizenship: Writing the Future' (2007) 13 *ELJ* 623–46; S Benhabib, 'Another Cosmopolitanism' in R Post (ed), n 3 above, at 13–80; S Sassen, *Territory, Authority, Rights* (Princeton NJ, Princeton University Press, 2006).

dwelling may be more accessible, either without a membership card or with one increasingly easily acquired (perhaps through brief residence). The sense of membership may become less tied to the broader practical identity of the resident right-holder. And finally, the affirmative recognition of the member *qua* member by other members and, equally, the pejorative recognition of the non-member *qua* non-member by members, and the associated conveyance of symbolic capital or deficit, may gradually diminish or dilute.

Overall, then, whereas in the other two transcendent models of denizenship—the transnational and the post-national models—the rights associated with membership are split and diversified, here membership ceases to be a significant status-shaping code and medium at all. The very idea of membership, with its ordering of a binary legal distinction (member/non-member), with its connotation of highly specified entry and exit rules and regimes, and with its symbolic self-and other-interpolation of belonging and not-belonging, is arguably too rigid and too enveloping a notion for a world of more diverse and fluid commitments. Of course, considerations both of continuity and security of social identity at the individual level and of a viable threshold of capable-of-putting-things-effectively-in-common political community at the collective level—with a premium placed on the generation and sustenance of the minimum of trust, respect, and mutual sympathy necessary for that viability—mean that such common commitments will inevitably remain important.[16] Political community can never be made out of co-presence alone. But arguably a graduated language that speaks, through the receptive medium of denizenship, of (degrees of) association and (levels of) investment is better able to depict the nuances of our increasingly non-exclusive and fluctuating relationship to collective community than is the dichotomising language of membership.

And as one consequence of this, it may be that the very idea of a distinction between citizenship and denizenship becomes increasingly fuzzy (at the objective level) and overstated (at the subjective and inter-subjective levels), and perhaps in time even redundant. In these circumstances, denizenship, or its functional and imaginary equivalent, might even seek to assert itself as the master category of association with and investment in political community rather than a residual sub-category.[17] In other words, within its most

[16] See, eg, M Canovan, *The People* (Cambridge, Polity Press, 2005).

[17] Of course, other labels might be preferred. In particular some, while sharing the view that the position of 'denizens' within the 'political community' should be significantly upgraded, would prefer to retain the notion of 'citizenship', now conceived of much more inclusively, as a master category to mark and embrace this upgrading. See, eg, R Baubock's discussion of inclusive third country national initiatives within the EU under the rubric of 'civic citizenship' in 'Civic Citizenship: A New Concept for a New Europe', Report commissioned by the Bertelsmann Foundation, Brussels in R Süssmuth and W Weidenfeld (eds), *Managing Integration. The European Union's Responsibilities towards Immigrants* (Gütersloh, Bertelsmann Stiftung, 2005). See also the ground-breaking earlier discussion of J Weiler, *The Constitution of Europe* (Cambridge, Cambridge University Press, 2009) especially

radically transformative trajectory, the idea of denizenship ceases simply to be a label for describing, emphasising and reordering known dimensions of regulation and experience, and instead becomes the key to a new regulatory and experiential map.

So, in summary, the denizen can be imagined, conservatively, within a proto-citizenship trajectory or an indefinitely tiered membership trajectory. Or, in a more transformative vein, the denizen may be imagined within a transnational membership trajectory, a post-national membership trajectory and even, albeit in a more embryonic fashion, within a post-membership trajectory. In the first case the denizen is climbing the ladder to the highest political status known in the global Westphalian system—national citizenship—and in this regard the only novelty prompted by the renewed prominence of the idea of denizenship is the increased visibility, internal order and, perhaps, accessibility of the rungs on the ladder. In the second case the denizen is nested between the citizen and the visitor and alien in a new but relatively fixed graduated hierarchy of national membership status. In the third case, as we move to the transformative side of the divide, the denizen is a mobile player on the transnational circuit and seeks to take at least some advantage of membership rights and status at all her staging posts. In the fourth case the denizen is a typical inhabitant of a more complex post-national constellation, simultaneously present within and belonging to different and overlapping political communities. And in the fifth and final case the denizen reflects and helps precipitate the marginalisation or demise of the very idea of political membership. She possesses a status that transcends fixed status, a membership only of the society of non-members, in a new and more fluid configuration of political association and investment.

III. THE DENIZEN AND THE FUTURE OF THE EUROPEAN UNION

In this final section, I want to draw out some of the implications of the open-endedness of the idea of denizenship for the remaking of political community in the multi-level polity of the EU. Three linked and cumulative points will be developed. These will deal in turn with the strategic, the ideological and the generative dimensions of the debate over denizenship. In each case, as we can see, the idea of denizenship, reflecting the uncertainty and contestation at the heart of this 'in-between' concept, has an ambivalent

ch 10. But given the importance of the subjective and inter-subjective dimensions within membership status, it is arguable that the concept of citizenship, however carefully qualified, simply carries too much 'Westphalian' freight to capture the novel 'in-betweenness' of denizenship as a self-identifying and reputational category.

significance, suggesting both new openings as well as very old forms of closure of political community.

Let us start with the strategic dimension. The key point to stress here is that of deferral. Particular policies and legal initiatives associated with the membership politics of the European Union have for a long time been fragmented across different national sites (given the general reservation of national jurisdiction over the constitutional core of membership status) and supranational sites (in the EU, both within and outside the context of the Area of Freedom, Security and Justice, and across First, Second and Third Pillars;[18] and also in the Council of Europe, particularly in the area of electoral law through its Venice Commission[19]), as well as within different functional registers—political rights, social welfare provision, free movement, migration, crime. Therefore there remains little sense either of co-ordinated policy projection, or of co-ordinated opposition. Particular policy moves, such as the 2003 EU Directive on Third Country Nationals, or the development of a common visa and asylum policy, or various national, supranational and international initiatives on voting rights, may thus, if considered discretely, be compatible with very different models and trajectories of membership politics—trajectories that, as we shall develop below, may or may not stress the idea of denizenship or an equivalent term or sensibility. What is more, the projected and somewhat speculative quality of all such models—they presuppose (highly contingent) concerted effort to produce long-term consequences—together with the fact that they are more often left implicit than made explicit—they do not specify the idea of political community on which they are based (and may indeed lack any coherent idea)—reinforces the scope for ambiguity-in-the-present and deferred conflict. In this regard, the discourse of denizenship joins a number of other contemporary discourses on the EU—including these on enlargement (deep and wide for integrationists, shallow and wide for intergovernmentalists), on differentiated integration (multi-speed for integrationists, deep diversification for intergovernmentalists), and on subsidiarity (integrationist administrative decentralisation, state-based intergovernmentalism or regionalism)—where the key concept may give nominal direction to, but actually radically underdetermines quite diverse, and often opposing, polity visions.[20]

In that strategic deferral and open-endedness, moreover, lie the seeds of starkly different patterns of overall policy development. We can see both

[18] See, eg, N Walker, 'In Search of the Area of Freedom, Security and Justice: A Constitutional Odyssey' in N Walker (ed), *Europe's Area of Freedom, Security and Justice*. (Oxford, Oxford University Press, 2004) 3–41, 5–28.

[19] Shaw, above n 14.

[20] See, eg, N Walker, 'Constitutionalising Enlargement, Enlarging Constitutionalism' (2003) 9 *ELJ* 365–85.

the possibilities for positive reconciliation across discrete policy fields—a gradually emerging permissive consensus—and the dangers of incoherent or unacknowledged drift which could result in a conflicted or stalled mobility politics or even an incremental creep towards a highly restrictive approach. Yet if we introduce our second dimension of debate, and add to the strategic issue of deferral an ideological propensity towards positive symbolic investment in a generous politics of mobility in the EU, the picture becomes more nuanced.

What is meant by this idea of a positive symbolic investment is the emergence of an overlapping commitment across most (if by no means all) shades of political opinion in the European Union to portray and present its mobility and membership politics in affirmative terms. Why is this so? In the first place, it is the compensatory flip-side to the coin of immigration restrictions. It represents the 'light-side' of relatively generous inclusion of those who have already established some level of settlement in the EU to accompany and mitigate the 'dark-side' of a politics which, in its economic-and security-driven sensitivity to the possibility of mass movement to the EU from both the South and the East,[21] has developed a strong 'first gate'[22] of primary immigration regulation through common and lowest common denominator visa and asylum policies and procedures and, indeed, increasingly through the extra-territorialisation of control under the auspices of Frontex. The counterbalancing pressure for mitigation towards those who have successfully negotiated the strong first gate is reinforced by the perceived need to counter allegations of double standards, and, indeed, to answer charges of a more general betrayal of the EU's founding principles. The post-Maastricht dual citizenship model, whether portrayed in expansive post-national terms or in more restrictive transnational terms or even in the state-conservative terms of liberal national proto-citizenship, undoubtedly speaks to an openness to progress beyond the stark dichotomies of singular and exclusionary citizenship *within* the EU, especially given its original and abiding commitment both to the 'four freedoms' and to an open-ended mission of Europe-wide enlargement. So it becomes difficult not to countenance the overcoming of that same binary logic in respect of third country nationals themselves with a strong de facto claim to be considered similarly 'internal' to the EU.

Yet, for all the spread of a more inclusive membership discourse, the danger with such an ideologically inflected politics is obvious. The division between citizen and alien may no longer look so stark, yet this does not mean that an axiomatic distinction between insiders and outsiders no longer holds. Rather, it may simply be in the process of being displaced, the neuralgic point of migratory politics and membership access gradually

[21] V Guiraudon, 'The constitution of a European immigration policy domain: a political sociology approach' (2003) 10 *Journal of European Public Policy* 263–82.
[22] Hammar, above n 1.

shifting backwards from the phase of settlement to questions of initial entry and reception.[23] On this view, denizenship is no longer an impossible category, but it is still liable to be treated as a scarce resource and as an exceptional condition. It threatens to become an elite—and thus marginal—status within a multiple lock system of movement rather than the emblem of a commitment to move beyond such a restrictive regime.

This ideological reinforcement of the double-edge of membership and mobility politics brings us, finally, to what may be termed the generative dimension of the denizenship debate. What we are concerned with here is the way in which perspectives on denizenship are both informed by and in their turn inform broader 'existential' contestation about the nature of the EU polity. If we treat the emergence of the EU constitutional debate in the opening years of this century not as an isolated 'moment' but as the product of a deeper historical dynamic, what may prove to be its most telling legacy is the way in which it has helped to establish as a lasting item on the supranational political agenda a type of reflexively generative politics (even allowing for the symbolic banishment of the Constitutional Treaty in by the European Council in the summer of 2007 following the prolonged ratification crisis and its replacement with an old-fashioned and as yet unratified Reform Treaty).[24] By this I mean a politics which, on account of the cumulative growth in the breadth and depth of the supranational economic and social agenda over 50 years, has undergone a qualitative shift. It is a politics which, in the face of such remorseless expansion, can no longer treat the EU as the simple creature or delegate of other (national) polities, and so has been gradually forced to confront and engage with the question of the EU's own status as a distinct (and distinctive) polity, and therefore with its *constituent* arrangements *qua* polity, that is, with the proper generative source of its programme politics. It is a politics in which, therefore, any attempt to ignore or avoid this 'polity turn' by sticking to or reverting to an older and more modest model whereby the legitimacy of the EU among *all relevant constituencies* may be secured or sustained in purely programme content and 'output'[25] terms, seems doomed to insufficiency. It is a politics, moreover, which, just by virtue of this 'polity turn,' has come to posit and presupposes a collective 'we' as the ongoing author and subject of the EU—a first person plural which both frames and is reframed by the generative process.[26]

[23] See, eg, the essays collected in D Bigo and E Guild (eds), *Controlling Frontiers* (Aldershot, Ashgate, 2005).

[24] N Walker, 'After finalité? The Future of the European Constitutional Idea' in G Amato, H Bribosia and B de Witte (eds), *Genèse et destinée de la Constitution européenne* (Brussels, Bruylant, 2007). See also A Somek, 'Postconstitutional Treaty' (2007) 8 *GLJ*.

[25] F Scharpf, *Governing in Europe: Effective and Democratic?* (Oxford, Oxford University Press, 1999).

[26] See, eg, H Lindahl, 'The Paradox of Constituent Power: The Ambiguous Self-Constitution of the European Union' (2007) 20 *Ratio Juris* 485–505.

The politics of denizenship impact upon this broader generative process at two levels. First, and most obviously, denizenship politics provides a tangible instance of contestation over the reflexive 'we' of the EU polity. As the complex, uneven, multi-site debate over electoral rights at subnational, national and European levels demonstrates, part and parcel of a generous recognition of the status of denizens is the permission and encouragement of them to become co-legislators of their own developing status, practical identity and rights provision. Equally, part and parcel of a less generous recognition is to deny this self-legislating imperative.[27] In either case, of course, there may be a (virtuously or viciously) circular tendency for the method of inclusion/exclusion chosen in pursuit of the politics of membership to corroborate the conception of membership which underpins the method chosen.

Yet this is just the most visible tip of the iceberg. The idea of denizenship is important not only for denizens themselves—and for their place in the generative politics of the EU, but also for the fate of these generative politics more generally. As the constitutional debate demonstrated, a reflexively generative politics both requires and stimulates different conceptions of the compound European *demos*—different models or imaginaries of self-authorisation. And paradoxically, precisely because the question posed is concerned to identify the deepest basis of supranational authority and the most authentic expression of collective selfhood, there can be no *pre-authorised* way to secure a definitive resolution to the contest between these different imaginaries. The recent and more intense constitutional phase of the reflexively generative politics is indeed witness to this. It has seen the stressing and reinforcement of the lines—always part of the background shading of EU politics—separating one cluster of views which—under the liberal national sign—holds that the EU should remain largely a state-derivative organisation based on the aggregation of *demoi*, from another cluster of views which—under the liberal national-transcendent sign—holds that the EU should rest on a multi-level and overlapping configuration of *demoi* at both national and supranational levels. These in turn are separate from a third perspective which—in a manner which threatens to become liberal nationalism writ large—tends to comprehend the EU in terms of the incipient development of a single, all-embracing EU-wide *demos*.[28] The danger is that the EU's existential question becomes an existential crisis: that its reflexively generative politics becomes stalled—stuck in an antagonistic

[27] Shaw, above n 14.

[28] For discussion of the different polity visions pursued in the Constitutional Treaty debate, see eg, N Walker, 'Europe's Constitutional Momentum and the Search for Polity Legitimacy' (2005) 4 *International Journal of Constitutional Law* 211–38. For a taxonomy of views on EU citizenship which closely tracks the three main polity visions, see S Besson and A Utzinger, 'Introduction: Future Challenges of European Citizenship—Facing a Wide-Open Pandora's Box' (2007) 13 *ELJ* 573–90, at 588.

groove. This danger became palpable in the public reception of the Constitutional Treaty and, since the polity legitimacy of the *existing* EU order was precisely what was put squarely at issue there for the first time, it can find no long term relief and resolution in the failure of that Treaty.

On what basis, if at all, is a movement towards reconciliation of the different imaginaries of self-authorisation possible? What is telling is the extent to which the dominant imaginaries of self-authorisation, or at least those that dominate public debate, continue to be coded and calculated through citizenship. Whether or not a confederal, a multi-level or a proto-federal solution is imagined, the basic ingredients of the various self-authorising solutions tend to be understood in terms of citizenship and the kinds of fixed and high qualification criteria and encompassing modalities of status and self-understanding, and so strong conceptions of political identity, we associate with citizenship—even under the EU's explicitly postnational and dualistic model. And given that these putative solutions tend to distinguish and distance themselves from the others in just such terms—either by virtue of attachment to a dominant collective political identity (in the confederal and federal models) or in recognition of a particular accommodation of multiple but strong collective political identities (as in the multi-level model), the contributory influence of the basic ingredient of citizenship towards a fractured generative politics is hard to deny.

It is against this backdrop that it becomes possible to imagine the idea of denizenship being introduced as a more or less significant leavening agent in the recipe of polity legitimacy. The emergence of a new basic template (or even of a significant supplementary template) of political attachment by voluntary association and investment rather than by fate or affinity, and one that operates as a matter of degree rather than kind, simply provides far fewer cues for the kind of antagonistic posing of different imaginaries of supranational self-authorisation than do more traditional templates of collective identity.

But of course, even to voice the potential of the denizenship idea to unblock the generative politics of the EU is to underline how difficulty it would be for that potential to be fulfilled. If the strategic and ideological politics of denizenship, for all their limitations, possess a progressive dimension, the connection between denizenship politics and more fundamental generative politics seems at first sight less promising. For what makes the denizenship solution attractive here, namely its apartness from the powerful and resilient tendency of contemporary generative politics to be coded in the less fluid and more distinguishing and divisive language of citizenship, is the very same factor that makes us doubt its plausibility. The danger is that the denizenship question will, at best, remain marginalised from and overshadowed by the concerns of generative politics, and at worst will be used negatively to reaffirm certain fixed positions, especially those on the nationalist end of the spectrum of imaginaries of self-authorisation. For instance, if we look at the French and Dutch referendum debates of 2005, the denizen, whether as Polish plumber, secular Turk or Middle Eastern Muslim, was often employed as a key negative archetype—an important figurative resource in the offensive against more inclusive positions within the EU's generative politics.[29]

Yet we should not conclude from this experience that the denizenship discourse is fated to marginalisation or pejorative manipulation. We should not make light of the strategic and ideological considerations in favour of a more progressive use of the denizenship discourse, nor dismiss the cumulative impact of the gradual recognition of the denizen voice within European electoral laws. Neither should we underestimate the significance of the hour, nor of supranational Europe's rising and unabated anxiety of collective identity. The idea of denizenship may remain an unlikely medium for overcoming old and resilient oppositions within the European polity debate, but it is both the predicament and the opportunity of such a frame-breaking 'in-between' concept to suggest 'unlikely' new legal and political horizons where the more 'likely' candidates remain in thrall to the old.

[29] See, eg, M Berezin, 'Appropriating the "No": The French National Front, the Vote on the Constitution, and the "New" April 21' (2006) 39 *Political Science and Politics* 269–72; R Dehousse, 'The Unmaking of a Constitution: Lessons from the European Referenda' (2006) 13 *Constellations* 151–64.

Index

abolition of internal borders, 34–5
access to justice, 65, 82
  and access to territory, 89–90
access to territory, 6, 89–92
accountability, 62, 155, 219–20, 226
  democratic, 63, 65, 80
actual space, 105–6
added value, 50, 52, 60, 194
addressees, 92, 165, 218, 235–7
adequacy decision, 45–7
admission, 66, 139–40, 181, 186, 191, 194–5, 202
Advance Passenger Information *see* API
Africa, 3, 18, 28, 115
AFSJ *see* Area of Freedom, Security and Justice
Agamben, G, 159, 227
agonistic cosmopolitics, 6, 230–6
air passengers, 42, 45–6, 50
  see also API
aircraft, 86–7
airline crew, 86, 88
Albanians, 88
Algeria, 18, 88, 226
alien suffrage, 224–5
alien world, 4, 100, 112
alienness, 96–7, 103
  see also otherness
aliens, 9–10, 29–30, 96–7, 100, 110–12, 137–44
  and citizens, 7–8
  unwanted, 84–6
alterity, 128–30
ambiguities, 9, 141, 161, 172–8, 226
Amnesty International, 158–9
Amsterdam Treaty, 20, 65, 71, 151, 187–90, 266
antinomy, 123, 131–4
apartness, 123, 202, 273
API (Advance Passenger Information), 42–4, 47, 49–50
Area of Freedom, Security and Justice (AFSJ), 36–7, 70, 72–3, 185–207, 269
  and belonging, 199–207
  institutional architecture, 187–99
  and political morality of migration/integration, 185–207
Arendt, H, 167, 169–70, 174–6, 179–80, 210–12, 215–17, 234–6
Aristotle, 97–8, 109, 164
artificiality, 202–3
Aruba, 253–5, 257
asylum, 65–7, 71–3, 87, 119, 165, 187, 197–9
  law, 80–3, 153
    in practice, 82–90
  policy, 2, 5–8, 71, 90, 185, 199, 269–70
  rights, 66–7, 82, 89–90, 188
    judicial protection, 70–80
  seekers, 2, 9, 54, 56, 66, 79, 119
asymmetry, political, 137, 143–4
atopia *see* non-places
Austria, 20, 36, 190, 247
authorities, 35, 43, 45–7, 51, 58–9, 63, 265–6
  national, 42, 56–8, 76–7, 120
automated gates, 41, 60
autonomy, 124, 230
  procedural, 74–5, 91

Baldaccini, A, 36, 53, 66
Balibar, E, 215–17, 227, 234
basis, legal, 42–3, 46–7, 53, 57–8, 60, 95, 197
Baubock, R, 203, 261, 264, 267
being-in-common, 11, 116, 130–5
beings, singular, 133–4
Belgium, 88–9, 242, 247
Beljin, S, 67–8
Benhabib, S, 81, 118, 143, 209–12, 216–21, 223–32, 234–9
Besselink, L, 252–3, 257
Besson, S, 253–4, 272
biometrics, 34, 39–41, 52–62, 196
birth, 43, 106–7, 166, 170, 242, 245
blind spots, 107, 112
body politic, 9, 111, 173
bona fide passengers, 60–1
bonds, 131, 233, 244–5, 257
border controls, 4–5, 28–9, 33–8, 40–4, 50, 52, 62–3
  external, 42, 47, 53, 60, 187, 193, 198
  internal, 35, 188
  reintroduction of, 35–7
border crossings, 2–5, 11, 17, 21, 29, 55, 60
  unauthorised/illegal, 29, 36
border guards, 20, 56, 83, 87
border security, 34, 36, 38–59
  and monitoring of movement, 42–52
  and passenger data, 42–52
  United Kingdom, 38–42
  United States, 38–42

borders, 2–5, 15–20, 25–31, 126–7
  emergence of, 11–12
  and emergence of a European Political Community, 28–31
  external, 33, 37, 60, 71–2, 82–4, 88–9, 197–8
  functions of, 27–9
  management of, 15–16, 30–1, 41, 60, 83
  national, 35, 119, 202, 224
  paradox of, 4–5, 33–63
  political, 20, 30, 165
  political disourses about, 15–31
  Southern, 17–20, 28
boundaries, 3, 6, 56, 221
  of distributive justice, 137–59
  logic of, 150–5
boundary crossings, 3, 140, 146, 153–4, 156, 158
bounded communities, 200, 220–2, 231
bounded justice and immigration, 138–40
boundless justice and immigration, 140–4
boundlessness, 128, 143–4, 147
Bratman, M, 147, 157, 174
breaking of promises, 137–59
British citizenship, 244–6
Brouwer, E, 53, 74, 78–9, 85

calculable apparatus, 121–2
call effects, 20, 26
Canary Islands, 17, 19–20
carriers, 42–4, 46–8, 51, 83, 86, 89
cayucos, 17, 20
CBP *see* common basic principles
Ceuta and Melilla, 17–19
circularity, 1–12, 90–2, 138, 151–3, 155
cities, 7, 97, 117, 217, 231, 234, 265
  of refuge, 7, 117, 231
citizen/alien distinction, 2, 5, 7–10, 63, 262
citizenisation, 8, 204
citizens, 7–10, 29–30, 69–72, 117–19, 137–44, 162–4, 242–4
  and aliens, 7–8
  Commonwealth, 243–4, 246, 249, 256–7, 259
  democratic, 216, 235
  EU, 36–8, 60–2, 70–2, 242–4, 246–9, 255, 257–8
  and humans, 9–10
  national, 195, 242, 265–6
citizenship, 199–200, 204–7, 234, 241–59, 262–8, 273
  debates, 244–52
  EU, 257–9, 265, 272
  and Euro-polity, 252–8
  national *see* national citizenship
  nature of, 243, 252
  rights, 53, 243–4, 250
  United Kingdom, 241–59
closure, 2–3, 11, 81, 139–40, 143, 151–2, 158–9
  founding, 11, 151, 153–4, 159
co-operation, home affairs, 187–8
collective self, 3, 9, 157
collective self-legislation, 141, 147–8
collective selfhood, 128, 148, 156, 158, 272
Commission, 19, 45, 49–53, 55–8, 60–1, 73, 189–96
common basic principles (CBP), 45, 191–4, 205
common cause, 6, 210, 222, 235
common immigration policy, 195–6
common interest, 145, 148, 151, 155, 179
common migration policy, 193, 196–7
common space, 11, 145, 152
commonality, 11, 134, 146, 149–50, 154–5, 157
Commonwealth citizens, 243–4, 246, 249, 256–7, 259
communities, bounded, 200, 220–2, 231
Community law:
  see also Introductory Note
  notion of rights, 67–8
Community loyalty, 74, 76
Community rights and legal remedies, 74–7
compromise, 118, 120, 123, 230
concentric circle model, 6, 82–4, 89
conditional hospitality, 214, 219, 225
consciousness, 112, 236
  false, 229
  popular, 235–6
constitutional change, 246–7
constitutional democracy, 227–8
constitutional orders, 230, 257
constitutional traditions, 76–7, 80, 186, 218, 257
constitutionalisation, 226, 258
constitutionalism, 128, 156, 228
contestation, 10, 138, 152, 263, 268, 272
contingency, 6, 99, 210, 221, 231
control and security, 199–207
cosmopolitan norms, 209, 211, 216, 220–1, 227
cosmopolitanism, 118, 123, 131–4, 209–13, 216–20, 223–9, 234–7
  normative, 231, 235
cosmopolitics, 213, 230–1
  agonistic, 6, 230–6
cosmos, 97, 102–3, 111
counter-terrorism, 34, 43–4, 50, 53, 61, 192
  see also terrorism
CPTAs, 158–9
credibility, 178, 206–7
crime, 41, 44, 55, 57–8, 187–8, 211
  and marginalisation, 23
  organised, 50–1, 187, 189, 192

cultural conflict and economic conflict, 22–3
cultural rights, 223
cultures, 23–4, 100, 105–6, 131, 201–2, 205, 238

data exchange, 44, 57, 83–4, 89
data protection, 43, 45, 48–9, 51
databases, 34, 39, 44, 46, 53–6, 59–60, 62–3
de facto immigrants, 11, 138, 153–4, 156, 158–9
de-politicisation of European immigration policy, 4–5, 56
democracy, 176–9, 200, 202, 213–15, 220–1
  constitutional, 227–8
  and effective remedies, 90–2
  and rule of law, 80–2
democratic accountability, 63, 65, 80
democratic citizens, 216, 235
democratic institutions, 71–2, 92, 163
democratic iterations, 7, 216–17, 219, 221, 228–30, 236
democratic legitimation, 219, 221, 223, 227–8
democratic politics, 186, 221, 230, 237
democratic self-determination, 200, 218
demoi, 80, 176–7, 202, 251, 258, 272
denizens:
  and future of European Union, 268–74
  location, 261–3
denizenship, 9–10, 152, 243, 261–74
  discourse, 269, 274
  politics, 272–3
  trajectories of, 263–8
Department of Homeland Security (DHS), 39, 46–9, 233
departure, 33, 42–3, 50–1
deportation, 19, 66, 115, 198, 224, 232–3
Derrida, J, 11–12, 121–4, 127–35, 212–15, 225, 229, 238–9
detention, 159, 162, 232
determinacy, 3, 11, 119, 121, 124, 126, 128–9
determinate existence, 11, 118, 130
deterritorialisation, 261–74
devolution, 248–9
devolved bodies, 247–8, 258
DHS *see* Department of Homeland Security
dimensions of law, 121, 125, 130
discretion, 91, 217, 236
distance, 102
distribution:
  of places, 4, 10
  of rights, 11, 159
distributive acts, 11, 138, 140, 149–54, 156, 159
distributive justice, 7, 10–11, 28–9
  acts of, 138, 140, 148, 150
  boundaries of, 137–59
  boundedness of, 140
  and immigration, 137–59
  spatiality of, 138, 148, 157
  theory of, 137, 139–41, 143, 150, 154
  thresholds, 158–9
diversity, 197, 202, 206
double gesture, 7, 212, 215, 230
  paradoxes of, 219–27
duties, 21, 82, 92, 103, 166, 170, 186
  positive, 142
dynamic learning, 206–7

e-borders programme, 40–1, 44
EC Treaty, 7, 42, 45, 47, 53, 70, 82, 92, 151–3
ECHR *see* European Convention for the Protection of Human Rights and Fundamental Freedoms
economic conflict and cultural conflict, 22–3
economic immigrants, 153–4
effective judicial/legal protection, 73, 76–80, 82, 91
effective remedies, 5
  and effective rights, 90–2
effective rights:
  Community right to enter EU, 67–70
  and effective remedies, 90–2
  rights in Community law, 67–8
  for third-country nationals, 65–92
effectiveness, 6, 55, 67, 70, 75
Eichmann case, 209–12, 235
Eilmansberger, T, 65, 67–8, 74, 80
EIP, 65–7, 71, 73, 77–8, 80–2, 89–92
  see also European immigration policy
elections, 242, 245–9, 255–6, 258, 266
  European Parliament, 242, 249, 254–7
  fair, 255–6
  local, 242–3, 249
  national, 242–3, 258–9
electoral rights, 8, 152, 241–59
  see also voting rights
emergence of borders, 11–12
emigration, 18, 22, 28, 147, 175, 181
emplacement, legal, 144, 146
employment, 70, 115, 181, 191, 203, 262
entry, 6, 60–1, 65, 69, 84–5, 150, 195–8
entry conditions, 68–9, 83, 85, 88, 196
entry-exit system, 55, 60–2
entry permission, 68, 84–5
equality:
  moral, 141–2
  political, 141, 146

ethics, 4, 29–30, 118, 202, 238
EU citizens, 36–8, 60–3, 70–3, 242–4, 246–9, 252–3, 255
EU citizenship, 7, 151, 217, 252–3, 257–9, 265, 272
Euro-polity, 241, 243, 245, 247, 249, 259
  see also European polity
  and citizenship, 252–8
Eurodac, 52, 54–5
European Border Agency (FRONTEX), 36, 86
European citizens *see* EU citizens
European citizenship *see* EU citizenship
European Commission *see* Commission
European Convention for the Protection of Human Rights and Fundamental Freedoms(ECHR), 66, 76–7, 80–2, 88, 91–2, 162, 255–6
European Council, 35, 52, 60, 190, 192, 197, 199
  Tampere, 71–3, 80, 190
European Data Protection Supervisor, 49, 59, 61
European immigration policy, 4–5, 63, 151, 155
  see also EIP
European integration, 33, 71, 243, 247
European migration policy, 16–17, 20, 30, 190
European Pact on Immigration and Asylum, 8, 60, 185, 197, 199
European Parliament, 8, 19, 45–6, 49, 57–9, 68–9, 256
  elections, 242, 249, 254–7
European political community, emergence, 15–31
European polity, 2–3, 5, 7, 10–11, 151–2, 154–5, 206–7
  see also Euro-polity
Europol, 57–8
exchange of information, 38, 55, 71
exchange of personal data, 34, 54–5
exclusion, 2, 5, 81, 102, 138–40, 145–6, 221
exclusivity, 264–5
  mutual, 264–5
exit, 60–1
exit effect, 26
external border controls, 42, 47, 53, 60, 187, 193, 198
external borders, 33, 37, 60, 71–2, 82–6, 88–9, 197–8

fair elections, 255–6
fair treatment, 190–1, 198
false consciousness, 229
family members *see* family reunification
family reunification, 66–70, 78, 90, 190–1, 194, 196–8, 200

fingerprints, 39, 52–4, 58
first person:
  and human rights, 168–9
  plural, 9, 138, 148–50, 153, 156, 159, 172–3
  singular, 172–3
first pillar, 43, 47, 49
football matches, 37–8
force of law, 121–3, 214
foreigners, 12, 66, 110, 200, 213–14, 218–19, 234
  see also aliens
forgiveness, 123, 133, 213, 231, 234
Foucault, M, 12, 105, 112, 127
founding closure, 11, 151, 153–4, 159
fragmentation, 23
France, 16, 19–20, 36, 84, 168, 177, 224–5
franchise, 246–7, 256, 259
  see also elections
free movement, 9, 33–4, 70–2, 161–9, 171, 178–81, 187–90
freedom, 36, 63, 70–3, 161–71, 178–81, 187–9, 191–2
freedom of movement:
  actors and authors, 173–6
  normative anchor-points, 178–82
  as right to land, 169–72
  rights, 162–7
    and human rights, 167–73
freedoms, negative, 63, 162, 262
friendship, 109, 123, 131, 133
FRONTEX (European Border Agency), 36, 86–7
functions of borders, 27–9
fundamental freedoms, 77, 92, 255
fundamental rights, 38, 46, 51, 56, 61, 73, 81
  protection of, 56, 61

generalised surveillance, 34, 38, 51, 60, 62–3
generative politics, 271–4
genocide, 209–11
Germany, 16, 20, 35, 37, 85, 187, 190
Gibraltar, 255–7
global justice and local justice, 26–7
globalisation, 96, 108–13, 201, 206, 226
globalism, 4, 108–11
God, 127–8
Goldsmith, Lord Peter, 8, 244–5, 247, 249–51, 257–8
Groenendijk, K, 35, 37, 83
Guild, E, 33, 35–6, 63, 66, 83, 89, 188
Guirandon, V, 83, 86–9

Habermas, J, 141–4, 146–7, 150–2, 179, 225, 227–8, 231
habits, 100, 111, 238–9

habitual space, 105–6
Hague Programme, 36, 55, 72–3, 192–3
health, 164, 168–9
history, 95–8, 105, 116, 122, 193–5, 204–5, 224
home affairs co-operation, 187–8
Home Affairs Council, 51, 54, 56–7, 191
Home Office, 40–1, 44, 50, 245
home-world, 4, 100, 112
homogeneous space, 100–3
hospitality, 4, 7, 112, 131–2, 212–15, 218–19, 229–31
  conditional, 214, 219, 225
  and rights, 213–19
  unconditional, 132, 215
host languages, 204–5
host societies, 192–3, 195–6, 203
human rights, 9, 27–30, 71–2, 161–5, 167–9, 171–3, 179–81
  discourse, 161, 167, 176
  and first person, 168–9
  and migrants, 161–82
  protection of, 27, 67, 77, 79, 200
  and security, 25
  universal, 7, 215, 219–20, 222–3, 227, 230
humanity, 9, 131, 175, 211, 221
humans:
  and citizens, 9–10
  and migrants, 161–82
Husserl, E, 96, 98–101, 105, 107

identification, 39–41, 52, 56, 206
identity, 15, 39–40, 148, 157, 168–70, 186, 200–1
  national, 139, 141–2, 146, 201, 204–5, 252
illegal immigrants, 19, 41, 59, 119–20, 198
illegal immigration, 18–20, 42–4, 47, 55, 72, 156, 196–8
imaginaries, 10, 267, 272–3
  political, 262–3, 266
  of self-authorisation, 272–3
immigrants:
  de facto, 11, 138, 153–4, 156, 158–9
  economic, 153–4
  illegal, 19, 41, 59, 119–20, 198
  would-be, 9, 89, 119, 155, 232, 234
immigration, 4–8, 18–27, 79–82, 110–12, 195–7
  see also Introductory Note; migration
  and bounded justice, 138–40
  and boundless justice, 140–4
  and distributive justice, 137–59
  illegal, 18–20, 42–4, 47, 55, 72, 156, 196–8
immigration control, 34, 36, 41, 44, 49, 56, 86
immigration databases, transformation of, 54–9
immigration law:
  see also migration law
immigration law in practice, 82–90
immigration policy, 3, 6, 9, 11, 111, 141–2
  common, 195–6
  and normative formation, 115–35
  as a wager, 155–8
immigration rights:
  judicial protection, 70–80
  and legal remedies, 78–80
implementing measures, 187, 192–3
in place and out of place, 106–8
inclusion, 2, 5, 56, 118, 138–40, 142–6, 151
  see also Introductory Note
inclusiveness, 142, 207
indexical expressions, 4, 100–1, 107, 148
individual rights, 65, 67–9, 74–5, 77, 83, 91
information, 34, 36–7, 39, 42, 44, 50–1, 55
  exchange of, 38, 55, 71
inner circle, 84–6
inside/outside distinction, 2, 4–5, 63, 96, 102–3, 144, 166
insitutional context, 15–92
institutions, 74, 92, 193–4, 205–6, 211–12, 234, 236–8
  democratic, 71–2, 92, 163
  interstate, 234–5, 237
Integrated System of External SurveillanceÆ (SIVE) *see* SIVE
integration, 8, 111, 241–2, 245
  and Area of Freedom, Security and Justice, 185–207
  conditions, 191, 194–5, 204
  European, 33, 71, 243, 247
  policies, 190–5, 207
  political morality of, 185–207
intentions, 61, 84, 127–8, 147, 157, 174, 229
interest, common, 145, 148, 151, 155, 179
internal border controls, 35, 188
internal borders, 20, 35, 37, 83, 192
  abolition of, 34–5
internal market, 10, 71, 152, 154, 201
internal security, 35, 55–8
international airports, 86–8
international institutions, 210, 212, 215
international law, 29, 66, 92, 117, 126, 142, 222
international obligations, 91–2
interoperability, 52, 54–6, 61–2
interstate institutions, 234–5, 237
investment, 10, 264, 267–8, 270, 273
ipse-identity, 148, 157
Ireland, 242, 246–7, 250, 258
  Northern, 246–50

Irish citizens, 246–7, 250, 258
irregular migration, 192–3, 195, 198–9
Israel, 170, 211–12
Italy, 19, 36, 88, 158–9, 242
iterability, 7, 229–30
iterations, democratic, 7, 216–17, 219, 221, 228–30, 236

JHA Council *see* Justice and Home Affairs Council
Johnston case, 76–7
judicial protection:
  effective, 76–7
  immigration and asylum rights, 70–80
judicial review, 6, 70, 81–2, 92
juridification, 142–3
jurisdiction, 73, 168, 203, 264–5
  territorial, 262, 264–5
jus includendi et excludendi, 2, 6, 153
justice, 8–12, 70–3, 89–92, 121–4, 130–3, 187–92, 254–7
  access to, 65, 82, 89–90
  bounded *see* bounded justice, 138–9, 141
  boundless *see* boundless justice
  distributive *see* distributive justice
  genuine area of, 71–2
  and law, 10–12
Justice and Home Affairs, 55, 187
Justice and Home Affairs Council, 51, 54, 56–7, 191, 193, 197

Kant, I, 101–2, 109, 213–14
knowledge, 40–1, 55, 79, 198, 205–6
  basic, 194, 205
Kymlicka, W, 143, 201, 263–4

language, 95–6, 100–1, 112–13, 192–5, 205–6, 218–19, 229
  host, 204–5
law:
  see also Introductory Note
  and justice, 10–12
  and politics, 209–39
laws of Nature, 127–8
Lebenswelt see life-world
Lefort, C, 129, 179
legal aid, 79, 89
legal basis, 42–3, 46–7, 53, 57–8, 60, 95, 197
legal emplacement, 144, 146
legal migration, 195–6, 198
legal obligations, 5–6, 67, 74, 78, 80, 90
legal order, 3, 10, 35, 128, 137, 142, 146
legal remedies, 6, 82, 90
  see also remedies
  and Community rights, 74–7
  and immigration rights, 78–80
legal space, 6, 104, 156, 159
  genesis of, 150–5
  structure of, 144–7
  'to each their own place', 147–50
legality, 11, 43, 53, 60–2, 78, 92, 117
legislation, 8, 42, 44–5, 49, 62, 247, 258–9
legitimation, democratic, 219, 221, 223, 227–8
liberty, 92, 163–4, 189, 202
life-world, 96, 112
  multiplicity of, 98–100
living-in-common, 6–7
local elections, 242–3, 249
local justice and global justice, 26–7
local, the, 248
localisation, 108–13
localism, 4, 109–11
logic, 10, 15, 24–5, 33–4, 61, 152–3, 178–9
  of boundaries, 150, 152–3
long-term residents, 79, 190–1, 262, 265

management:
  of borders, 15–16, 30–1, 41, 60, 83
  of migration flows, 27, 55, 181, 193
manifold of ought-places, 145, 149
marginalisation and crime, 23
marriage, 234
Marx, K, 110, 171
Matthews case, 256
Mauritania, 17–18, 27
membership, 7–9, 200, 202–3, 205–7, 220–2, 250–2, 264–8
  politics, 10, 221, 265, 269–70, 272
  rights, 254, 258, 265–6, 268
  status, 268–9
Merleau-Ponty, M, 96, 107–8, 112, 124, 153, 170
middle circle, 84–6
migrants, 115–16, 161–7, 175, 177–81, 193–5, 197–9, 203–5
  as category, 162–7
  and human rights, 161–82
migration, 19, 180–1
  see also immigration; *Introductory Note*
  and Area of Freedom, Security and Justice, 185–207
  control, 185, 196, 198, 203, 207
  flows, 25, 83–4, 86, 88, 190
    management of, 55, 181, 192
  irregular, 192–3, 195, 198–9
  legal, 195–6, 198
  political morality of, 185–207
migration law, 166, 188, 203
  see also immigration law
  ambiguities, 173–8
  freedom of movement, actors and authors, 173–6
  spokesmen and beneficiaries, 176–8
migration policy, 15–17, 20–1, 181, 204
  European/common, 16–17, 20, 28, 30, 153, 193–4, 196–7

liberal, 186, 203
normative challenges, 27–31
Miller, D, 203, 251
Minderhoud, P, 35, 83
misplacement, 144, 146
mobility, 116, 207, 250, 266, 270
Moon case, 85
moral conversation, 220–1
moral equality, 141–2
moral reciprocity, 143
morality, 137, 142, 167, 179, 202, 235
political, 7, 30, 186–7, 189, 191, 193, 207
Morocco, 17–19, 22, 88, 115
movement, monitoring, 42, 60
movement politics, 230, 236–7
movements, social, 228–9, 237–8
multi-level polities, 244, 265, 268
multiculturalism, 16, 204
multiplicity, 96–8, 103, 252
mutual promises, 138, 157

Nächste, der/das, 233
Nancy, J-L, 123–4, 129, 131, 134
nation-states, 128, 134, 142, 144, 252
national authorities, 42, 56–8, 76–7, 120
national borders, 35, 119, 202, 224
national citizens, 195, 242, 265–6
national citizenship, 245, 249, 253, 259, 262, 264–5, 268
transformation of, 253–4
national elections, 242–3, 258–9
national identity, 139, 141–2, 146, 201, 204–5, 252
national law, 43, 59, 75, 79, 89, 190, 193
national security, 35, 41, 43–4, 47, 85, 173, 188
see also public security
nationalism, 141, 144, 169–70, 201
nationality, 17, 25, 66, 69, 166–7, 203, 251–3
country of, 87–8
nationals, 65, 69, 71, 78–9, 88–9, 221–2, 255
see also citizens; national citizens
nature, laws of, 127–8
nearness, 102
negative freedoms, 63, 162, 262
neighbours, 6, 173, 203, 209, 222, 232–4
Netherlands, 12, 20, 35, 85, 194, 253–4, 257
networks, 59, 108–9, 230, 232
New Europe, 209–39
newcomers, 8, 170, 206–7, 245, 250
Nietzsche, F, 109, 128, 132, 239
nomos, 125–6, 234
non-citizens, 164, 242–3, 246, 261
see also aliens; non-nationals
non-members, 63, 142, 153, 207, 267–8
non-nationals, 162–3, 243
see also aliens; non-citizens
non-places, 11, 96, 111–12, 159
normative anchor-points, 178–82
normative challenges, 27–31
normative cosmopolitanism, 231, 235
normative dissolution, 120–5
normative formation and immigration policy, 115–35
normative foundations, 16–17, 21, 141
normative interpretation of immigration, 22–5
normativity, 3, 5, 11–12, 115–35
being-in-common, 130–5
dimensions of, 125–6
normative dissolution, 120–5
place of, 116–20
polity as normative, 126–30
resolving the normative, 125–35
norms, 5, 7, 10, 68, 110, 112, 116–17
cosmopolitan, 209, 211, 216, 220–1, 227
and facts, 5–7
legal, 68–9, 74–5, 77, 149
universal, 210
Northern Ireland, 246–50

obligations, 24, 29–30, 65–6, 68–9, 74–6, 78–82, 85–6
international, 91–2
legal, 5–6, 67, 74, 78, 80, 90
oikeios, 97
oikos, 97–8, 112
oppression, 163, 165, 180
organised crime, 50–1, 187, 189, 192
Orient, 100–2
orientated space, 100–3
otherness, 96–7, 106–7, 112, 172–3
ought-places, 111, 144–5, 150
manifold of, 145, 149
outer circle, 88–9
outside and inside, 4–5, 102–3
outsiders, 2, 4, 203, 207, 221, 270

Panayotova case, 76–7, 80–1, 91
paradoxes:
of borders, 4–5, 33–63
of bounded communities, 220–2, 231
of democratic legitimation, 219–21, 223, 227
of double gesture, 219–27
and proximity, 209–39
of representation, 155–6
of rights, 215–16
Parlak, Ibrahim, 232–3, 237
particularity, 30, 99, 219, 221, 223–4, 228, 239
partition, 123–4, 129
passenger data, 34, 86
advance, 42–4
and border security, 42–52
Passenger Information Units *see* PIUs

passenger name records, 44–53, 62
agreements, 47–51, 62
Commission proposal for EU system, 49–52
data, 44–6, 48–50
transfer of, 45–7, 49–50
EC/US Agreement, 44–6
ECJ PNR judgment, 46–7
EU-US Agreements, 47–9
passengers, 34, 39–42, 44, 46, 51, 62–3, 86–7
passports, 50, 52–4, 169, 249
pateras, 17–18, 20
PD *see* proactive discourse
people, the, 128–30, 133, 174, 177
perception, 101, 105, 112, 135, 144, 203
personal data, 42, 45–6, 50, 56, 58, 62–3
see also passenger data
exchange of, 34, 54–5
Pettit, P, 147–8, 157
phantasms, 238
phenomenology of space, 4, 95–113
pillars:
first, 43, 47, 49
third, 43, 50, 57–8, 62, 187, 197
PIUs (Passenger Information Units), 51
Plato, 126, 169–70
plural self, 175, 177, 179
plurality, 99, 179
PNR Agreements *see* passenger name records, agreements
PNR data *see* passenger name records, data
PNRs *see* passenger name records
police, 35, 41, 44, 56, 187–8, 216, 237
police powers, exercise of, 35–6
policy answers to immigration, 25–7
political action, 6–7, 104, 229, 237
political arguments, 139–40
political asymmetry, 137, 143–4
political authority, 8, 244, 262, 264–5
political borders, 20, 30, 165
political communities, 3–5, 8–10, 15–16, 21–5, 30–1, 139–41, 265–9
European, 15–17, 27–30
political disourses about borders, 15–31
political equality, 141, 146
political events, 5, 62, 239
political imaginary, 262–3, 266
political judgment, 156–8
paradoxical temporality of, 138, 157
political membership, 10, 28, 203, 268
political morality, 7, 30
of migration/integration, 185–207
political participation rights, 242–3, 249, 262
political reciprocity, 62, 139, 142–3, 145–6
political reflexivity, 145, 148, 151, 153–4, 159
political rights, 162, 164, 191, 247, 252, 258, 264
see also political participation rights
politicisation, 5, 8, 63
see also de-politicisation
politico-legal alternatives, 185–274
politico-legal space, 2, 4
politics, 30
democratic, 186, 221, 230, 237
denizenship, 272–3
and law, 209–39
post-reflexive, 11, 158–9
see also European polity
polities, 9–11, 117, 125–30, 137–9, 154–9, 177–8, 202–3
see also Euro-polity; European polity
multi-level, 244, 265, 268
and normativity, 126–30
polity, world, 142–3
popular consciousness, 235–6
positive duties, 142
possession, 95–6, 223
post-national membership models, 264–6
post-reflexive politics, 11, 158–9
poverty, 23–4, 115, 163, 181
power, 17, 27, 36, 124, 157, 179–80, 248–50
power relations, 24, 221–2
Prague Airport case, 87–8
Prechal, S, 67–8, 74–5, 82, 91–2
priorities, 40, 54, 73, 190, 192, 198
privacy, 5, 34, 39, 45, 51, 59, 63
private sphere, 173–4
proactive discourse (PD), 21–7, 29–30
procedural autonomy, 75–6, 91
profiling, 34, 39, 50–1, 59, 61, 63
proliferation of controls, 33–4
promises, 116, 131, 218–19, 225–6
breaking in order to keep, 137–59
mutual, 138, 157
protection, 27, 44–6, 63, 80, 83, 200–1, 262
of fundamental rights, 56, 61
of human rights, 27, 67, 77, 79, 200
judicial, 75–6, 79
proto-political reflexivity, 11, 153, 158–9
proximity, 6, 18, 102
and paradox, 209–39
public opinion, 21, 27
public order, 22, 61
and risk, 35–8
public policy, 35, 44, 78
public security, 46–7, 49
public sphere, 167, 174–5, 235
Qualification Directive, 66, 68–70, 90
quasi-federal states, 247–8

RD *see* reactive discourse
re-politicisation, 5
 see also de-politicisation; politicisation
reactive discourse (RD), 3, 21–6, 29, 124
real space, 104–5
reception centres, 17–18
receptive political community, 24–5
reciprocity, 48, 137, 142, 147, 174, 179–80, 246–7
 moral, 143
 political, 62, 139, 142–3, 145–6
recognition, 53, 73, 142, 172, 202, 216–17, 265–6
rectitude, 127–9
referendums, 246–8
reflexivity:
 political, 145, 148, 151, 153–4, 159
 proto-political, 11, 153, 158–9
refuge, cities of, 7, 117, 231
Refugee Convention, 66, 81–2, 87, 91–2
refugee status, 66, 78, 175
refugees, 66, 68–9, 163–6, 175, 180–1, 225–7, 231–2
reintroduction of border controls, 35–7
religions, 22, 121, 164, 201, 205, 214
remedies, 65, 74–6, 78, 89–91
 effective, 5, 65, 67, 73–4, 76–7, 80–4, 89–91
 legal, 6, 74–5, 78, 80, 82, 90
repatriation agreements, 17–18
repetition, 104–5, 239
representation, 79, 145, 156–7, 173, 175–7, 220, 246
 paradox of, 155–6
representatives, 79–80, 128, 161, 171, 176–7, 233, 237
residence, 53–4, 65, 68–9, 119, 162, 203–4, 261–2
 permits, 53–4, 69, 190
 rights, 70, 190, 264, 266
residents, 8, 36–8, 69, 242, 246–7, 254–5, 266–7
resources, 8, 26, 28, 79, 180, 182, 195
responsiveness, 11, 120–2, 124–5, 130, 154, 156
reunification, family, 66–70, 78, 90, 190–1, 194, 196–8, 200
review, judicial, 6, 70, 81–2, 92
Ricoeur, P, 148, 156–8
right balance, 188–9, 198
rights:
 cultural, 162, 223
 electoral *see* electoral rights
 and hospitality, 213–19
 human *see* human rights
 to land, freedom of movement as, 169–72
 membership, 254, 258, 265–6, 268
 to move/free movement, 161–82
  and human rights, 167–73
 notion of rights in Community law, 67–8
 paradox of, 215–16
 political, 162, 164, 191, 247, 252, 258, 264
 social, 203, 225, 264
 to stay, 161–82
 voting *see* electoral rights; voting rights
risk, 40, 49, 61, 80, 189, 226–7
 and public order, 35–8
risk assessments, 39, 50
risk-based approach, 34, 38
Rome, Treaty of *see* EC Treaty
Rosenzweig, F, 6, 209–10, 213, 231–3, 239
Rousseau, J-J, 128, 177–9
rule of law, 63, 71–2, 120, 177–8, 227–8
 and democracy, 80–2
 and effective remedies, 90–2

SBC (Schengen Borders Code), 35–7, 68–70, 79, 83–6, 88–90
Schengen, 20, 34–5, 37, 41, 51, 195
Schengen Borders Code *see* SBC
Schengen Implementing Convention, 35–7
Schengen Information System *see* SIS
Schengen rules, 84–5
Schuster, L, 115–16
Scotland, 245–9, 251
sea borders, 83, 87, 95
security, 20, 22, 37–40, 187–9, 191–2, 195–9
 and control, 199–207
 and human rights, 25
 national, 35, 41, 43–4, 47, 85, 173, 188
 public, 46–7, 49
self, 63, 108, 134, 147–8, 158, 161, 168
 collective, 3, 9, 157
 plural, 175, 177, 179
self-authorisation, 272–3
self-determination, democratic, 200, 218
self-legislation, collective, 141, 147–8
selfhood, 106, 148
 collective, 128, 148, 156, 158, 272
selfishness, 9, 168–9
Senegal, 18
settlement, 119, 186, 203–4, 206, 246, 270–1
Sevinger and Eman case, 253–4, 257
singular beings, 133–4
singularity, 106, 134, 180
SIS (Schengen Information System), 52, 54–5, 58–9, 74, 84–6
sites, 4, 100, 116, 225–6, 235–6, 251, 254
SIVE (Integrated System of External SurveillanceÆ (SIVE), 18–19, 27
Slow Food, 231, 236

social contract, 178–9
social movements, 228–9, 237–8
social rights, 203, 225, 264
Socrates, 168–70
solidarity, 7, 25, 192, 196, 207, 221–2, 234–5
soul, 164, 209, 232
Southern borders, 17–20, 28
sovereignty, 117–18, 120–1, 124–5, 133–4, 199–200, 220–1, 226–7
  legislative, 248
space, 95–101, 103–7, 109–11, 113, 125, 144–5, 148–50
  actual, 105–6
  common, 11, 145, 152
  dimensions, 101–2
  distance, 102
  experience, 100–1
  globalisation, 108–13
  habitual, 105–6
  homogeneous, 100–3
  legal *see* legal space
  localisation, 108–13
  nearness, 102
  orientated, 100–3
  paradigms, historical, 96–8
  phenomenology of, 95–113
  in place and out of place, 106–8
  politico-legal, 2, 4
  real, 104–5
  spatial dispositions, 103
  symbolic, 104–5
  virtual, 105–6
Spain, 15–20, 26–30, 242, 247, 255–7
  Parliament, 17, 20–1, 27
spatial dispositions, 103
spatial unity, 145–6, 150–2, 154, 156
spatiality of distributive justice, 138, 148, 157
spheres:
  private, 173–4
  of validity, 149–50
Spijkerboer, T, 83, 87, 175
standards, 42–3, 45, 48, 51–2, 78, 91, 181
state sovereignty *see* sovereignty
stateless persons, 68–9, 167, 216–17
statism, 224, 227–8, 237
strange places, 144–7, 152
strangers, 103, 110, 118, 143, 202, 227
students, 163, 165, 196
surveillance, 4–5
  generalised, 34, 38, 51, 60, 62–3
  of movement, 33–63
suspensive effect, 79, 89
symbolic space, 104–5
synergies, 52, 54–5, 198
Tampere European Council, 71–3, 80, 190
TCNs *see* third-country nationals
territorial jurisdiction, 262, 264–5
territory, access to, 89–90
terrorism, 39–41, 44, 49–52, 55–8, 85, 187, 232
TEU *see* Treaty on European Union
theoretical issues, 95–182
third countries, 33, 41, 47–50, 58, 62, 78, 187
third-country nationals, 52–4, 60–1, 190–1, 242–3
  effective rights for, 65–92
  status of, 79, 190
third pillar, 43, 50, 57–8, 62, 187, 197
threats, 35, 37, 40, 51, 57, 85, 189
thresholds, 11, 58, 110, 112, 153, 158–9, 162
togetherness, 134, 202
Toner, H, 36, 66
topos, 96–7, 111–13
torture, 66, 169
trade, 116, 181–2, 234
traditions, 24, 72, 96, 112, 176, 204–5, 213–14
transfers of PNR data, 45, 47–50
transformation of national citizenship, 253–4
Treaty of Amsterdam *see* Amsterdam Treaty
Treaty of Rome *see* EC Treaty
Treaty on European Union (TEU), 47–8, 187
trust, 35, 37, 187, 215, 258, 267
truth, 109, 129, 134, 172

UDHR *see* Universal Declaration of Human Rights
UK *see* United Kingdom
unconditional hospitality, 132, 215
United Kingdom, 8, 43–4, 49–51, 87
  border security, 38–42
  citizenship, 241–59
    debates, 244–52
  electoral rights, 241–59
United States, 47–9, 120, 127–8, 204, 214, 232
  border security, 38–42
  Bureau of Customs and Border Protection, 45–6
unity, spatial, 138, 144–7, 149–52, 154, 156
Universal Declaration of Human Rights (UDHR), 66, 162, 169
universal human rights, 7, 215, 219–20, 222–3, 227, 230
universalism, 6–7, 143, 213, 219–22, 228
universality, 7, 30, 99, 119, 218–19, 221–3, 231

unwanted aliens, 84–6
Utzinger, A, 253, 272

validity, spheres of, 149–50
values, 50, 52, 60, 84, 139, 194–5, 205–6
  basic, 193–4
Van Gend en Loos case, 66, 75
violence, 111, 125, 163, 180, 189, 222
virtual space, 105–6
VIS *see* Visa Information System
Visa Information System (VIS), 52, 54–8, 60, 198
visa requirements, 60, 83–4
visas, 6, 71, 88–9, 192, 195, 198
voting rights, 8, 129, 224–5, 242–4, 246–51, 254–9, 266
  see also electoral rights

Waldenfels, B, 4, 103, 105, 112, 146, 156, 177
Walzer, M, 111, 138–40, 143, 147–8, 150–2, 200
war on terror, 46, 52, 54–5
  see also terrorism
well-nigh nighest, 209, 232–3
women, 139, 223–4, 229, 246
world polity, 142–3
world state, 144–7, 151
worldliness, 234–5, 237
would-be immigrants, 9, 89, 119, 155, 232, 234

xenophobia, 23, 187, 203, 224

Zapata-Barrero, R, 3, 16, 21, 27

11123508